REGULATING THE MEDIA

AUSTRALIA
LBC Information Services
Sydney

CANADA and USA
Carswell
Toronto

NEW ZEALAND
Brooker's
Auckland

SINGAPORE and MALAYSIA
Thomson Information (S.E. Asia)
Singapore

REGULATING THE MEDIA

[Second Edition]

THOMAS GIBBONS,

B.A., L.L.M., Dip.Crim.

London
Sweet & Maxwell
1998

[First edition 1991, second edition 1998]

Published by
Sweet & Maxwell Limited of
100 Avenue Road,
Swiss Cottage, London NW3 3PF
http://www.smlawpub.co.uk
Typeset by Dataword Services Limited by Chilcompton
Printed and bound in Great Britain by MPG Books Ltd, Bodmin, Cornwall

A C.I.P. catalogue record for this book
is available from the British Library

ISBN 0421 60660 6

No natural forests were destroyed to make this product,
only farmed timber was used and replanted.

To Judy

Preface

This book is a study of regulation in the British media industry. Although it is possible to make some generalisations about regulation, for the most part it must be understood in the context of the traditions and aspirations of a specific sphere of activity. In the case of the media, there is a complex relationship between their political and cultural roles and their commercial objectives. That has led to the development of a particular set of institutions and practices to guide their behaviour. Whilst the book is written primarily from a legal perspective, it draws on political, social and economic theory to examine the way that law blends with other ways of shaping such behaviour. In the media industry, as in other areas of regulation, the formal law provides only a skeletal indication of the norms and values which actually guide decisions. My aim has been to given an account of the regulatory framework and the way in which different sources of guidance relate to each other for different purposes.

In writing, I have tried to reflect the great wealth of argument and deliberation which has been generated in the political arena generally, in Parliament, in various committees and within the media themselves. As might be expected in such an industry, changes in regulation have largely been accompanied by an articulate examination of the policies at stake. It is clear that many problems are intractable and similar kinds of argument continue to resurface over the years. The book reflects this process of debate, which has been one of the strengths of the media tradition in this country, by organising the material around a series of focal issues which reflect the public interest in the media's work. While the book is aimed primarily at students of regulation and of the media, I hope that it will also be of interest to both the media practitioner and the general reader.

This is an exciting time to be commenting on media regulation. Hardly a day passes without another development in the industry, whether it be an advance in technology, the creation of a new media product, or further modification to patterns of ownership, control and finance. The rapid pace of change presents its own challenges. One is the diverse range and considerable number of sources which must be monitored to analyse what is happening. To meet that challenge, I have rewritten and expanded much of the material whch appeared in the first edition and I have tried to incorporate major developments up to May 31, 1998. The other challenge is substantive and concerns the implications of new forms of media for the continued relevance of a special body of regulation. When the first edition was published, the Broadcasting Act 1990 had paved the way for a transition in the electronic media from public service broadcasting to a lightly regulated, commercialised industry. Much has occurred in the last seven years and the adoption of digital technology, and the possibilities of convergence between the traditional media and other forms of communication, such as telephony and the internet, are now being heralded by some commentators as reasons for dispensing with media regulation altogether. I remain unconvinced by such claims. Convergence and the achievement of a multi-media environment are inevitable, even if the speed of their arrival may be slower than some are currently predicting. However, the social and cultural roles of the media will be no less significant with new forms of delivery. There will continue to be a need for institutions and mechanisms, other than the market process, to enable discourse about those roles to take place between media professionals, politicians and the public, and to preserve the values that all of them represent.

Writing this book would have been impossible without the kind assistance and encouragement of many people. Over the years, discussion with colleagues at Manchester has been invaluable and particular thanks are due to Peter Humphreys and to Anthony Ogus. I have also benefited greatly from the insights provided in conversations and interviews with media practitioners and regulators in all sectors of the industry. The editorial staff at Sweet and Maxwell have been especially generous in their help and forbearance. Not least, I am grateful to Judy, Beth, Tim and Andy for their support and understanding, and for making it all worthwhile.

Thomas Gibbons
Manchester University
June 1998

Contents

Table of Cases

Table of Statutes

Table of Statutory Instruments

Abbreviations

BBC	British Broadcasting Corporation
BCC	Broadcasting Complaints Commission
BSC	Broadcasting Standards Commission
IBA	Independent Broadcasting Authority
ITA	Independent Television Authority
ITC	Independent Television Commission
ITV	independent television
ITVA	Independent Television Association
OFTEL	Office of Telecommunications
PCC	Press Complaints Commission
R.A.	Radio Authority
the 1981 Act	Broadcasting Act 1981
the 1990 Act	Broadcasting Act 1990
the 1996 Act	Broadcasting Act 1996

Chapter One

Introduction

Communication through the mass media has become a dominant part of our lives. Not only is a considerable amount of our leisure time spent in reading newspapers, listening to the radio and watching television, but we have also come to rely on the media as a major source of knowledge about the society that we live in. As such, the media influence our attitudes and opinions, they provide a forum for political debate and they shape our choices.

Although there is much contemporary discussion about the implications of the "information society",[1] it is more appropriate to describe us as living in a "knowledge society," one in which "the production of information and its conversion into knowledge is a primary activity and knowledge is a key aspect of organisational power and social stratification."[2] This is why the media are so important: they play a central role in bringing information to our attention and then placing it in some context, offering interpretations of it and suggesting a proper meaning for it. The media are able to contribute, therefore, to our understanding of what is normal and deviant, acceptable and unacceptable. To the extent that knowledge is used by the state, by politicians and by public and private organisations, it may be seen as a powerful means of exerting social

[1] High Level Group on the Information Society, *Europe and the Global Information Society: Recommendations to the European Council* (1994) (The Bangemann Report). See also R. Collins & C. Murroni, *New Media, New Policies* (1996).

[2] R. V. Ericson *et al.*, *Visualizing Deviance: A Study of News Organization* (1987), p. 11 and see chap. 1 generally. See also M. Gurevitch *et al.* (eds.), *Culture, Society and the Media* (1982); P. Berger and T. Luckmann, *The Social Construction of Reality: A Treatise in the Sociology of Knowledge* (1966).

control, creating social cohesion and both seeing and serving particular interests. In contributing to these processes, the role of the media is to bring information to their readership and audience in a form that makes it intelligible. In particular, the role of the journalist in reporting news may be seen as one of creating common sense out of specialised knowledge. But a similar task is undertaken with other media activity too, whether it be entertainment, both popular and highbrow, or political analysis.

Nevertheless, it is by no means certain exactly what effect the media have on their public. It is no longer thought that the media have a direct effect on behaviour; for example, the watching of violence on television has not been demonstrated to promote or encourage violence in everyday life. But neither are the audience indifferent to the knowledge portrayed by the media, even if it represents a relatively small amount of the knowledge that they accumulate. The more recent tendency in research has been to emphasise the way in which messages are moulded by the media, and then adapted by the audience or readership and integrated into their lives.[3] Equally, it is no longer thought that the media act as "mirrors" of society, although it is recognised that influential groups may use the media to convey their definitions of reality.[4]

Generally, if a clear message exists at all, it is that the relationship between the media and the production of knowledge is a complex and subtle one. It may not be surprising, then, that the form of regulation which has emerged for the media tends to reflect that ambiguity, a curious blend of optimism that mass communication will bring greater understanding, together with a deep suspicion that there is a potential for distortion and manipulation. In the United Kingdom, media structures and traditions have grown in only a piecemeal fashion, responding to new forms of communication as and when they have become available. Originally, the press was the only form of mass media. Initially it was owned by the political parties, later it came to be ruled by the media barons,[5] and now it is

---

[3] See J. Curran *et al.*, "The Study of the Media: Theoretical Approaches" and T. Bennett, "Media, 'Reality', Signification" in *Media, Culture and Society* (M. Gurevitch *et al.*, eds. 1982); R. Negrine, *Politics and the Mass Media in Britain* (2nd ed. 1994), chap. 1.

[4] See J. Curran *et al.*, above, n. 3. See also J. G. Blumler and M. Gurevitch, "Journalists' Orientations to Political Institutions: The Case of Parliamentary Broadcasting" in *Communicating Politics* (P. Golding *et al.* eds., 1986); S. Hall *et al.*, *Policing the Crisis* (1978).

[5] For an overview, see J. Curran and J. Seaton, *Power Without Responsibility: The Press and Broadcasting in Britain* (5th ed., 1997).

an extension of corporate empire. Throughout, its need to maintain efficiency and secure profitability has been held in tension with its journalistic aspirations to free speech and editorial independence. The consequent pressures on journalists have not diminished in the face of increased competition from newer forms of media. Although improved technology in typesetting and printing, together with developments such as freesheets and Web sites on the Internet, have provided new opportunities for the press, the newspaper industry is experiencing a general decline.

It is, therefore, electronic media which are likely to have the most pervasive influence in contributing to our knowledge in the future. Broadcasting was established in 1926 and, under a shadow of government control which still persists,[6] the British Broadcasting Corporation initiated the "era of radio." Radio was regarded as a medium more truly for the masses and it was used by the BBC to disseminate its particular brand of consensual values and artistic creativity unchallenged for 30 years.[7] Although the BBC developed a television service after the Second World War, it was only in 1954 that an independent (or commercial) sector was allowed to share control with it in a "comfortable duopoly"[8] that has not yet been broken up. At that time, the Independent Television Authority was created as a regulatory body to oversee the initiative and, when radio was introduced to the independent sector in 1972, it became the Independent Broadcasting Authority and began to consolidate its supervision of the industry. The most exciting innovation during this period was the creation of Channel 4 in 1980, allowing the smaller, independent producers to enter the sector.

The contemporary period of development began in 1982 as the attractions of the new age of information technology encouraged the decision to exploit the possibilities of cable television and satellite.[9] A Cable Authority was established in 1984 with a brief to promote the expansion of systems that would enable home shopping and

---

[6] Wireless Telegraphy Act 1949.

[7] See A. Briggs, *The History of Broadcasting in the U.K.*, Vol. I *The Birth of Broadcasting* (1961), Vol. II *The Golden Age of Wireless* (1965).

[8] See B. Sendall, *Independent Television in Britain: 1. Origin and Foundations 1946–62* (1982); A. Briggs, *The History of Broadcasting in the U.K.*, Vol. IV *Sound and Vision* (1979); Home Office, (Peacock) *Committee on Financing the BBC* (1986) Cmnd. 9824, chap. 4.

[9] See R. Negrine, "Cable Television in Great Britain" in *Cable Television and the Future of Broadcasting* (Negrine ed., 1985); T. Hollins, *Beyond Broadcasting to the Cable Age* (1984).

information transfer to be provided alongside specialist entertainment.[10] At the same time, political support for the use of the market as the principal allocative mechanism led to the major shift to deregulation which was effected by the Broadcasting Act 1990. That statute established the Independent Television Commission to supervise television programmes, replacing the IBA and the Cable Authority, together with the Radio Authority to supervise sound programmes. It was intended to provide a flexible framework for a whole range of new technologies to be adopted as the future media of mass communication[11] but the rapid pace of development required further legislation, in the Broadcasting Act 1996, to create a framework for digital terrestrial broadcasting and to make more flexible provision for ownership regulation.

Currently, the major challenge for the media is their response to convergences between themselves and other forms of communication, such as telecommunications and the Internet. The introduction of digital technology has altered the parameters of debate about the media because it promises to recast the relationships between producers and audiences, broadcasters and narrowcasters, and programming and interactive capabilities.[12] Before discussing these issues, it will be helpful to consider some perspectives on regulation in general.

A. Regulatory Approaches

The Nature of Regulation

In an abstract sense, the regulation of any practice that is socially beneficial consists of shaping and guiding it to achieve the ends that are thought desirable for it.[13] In doing so, particular forms of regulation reflect the values that have come to dominate the practice

---

[10] Cable and Broadcasting Act 1984, Part I. Satellite television was regulated by the IBA under Part II of that Act.

[11] See Home Office, *Broadcasting in the 90s: Competition, Choice and Quality* (1988) Cm. 517 (White Paper); Home Affairs Committee, *The Future of Broadcasting* 3rd Report (1987–88) H.C. 262-I and II; Broadcasting Research Unit, *A Report From the Working Party on the New Technologies* (1983).

[12] See J. Steemers (ed.), *Changing Channels: The Prospects for Television in a Digital World* (1998).

[13] See also A. I. Ogus, *Regulation: Legal Form and Economic Theory* (1994) p. 1.

and the way in which power has come to be allocated in determining its objectives. A study of regulation will be concerned, then, with examining the various normative sources that are available to constitute or constrain action and to note where effective control of the practice appears to be located. Those norms are often thought to be legalistic in form, but they may equally involve political convention, commercial custom or professional discipline. They may be contrasted with proscriptive legal rules and principles which are intended to eliminate practices that are regarded as anti-social, such as those contained in the general law relating to, for example, crime or torts. More specifically, the laws on defamation, obscenity, contempt of court, confidentiality and official secrecy are instances of proscriptive norms which are especially important for a full understanding of media activity. They are, however, beyond the scope of this book. The focus here will be on forms of regulation that supplement the general law, a specialist body of guidance and processes which, in this case, is characterised by the particular concerns of the media industry and its traditions. For example, journalists have their own set of values, the media's role in the political process means that democratic principles should be considered, and the media's cultural and moral potential raises questions about its production values and basic standards. Much discussion will centre on the programming media, since that is where most of such specialist guidance is to be found. But, throughout, the press will provide a useful standpoint for assessing the need for provisions that go beyond the general law.

Rationales for Media Regulation

Why should there be special provision for the media? One set of reasons deals with economic grounds for regulating in the public interest. It points to market failures which are exemplified in the media but which would also justify regulatory intervention in other industries. The assumption is that the media are engaged in commercial behaviour and that, ideally, the market will allocate resources efficiently by matching production to consumer demands through the price mechanism. Where the market is unable to do that, alternative mechanisms may need to be introduced to correct the failure and they have some bearing on the way in which the media might be regulated.[14]

First, there may be a need for "social regulation" to correct information gaps about the quality of services provided or to deal with externalities ("spillover" effects). The problem of information failure has been singled out for particular attention. Where consumers do not have adequate information, they are unable to obtain what they want and producers are unable to supply it. Information gaps make it difficult for the buyer to judge the worth of the product before it is too late. In relation to the media, the regulation of advertising is a response to this problem. But the market often fails also to provide the means to assess the worth of the media product itself, for example, in the case of programming content which is often not appreciated until it is received. In those cases, or where the transaction costs of providing the information are too high, an alternative mechanism may be the regulatory provision of some minimum guarantee of the standard of material that can be expected.

In the case of externalities — that is, effects whose costs or benefits are not fully reflected in the market price of a product or service — the aim of regulation is to correct the deficiency. A general example would be pollution caused by an industrial process; in the media, interference caused by overlapping frequencies or the disturbance caused by laying a cable system would have a similar impact. Given the high transaction costs which would be entailed by requiring all the affected parties to bargain with each other to secure compensation for losses incurred, it may be more efficient to control the activity through regulation which minimises its disruptive effects.

More significantly for the media, there may be positive externalities caused by there being an insufficient nexus between buyer and seller. Where goods are preferred, not only because individuals desire them for their own enjoyment, but also because they benefit the community at large, it will be difficult for the market to allocate them through the price mechanism. Broadcasting is an example of such "public goods." They benefit the whole community but it is difficult to determine particular individuals' willingness to

[14] The following summary draws on the analysis offered by Ogus, above, n.13, chap. 1. See also I. Ramsay, *Rationales for Intervention in the Consumer Marketplace* (1984) Occasional Paper for the Office of Fair Trading, pp. 15 *et seq.*; S. Breyer, *Regulation and Its Reform* (1982), chaps 1–4. See also W. Hoffman-Reim, *Regulating Media* (1996).

pay for them. This is because, knowing they will receive the goods in any case, individuals have an incentive to "free ride" and let others pay. In such cases, it may be better to finance the provision of the good publicly, rather than have it not provided at all.

Even where broadcasting can be supplied and bought in the market, it may still be unable to secure an adequate nexus between buyer and seller and may have some "impure" public good characteristics. For example, where broadcasting has been financed by advertising, responsiveness to the product has been measured principally through the cruder mechanism of average audience ratings. In such a case, as with publicly financed broadcasting, there will be a need to impose some public standards of quality. Not all forms of media involve public goods in this sense, however. Where it is possible to exclude free riders, there are economic grounds for allowing the market process to operate unhindered. Thus, as the Peacock Committee stressed,[15] the greater the technological potential for subscription services, including "pay-per-view", the closer the electronic media will become to publishing in the print media.

A second kind of regulation is "economic regulation" and it covers goods or services which are supplied through a monopoly or oligopoly. In such cases, there is a lack of competition which may result in prices being raised with no incentive to keep production costs down, or a reduction in the range of goods and services available, or both. In relation to the media, this manifests itself in concern about concentrations of ownership and the control of programme making. It also raises issues about barriers to entry to the market and, in the broadcasting media, the existence of technological limitations on the number of services that can be provided has been the basis of the so-called "scarcity rationale" for regulating it.

The scarcity rationale has played an important role in justifying a different approach to broadcasting compared with the press. It is said that, unlike the situation with the press, where there are no technical limits on the number of newspapers that might be produced, there are only a limited number of frequencies available for broadcasting transmissions. Beyond that number, transmissions will tend to interfere with each other and to allow unlimited access to the spectrum would result in chaos. Interference by government in the market process is justified, then, in order to secure an orderly development of the medium and to ensure that its potential is not wasted.

---

[15] (Peacock) *Committee on Financing the BBC* (1986) Cmnd. 9824, para. 131.

However, the argument has not been found persuasive by economists[16] Almost all resources are limited and relatively scarce and the function of the price mechanism is precisely to determine who is to be allowed to use them. For Coase, the difficulty was that "no property rights were created in these scarce frequencies." Just as land or rare works of art are in relatively short supply but can be allocated through the market, so it was the case with electromagnetic frequencies. The point applies whether or not the whole, albeit limited, spectrum is available or whether government reduces it even further by reserving certain portions of it for the use of, for example, the military or emergency services.

The Peacock Committee reached no conclusion on the question of whether or not property rights in frequencies should be introduced. Instead, it focused on the use of new cable and satellite technologies to circumvent scarcity.[17] But the assumption that the market would locate electromagnetic resources efficiently has not gone unchallenged and it is recognised that there are some problems associated with it.[18] One is that it may be difficult, technically, to specify property rights in the spectrum. Another is that the cost of preventing interferences between transmissions may be too high to be borne by frequency owners. Similarly, high transaction costs in terms of time and money may prevent all users of the spectrum, consumers as well as producers, from organising in a market sufficiently perfect to enable them to negotiate transfers of ownership of the spectrum to reflect their preferences. Furthermore, as a matter of equity, it may not be appropriate to allow control of socially valuable assets such as spectrum to be allocated by reference to wealth and power.

These technical objections may suggest strong reasons for removing spectrum allocation from the market process. But the issue of spectrum scarcity also relates to the use to which the spectrum is put, that is, the programming which is transmitted. In this context, a second set of reasons for regulating the media becomes relevant. It questions whether the market process is relevant at all for

---

[16] R. Coase, "The Federal Communications Commission" (1959) 2 *J. Law & Econ.* 1. See also Peacock, above, n. 15, paras 134–138.

[17] Peacock, above, n. 15, para. 136.

[18] See N. Johnson, "Towers of Babel: The Chaos in Radio Spectrum Utilization and Allocation" (1969) 34 *Law and Contemporary Problems* 505. Johnson was a former Commissioner with the Federal Communications Commission. See also Peacock, above, paras 125–134.

determining the crucial issues of media practice and it stresses, instead, the use of political and philosophical argument in identifying ideals, values and interests. Although in economic terms such argument is about "merit goods" which are to be secured at the expense of efficiency, whether or not for paternalistic reasons, the emphasis is actually on non-economic grounds for treating the media as special. In political theory, these reasons are framed in terms of discussions about freedom of communication and the imposition of media standards. Since they have played such an important part in shaping media objectives, their examination will be postponed to a fuller treatment in chapters two and three.

Describing Regulation

Generally, economic considerations do not present a full picture of regulatory schemes, but they do provide a useful basis for understanding regulation provided it is recognised that they reflect a form of individualism which assumes the desirability of the market as the starting point for discussion.[19] From the perspective of political science, regulation has a less singular goal, and the idea of public constraints being imposed on a private sphere of activity is seen as unrealistic.[20] Instead, there is an emphasis on the complex and shifting relationships that characterise contemporary mixed economies. Descriptively, the image of "regulatory space" has been suggested to depict the arena of power within which groups and organisations vie for control. Within any particular space, the form of regulation will both reflect and determine the extent to which goals continue to be sought through political debate or become routinely organised in institutionalised procedure.[21] What is particularly helpful about this approach is that the regulatory process is not to be seen as distinct from the market and nor is it taken that the market should be regarded as the natural order from which departures should be justified.[22] Rather, the use of market mechanisms is to be viewed as

---

[19] *cf.* M. Hollis and E. Nell, *Rational Economic Man: A Philosophical Critique of Neo-Classical Economics* (1975). See also J. Rawls, *A Theory of Justice* (1971), pp. 259–263.
[20] See L. Hancher and M. Moran, "Introduction" in *Capitalism, Culture and Economic Regulation* (Hancher and Moran eds., 1989).
[21] See L. Hancher and M. Moran, "Organising Regulatory Space" in Hancher & Moran, *op. cit.*
[22] See I. Ramsay, *Consumer Protection* (1989), pp. 24–32. See more generally, M. Hollis and E. Nell, and J. Rawls, above, n. 19.

one type of institutional response amongst many, reflecting the truism that markets are not defined in the absence of regulation but are constituted through it.

In a similar vein, it should not be assumed that there is only one kind of normative response which is appropriate for securing regulatory objectives. In responding to the needs of contemporary society, with its complex and diverse organisation, interests and values, it has been suggested that the law is evolving from a type characterised as autonomous, in which formal and universal principles are provided for all practices, to one that stresses instead the implementing of specific and specialised social policies.[23] In some cases, it may be that those policies cannot or should not themselves be determined in advance and the law may then take on a more reflexive form, in which "attention focuses on creating, shaping, correcting, and redesigning social institutions that function as self-regulating systems." Rather than seeking to achieve particular results, legal norms are directed towards "organisation, procedure and competence."[24] Such an approach is enabling and facilitating rather than stipulative.

However, this does not necessarily entail that law should be characterised as an entirely separate system of norms, one which consists of a self-contained doctrine that co-ordinates but does not directly engage with the norms of the practice it regulates.[25] As will be seen, in media regulation there is a subtle interplay between different layers of policy formation and decision making, drawing on a wide range of normative sources. The statutory framework and judicial determinations are very important, but so are political debate and the expert discourses of relevant disciplines such as media production, economics, administration and technology. What are significant are the points at which each of these normative sources has an influence on the shape of regulation. Partly, that is a matter of institutional design,[26] but it is also dependent on the values and

[23] See P. Nonet and P. Selznick, *Law and Society in Transition: Toward Responsive Law* (1978).

[24] G. Teubner, "Substantive and Reflexive Elements in Modern Law" (1983) 17 *Law and Society Review* 239–285, pp. 251 and 266 *et seq.*

[25] For such an "autopoietic" account of law, see G. Teubner (ed.), *Autopoietic Law: A New Approach to Law and Society* (1988). See also R. Cotterrell, *Law's Community: Legal Theory in Sociological Perspective* (1995) pp. 105–108; M. Loughlin, *Public Law and Political Theory* (1992), pp. 255–257.

[26] See T. Prosser, "Democratisation, Accountability and Institutional Design: Reflections on Public Law" in *Law, Legitimacy and the Constitution* (P. McAuslan and J. McEldowney eds., 1985).

actions of the individual actors who make the regulatory system work.[27] Certainly there will be some "partial closure" where one particular kind of normative guidance, whether it be rules of statutory interpretation or economic arguments or technological necessity, is given a leading part in finalising outcomes. But, generally, there will be a complex interrelationship between the different sources of guidance. What characterises regulation, then, is the existence of a set of institutionalised normative constraints which are applied to a specific social sphere. Furthermore, it is implicit that there should be developed principles and reasoning which are appropriate to its practices.[28] In this sense, regulation is synonymous with a broader conception of law itself.[29] The expectation must be that a regulatory scheme will be capable of being rationally justified, as will the particular policies that it promotes or allows to be developed. To that end, the ideas of participation and accountability are important concepts for the development and evaluation of regulatory forms.[30]

Assessing Media Regulation

An important question is how any regulatory scheme is to be judged. One set of criteria relate to the practicalities of institutional design.[31] The relative costs of different options need to be assessed, in so far as that can be done. Then the forum for regulatory decision-making, be it the courts, a regulatory agency or some less formal body, must be determined. Here, a regulatory agency has many advantages.[32] It enables expertise to be utilised in a form that is independent from government and direct political influence and it can facilitate greater participation by the public, although there are possible disadvantages of remoteness and a lack of accountability. Another important issue is

---

[27] See Cotterrell, above, n. 25, p.107.

[28] See Cotterrell, above, n. 25, pp. 320–325.

[29] See Loughlin generally, above, n. 25, and his elaboration of a "functionalist" conception of public law.

[30] See T. Prosser, "Towards a Critical Public Law" (1982) 9 *Journal of Law and Society* 1–19; Prosser, above, n. 26.

[31] See R. Baldwin and C. McCrudden, *Regulation and Public Law* (1987); I. Harden and N. Lewis, *The Noble Lie* (1986); J. Jowell, *Law and Bureaucracy* (1975); K.C. Davis, *Discretionary Justice* (1969).

[32] See Baldwin and McCrudden, above, n. 31, pp. 4–7, 9–12.

the scope of any discretion which is allowed when allocating various duties, powers and standards; the more tightly drafted rules will have a more predictable effect but may be inflexible and contain loopholes, whereas the more principled guidance will be flexible but less easy to control.[33]

A broader set of criteria for judging a regulatory scheme may depend on observing a particular model of society — for example, whether it is to be seen as a hierarchical order, a competitive market or a co-operative community.[34] That, in turn, may indicate the extent to which the scheme can be regarded as legitimate. In one sense, the idea of legitimacy amounts to little more than the description of a general acquiescence in the authority of the political order. The reasons why such authority is accepted are not significant for attributing legitimacy in this sense, although it may be implied that the fact of legitimacy serves to confer normative validity. Another meaning of legitimacy is more substantive, however, and implies that there are good reasons for believing that the political order is worthy of allegiance. It requires a sensitivity to critical reflection on the way in which a society is organised and on its most basic principles.[35]

Both senses of legitimacy may be applied, by analogy, to the status of a regulatory scheme. It has been suggested, for example, that the performance of regulatory agencies should be judged in terms of their legislative mandates, accountability, expertise, efficiency and respect for due process.[36] Such criteria are helpful for clarifying possible grounds for disaffection with the way in which agencies carry out their functions. While failure to command the respect of those whom it organises would not jeopardise the existence of the

---

[33] See J.M. Black, "'Which Arrow?': Rule Type and Regulatory Policy" [1995] *Public Law* 94–118; E. Rubin, "Law and Regulation in the Administrative State" (1989) 89 *Columb. L.R.* 369–426. These issues have also been considered in the economics of law literature: see A. I. Ogus, "Quantitative Rules and Judicial Decision Making" in *The Economic Approach to Law* (P. Burrows and C. Veljanovski eds., 1981); I. Ehrlich and R. Posner, "An economic analysis of legal rulemaking" (1974) 3 *J. Legal Studies* 257–286.

[34] See K. Dyson, "The Debate about the Future of Broadcasting: An Analysis" in *Broadcasting and New Media Policies in Western Europe* (K. Dyson *et al.* eds., 1988), at pp. 65–69.

[35] See W. Connolly, "The Dilemma of Legitimacy" in *Legitimacy and the State* (W. Connolly ed., 1984).

[36] On this theme, see R. Baldwin, *Rules and Government* (1995); R. Baldwin and C. McCrudden, *Regulation and Public Law* (1987), chaps. 1–3; R. Baldwin, M. Cave and T. Jones, *The Regulation of Independent Local Radio and its Reform* (1986) Brunel Discussion Papers in Economics No. 8603, pp. 8–28. See also T. Jones, "Administrative Law, Regulation and Legitimacy" (1989) 16 *J. Law & Soc.* 410–425.

agency, let alone the political order itself, the acceptance of regulatory arrangements is clearly important in assessing their value. Yet it may be that those criteria can only enhance our understanding when they illuminate the idea of legitimacy in a substantive sense. Certainly an emphasis on procedural regularity through legality, with or without the assumption that it reflects general democratic approval, does not serve to justify any particular form of regulation.[37]

These varying perspectives show that it is not possible to examine a practice with only one regulatory approach in mind. Rather, regulation may be seen as a means of integrating a complex pattern of spheres of action and its success will be judged by reference to the purposes that the practice is intended to secure. Thus, in relation to the media, it will be important to notice the way in which forms of regulation are likely to have an impact on their central function, the distribution of knowledge in the broadest sense. Some indication has already been given of the role that mass communication may play in that task, and the ideas of free speech and of public service are important focal issues for settling upon an appropriate regulatory scheme. Of particular interest will be the implications of different bases for decision-making for controlling the knowledge that the media disseminate and the extent to which professional expertise can shape that knowledge. One feature of contemporary society is the way in which areas of knowledge appear to become ever more specialised, with the consequence that the distance between expert cultures and the general public grows greater.[38]

As a practice, the media do not have a set of absolute principles to govern their operations. But practical choices about the material that they produce and the way in which they are organised have raised a number of central issues, about which differing aims and interests can be resolved through discussion. This book examines that discussion and the axes about which justifications for different forms of regulation may emerge. Decisions as to how to regulate may be thought of as constituting the domains — political, institutional, professional or the market — within which the focal issues of the practice are settled and its internal doctrine developed. They determine where power should lie, and where effective decision-making should occur.

---

[37] On the distinction between legality and legitimation, see J. Habermas, *The Theory of Communicative Action*, Vol. 1 *Reason and the Rationalization of Society* (1984), pp. 264 *et seq.*
[38] See J. Habermas, *The Theory of Communicative Action*, Vol. 2 *Lifeworld and System: A Critique of Functionalist Reason* (1987), pp. 326 *et seq.*

B. Convergences

In deciding whether, or what kind of, regulation is appropriate, it is important to keep in mind a set of convergences which are evolving in the media industry. Technological convergence raises questions about the nature of the media product and its dissemination. Transfrontier convergence is a response to the increasingly international character of media activities. Regulatory convergence is a reaction to each of those developments. Since these convergences are still in a state of evolution, much discussion about their implications for the industry and policy-makers is necessarily speculative.[39] But it is possible to identify a series of trends and they will undoubtedly shape further progress.

Technological Convergence

It is the development of computer technology which has created the potential for convergence in media forms. Information, including text and pictures whether moving or still, can be converted to a common form, digital bits, and they can be packaged and distributed in common ways. The limitations of the older bases of media dissemination, such as paper and analogue radio frequencies, thereby become minimalised. The way that material is originally created does not necessarily have implications for the way it can be disseminated and the audience that it can reach, and new products and new markets for them can be established. One of the most significant aspects of such digitalisation is that it enables the flow of material to be much more closely controlled by both producers and consumers. Material can be bundled into discrete elements which can be marketed separately. Consumers can choose to obtain precisely the type and amount of material that they want. This interactive potential

---

[39] For discussions, see R. Collins (ed.), *Converging Media: Converging Regulation?* (1996); T. Prosser *et al.*, "The Impact of New Communications Technologies on Media Concentrations and Pluralism" (1996) Final Report of a Study prepared for the Council of Europe. See also A. Weymouth & B. Lamizet (eds.), *Markets and Myths: Forces for Change in the Media of Western Europe* (1996). For a view from the United States, see T. G. Krattenmaker and L. A. Powe, "Converging First Amendment Principles for Converging Communications Media" (1995) 104 *Yale Law Journal* 1719–41.

has important ramifications for traditional mass media which, by definition, have provided a varied diet of writing and programmes to a relatively undifferentiated readership and audience.

In deciding what form of regulation is appropriate for digitalised media, however, it is important not to be driven by the technical form. Newspaper articles may be word-processed on computers and sent by e-mail (using a telecommunications system) to the printing works. A film may be ordered by telephone and sent down the telephone line for viewing on demand. One programme may be sent by terrestrial broadcasting as both an analogue and a digital transmission. Computer users may surf the Internet and select the pages they want to see, watching films and listening to music. But they may also choose a "webcasting" site which sends programmes to them at the site's discretion until they sign off. In each of these cases, the digital basis of the item is less fundamental than its nature as a mass-oriented or interactive product.

Technological convergence can be deceptive, therefore. It can encourage the impression that, not only is the method of communication changing, but that the character of mass media itself is altering too. Yet the issues to be resolved in shaping media practices and standards remain the same, whatever the form of delivery.[40] The claims of free speech and editorial independence still have to be ranged against the demands of quality and accountability, and the appropriate means of organising media activity decided. This book is primarily concerned with the way in which those issues are manifested in the media tradition.

Transfrontier convergence

A number of transfrontier issues have arisen in the media industry. Some of them have been prompted by technological developments. Satellite and telecommunications advances have challenged the integrity of national boundaries; satellite footprints are simply too broad and the traffic on telecommunications systems, including the Internet, is so busy and diverse that it is difficult to contain. In addition, the developing political structure of Europe, manifested in

---

[40] See also J. Steemers, "Broadcasting is Dead. Long Live Digital Choice. Perspectives from the United Kingdom and Germany" (1997) 3 *Convergence* 51–71.

the Council of Europe and especially the European Community, has had a dominant influence on the media industry.[41]

At an international level, the allocation and co-ordination of frequencies and the organisation of satellite provision is regulated through a number of international treaties.[42] They do not attempt to deal with the content of the material which is broadcast and that has been tackled at the European level in two ways. One is through the Council of Europe's Convention on Transfrontier Television of 1989.[43] The other is the European Community's "Television Without Frontiers" Broadcasting Directive.[44] In addition, the European Community has issued directives which deal with satellite and telecommunications standards and European competition law is becoming increasingly relevant to media activities.

The problem with transfrontier transmissions is that, in the absence of co-ordinated action, the creation and reception of programming will be governed by different regulatory jurisdictions. This means that the programmes are likely to comply with some country's standards of quality or advertising but not with others. Programme makers will have to restrict the reach of their material, if possible, or else satisfy the demands of the strictest regulator. The solution to this difficulty, in both the Transfrontier Convention and the Broadcasting Directive, is to require that broadcasts from one member state should be allowed to be transmitted to and received in every other member state, provided they satisfy a set of minimum standards which apply to all. It is a principle of mutual recognition resting on some basic harmonisation.

With the Council of Europe having a wider remit than the European Community, the Transfrontier Convention was the initial focus for discussion of these issues. But it was also more concerned with cultural policy and individual rights and these issues naturally found their way into the Convention. Most of the overall framework is reflected in the Broadcasting Directive, however, since discussion

---

[41] See generally P. Humphreys, *Media and Media Policy in Western Europe* (1996). See also L. P. Hitchens, "Identifying European Community Audio-Visual Policy in the Dawn of the Information Society" (1996) 2 *Yearbook of Media and Entertainment Law* 45–73.

[42] See S. White *et al.*, *Satellite Communications in Europe: Law and Regulation* (2nd ed., 1996).

[43] European Treaty Series No. 132. (hereinafter, the "Transfrontier Convention").

[44] Council Directive (89/552/EEC) of October 3, 1989 and Directive 97/36/EC of the European Parliament and of the Council (Consolidated Version, 1997) (hereinafter, the "Broadcasting Directive").

in the European Community was conducted in parallel, and there was strong pressure to harmonise the two measures as far as possible to minimise jurisdictional conflicts and assist enforcement. Some provisions in the Convention are not found in the Directive, namely those relating to freedom of information, programme standards, access to public events and marketing in a single jurisdiction, but the remainder are virtually duplicated.[45]

The Broadcasting Directive was formulated within the broader context of European audio-visual policy.[46] There were demands for the promotion of European industrial standards against overseas competition and the protection of European culture through the expansion of an indigenous production industry. But there were also demands for liberalisation of the broadcasting sector and the breaking of the public service broadcasters' hold over national media. There was, indeed, a complex political debate about its eventual content, with claims for cultural diversity being opposed by those for cultural unity, with liberal (market) policies being countered by interventionist policies, and with different institutions and pressure groups seeking to augment their own positions. Not surprisingly, the Directive turned out to be quite different from the proposals first suggested in the Green Paper.[47] It does not extend to copyright, for example, and it does not require states to insist on advertising in all broadcasting, but it does include provisions for programming quotas and a strong right of reply. There are only limited public service provisions, principally relating to the protection of minors, but states are allowed to impose stricter requirements on programming directed solely within their own jurisdiction. The main provisions of the Broadcasting Directive that emerged were as follows. As mentioned, a quota of a "majority" of European programming was required. Ten per cent of programming had to be reserved for independent productions. There was a two-year "window" between the release of a film and its showing on television. The major part of the Directive dealt with advertising and sponsorship, but the provision for the protection of minors and a right of reply was included in the final version.

---

45 For a discussion of the Convention, see E. Barendt, *Broadcasting Law: A Comparative Study* (1993), pp. 222–229.

46 See R. Collins, *Broadcasting and Audio-Visual Policy in the Single European Market* (1994). See also C. O'Leary & D. Goldberg, "Television Without Frontiers" in T. Daintith (ed.), *Implementing E.C. Law in the United Kingdom: Structures for Indirect Rule* (1995).

47 *Television Without Frontiers* (1984) COM(84) 300 final.

In 1995, a new round of discussions started as the outcome of the European Commission's regular review of the Directive's implementation. The Commission made proposals relating to jurisdictional problems, the need to regulate "teleshopping" and the desirability of strengthening the protection of children. Following amendments introduced by the European Parliament, a new Directive has now been issued.[48] Some changes involve clarifications of the previous position. For example, it is confirmed that Member States' jurisdiction over television broadcasters is dependent on the latters' place of establishment, which is determined mainly by the location of their central administration and their programme decision-making.[49] There is provision for improved legal remedies and for the protection of free-to-air broadcasts of important public events. In addition, teleshopping has been brought within the purview of the Directive in response to ambiguity about its status as programming or advertising. Furthermore, at the instigation of the European Parliament, there is much enhanced protection for minors and a strengthened right of reply. Generally, the Directive will be implemented in due course through the broadcasters' and regulators' codes of practice. There will be detailed discussion of the application of its provisions to substantive issues, where relevant, in later chapters.

Other areas of European Community influence may be anticipated here also. The desire to promote the single market has prompted an important measure relating to digital transmissions.[50] More generally, the requirements of European Community competition law also impinge on media transactions, although they are usually applied indirectly as part of the British regulators' responsibilities.

Regulatory convergence

Both technological convergence and transfrontier convergence raise questions about the regulatory approach that is best for the media. To

---

[48] See above, n. 44. See P. Keller, "The New Television Without Frontiers Directive" (1997–98) 3 *Yearbook of Media and Entertainment Law* 177–195.

[49] This endorses the decision of the European Court of Justice in *Commission of the European Communities (France intervening) v. United Kingdom* Case 222/94 [1996] 3 C.M.L.R. 793, *The Times*, September 30, 1996. The ITC had already indicated that it would comply with the ruling and would no longer license on the basis of uplink. But it maintained that there would be little practical effect because most uplinking services are connected with the U.K. by establishment in any event.

[50] Council Directive 95/47/EC.

the extent that methods of dissemination increasingly employ telecommunications systems, for example, and to the extent that the problems of media regulation increasingly involve competition issues, is there any need for specialist media regulators? The latter issues mean that, in recent years, there has been greater involvement in media regulation by such bodies as the Office of Telecommunications (OFTEL), the Director-General of Fair Trading and the Monopolies and Mergers Commission. The ITC and the R.A. are usually required to consult with those bodies when deciding matters relevant to competition and are clearly junior partners on such issues. More generally, as the media have developed and the means of delivery have become more sophisticated, there has been an increase in differing regulatory regimes without much effort to rationalise them. These kinds of overlap make a reduction in the proliferation of regulators very attractive. However, rationalisation is not a neutral process and should not pre-empt reform without deeper consideration. The aims of media regulation need to be considered first and, if the promotion of certain democratic and media values are thought important, it is those values which should determine the form of regulation, whether within or outwith a competitive environment, and regardless of the media's technological base. The scope of those values is, naturally, open to debate and will be taken up the next two chapters.

Chapter Two

Political Values

A. Freedom in Communication

Absence of State Interference with Free Speech

Arguments for regulating the media have to be considered in the context of the political value most closely associated with media activities, that of free speech. At the outset, it must be recognised that the media are mainly concerned with the commercial activities of providing entertainment and securing financial success, and their output may not necessarily have any special worth which merits protection. Nevertheless, they do provide the most important commercial and institutional channels for disseminating information, for conveying opinion and for enabling exchanges to take place between individuals and groups.[1] While they are not the sole avenue of expression, any restrictions on the media's ability to communicate will broadly tend to interfere with speech. For that reason, in determining whether there can be any justification for the state to impose such restrictions, both politicians and the media have drawn on the privileged status accorded to free speech in the liberal tradition. Freedom of speech is considered to be an important principle, not only because its protection may be regarded as a consequence of securing liberty for the individual in general,[2] but

[1] For a study of television's potential and limitations in this respect, see S. Livingstone & P. Lunt, *Talk on Television* (1994).

[2] See J. S. Mill, *On Liberty* (1859); F. Schauer, *Free Speech: A Philosophical Enquiry* (1982) pp. 5 *et seq.*

also because it is thought to safeguard in particular the values of discovering truth, participating in a democracy and promoting human dignity.

The argument from truth is expressed in Mill's two "hypotheses" that "We can never be sure that the opinion we are endeavouring to stifle is a false opinion; and if we were sure, stifling it would be an evil still."[3] The first of these has been described as the "avoidance of mistake argument"[4] and makes the point that since we can never be sure that what we suppress as false is in fact false, we must allow free discussion as a method of testing for errors in beliefs and opinions. The argument is based on a number of assumptions. First, is supposed that the purpose of speech and discussion is the discovery of truth. Secondly, it is believed that the pursuit of truth is an absolute value which must be achieved at the expense of other goals. Thirdly, it is assumed that all suppression of discussion occurs because the opinions expressed are thought to be false.[5] Where these conditions do not apply, however, the avoidance of mistake argument provides no compelling support for giving priority to free speech.[6] Similarly, if the pursuit of truth is the prime value, it must follow that where knowledge is not advanced by discussion or could be secured by other more effective means such as indoctrination, free speech has no claim to special protection either.[7] In any event, it may be doubted whether discussion does always lead to truth. The argument incorporates a view of knowledge as the product of competition between opposing opinions in a "marketplace of ideas." Since truth cannot plausibly consist of a consensus arising from discussion,[8] it must be assumed that some objective notion of truth will flourish and will emerge and be recognised, given the opportunity for differing claims to truth to engage with each other. Mill thought that a sufficient condition for this to happen would be to prohibit the persecution of speech, but history has not demonstrated that truth will always surface in this way and there is

---

[3] J. S. Mill, *On Liberty* (Penguin ed., 1974), p. 77.
[4] C. L. Ten, *Mill on Liberty* (1980), p. 125.
[5] Schauer, above, n. 2, p. 23.
[6] See also E. Barendt, *Freedom of Speech,* (1985), p. 11.
[7] See Ten, above, n. 4, pp. 128 *et seq*. Ten regards the value of toleration as a more important reason for protecting free speech, however; see pp. 142 *et seq*.
[8] Although discussion is an important element in securing rational assurances that beliefs are true. See n. 13, below.

no reason to suppose that a free media would make a special contribution to the process.[9]

Mill's second hypothesis has as its main component what has been described as the "assumption of infallibility argument."[10] This also depends for its force on a belief about human rationality, but the emphasis is on the conditions which are necessary for individuals to be confident that, for the purpose of action (including the expression of the belief), what they believe to be true is to be taken as actually true. Rational assurance in a belief, not certainty that it is true, is what is being sought.[11] On that basis, freedom to engage in discussion, in order to expose beliefs to contradiction and refutation, is seen as the best way of securing that rational assurance. Schauer characterises this argument as one from uncertainty, noting that it stresses falsifiability rather than verifiability: "allowing the expression of contrary views is the only rational way of recognising human fallibility, and making possible the rejection or modification of those of our beliefs that are erroneous."[12] A more positive way of putting it, however, would be to emphasise that it is through discussion and argument that we can examine the very criteria that are to be used in justifying the beliefs that we understand to be true.[13] This offers strong grounds for denying interference with the types of speech that provide such assurances. Here, the media may have ambivalent roles. On the one hand, they can contribute to the range of ideas and information which is needed to provide confidence in beliefs. On the other hand, the media may promote a view of the world, an ideological perspective, which itself amounts to an "assumption of infallibility." It must not be presumed, then, that the interests of the media are identical with the pursuit of free speech. Rather, some regulation of the media may well be justified in order to secure freedom in communication.[14]

---

[9] See Schauer, above, n. 2, pp. 20–30; S. Ingber, "The Marketplace of Ideas: A Legitimizing Myth" (1984) 1 *Duke Law Journal* 1.

[10] Ten, above, n. 4.

[11] "Whereas Stephen merely wanted men to have true beliefs, Mill wishes them to know the truth": Ten, above, n. 4, p. 130.

[12] Above, n. 2, p.25.

[13] For differing perspectives on this theme, see R. Bernstein, *Beyond Objectivity and Truth* (1983); J. Habermas *Communication and the Evolution of Society* (1979); A. MacIntyre, *After Virtue* (2nd ed., 1984); H. Putnam, *Reason, Truth and History* (1982); (William) *Report of the Committee on Obscenity and Film Censorship* (1979) Cm. 7772, para. 5.21.

[14] See E. Barendt, *Freedom of Speech* (1985), p. 83.

A different justification for free speech, and one which suggests a special role for the media, however, is the argument from democracy.[15] Like the argument from truth, it is consequentialist in form, depending for its force on acceptance of the value of democratic government and, in particular, a version of such government which allows ultimate decision-making *by* the people, as opposed to *for* the people.[16] What this entails is that the electorate should be able to discuss the government's actions and policies in order to secure a measure of accountability and responsiveness, with a real possibility that the government might be removed from office. Ultimately, it is the people's considered view of what policy is right or wrong that ought to prevail. In order to secure a consensus of policy, free speech is required so that there might be the greatest opportunity for differing points of view to be aired and for sufficient information to be available as a basis for making decisions. In the interests of the audience, then, speakers should not be inhibited from offering their opinions.

As Schauer points out, the argument resembles a specialised version of the argument from truth; it is accepted that the government cannot be regarded as infallible in matters of political truth and that the only way to discover that truth, or at least to be confident that all erroneous avenues have been eliminated, is to prevent speech from being curtailed. In a different respect, where the weight of the democratic argument rests more on the value of participation in the political process, its strength as a justification for protecting free speech depends on the fact of experiencing a particular type of democracy, one in which people engage in discussion about policy and thereby have some real influence on decision-making. The argument from democracy is weakened to the extent that people are removed from the policy-making process and, similarly, to the extent that rational decision-making has no influence on policy-making. Furthermore, where majority rule alone characterises a democracy, and the majority's wish is to suppress free speech, there will be no democratic basis for protecting it. As a principle based on democratic theory, freedom of speech derives its

---

[15] See generally, A. Meiklejohn, *Political Freedom: the Constitutional Powers of the People* (1965); Schauer, above, n. 2, chap. 3. From different perspectives, see also J. Curran, "Mass Media and Democracy Revisited" in J. Curran & M. Gurevitch (eds.) *Mass Media and Society* (1996); J. Keane, *Media and Democracy* (1991); T. Campbell, *The Left and Rights: A Conceptual Analysis of the Idea of Socialist Rights* (1983), chap. 8.
[16] See J. Lively, *Democracy* (1975), pp. 29–49.

force much more from a sceptical tendency which stresses the fallibility of those in power and displays a healthy attitude of incredulity towards the claims of authority. The need is for political choices to be justified and for mistakes, with their potential for serious and wide-reaching consequences, to be avoided. In this task, the media have come to play a significant part, both in providing a platform for political debate and in helping to mould opinion.

The arguments from truth and from democracy are intended to counter restrictions on expression without depending on more general arguments which may establish the citizen's liberty from interference by society or the State. They also focus on the benefits that will accrue to the listener when speech is unrestrained.[17] Other grounds for free speech do not provide independent arguments in the same way and concentrate rather on the speaker's interests. For example, it may be argued that individual autonomy or the right to equal concern and respect require protection for freedom of speech,[18] but they do not provide grounds for giving speech such a special place in promoting the good life or in leading to self-fulfilment that it should be given priority over other activity.[19] Rather, protecting speech may be one of many ways of achieving broader conceptions of moral or political aspiration and these may also be served by actually curtailing speech.[20] Arguments of this type, then, depend on the particular version of human flourishing that is being claimed for the speaker and are not confined to the liberal tradition, since the value of free speech is recognised in a range of approaches.[21] But there is a central place for communication in securing truth and democracy and, for that reason, it is the promotion of those values which have been most emphasised in the relationship between the media and freedom of speech.

---

[17] On the differing interests in free speech, see Barendt, above, n. 6, pp. 23–28.

[18] T. Scanlon, "A Theory of Free Expression" (1972) 1 *Public Affairs* 204–226; R. Dworkin, "Is There a Right to Pornography?" (1981) 1 *Oxford Journal of Legal Studies* 177–212.

[19] F. Schauer, above, n. 2, chaps. 4 and 5; Barendt, above, n. 6, pp. 14–20.

[20] Scanlon later modified his view in this direction; see "Freedom of Speech and Categories of Expression", (1979) 40 *U. Pittsburg L. R.* 519–524.

[21] See Campbell, above, n. 15; S. Hall, "Media Power and Class Power" in *Bending Reality: The State of the Media* (J. Curran *et al.* eds., 1986); P. Lind, *Marcuse and Freedom* (1985); A. Walicki, "The Marxian Conception of Freedom" and J. Bernstein, "Habermas" in *Conceptions of Liberty in Political Philosophy* (Z. Pelczynski and J. Gray eds., 1984).

The Legal Status of the Media

Freedom of speech operates as an independent principle for assessing claims that the media should be free from regulation. It requires that there should be particularly strong reasons for controlling or interfering with communication — reasons which go beyond those typically used specify the State's interest in regulating conduct. Nevertheless, for the law in general, there is no tradition of giving preferential status to free speech.[22] Furthermore, with only a few exceptions, the law does not accord any special treatment to the media in recognition of their close relationship with free speech. The formal approach is libertarian, there being no prior restraint on speech, so that an individual may communicate without first seeking official approval and thereby risking unpredictable, possibly ill-motivated and bureaucratic exercises of discretion.[23] If, however, as Blackstone put it, "he publishes what is improper, mischievous or illegal, he must take the consequences of his own temerity."[24] As a result, the extent of freedom for speech has to be judged against the restraints intended to protect what the legislature and judiciary consider to be more valuable interests.

Thus, for the timorous at least, the law effectively inhibits speech in the interests of preserving reputations, official secrets and confidences, and safeguarding intellectual property. It penalises obscenity and the giving of moral or religious offence. It prevents speech from compromising the administration of justice. For the most part, the balance between these interests and the pursuit of truth or participation in a democracy has been merely reflected in settled principles or rules. Until relatively recently, there have been only limited circumstances when it has been possible directly to invoke the free speech principle, for example, in determining what constitutes fair comment as a defence to defamation or the public interest as a defence to breach of confidence or copyright. Even then, the courts' attitude, in so far as any pattern could be discerned, tended to diminish the importance of the principle.[25]

---

[22] A detailed treatment of the law relating to all aspects of speech is beyond the scope of this book, and has been well discussed elsewhere. See G. Robertson and A. Nicol, *Media Law* (3rd ed., 1992); S. Bailey, D. Harris and B. Jones, *Civil Liberties* (4th ed., 1995) chaps. 5–8; E. Barendt, above, n. 6.

[23] For a discussion of prior restraint, see Barendt, above, n. 6, chap. 4.

[24] *Blackstone's Commentaries* (1765), Book IV, pp. 151–152.

[25] See A. Boyle, "Freedom of Expression as a Public Interest in English Law" [1982] *Public Law* 574–612.

A different approach has emerged during the past decade, however, as a result of the influence of the European Convention on Human Rights. Article 10 of the Convention provides a right to freedom of expression, one which includes the freedom to hold opinions and to receive and impart information. It does not prevent the licensing of broadcasting, however, and it is subject to exceptions, prescribed by law and necessary in a democratic society, in the interests of national security and territorial integrity, the prevention of disorder or crime, the protection of health and morals and of reputation or confidentiality, and upholding the authority of the judiciary. These interferences must be justified by a "pressing social need."[26] Until recently, the courts treated the Convention as having only persuasive authority in deciding free speech issues but they have now altered their position. They have decided that Article 10 actually reflects the common law's position on free speech[27] and this is beginning to have some effect in protecting the media's interests.

Although there are indications that the law is beginning to acknowledge the free speech principle, the media's position is generally not regarded as being different from that of any individual. At most, there is some recognition of their role as a surrogate for the public's interest in the dissemination of information and the scrutiny of official behaviour. Thus, in the law of defamation, the media have secured certain preferential treatment in relation to the defences of absolute privilege, for example the contemporaneous publication of a fair and accurate report of judicial proceedings, and qualified privilege, for example non-malicious, fair and accurate reports of certain public proceedings and announcements.[28] In the law of contempt, while the media attract strict liability for creating a substantial risk that the course of justice will be seriously impeded or prejudiced, it is a condition of liability that such a risk is created only incidentally in the course of discussion of matters of public

---

[26] See *Sunday Times v. United Kingdom* [1979] 2 E.H.R.R. 245. See generally, D. J. Harris *et al.*, *Law of the European Convention on Human Rights* (1995) pp. 372–416.

[27] *Attorney-General v. Guardian Newspapers (No. 2)* [1988] 3 All E.R. 545 (balance of public interest in disclosing a confidence); *Derbyshire County Council v. Times Newspapers* [1993] 1 All E.R. 1011 (council's inability to sue in defamation for political criticism); *Rantzen v. Mirror Group Newspapers* [1993] 4 All E.R. 975 (chilling effect of excessive damages awards in libel); *Goldsmith v. Bhoyrul* [1997] 4 All E.R. 268 (political party cannot sue in libel). See generally, E. Barendt, "Libel and Freedom of Speech in English Law" [1993] *Public Law* 449–464.

[28] Defamation Act 1996, ss. 14 and 15. In respect of contempt, there is a not dissimilar provision in Contempt of Court Act 1981, s. 4.

interest.[29] Where public access to some types of court hearings is restricted, journalists are allowed to attend juvenile courts, domestic hearings in magistrates' courts, and the presentation of some sensitive evidence, although there are restrictions on what may be reported.[30] For some, the existence of the press bench in courts is an important symbol of the media's role here.[31] In the law relating to breach of confidence, the function of the media has been specifically taken into account, if not always endorsed, when balancing the public interest in obtaining information against the claim that it would be wrong to disclose it.[32]

Generally, then, the media's position under the law is the same as that of any individual, although in some limited respects it is rather better. Does it need additional protection as an institution, in recognition of its special role in providing opportunities for mass debate and discussion?[33] The media may want to claim that their interests are identical with the protection of free speech but, often, their association with truth and participation in a democracy is only incidental. An advantage of giving special status to the media as an institution would be to provide a more tangible safeguard for free speech in order to prevent it from being balanced too easily by other interests. This might be especially pertinent if the media were to assume special responsibilities for informing the public about government activities. Then the question would go beyond the matter of protecting publication and dissemination to include the possibility of positive rights to investigate, perhaps with duties being imposed on officials to co-operate with the media. The result would be to institutionalise the role of the media as the Fourth Estate,[34] a watchdog representing the people in an inefficient democracy. There are a number of difficulties, however, about allowing the media such a special place in the formal democratic process. The relationship between the media and Parliament would need to be clarified to

---

[29] Contempt of Court Act 1981, ss. 1 and 5.

[30] See respectively: Children and Young Persons Act 1933, s. 47(2); Magistrates Courts Act 1980, s. 69(2); Children and Young Persons Act 1933, s. 37(1). For a statement of judicial attitudes, See *R. v. Waterfield* [1975] 1 W.L.R. 711, C.A.

[31] Robertson and Nicol, above, n. 22, p. 17.

[32] See *Attorney-General v. Guardian Newspapers* [1987] 1 W.L.R. 1248; *Attorney-General v. Guardian Newspapers (No. 2)* [1988] 3 W.L.R. 776. See also E. Barendt, "Spycatcher and Freedom of Speech" [1989] *Public Law* 209–212.

[33] See Schauer, above, n. 2, pp. 106–109.

[34] See J. Curran & J. Seaton, *Power Without Responsibility: The Press and Broadcasting in Britain* (5th ed. 1997) p. 7.

prevent the latter's function from being usurped. In addition, doubts about the media's own accountability and responsiveness would have to be satisfied. At a more practical level, there may be uncertainty about what should count as journalism for the purposes of protection and the possibility that too much material would be included regardless of content. There is, too, the probability that the claims of journalists, editors and proprietors would not coincide.[35] On balance, the arguments do not show why the media should be given preferential treatment in the law relating to free speech. Indeed, many journalists would not want it since the profession's legitimacy is regarded, perhaps somewhat romantically, as depending on its identification with ordinary people.[36]

Nevertheless, as Barendt notes, the idea of broadcasting freedom has been given constitutional recognition in some European jurisdictions.[37] It entails that, in order to safeguard free speech in the context of broadcasting, some regulation is actually necessary to ensure that the interests both of those who communicate through the medium and of their audiences are secured. One element of this freedom is protection for broadcasters against state censorship,[38] but another is a set of "institutional" rights whereby broadcasters are free to discharge their responsibilities to satisfy programme standards without state interference.[39] In fact, broadcasting freedom is closely associated with public service aims, and its acknowledgement assumes that some broadcasters should have the responsibility to provide a public service and that they can be held to account for it. A similar notion of editorial freedom can be envisaged for the press if it is recognised that journalistic ideals of fair and accurate reporting may need to be protected against proprietorial interference.[40] It is in considering regulation to secure both kinds of freedom, broadcasting and editorial, that arguments about the value of media pluralism are especially relevant.

---

[35] Barendt, above, n. 6, pp. 66–77, especially at p. 71.

[36] This has been a constant theme in submissions by the press to successive Royal Commissions. It has also been apparent in editorial responses to Parliamentary debate about the case for special treatment, for example, in relation to the Contempt of Court Act 1981 and the Police and Criminal Evidence Act 1984.

[37] E. Barendt, *Broadcasting Law: A Comparative Study* (1993), chap. 2.

[38] See the discussion later in this chapter. Barendt points out that the British position would not satisfy the German constitutional court.

[39] See also E. Barendt, "Press and Broadcasting Freedom: Does Anyone Have Any Rights to Free Speech?" (1991) 44 *Current Legal Problems* 63.

[40] See T. Gibbons, "Freedom of the Press: Ownership and Editorial Values" [1992] *Public Law* 279–299.

REGULATING FOR PLURALISM

While the law in general makes few concessions to the media as such, neither does it make free speech more difficult for the media. A major objection to regulating the media, however, is that regulation consists of burdens which amount to censorship.[41] In particular, it may be said that the media are being subjected to unacceptable prior constraints when standards are imposed on the material that they produce, or when they are asked to give an account of their activities, or when their economic arrangements are controlled. Arguments for a free speech principle are not an absolute bar to these types of constraint, however. They provide a presumption against regulation but one which can be resisted by other arguments that justify intervention. Regulation may actually be adopted to advance the types of interest that a free speech principle aims to protect — for example, in attempting to secure accuracy or in enabling democratic discussion to take place — or it may simply reflect the belief that other values are more important than free speech. These matters have been most fully discussed in the context of broadcasting and the significance of public service, in particular, will be taken up in the following chapter. However, in terms of freedom of communication, it is the issues of access to the media and pluralism in the media which suggest positive grounds for regulation.

Taking pluralism first, it is the recognition that journalists and broadcasters control an important cultural and political resource which underpins the claim that the free speech interests of the audience (and readership) should be given priority when assessing the use to which the media are put.[42] It rests on a sceptical belief that the mere absence of state censorship will not encourage media controllers to advance knowledge or promote democratic debate. Rather, they will enjoy the liberty to dominate the means of communication, so some State interference in the media may be justified to enrich public debate. As Fiss observes, "the issue is not market failure but market reach."[43] In developing the idea of media pluralism, therefore, a distinction may be drawn between a "non-interference or no censorship principle" and a "multiplicity of voices

[41] See Robertson and Nicol, above, n. 22; C. Munro, *Television, Censorship and the Law* (1979); P. O'Higgins, *Censorship in Britain* (1972), chap. 4.
[42] See Gibbons, above, n. 40.
[43] O. Fiss, "Why the State?" (1987) 100 *Harv. L.R.* 781–94, at 788.

principle,"[44] the latter encapsulating the idea that the purposes of free speech can only be fully achieved where there is a diversity of viewpoints available to the listener. Rather than only being a means for speakers to convey their messages, this kind of perspective sees the media as providing a forum for public debate.[45] For some writers, indeed, the modern media are well placed to represent a "public sphere" where there is free, equal and fully informed discussion without domination by particular groups or the state.[46] Arguments for media pluralism, then, are derived from the principle that points of view should not be allowed to eclipse others simply because those with contrary views do not have the power to challenge them. The aim is contestability of beliefs and, insofar as the media may be able to exclude opinions for reasons unrelated to their cogency or validity, it may be justifiable to require them to diversify their output.

A demand for media pluralism is a realistic response to the contribution that the media do make to political debate in our democracy. It does not depend on the media being the primary forum, nor does it imply that the place of Parliament has been usurped by the media. It is, rather, a practical recognition of the way that complex democracies work, with ideas and opinion being channelled into the constitutional process through the media, from discussions taking place in a whole range of overlapping constituencies and representative groups. The more important this role as a subsidiary forum becomes for the media, the more urgent will be the need to allow a sufficient range of views to be promulgated by the media. For public service broadcasting, the objective of universality, catering for the needs of the whole audience, will normally be sufficient to provide a diversity of programming content within the service (internal pluralism). For private media enterprises, the grounds for regulating media content are less strong but there may still be a need to secure a diversity of media sources (external pluralism), whether through special media

---

[44] J. Lichtenberg, "Foundations and Limits of Freedom of the Press" (1987) 16 *Philosophy and Public Affairs* 329–355.

[45] E. Barendt, "Press and broadcasting freedom: Does anyone have any rights to free speech?" (1991) 44 *Current Legal Problems* 63–82, at 66–67.

[46] For discussion of this approach, which is informed by Habermas' theory of communicative action, see J. Curran, "Mass media and democracy: a reappraisal" in *Mass Media and Society* (J. Curran and M. Gurevitch eds., 1991). For earlier work, see N. Garnham, "The Media and the Public Sphere" in *Communicating Politics* (P. Golding *et al.* eds., 1986); P. Scannell, "Public service broadcasting and modern public life" (1989) 11 *Media, Culture and Society* 135–166.

regulation or competition law. At the European level, the importance of media pluralism has been recognised by the Italian and the French constitutional courts, the former placing greater emphasis on the public broadcasters' responsibility for securing pluralism.[47] In Germany, the continued existence of the public service broadcasters is constitutionally protected, at least for so long as private broadcasters do not provide a comprehensive range of programming.[48] Such a principle of complimentarity has, if only implicitly, been accepted in the United Kingdom in preserving the BBC as the cornerstone of British broadcasting during the process of deregulating the rest of the sector.[49] Interestingly, a right to pluralism of information has not been directly recognised by the European Court of Human Rights, notwithstanding that Article 10 of the Convention refers to the right "to receive and impart information and ideas." However, the same phrase seems to support the view that regulation which is intended to advance pluralism will not be regarded as an interference with freedom of expression.[50]

Related to the promotion of media pluralism is the issue of a speaker's access to the media to convey his or her own message. Again, it is the fact of journalists' and broadcasters' power that is significant.[51] The claim has two main grounds, one an expansive notion of freedom of communication and the other more closely associated with democratic aims. The free communication arguments go beyond the negative liberty to speak, those concerned with protecting speech from unjustifiable interference, and stress that such protection provides only the opportunity to communicate. The way that the freedom is used — its actual value, it is said — will depend on the economic, social and natural resources available to the speaker. From the latter's perspective, whilst some speech may be purely expressive, its worth[52] usually rests on its capacity to reach the audience at whom it is directed. Furthering the interests promoted by free communication, therefore, may require access to a mass

[47] For an excellent analysis, see R. Craufurd Smith, *Broadcasting and Fundamental Rights* (1997), chap. 7.
[48] See Barendt, above, n. 37, chap. 3.
[49] Home Office, *Broadcasting in the '90s: Competition, Choice and Quality* (White Paper) (1988) Cm. 517, para. 3.2.
[50] See Craufurd Smith, above, n. 47, pp. 174–183.
[51] See T. Gibbons, "Impartiality in the Media" (1985) *Archiv fur Rechts-und Sozialphilosophie* Beiheft Nr. 28, pp. 71–81; D. Goldberg, "Freedom of Speech and Access to the Media" *ibid.* at pp. 82–85.
[52] On the worth of liberty, see J. Rawls, *A Theory of Justice* (1971), pp. 204 *et seq.*

audience, implying the use of the mass media.[53] One objection to this claim is that neither the mere wish to use the mass media nor the belief that a particular message is especially important are sufficient grounds for giving one person's speech priority over another's.[54] Alternatively, the media may be seen as an important resource which should be distributed fairly amongst all citizens. But a similar point could be made about other resources, such as wealth or education, and justice does not require that special weight should be given to the facility to communicate. Another argument is that access by a speaker would contribute to the range of viewpoints available to the audience, although focusing on the benefits of access could make viewpoints vulnerable to the audience's preferences — they may simply say that they do not want to listen — albeit only if the acquisition of knowledge or a strong version of democratic participation were not accepted to be of independent value. However this would not entail the contribution of a particular speaker, but merely imply that the views held by any speaker ought to receive an airing; this is really an argument in favour of media pluralism. The general point is that access to the media as a democratic forum does not entail a right of personal access.[55] The reasons are the same practical ones that underlie representative democracy itself: the limitations imposed by size, time and specialisation on the creation of an assembly of the whole electorate.

In situations where access is conceded, whether to introduce diversity of viewpoint or to allow individuals to speak or reply, it will have been gained at the expense of those who would otherwise have used the media. This raises a problem which is often characterised in terms of censorship, with editors complaining that their autonomy would be compromised by being required to publish opinions that they would rather disregard, and prospective speakers complaining that editors are preventing their views from being aired.[56] This is

---

[53] For an early review of the literature, see D. Caristi, "The Concept of a Right to Access to the Media: A Workable Alternative" (1988) 22 *Suffolk University Law Review* 103–130, at 105–118. See also E. Barendt, above, n. 6, pp. 83–86. For an early, seminal discussion, see J. Barron, "Access to the Press — A New First Amendment Right" (1967) 80 *Harv L.R.* 1641, and his *Freedom of the Press For Whom?* (1973).

[54] To use Barry's expression, such grounds would be essentially "want-regarding." See B. Barry, *Political Argument* (1965), pp. 38–17.

[55] Barendt, above, n. 6, emphasises that recipient interests in speech do not compel individual rights to use the media and nor does the public's "right" to know; see pp. 81–83.

[56] For a discussion of this issue see D. Tucker, *Law, Liberalism and Free Speech* (1985), chap. 3. See also A. Ward and R. Redmond-Cooper, "The Right to Reply in England, France and the United States" (1985) 4 *J. Media Law and Practice* 205–223.

liable to cause confusion. In associating the editorial role with freedom of speech, it is implied that interference with one is interference with the other. In relating editorial control to prohibition on speech, it is implied that expression itself is identical with the media. But in each case, the issue is not whether the liberty to speak, in the negative sense, has been curtailed — because it has not. Rather, the question is who can use the media as an effective means of making speech worthwhile. Here, social and economic constraints are as likely to suppress or inhibit the dissemination of information and opinion as legal prohibitions on speech. The extent to which there should be access to the media is related, therefore, to the way in which media content is controlled, or the way that power in the media has been distributed.[57] However the practical issue is access for different points of view rather than individual expression and, in deciding this, it will be appropriate to examine the purposes of different media in order to determine the target audience to which access is sought. If television services are broadcast to reach a broad audience, for example, then widespread access may be required. To the extent that segmented services, such as cable or satellite, can serve more particular audiences, access to them will be narrower. Similarly, in relation to the press, the greater the monopoly of public debate and comment, the stronger is the case for access; and the more specialised and diversified the publication, the greater is the scope for editorial autonomy in deciding what to include.

How far are these ideals realised in media practice? Provision for media pluralism will be discussed, in later chapters, in relation to media standards and the regulation of ownership and competition. In terms of individuals, access is confined to a relatively small number, mainly consisting of proprietors and broadcasters, journalists, expert commentators, entertainers, the newsworthy (indicating human interest or political significance), and some members of the audience or readership who provide feedback. In terms of substantive content, the function of defamation law in enabling apologies and corrections has already been noted. There have also been experiments with

---

[57] In the United States, for example, the Supreme Court has stressed the private ownership of newspapers in upholding absolute editorial autonomy in determining what to publish; see *Miami Herald Publishing v. Tornillo* 418 U.S. 241 (1974). As Barendt notes, above, n. 6, p.100, this makes press freedom look more like a "quasi-property right." By contrast, the public interest in broadcasting had led the court to uphold the constitutionality of the Federal Communication Commission's "fairness doctrine"; see *Red Lion Broadcasting v. F.C.C.* 395 U.S. 367 (1969).

public access programming and some feedback programming. In the press, the Press Complaints Commission's code provides for limited concessions to reply to inaccuracies or unfair treatment and that allows access to some, albeit largely in the interests of accuracy. In addition, the correspondence pages of the broadsheet newspapers may be seen as providing opportunities for some issues to be aired in public. Generally, however, the press have not acknowledged any obligation to provide wide access, nor a more limited right of reply, because it is regarded as interfering with proprietorial and editorial freedom. In broadcasting, there is an obligation to provide a right of reply under the European Broadcasting Directive and the European Convention on Transfrontier Television and, curiously, the Broadcasting Complaints Commission believed that its power to require publication of its adjudications on fairness was sufficient to comply with this.[58] The revised Broadcasting Directive has a stronger statement of the right of reply, but it remains to be seen whether the BSC will alter its fairness code to ensure compliance.

B. Independence

An important theme in democratic theory is the idea that State power should not be absolute. One general limitation is the requirement that government action to restrict liberty must be justified,[59] a particular example being the free speech principle discussed above. In addition, the theme of limited power underlies the principle of constitutionalism, including the doctrines of the rule of law and the separation of powers, as a means of checking State action.[60] In the same tradition, because the communication of ideas is widely recognised as being central to the control of power, both government and the media themselves have accepted the convention that the media should be independent from the State. The arguments are closely associated with those relating to free speech, but they concentrate on the identity and interests of the speaker, in the shape of government, rather than the restrictions which are placed on the speech.

---

[58] B.C.C., *Annual Report*, H.C. 490, 1989, para.14. However, it is difficult to understand how the wording in the Directive can be read into the British legislation.
[59] See Lively, n. 16, above, chap. 2.
[60] See P. McAuslan and J. F. McEldowney, *Law, Legitimacy and the Constitution* (1985); I. Harden and N. Lewis, *The Noble Lie* (1986).

The underlying assumption is that the media are powerful and authoritative means of channelling information and opinion. They form an important forum for discussion of policy, extending to a large proportion of the democratic constituency, and enabling government activity to be scrutinised. If that is so, then, while government and state officials may speak freely like anyone else, they should not adopt the institution of the media as their own. The principle of independence requires, therefore, that the State should not seek to control the content of material that is published or disseminated. It is a corollary of the view that the goals of truth and participation in a democracy can best be achieved when communication is free from domination by particular concentrations of power. It also reflects what democratic defences of the media's independence[61] have emphasised, that the media may perform a special role, more especially manifested in the press, in acting on behalf of the people to call government to account. From this perspective, the function of the media as the Fourth Estate is to oppose government, not collude with it. For these reasons, it is a general theme in democratic theory that ownership and influence of the media should be distanced from the State, so that governments' objectives cannot dictate editorial policy.

In practice, the media's independence from the State is mainly respected and followed as a public standard for government and official behaviour, but there are a number of areas of tension where the precise relationship remains ambiguous. In relation to the press, the principle was formally established when the licensing of publications stopped in 1694.[62] From then onwards, any coincidence of views between government and editorial policy has been largely fortuitous. That has not meant, however, that governments have been indifferent to what the press has published; they have expended much effort in securing favourable circumstances, mainly economic and through taxation, for a type of "responsible" press that would not be too critical of them. The role of the media as the champion of the people emerged in the eighteenth century, when the press evolved as a platform for popular political discussion which an unreformed and authoritarian Parliament could not provide.[63] Since then, the press

---

[61] See A. Meiklejohn, above, n. 15.

[62] Sir William Holdsworth, *A History of English Law* Vol. 6 (1924), pp. 360 *et seq.*

[63] See Curran and Seaton, above, n. 34, Part I. See also, T. Burns, *The B.B.C.: Public Institution and Private World* (1977), p. 176.

has jealously guarded its status and, ostensibly, this has been justified by reference to the principle of independence. In some respects, that may simply provide a convenient ideal to rationalise the commercial freedom and success that newspapers represent; it must not be forgotten that they are primarily sources of entertainment and not constitutional weapons but that, at the same time, they are prepared to use their resources to lobby for their favoured political goals, not least in respect of media policy.[64] From a government's standpoint, the principle of independence may be respected not from its own wish to encourage free expression, but because its political credibility may be thought to depend on a prudent regard for democratic ideology. Similarly, a government is likely to anticipate that it may lose office and it would not want the press denied to it as a vehicle for publicising its own policies during a period in opposition. Despite the fact that respect for the principle may be tempered with some cynicism, the independence of the media has continued to be an ideal that is invoked to resist what the media regard as censorship of their activities; examples are the debates in Parliament and the press which were prompted by the passing of the Contempt of Court Act 1981, the Official Secrets Act 1989 and, to a lesser extent, the Defamation Act 1996, together with the current discussion of proposals to introduce a law of privacy and of the implications of the Human Rights Bill 1997 and the Data Protection Bill 1998.

In relation to the press, independence is realised primarily through its commercial freedom. In addition, it has been distanced from direct political involvement in its affairs and there has been a reluctance to use the law to regulate it. Thus, discussion of broad issues relating to its organisation and practices has taken place under the auspices of Royal Commissions. Self-regulation in the form of the voluntary codes of practice, operated by the former Press Council and the present Press Complaints Commission, have been preferred to statutory intervention. Furthermore, the management of information about sensitive matters of political policy or national security was achieved by co-operation with the press, through the Lobby[65] and the issue of D-Notices respectively, with broadcasting simply acceding to the practices thereby established. Yet despite these

---

[64] See J. Tunstall, *Newspaper Power: The New National Press in Britain* (1996).

[65] See P. Hennessey and D. Walker. "The Lobby" in *The Media in British Politics* (J. Seaton and B. Pimlott eds., 1987); J. Tunstall, *The Westminster Lobby Correspondents* (1970).

processes intended to institutionalise independence, the political reality is that all journalists, including those from the press, cannot be immune from government power. For example, they depend on the government for much of their political material and they know that, if they do not co-operate in responding to unattributed comments, embargoes on publication and official attitudes to what should remain secret, they run the risk of isolation. The co-operation is mutual, however, and attempts by government to alter the arrangements, by limiting lobby correspondents' discretion to use material and by ignoring decisions of the D-Notice committee,[66] have caused some friction and renewed calls for the press to stop what is regarded by some as collusion with the State.

Independence from the State supplements the free speech principle in preventing restrictions on the dissemination of material. But just as regulation to ensure a diversity of media sources may be needed to support a broad conception of freedom in communication, so regulation of the economic base of the media may be justified for the same reason. The commercial independence of those who have the resources to enter the media market does not guarantee that power to control communication will be dispersed. Rather, the media themselves may become a seat of extra-constitutional power instead of enhancing democratic government.[67] Indeed, the history of the modern press illustrates the point. It was initially the political parties who were the proprietors of newspapers and, not surprisingly, their papers were able to prevail over the radical press which was suppressed throughout the last century. While the later rise of the press barons, together with financial dependence on advertising revenue, led to the removal of direct political influence on the press, those developments did not encourage a diversity of opinion or easy access to the medium.[68] The industry's present corporate structure has tended to exacerbate the problem, and it has been accepted for some time that some regulation on holdings in the press is required to limit monopoly power and to enhance competition. Similar considerations now apply to cross-ownership within and between the press and other forms of media. As will be discussed in a later

---

[66] D. Fairley, "D-Notices, Official Secrets and the Law" (1990) 10 *Oxford J.L.S.* 430–440. The remarks in the text apply equally to the DA-Notice system which has replaced the previous arrangements.
[67] See Burns, above, n. 63; J. Curran & J. Seaton, above, n. 34, pp. 105–106, 299–300.
[68] See Burns, above, n. 63, pp. 173–180; O'Higgins, above, n. 41.

chapter, the main issue is no longer the existence but the scope of such regulation.

Independence in broadcasting developed from the tradition of independence in the press. From the beginning, both broadcasting committees and politicians accepted that the BBC should be an independent organisation and it was deliberately established in a form that distanced its day-to-day operation from political interference. The principle was never doubted when the independent sector was established in 1956 and the issue simply never arose when the framework for cable was introduced in 1984. Since then, it has been reaffirmed many times by Ministers and other politicians, both in and out of Parliament.[69]

However, the idea of independence has a much more precarious status in broadcasting, for the state has never relinquished the potential for control that is entailed in the allocation of broadcasting frequencies and, in the case of public service broadcasting, the use of public finance and the guarantee of protection from competition in the market place. Independence has had a more negative aspect, being concerned with preventing direct interference from government rather than promoting the more critical tradition which the Press had claimed for itself and which broadcasting has attempted only relatively recently.[70] Indeed, the scope for broadcasters to assert a "Fourth Estate" role has always been ambiguous, especially for the BBC whose constitution has never clearly defined the nature of its association with government. Its independence has been secured in exchange for an understanding about what is acceptable political reporting and comment. The result has been what Burns has described as the BBC's "politics of accommodation": serving the national interest, as Parliament sees it, on the one hand and the public good on the other.[71]

---

[69] See Home Office, *Broadcasting in the '90s: Competition, Choice and Quality* (White Paper) (1988) Cm. 517, para. 2.6 (but *cf.* para. 7.15 on the banning of direct statements by terrorists' representatives); the Home Secretary's position, outlined in (Peacock), *Committee on Financing the BBC* (1986) Cmnd. 9824, paras 14 and 15; Third Report of the Home Affairs Committee, *The Future of Broadcasting* (1987–88) H.C. 262–I and II, paras 11–15, 24–25; BBC, *BBC Annual Report and Accounts 1986–87* (1987), p. 63; (Pilkington), *Report of the Committee on Broadcasting 1960* (1962) Cmnd. 1753, paras 22–23.

[70] See generally, Burns, above, n. 63, pp. 180–185.

[71] It is interesting to note that only in 1986 did the BBC stop vetting most of its staff for security clearance, soon after the existence of the practice had been revealed in the press.

More generally, and remarkably, both the BBC's Licence and Agreement and the legislation which governs commercial broadcasting have always contained provision for direct interference by government. Under clause 8.2 of the present Agreement,[72] the Secretary of State "may from time to time by notice in writing require the Corporation to refrain at any specified time or at all times from broadcasting or transmitting any matter or matter of any class specified in such notice, and the Secretary of State may at any time or times vary or revoke any such notice." However, the Corporation "may at its discretion announce or refrain from announcing that such a notice has been given or has been varied or revoked," a provision which is intended to provide a safeguard by enabling the BBC to resist through public protest any attempt to exert pressure upon it. Almost identical provisions are contained in sections 10(3) and (4) and 94(3) and (4) of the 1990 Act. The power has never been used in relation to specific programmes and, although its use was threatened against the BBC in connection with a documentary about Northern Ireland in 1972, it was not implemented when the Chairman of the Governors indicated that he would reveal the Government's action.[73]

As a general veto on broad classes of programme, however, the power has been used all too often. In 1927, the co-operation which Reith had afforded the Government during the General Strike was formalised into a prohibition on the broadcasting of matters of political, industrial or religious controversy.[74] The restriction was lifted in 1928, but only when the Government accepted the recommendations of the Crawford Committee, made three years earlier, that controversial matter could be broadcast if it was of high quality, not too lengthy or insistent and distributed with "scrupulous fairness",[75] and the BBC had undertaken to deal with such matters on an impartial basis. Another matter which was also the subject of a veto, imposed in 1927 and never actually lifted, was a prohibition on the broadcasting of editorial opinion on current affairs or matters of public policy. The subjects of these vetoes were incorporated into

---

[72] Department of National Heritage, *Copy of the Agreement Dated the 25th Day of January 1996 Between Her Majesty's Secretary of State for National Heritage and the British Broadcasting Corporation* (1996) Cm. 3152, (hereinafter "BBC Agreement"). For discussion of the BBC's constitution, see chap. 5.

[73] (Annan) *Report of the Committee on the Future of Broadcasting* (1977) Cmnd. 6753, para. 5.15.

[74] Burns, above, n. 63, p.16; Annan, above, n. 73, para. 5.10.

[75] (Crawford) Broadcasting Committee, *Report* (1925) Cmd. 2599, para. 15.

undertakings which became attached to the Licence and they are now reflected in the duty of impartiality imposed by the current Agreement.[76] They correspond with the similar duties which are placed on the ITC and the R.A.[77] Interestingly, the BBC has regarded its obligation as the mainstay of its position and defended it thus at the time of the Peacock inquiry:

> "Without genuine independence, it is difficult, if not impossible, for broadcasters to maintain the highest standard of truthfulness and impartiality. Conversely, without having established a reputation for just those qualities it is difficult for any broadcasting organisation to be recognised as being truly independent and worthy of trust."[78]

This is a defensible rationalisation of the values of the Corporation, or indeed of public service broadcasting, but the genesis of such independence shows that a high price has been paid in the removal of any threat that the perceived power of the new medium would be used against politicians, whether in government or opposition.

The legal and regulatory basis for the independence of the broadcasting media is, therefore, dependent on the goodwill of the government of the day. Where that goodwill is strained, the veto power is all too readily available. Its most significant use in recent times was the "broadcasting ban" which occurred when the Secretary of State issued directives, in 1988, prohibiting the broadcasting of direct statements not only by members of terrorist organisations, but also by nationalist and loyalist political parties connected with Northern Ireland.[79] The vagueness of the ban played on the broadcasters' reluctance to be branded as IRA sympathisers and, initially, they adopted a very restrictive interpretation of its effect. It was also difficult to tell whether material was being excluded from programmes; not every exclusion would necessarily carry a warning that it was being forced by government restrictions. Eventually, the broadcasters became less timid and they developed increasingly

---

[76] BBC Agreement, cl. 5.1(c). The obligations of impartiality in the current Agreement replace those in the Resolution of the Board of Governors which was attached to the Licence and Agreement of 1981 (Cmnd. 8233). They, in turn, replaced the "prescribing memoranda," a set of assurances given by the BBC and incorporated into a letter from Lord Normanbrook, then Chairman of the Governors, to the Postmaster-General in 1964; see C. Munro, above, n. 41, pp. 10–11.

[77] Under the 1990 Act, ss. 6 and 84, respectively, reflecting the 1981 Act, s. 4.

[78] BBC, *BBC Annual Report and Accounts 1986–87* (1987), p. 63.

[79] *Hansard*, 138 H.C. Deb., col. 885 (October 19, 1988).

sophisticated means of dubbing actors' voices over film of the speakers. Yet it is clear that, despite the broadcasters' ability to publicise the fact that they were constrained by government restrictions, their editorial choices about matters concerning Northern Ireland were compromised.[80] Some journalists did challenge the legality of the veto although, interestingly, the broadcasters themselves did not. Regrettably, the House of Lords was not prepared to hold that the Secretary of State had exercised his power unreasonably in his wish to combat terrorism and they refused to test the issue by reference to the proportionality test adopted by the European Court of Human Rights for applying Article 10 of the Convention.[81]

Another potential source of control of broadcasters lies in the power, contained in clause 8.1 of the Agreement and sections 10(1) and (2) and 94(1) and (2) of the 1990 Act, for any Minister to require the broadcasting of any announcement. Again, the broadcasters have a discretion whether or not to reveal the existence of the request. In practice, these arrangements are not invoked, at least in peacetime,[82] since major announcements are likely to be a matter of news interest. Others are made as public service announcements, the result of informal consultations in which the broadcasters' co-operation is obtained.[83] For ministerial broadcasts, a special agreement was reached, the so-called "Aide-Memoire", incorporating rights of reply and discussion.[84] It originally resulted from the desire of parties in opposition not to be disadvantaged by government's access to the medium, but also from the BBC's wish to pass responsibility for an impartial presentation to the political parties themselves. So reluctant, in fact, was the BBC to encourage political discussion in broadcasts, for fear that it would stir up antagonism which would compromise its position, that it introduced the notorious "fourteen day rule" whereby no discussion or *ex parte* statement was allowed to be broadcast on any issue for a period of a fortnight before it was due to

---

[80] See B. Rolson (ed.) *The Media and Northern Ireland* (1991).

[81] *R. v. Secretary of State for the Home Department, ex p. Brind* [1991] 1 A.C. 696. Regrettably, too, the European Commission on Human Rights rejected the admissibility of a claim that the Republic of Ireland's similar ban was an infringement of Art. 10 of the Convention: *Purcell v. Ireland* (1991). See D. J. Harris *et al., Law of the European Convention on Human Rights* (1995), pp. 386–416, esp. p. 408.

[82] Curran and Seaton, above, n. 34, chap. 9.

[83] For example, an agreement about public service announcements concerning Northern Ireland was reached in January, 1988.

[84] For further discussion, see chap. 3.

be debated in Parliament.[85] This restriction actually became the subject of a general veto in 1955 but that was withdrawn two years later.[86] In theory, the power to demand programme time could also be used for the purposes of making party election announcements but these are, in fact, arranged by agreement.[87]

While there may be consensus between broadcasters and politicians in the rhetoric of political independence, the reality is that broadcasters' freedom has existed in the shadow of governmental readiness to censor when expedient. It is inevitable that there has been much friction in practice. Broadcasting is considered to be the more influential medium and has emerged as the preferred platform for demonstrating and rehearsing policies. There will always be a temptation to control it. Indeed, it is misleading to concentrate unduly on the formal independence of broadcasters since it is more their attitude which determines the extent to which the state's interests are served by their programmes.[88]

In the early years of the BBC, independence seems to have been won at a very high cost, with too great an enthusiasm for self-censorship in anticipation of political displeasure. It was only after the Second World War that a more confident mood emerged, partly as a reaction to the Corporation being used as the government's mouthpiece during hostilities and demonstrated by its impartial stance during the Suez crisis.[89] Burns attributed that to the consolidation of a more professional journalism, noting the way that the Corporation survived critical moments such as controversies over *Yesterday's Men* and *A Question of Ulster*.[90] Yet that mood cannot be assured, for part of the Reithian legacy is that the BBC, at least, is still identified with the interests of the nation as politicians define it, and it has seemed particularly vulnerable to criticisms directed at its treatment of news and current affairs.[91] This seems to be especially so

---

85 See A. Briggs, *The History of Broadcasting in the United Kingdom,* Vol. IV *Sound and Vision* (1979), pp. 613–686.

86 See G. W. Goldie, *Facing the Nation: Television and Politics 1936–76* (1977).

87 From 1955 to 1964, a veto was imposed on party political broadcasts other than those agreed between the leading political parties: see Munro, above, n. 41. The position has now been reversed, with discretion to allow such broadcasts having passed to the broadcasters. See the discussion in chap. 3.

88 See R. Negrine, "Great Britain: The End of the Public Service Tradition?" in *The Politics of Broadcasting* (R. Khun ed., 1985).

89 Briggs, above, n. 85, pp. 17–18; A. Briggs, *The History of Broadcasting in the Golden Age of Wireless* (1965), pp. 42 *et seq.*, 625 *et seq.*

90 Burns, above, n. 63, p.14.

91 See P. Scannell & D. Cardiff, *A Social History of British Broadcasting,* Vol. I, *1922–1939 Serving the Nation* (1991), chap. 3.

where both government and opposition share a consensus about appropriate national policy in times of crisis, for example in relation to Ulster or the Falklands war. In the atmosphere of uncertainty created by renewed debate about its future financing and very existence, during the late 1980s, the BBC adopted a rather defensive posture to government and doubts were voiced about its willingness and ability to stand up to sustained pressure.[92] Publicly, however, the BBC has not accepted that view of itself and has continued to make programmes which attract governmental criticism.[93] It has also issued a series of strong statements reasserting its independence.[94]

Discussion has concentrated on the BBC because its experience has provided the basis for the independent sector's relationship with the state. In addition, that sector's commercial base and its relatively smaller, and arguably less incisive, output in current affairs has provided fewer opportunities for government to interfere. Yet it has also been subject to government pressure whereby, in anticipation of legislation, it was indicated that the economic structure of the industry was open to review and would have to change in order to promote competition and reduce state subsidy. The process was started with the establishment of the Peacock Committee and emphasised in an unprecedented "seminar", held in the autumn of 1987, in which the Prime Minister met leading broadcasters in order to discuss the state of the medium. This was followed by voluntary moves to introduce more programmes made by independent producers, in both ITV and the BBC, and attempts to improve efficiency in levels of manning and salaries in independent television.[95] A further source of indirect pressure, intended to produce greater sensitivity to standards of taste and decency, was the announcement that the Broadcasting Standards Council would be set up, again in anticipation of legislation, to take responsibility for those

---

92 The case was persuasively put in "Taming the Beeb", *World in Action,* Granada Television, February 29, 1988 (file with author).

93 See below, n. 97.

94 For example, the programme "Open Air Special" broadcast on January 3, 1988, the annual reviews in the late 1980s called "See For Yourself" and their accompanying pamphlets (since discontinued), its Annual Reports and its policy statements issued prior to its latest renegotiation of the Charter and Agreement.

95 See BBC, *Annual Report and Accounts* (1988); IBA, *Annual Report 1988–89* (1989). In 1988, the Monopolies and Mergers Commission was asked to investigate possible restrictive practices relating to manning levels and salaries in the independent television sector. It was unable to find evidence of such practices, but its report has not been published. See *The Guardian*, April 13, 1989.

matters from the broadcasting authorities.[96] Together with the changes introduced by the Broadcasting Act 1990, the effect was to create a sense of instability and even apprehension likely to make broadcasters all the more deferential to government wishes. In that way even more diffuse, but no less insidious, vague expressions of displeasure by government may lead to cautious self-censorship; the BBC has been especially sensitive to such pressure and has stopped various documentaries apparently for fear of offending the Government.[97]

Nevertheless, these developments do raise questions about the nature of the independence that broadcasters are entitled to expect.[98] The general principle reflects the belief that it is undesirable for the State to commandeer the messages which are carried by a medium which pervades our lives, but it does not serve to entrench any particular economic arrangements and nor does it undermine demands that broadcasters should be made more responsive and accountable to their audiences. However, there continues to be a need for greater clarification of the relationship between government and broadcasters, particularly the minimising of opportunities for hidden intervention. As will be seen later, in Chapter 6, the line between censorship and accountability may be a fine one.

In the meantime, some further distancing of the BBC from government remains a priority. Placing its undertakings in respect of matters of controversy and quality on a statutory basis would go some way towards achieving that end. In the new Agreement of 1996, an attempt to protect the BBC's position has been made, although the nature of the document shows that it does not provide complete independence. Thus, it is agreed that the BBC shall be independent in all matters concerning the content of its programmes and the times at which they are broadcast or transmitted.[99] In addition, there are a number of clauses which set out the Corporation's programming obligations, and their very articulation may be seen as a shield for the BBC against partisan demands. Ultimately, however, the BBC needs to secure a stable economic base which is not directly

---

[96] It was reported in the press at the end of 1987 (see P. Fiddick, *The Guardian,* December 28) and was announced in the House of Commons on May 16, 1988: *Hansard* H.C., Deb. (1987–88) Vol. 133, cols. 689–698.

[97] See S. Weir, "Captain Courageous or Colonel Blimp?", *The Guardian*, February 13, 1995. The subjects of such documentaries have included the Iraqi supergun, and the Lawson economic miracle, as well as the Westminster local government scandal.

[98] *cf.* Barendt, above, n. 37.

[99] BBC Agreement, cl. 2.1.

related to fluctuations in governmental policy. For the press and the commercial sector, too, economic arrangements for ownership and control are crucial to their independence. None of this implies total autonomy for editors, however, because the public will continue to have a wider interest in the way that the media are organised to secure free communication.[1]

C. Accountability

Although a complex set of arrangements exists for the control and shaping of the media, there continues to be much ambiguity about the extent to which they should respond to public wishes. The media's principal function is to provide a satisfactory service to their readership or audience, and the general assumption is that the service should be responsive to public wants and needs. At the same time, it is very much conditioned by broadcasters' and journalists' own conceptions of their work, including their interest in matters such as creative autonomy, editorial independence, professionalism and the quality of programmes or copy produced. Historically, the public's influence has taken two forms, the market in the case of the press and the political process in the case of broadcasting and the other electronic media. Increasingly, however, the latter are being distributed through technologies which allow market transactions to occur between programme makers and the audience. Discussion of different types of responsiveness no longer depends, therefore, on the forms of the media which are involved. Rather, the issue is the kind of values and objectives which we wish to impose on media practice through regulation.

The Market Process

While its operation is not immune to political scrutiny and may, indeed, be used to secure political objectives, the main concern of the market is to satisfy the particular preferences of those for whom a product is provided. Ideally, producers will tend to supply those goods and services for which customers reveal their preferences

---

[1] *cf.* A. Smith, *The Shadow in the Cave* (1973).

through a willingness to pay, thereby offsetting the costs involved. Since failure to satisfy preferences will result in custom being taken elsewhere, there is a strong incentive for producers to discover and respond as far as possible to each individual consumer's wants. In this context, responsiveness implies a sensitivity to changes in consumer satisfaction, as manifested in public demand, and a recognition of the need to adapt accordingly. Producers may use advertising to change and mould consumer taste to a significant degree but, in general, that taste is an important constraint on the scope of their activity.

As the experience of the press demonstrates, the market process provides distinct advantages for the media. Not only does the market have the virtue of facilitating a direct relationship between the editor of a newspaper and its readership, but it also serves to secure responsiveness without compromising editorial independence. Although in a democracy few aspects of social life should be excluded from political deliberation, it is well recognised that political involvement in media practice is not consistent with the values of free speech and calling government to account. Ideally, at least, economic independence serves to distance the editor from governmental power and pressure.

For all that, the journalists in the press have continued to be subject to political pressures. Not unexpectedly, those who wish to exert power will tend to resist efforts to restrict its scope. From within, proprietors may wish to use the press to promote their own interests. Externally, Parliament is an obvious forum for those who wish to criticise editorial policy and reporting practices. More importantly, however, political pressures arise because the market is not able to deal adequately with certain types of public concern. Examples of these include the accuracy of reporting, the quality of material published and the protection of privacy. This has manifested itself in the deliberations of three Royal Commissions, the establishment of the Press Council and the Press Complaints Commission, and continued debate about the latter's role and effectiveness. So far, the political power of the press has held off legislative intervention in its affairs with the promise that self-regulation would be introduced and made to work. However, such regulation is regarded as secondary to market forces. Indeed, it is asserted that consumer action belies the need for regulation because circulation figures show that those who express dissatisfaction with the press are still prepared to buy newspapers. Such a view overlooks some important factors, however, such as the very marginal effect of an individual boycott of a paper, the limited availability of comparable alternatives, the fact that newspapers are complex packages of which only a portion might induce sufficient concern that this might be manifested in the market, and the external costs of press activity.

More generally, what the market fails to do is to enable broader issues of principle or policy to be addressed, issues concerned with the relationship between the media and the cultural, moral or political practices of society as a whole. It facilitates specific transactions between individuals or groups in order to satisfy their more immediate, mutual wants. Since acceptability of outcome is judged only in terms of efficiency, however, questions of motivation, justification or objective are irrelevant unless they can be manifested as tastes or intangible benefits that can be priced. Unless, improbably, a "hidden hand" operates, the cumulative impact of particular arrangements, or their contribution to any social trend, will be fragmented and incidental. Discussion of their political implications will necessarily lack any formal structure and be unfocused, even arbitrary, and without effect; for conceptions of public or community interest, albeit difficult to define, together with social organisation or even government, do not appear to make much sense in a context of personal advantage through competition.

Whether it is appropriate to rely on market responsiveness to determine the nature of media output depends, therefore, on the functions that the media are expected to fulfil. If they are considered to provide no more than a consumer product, the market will be the most appropriate means of enabling audiences and readerships to receive what they want. If the media are expected to promote other values in addition, then some other method of securing their accountability to the public is needed. What is important, however, is not to allow the mere possibility of market transactions to dictate the regulatory approach. For example, the development of new technology such as digital transmission, which enables direct producer-consumer relationships to be established, does not entail that public interests are no longer relevant.

The Political Process

In broadcasting, it was accepted from the outset that the service had a public dimension which required that it should be defined and supervised through political channels.[2] Broadcasting freedom, in

[2] (Sykes) Broadcasting Committee, *Report* (1923) Cmd. 1951.

Barendt's sense of an institutional right,[3] cannot be given unconditionally. Broadcasters were expected to account for their work in terms of the democratic principles which underlay its status as a public good. The use of the political process to render such accounts has the effect, however, of altering significantly the type of responsiveness that the public can expect from the media.

Whereas consumer sovereignty requires a simple responsiveness to demand in the market, democratic control is typically more indirect. A relationship of accountability rests on the responsibility which arises where decision-making is delegated or divided within defined limits.[4] Political actors are not expected simply to comply with their constituencies' demands. Accountability entails neither complete control by those who allocate a function, nor full autonomy for those who undertake it. Instead, there is an area of discretion whose exercise implies, first, that decision-makers are answerable for their choices and, secondly, that certain standards of propriety should be applied.[5] The central idea is that action and decisions should be justified by providing reasons acceptable to those with an interest in them. What this involves, however, is that choices are nevertheless to be made, and made independently, and this is why the derivation of accountability from responsibility should be emphasised. For this reason, accountability must be distinguished from simple control. While the nature of answerability will differ according to the parties concerned and their organisational relationships,[6] in a democracy, explanations will be required to be broadly acceptable to the electorate, whether they emerge through legal, institutional or political channels. In doing so, they will be expected to address, more or less explicitly, the criteria that are to be taken into account when justifying action.

That such justifications are needed, and are important, is to be understood by reference to responsiveness as an underlying context

---

[3] Barendt, above, n. 37.

[4] For discussions of accountability, see generally P. Craig, *Administrative Law* (3rd ed., 1994), pp. 88–92; J. Jowell, *Law and Bureaucracy* (1975), chap. 1; T. Prosser, "Towards a Critical Public Law" (1982) 9 *J. Law & Society* 1–19; B. Smith and D. Hague, *The Dilemma of Accountability in Modern Government: Independence versus Control* (1971). One of the best treatments of the subject remains W. A. Robson, *Nationalised Industry and Public Ownership* (2nd ed., 1966), chap. 8.

[5] J. R. Pennock, *Democratic Theory* (1979), chap. 7.

[6] See N. Lewis, "Regulating Non-Government Bodies: Privatization, Accountability, and the Public-Private Divide" in *The Changing Constitution* (J. Jowell & D. Oliver eds., 2nd ed., 1989).

for the political process. Connoting a readiness and willingness to react favourably to democratically expressed wants, it entails that a public body should not only keep within the bounds of its legislatively granted authority, but should also maintain the spirit of democratic government. This implies more than merely taking all interests and expectations into account,[7] suggesting instead that outcomes should reflect the general weight of opinion. Nevertheless, responsiveness must be regarded as only one element of accountability. In a spectrum of decision-making, it represents the more constrained end where little discretion is exercised. At the other end, where the criteria for offering explanations tend to reflect rational concerns about political ideals or technical expertise, accountability may be consistent with considerable autonomy. Generally, therefore, for an account to be acceptable to politicians and the public, it need not demonstrate a very high degree of responsiveness, provided that it shows convincing reasons why rational considerations should prevail.

Making broadcasters responsive through the political process has led to two opposing sources of difficulty, however. First, much greater effort has to be expended in resisting the use of political channels, which do not exist in the market, for political interference. This is possibly less of a problem for the regulators, who have a statutory remit to protect them, than for the BBC. Secondly, because there are only indirect ways of discovering audience preferences, it is easier for broadcasters to become remote and elitist. For regulators, also, there may be a tendency to introspection or an undue concern with the interests of the industry. In relation to political interference, the formal position is that decisions about programme making and dissemination should be distanced from direct political influence out of respect for editorial independence and free speech. Nevertheless, political influence, whether to represent public opinion or to further politicians' own ambitions, manifests itself in a number of ways. The most direct sources are the controls which have been reserved to ministers in the constitutions of the broadcasting authorities, discussed earlier. Although these powers are rarely invoked, their very existence makes their use easier and more tempting. Just as importantly, they serve to emphasise that, in the last resort, broadcasters and regulators may be required to be responsive rather than responsible. In a period of economic and structural flux, that can

---

[7] *cf.* J. Jowell, "The Rule of Law Today", J. Jowell and D. Oliver, above, n. 6.

foster caution and the second-guessing of government intentions, rather than a vigilant defence of broadcasters' independence. Equally significant, in terms of regulatory approach, is the pervasive influence that government has on the nature of the regulatory framework. The latter is shaped by primary and, increasingly, secondary legislation, and the regulators' function is often to implement that legislation rather than be independent.

Less visible as a source of political interference is the patronage used in appointing governors of the BBC and members of the regulatory bodies.[8] A particular difficulty with patronage is the suspicion that appointment to office carries with it a set of understandings about the way in which the job is to be carried out, and that they will tend to further the sectarian interests of government rather than the wider public interest. In a democracy, it is proper that the people's representatives should choose office-holders and that they should reflect the political mood of Parliament for the time being. But choices which are politically partisan, advancing only the interests of one particular group in society, reflect a narrow majoritarian view of democracy. A broader view which recognises the interests of minorities favours the selection of persons who reflect a wide range of interests, particularly where the service in question is of universal appeal or where regulation is for the public interest. Some of these fears may be unfounded or mitigated by the arrangements in the programming sector, where governors and members hold office for only five years, though this is renewable, and their influence may be limited. There is, too, a tradition of professional domination — although that indicates a failure of democracy in a different way. Yet events at the BBC have given cause for concern, for example, when the appointment of new governors, including a new Chairman, was followed by the controversial resignation of the Director-General in circumstances which suggested that the government wished to secure personnel who were not unsympathetic to its interests.[9] The new practice of openly advertising for new governors will not stop that from happening again, but it indicates a welcome willingness to be seen to appoint on merit.[10]

---

[8] See P. Craig, *Administrative Law* (3rd ed., 1994), pp. 87.

[9] Towards the end of 1986, the B.B.C.'s governors were widely regarded in this light, especially after the appointment of Marmaduke Hussey as Chairman. Some months later, the Director-General, Alastair Milne, was forced to resign. See A. Milne, *DG: The Memoirs of a British Broadcaster* (1988).

[10] Department of Media, Culture and Sport, *Press Release*, February 25, 1998.

Some of the most awkward problems in securing responsiveness through the political process arise from ambiguities about its everyday balance with responsibility. The arrangements for programming in general do not indicate the extent to which programmers are required simply to respond to the demands made of them by way of comment and criticism, rather than being able to justify their choices on grounds of principle. It is never wholly clear, therefore, exactly when legitimate political interest becomes interference. That this is so in broadcasting, in particular, is not immediately apparent from the way in which its formal avenues of accountability operate. Amongst public enterprises, it is broadcasting that has best been able to implement the ideal, which it first articulated,[11] that government and the legislature should distance themselves from public corporations' activities because their functions would be hampered by direct political participation. The reasons are that initiative, technical competence and efficient decision-making are incompatible with ministerial supervision. It tends to be slow and bureaucratic, there is inconsistency in the way that delegated powers are reserved and many day-to-day matters are beyond the expertise of most politicians.[12] In addition, as a matter of principle, the outcome of political discussion should advance general interests rather than secure any unfair advantage through interventions in detailed decision-making.

As an ideal, therefore, it might be said that public bodies are expected to act responsibly in relation to day-to-day management or administration, and to be responsive in relation to general issues of policy. In practice, the distinction has not proved sufficiently compelling to exclude many enterprises from political scrutiny, with increased intervention by Ministers and, indirectly, Parliament, in their operations.[13] This is hardly surprising since even the most mundane and routine decision can have, or may be interpreted to have, broad implications to which the responsible body may be expected to respond. Broadcasting has appeared to be more resilient in maintaining support for its autonomy in the development and

---

[11] The "progress of science and the harmonies of art will be hampered by too rigid rules and too constant a supervision by the state": (Crawford) Broadcasting Committee, *Report* (1925) Cmd. 2599, para. 5.

[12] See J. B. D. Mitchell, *Constitutional Law* (1968), pp. 215 *et seq.*; Robson, above, n. 5, chap. 6; see also, R. Baldwin and C. McCrudden eds., *Regulation and Public Law* (1987), chap. 1.

[13] See T. Prosser, *Nationalised Industries and Public Control* (1986).

maintenance of a public service, although it has not been immune to interference. In part, this can be attributed to a genuine tradition of independence, including a respect for free speech, that developed from the early definitions of public service broadcasting as somehow being above politics. More ominously, however, broadcasters' autonomy has reflected, not so much an isolation from political interests, as an accommodation with politicians about what constitutes a proper, responsible attitude to political activity. Responsibility in this sense connotes a respect for certain values which are considered to be in some way fundamental to our society. Since it is a proper role for government also to protect such values, there is obvious scope for political considerations to become confused with the public interest involved.

Use of the political process to secure responsiveness to general social issues does leave public service broadcasters, in particular, vulnerable to improper political demands. At the same time, use of the political process can also have the effect of actually reducing responsiveness to public wishes. Giving responsibility to professional programmers rules out detailed political scrutiny and allows, indeed encourages, them to use their expertise to determine what is required by concepts such as due impartiality or quality. They are able, consequently, to give an account of their activity in terms that enable them to justify choices of programme-making and content that may differ from public preferences. Political comment becomes limited to questions such as the extent to which the broadcasters and regulators have turned their attention to those general objectives of the service, whether they have moved to implement them, and how efficiently. As a result, programmers have considerable scope to develop their own professional concerns and this has given rise to charges of elitism.[14]

Two ways have emerged for countering these tendencies to become isolated from the public, for whom the service is supposed to be provided. One is the encouragement of a professional self-awareness that responsibility to the audience may actually include taking their wishes into account, and that a quality programme is of no use without an audience. This has encouraged the development of competition for programme ratings. The other approach has been to establish some institutional means of bringing the audience and

---

[14] A notable example is (Beveridge), *Report of the Broadcasting Committee 1949* (1951) Cmd. 8116, paras 212–221.

programme-makers together in a way that reflects the proximity of the market. There exist a number of methods for discovering consumer preferences and hearing grievances, methods of acquiring information which might otherwise be obtained through the price mechanism. Together with the general tendency to deregulation, the effect may be to supplement the political process with the market, as information about audience preferences is taken as a signal to which broadcasters and regulators must respond, rather than a factor for them to use in the responsible exercise of their discretion. In doing so, a third way of dealing with political interference and remoteness may become attractive, and that is to accept that the market should determine relationships between the media and the public. Only if democratic and media values are not thereby jeopardised, however, would that be an acceptable trend.

The relationship between independence and accountability is one of the most difficult problems for media regulation to solve, especially for broadcasters and regulators. Where bodies are given responsibility for promoting values because of their expertise and experience, they require a reasonable degree of autonomy. Accountability will necessarily be indirect, therefore, and is likely to be best achieved through the articulation of clear objectives and a transparent process of policy making and decision making.

Chapter Three

Media Standards

The topic of media standards has been a recurring theme in discussion about the proper scope of regulation. Recognising that many areas of the law in general, for example, defamation, contempt of court, obscenity or official secrecy, will affect the content of journalists' and producers' output, the question is whether the media possess special characteristics which justify additional control of their work. Generally, the press have been able to resist demands for such regulation of content, whereas broadcasters have been subjected to quite rigorous obligations. Many of those have been entailed by the treatment of broadcasting as a public service but, apart from that, there are a number of basic standards which are said to be appropriate for any programming medium, however segmented its audience. For the press, the major issue has been the extent to which special regulation of intrusions into privacy should be introduced in the absence of a general law on the subject.

A. Public Service

The concept of public service has a number of interpretations and has been the subject of much debate which has led to a shift in emphasis in recent years. Nevertheless, a central core of meaning continues to be accepted by politicians, journalists and media management. While the principle has received most attention in relation to broadcasting, it has also been discussed in relation to the press and cable services.[1] As many as eight different elements of public service have been identified, at least in relation to broadcasting,[2] but two features are distinctive. One is the idea of universality, in the geographical sense that the material which is produced should be available throughout the country, and in the consumer sense that it should cater for all tastes and interests. The other feature is the idea of cultural responsibility, that material should have the object of informing and educating the public, offering a high standard of quality, as well as entertaining them. Connected with both ideas is a sense of cultural consensus, that the nation shares a common fund of values and preferences which give it an identity as a community, notwithstanding the existence of differences of opinion between various sections of the population, including minority groups. In addition, other elements have become associated with public service, although they can be regarded as analytically separate. These include the principle of independence from political influence, which has been discussed above. Having at least one part of the broadcasting system financed directly by its users has also been thought by some to be a prerequisite of public service provision, and it is a crucial axis of the contemporary debate about the future shape of the BBC. Almost as a corollary to these, a general distrust of the market as an appropriate mechanism for achieving the aims of public service has been a constant sub-theme.

The reasons for the emergence of a public service principle can be traced to the introduction of broadcasting in the early 1920s. It was claimed then that there was a public interest in communication which required special protection. In part, this was a response to the need to regulate the use of the limited number of frequencies available for radio transmission, but the recognition of that need was itself connected with the strong belief that the new medium was so powerful a means of disseminating knowledge and opinion that it should not be left to the market for its development.[3]

Thus, the Sykes Committee in 1923 took the view that "radio-telephony" was so far-reaching and relatively cheap that "the control

---

[1] Royal Commission on the Press, *Report* (1949) Cmnd. 7700, paras 87–89. 361–370; Royal Commission on the Press, *Final Report* (1977) Cmnd. 6810, paras 2.1–2.11; (Hunt) Inquiry, *Cable Expansion and Broadcasting Policy* (1982) Cmnd. 8679.

[2] Broadcasting Research Unit, *The Public Service Idea in British Broadcasting- Main Principles* (1985) See also M. Raboy, *Public Broadcasting for the 21st Century* (1996).

[3] Reith's early views are discussed in A. Briggs, *A History of Broadcasting in the U.K.,* Vol. I *The Birth of Broadcasting* (1961) pp. 234–240.

of such a potential power over public opinion and the life of the nation ought to remain with the State, and that the operation of so important a national service ought not to be allowed to become an unrestricted commercial monopoly."[4] The wavebands were to be regarded as "a valuable form of public property"[5] which had to be protected for the future, partly to prevent technical chaos in the use of such scarce resources but also to exercise potential control over the nature of the material disseminated. The theme was adopted by the Crawford Committee, two years later, in recommending that the BBC should be established as a public corporation, "as trustee for the national interest in broadcasting."[6]

Since then, the importance of public service has been taken as axiomatic in developing the scope and nature of broadcasting and, although it has coincided with and been informed by the existence of the BBC as one example of financing broadcasting,[7] its value has been assumed independently of arguments about the shape of particular institutions. The Beveridge Committee in 1949 regarded broadcasting, like the work of the universities, as directed to a social purpose, since it was "the most pervasive, and therefore one of the most powerful, means of affecting men's thoughts and actions."[8] Both the Pilkington Committee[9] in 1962 and the Annan Committee[10] in 1977 took the public service objective for granted, their deliberations being concerned with ways of adapting and improving it. The most recent review of broadcasting, by the Peacock Committee,[11] similarly considered its appraisal of the options for financing the BBC to be constrained by the principle of public service. Furthermore, support for the principle has continued to be evident in politicians' statements and in discussion by broadcasters.[12]

---

[4] (Sykes) Broadcasting Committee, *Report* (1923) Cmd. 1951, para. 6.2.

[5] *ibid.* para. 7.

[6] (Crawford) Broadcasting Committee, *Report,* (1925) Cmd. 2599, para. 4.

[7] The Peacock Committee emphasised the distinction between public service as a set of institutional arrangements and public service as a set of more general aims: (Peacock) *Committee on Financing the BBC* (1986) Cmnd. 9824, para. 575.

[8] (Beveridge) *Report of the Broadcasting Committee 1949* (1951) Cmd. 8116, paras 212–213.

[9] (Pilkington) *Report of the Committee on Broadcasting 1960* (1962) Cmnd. 1753

[10] (Annan) *Report of the Committee on the Future of Broadcasting* (1977) Cmnd. 6753.

[11] Above, n. 7. As the Committee noted, at para. 15, the Home Secretary stressed a commitment to public service when he announced its formation.

[12] See T. J. Nossiter, "British Television: A Mixed Economy" in *Research on the Range and Quality of Broadcasting Services* (West Yorkshire Media in Politics Group 1986), p. 7. This was one of the independent studies commissioned by the Peacock Committee.

This continuity in adopting the concept of public service in broadcasting does not mean, however, that it has been interpreted consistently over the years. It has fluctuated between conceptions based upon paternalism, elitism and consumerism, with the current trend being towards the latter. Early ideas of public service in broadcasting were shaped by Reith's approach to developing the new BBC.[13] He saw its role as dedicated to the "maintenance of high standards, the provision of the best and the rejection of the hurtful,"[14] and infused with a "moral and cultural zeal."[15] Successive Broadcasting Committees endorsed this vision. The Sykes Committee noted with approval the educative value and high standard of the broadcast matter.[16] The Crawford Committee also approved the emphasis on quality, although it was wary of too much highbrow material,[17] and the Ullswater Committee in 1935 particularly noted the function of the BBC in encouraging the playing and hearing of music.[18] After the Second World War, the aims of radio's Home Service were consolidated as a mission to "help raise the standard of taste, entertainment, outlook and citizenship of the British people."[19]

These sentiments provide constant themes in discussion of public service broadcasting by those involved in its production. The Pilkington Committee in 1962 maintained that "unless and until there is unmistakable proof to the contrary, the presumption must be that television is and will be a main factor in influencing the values and moral standards of our society"; this gave broadcasters a responsibility they could not evade.[20] The Committee reported apparent agreement between itself and broadcasters about what this might mean: it was to give a lead in choosing what the public should be able to select from, in order to enlarge their worthwhile experience and to broaden and deepen their taste.[21]

In this depiction of the public service approach, however, there were the beginnings of an awareness of the needs of the audience and

---

[13] See P. Scannell & D. Cardiff, *A Social History of British Broadcasting*. Vol. 1 *1922–1939 Serving the Nation* (1991) chap. 1.

[14] See A. Briggs, above, n. 3, p. 238.

[15] T. Burns, *The BBC: Public Institution and Private World* (1977), p. 36.

[16] Above, n. 4, para 9.

[17] Above, n. 6, para. 14.

[18] Broadcasting Committee, *Report* (1935) Cmd. 5091, paras 95–96.

[19] Beveridge Committee, above, n. 8, para. 35, quoting from the main memorandum that the BBC submitted to it.

[20] Above, n. 9, para. 42.

[21] *ibid.*, para. 49.

a recognition that broadcasters could not serve up just what they wanted and expect the public to accept it uncritically. A similar approach was to be found in the report of the Annan Committee in 1977 which explicitly rejected the notion that a consensus of "social and moral objectives could be formulated, agreed, and then imposed upon the broadcasters."[22] Consequently, "Broadcasters are wiser to see themselves as hosts to . . . individuals and organisations and, by inviting them to broadcast, help people to understand issues and what, if anything, can be done to resolve them."[23] In addition to the original objectives of providing entertainment, information and education for large audiences, the Committee offered another, described as enrichment, which it saw as being "To enlarge people's interests, to convey to them new choices and possibilities in life."[24] Diversity was to be the central aim in this new approach, with broadcasting to become a type of clearing house for communication between different sections of the population.

In adopting this approach, the Annan Committee has been criticised for actually abandoning the concept of public service broadcasting.[25] The argument seems to be that, by rejecting moral leadership as an appropriate role for broadcasters, the whole basis for the tradition has been eroded. This may be to see the tradition too narrowly, however. It has always been a feature of public service that broadcasting should have universal appeal, catering for all tastes and interests, and reaching the whole nation. However, the Crawford Committee had noted that the listener was entitled to some latitude in the balancing of tastes and the Beveridge Committee drew attention to the broadcaster's responsibility to the listener, noting that if the broadcaster were only responsible to his own conscience, his decision might better be described as irresponsible.[26] What does appear to have occurred is a shift in emphasis towards a greater appreciation of public needs whilst recognising that they do not represent a consensus. This makes the broadcaster's task of mediating public preferences much more difficult, especially in political debate, but does not diminish its public service aims, which continue to be manifested in areas such as national coverage, catering for minorities and maintaining professional standards of quality.

---

[22] Above, n. 10, para. 3.21.
[23] *ibid.*, para. 3.21.
[24] *ibid.*, para. 3.22.
[25] J. Curran and J. Seaton, *Power Without Responsibility* (4th ed. 1991), p. 296.
[26] Above, n. 8, para. 235.

The most recent official statement of public service objectives has been that of the Peacock Committee. Despite being established in order to explore the possibilities of a more market-oriented approach, the Committee accepted the central ideas that broadcasting is a national asset which must be directed to the public good, that broadcasters are responsible as trustees for the national interest, and that there should be freedom from government intervention in day-to-day affairs and programme content.[27] Its interpretation of what these statements entail, however, represents a further departure from the earlier, consensual notions of broadcasting objectives. Now, the public good is much more directly linked to the idea of consumer sovereignty and it is no longer maintained that all broadcasters should be required to provide, on a universal basis, programmes of cultural merit. Instead, public service "is simply any major modification of purely commercial provision resulting from public policy."[28] Such public policy embodies the provision of programmes which expand the knowledge of citizens, provide high quality programmes on the arts, offer critical and controversial commentary, and facilitate experimentation. In the interests of the collective benefit which results from access to a considerable range of programmes, "particularly those which concentrate on matters of serious national concern, including news, educational and current affairs programmes," there should be public patronage of such programmes by citizens in their capacities as taxpayers and voters, if not as consumers.[29]

The implications of this change of focus for the economic framework for public service broadcasting will be considered in chapter four but, for the moment, it may be noticed that, despite strong pressure to allow the market to dominate its organisation, the principle of public service continues to exert a major influence on thinking about the medium. It also continues to feature strongly in broadcasters' own views about their work.[30] This is especially so in their discussion of the standards of impartiality and quality to which they aspire, a matter which will be discussed below and which was surveyed more directly in a study by Nossiter commissioned by the Peacock Committee.[31]

---

27 Above, n. 7, para. 29.
28 *ibid.*, para. 580.
29 *ibid.*, para. 570. See also paras 562, 563 and 581.
30 See J. Morgan, "The BBC and the Concept of Public Service Broadcasting" in *The BBC and Public Service Broadcasting* (C. McCabe and O. Stewart eds., 1986).
31 Nossiter, above, n. 12.

Nossiter found considerable agreement amongst broadcasters about the idea of public service broadcasting. It stood for high standards and excellence, and a professional (but not necessarily "highbrow") interest in whatever interests, excites or illuminates feelings and relationships.[32] In addition, there was a marked feeling that British broadcasting should represent a coherent set of values which reflect Britain as a community, society, culture and polity; it was the principal forum which enabled the whole nation to talk to itself. Public service was also seen as involving an obligation to cater for all significant conditions and interests in society, including the articulation of regional consciousness, perspectives and identities.[33] Such objectives in range and quality were not regarded as inconsistent with the greater importance which is currently attached to maximising audiences, although that means that they must depend more upon professional commitment than institutional arrangements for their realisation.

These views of the broadcasters, taken with those of the various broadcasting committees and the support of politicians, demonstrate a remarkable unity of purpose in discussion of broadcasting. Public service may, indeed, be interpreted as a principle of constitutional dimensions, one which encapsulates a set of aspirations commonly accepted by the major constitutional actors in the field and which has exerted a long-standing influence on the regulation of broadcasting institutions. As Nossiter pointed out, Parliament continued to seek to foster the system as a service to the public despite the breaking of the BBC monopoly and the introduction of new channels reflecting new ventures. Similarly, the introduction of more recent changes has still been accompanied by the belief that public service should be retained as a major dimension of broadcasting. There has continued to be a requirement to provide comprehensive news coverage, current affairs, religious, children's and educational programmes, and there continues to be a policy on family viewing arrangements.[34]

There are, however, problems with the idea of public service. A major issue is the extent to which it is plausible to speak of a set of national, cultural values. Writing of the BBC some years ago, Maley voiced a frequently encountered view that the Corporation "is based

---

[32] *ibid.*, p. 21.

[33] *ibid.*, p. 18. See also Raboy, above, n. 2; K. Dyson & W. Homolka (eds.) *Culture First! Promoting Standards in the New Media Age* (1996).

[34] *ibid.*, pp. 9–10. This trend is reflected in the Broadcasting Act 1990.

upon centralisation and censorship, built upon complete control of the primary channels of culture and communication in a heterogeneous society which belies the homogenous image of that church whose mission is to create the illusion of unity where none exists in practical terms."[35] Certainly, as the discussion of media quality below demonstrates, there is a real danger that broadcasters and journalists can become elitist and too remote from the audience that they intend to serve, under the guise of developing professional standards. So, too, in a medium where access is necessarily limited, choices have to be made about which version of reality to include in describing or commenting on the state of the world or the political system, and there is a real risk of distortion, either by imposing the broadcaster's own interpretation of events, or by a failure to pay sufficient regard to the interests and opinions of marginal groups in society.

These points show that the idea of public service should not be accepted uncritically. Yet it provides an important foundation for constructing a system of media regulation. Not a mere adjunct, it has constituted the British broadcasting tradition in that it defines how broadcasting is practised and provides standards for evaluating it. Furthermore, public service ideals have grown out of, and are part of, a process of constructing a feeling of national cultural identity, which itself can be seen as being of constitutional proportions in a wider sense. This indeed was Reith's vision for the BBC,[36] but it has been argued to have even more relevance as a role for broadcasting in a more pluralistic society. Kumar, for example, put it this way:

> "It is . . . precisely because of the range and depth of its penetration that broadcasting has to conceive of itself primarily in public service terms. It can do what no other national institution can do. Neither education, religion, royalty, nor politics seem capable of providing that sense of participation in a national culture that a socially fragmented society requires."[37]

---

[35] W. Maley, "Centralisation and censorship" in C. McCabe and O. Stewart, above, n. 30, at p. 44.

[36] See A. Briggs, *The History of Broadcasting in the United Kingdom,* Vol. I *The Birth of Broadcasting* (1961), pp. 238–240.

[37] K. Kumar, "Public service broadcasting and the public interest" in C. McCabe and O. Stewart, above, n. 30 at p. 57. Kumar's perspective is a Durkheimian analysis of cultural purpose. For a different defence of public service broadcasting, based on Habermas' concept of the Public Sphere, see N. Garnham, "The Media and the Public Sphere" in *Communicating Politics* (P. Golding *et al.* eds., 1986).

There are good reasons for preserving and nurturing that tradition, for it expresses the sense of responsibility that broadcasters have for the worth and impact of their product, and it reflects the value attached to free speech and an independent media.

However, public service need not be monolithic, manifesting itself as a single conception and to the same extent in every broadcasting institution. As new forms of programme delivery are developed, enabling audiences to become more differentiated, the justification for imposing universal standards and for protecting the medium from market forces, the "scarcity rationale," does become weaker.[38] In the medium term, there will continue to be a relative scarcity of programming outlets, but there is increasingly more scope for purely commercial programming to serve audience demand. Yet the scarcity rationale is not, and never has been, the sole basis for the public service idea. Just as important are the broad benefits of informing, educating and entertaining, the provision of a common fund of diversity, and the "liberating" of programming from the need always to maximise audiences at the expense of innovation and experimentation.[39] Furthermore, a producer-consumer nexus is no substitute for the democratic relationship between the media and their audience.[40] For Curran, public television is the "core sector" which manifests that relationship.[41] Reflecting the importance of media pluralism, discussed in the previous chapter, public broadcasting may be seen as the principal forum for enabling the nation to communicate with itself. In doing so, it must cater for all significant conditions and interests in society, including the articulation of regional and minority consciousness, perspectives and identities. Notwithstanding the extent of segmented, commercial broadcasting — indeed, because of it — public service broadcasting

---

[38] See M. Cave, "Public Service Broadcasting in the United Kingdom" (1996) 9 *Journal of Media Economics* 17–30; C. Veljanovski, "Cable Television: Agency Franchising and Economics" in *Regulation and Public Law* (R. Baldwin and C. McCrudden eds., 1987).

[39] This is the eighth principle of public service identified by the Broadcasting Research Unit: see above, n. 2.

[40] See D. Beetham (ed.), *Defining and Measuring Democracy* (1994).

[41] J. Curran, "Mass Media and Democracy Revisited" in J. Curran and M. Gurevitch (eds.), *Mass Media and Society* (2nd ed. 1996), pp. 105–108.

remains a significant element of democratic participation in a pluralist society.[42]

B. Standards in the Press

While the professional standards of journalists establish much common ground between broadcasters and the press in the area of disseminating information and opinion, it is in the area of quality of programmes and publications that the greatest divergence between them exists. Broadcasting undertakes a certain responsibility in respect of moral and cultural considerations which the press does not fully recognise. For broadcasters, following a tradition established by the BBC, viewers and listeners must not be offended, images of violence and crime must be handled carefully in view of the possible effects of their transmission, and the public's tolerance and demand for intellectual and artistic endeavour should be stretched. By contrast, the press has not been so concerned with giving a lead in identifying some preferred notion of quality as with following the market in supplying the level of cultural sophistication that the readership is prepared to purchase. In their own different ways, therefore, the "quality" and "popular" newspapers are seen as giving the public what they want. Where standards of quality have been discussed in relation to the press, they have not been envisaged as a basis for regulation and have, in any event, been concerned with the requirements of information dissemination and discussion.

The first Royal Commission on the Press noted that most newspaper undertakings conceived themselves as rendering some service to the public. While it would be too strict to judge the press as if it were an agency for political education in a democracy, the Royal Commission considered that to allow it to pursue commercial advantage without limit would be unacceptable. It criticised the preoccupation of some newspapers with triviality and sensationalism and the high incidence of intrusions into privacy, but it saw the

---

[42] For discussions of this theme, see: J.B. Thompson, *Ideology and Modern Culture: Critical Social Theory in the Era of Mass Communication* (1990); C. Sparks, "Broadcasting and the public sphere", (1989) 11 *Media Culture & Society* 131–4; P. Scannell, "Public-service broadcasting and modern public life", (1989) 11 *Media Culture & Society* 135–66; J. Keane, "Citizenship and the freedom of the media", (1989) 60 *Political Quarterly* 285–96; Garnham, above, n. 37.

solution in an increase in the variety of intellectual levels provided, especially in the middle ground, and the establishment of a Press Council to deal with complaints and to build up a code of conduct in accordance with the "highest professional standards."[43] A realistic standard would be to require public affairs to be recorded and discussed truthfully, without triviality or sensationalism, and for the industry as a whole to allow a diversity of opinions to be ventilated, whilst protecting individuals from intrusions into their privacy. Some 30 years later, the third Royal Commission noted that the overlap between the press and broadcasting, in their functions, standards and the expectations made of them, suggested a need for the press to act according to some ideas of social responsibility. There was a consensus of evidence that it "should be neither subject to state control nor left entirely to the unregulated forces of the market."[44] It saw the answer in better professional training for journalists in providing an informed context for news gathering.

In practice, there has been a large gap between the rhetoric of the press' submissions to the Royal Commissions and its commercial aspirations. Where it is conceded that it is appropriate for the press to adopt some "responsible" standards, traditional concerns about free speech and the independence of the media — or at least the ability of the press to mobilise such arguments — have favoured self-regulation rather than legislation. This approach has often led, however, to standards being honoured more in the breach, and there are justifiable reservations about the industry's ability or wish to regulate itself.[45] Nevertheless, in recent years, the press has sought to respond to increasing public disquiet and the threat of legislation in the wake of the Calcutt Report,[46] by setting up the Press Complaints Commission (PCC) and publishing a new code of practice for journalists. The PCC's code[47] was first published in 1991 and it has been revised twice, most recently in 1997. The majority of its provisions deal with issues relating to accuracy of reporting and intrusions into privacy, and these will be considered below. In addition, there are clauses which deal with discrimination, financial

---

[43] Royal Commission on the Press, *Report* (1949) Cmd. 7700, paras 481–496, 561 and 640.

[44] Royal Commission on the Press, *Final Report* (1977) Cmnd. 6810, para. 2.11.

[45] G. Robertson, *People against Press* (1983).

[46] *Report of the Committee on Privacy and Related Matters* (1990) Cm. 1102.

[47] Press Complaints Commission, *Code of Practice* (1997). The Code can be accessed on the Commission's Web Site at http://www.pcc.org.uk/ .

journalism and payment for articles. Beyond imposing minimal ethical standards, however, there has been no enthusiasm to introduce more positive standards to promote quality or media pluralism.

C. Standards in Programming

General Approach

The initial concern to regulate the quality of broadcasting arose from the adoption of the scarcity rationale and the belief that the wavebands were such a "valuable form of public property"[48] that the right to use them should not be squandered by commercial interests. In addition, there was a strongly paternalistic attitude towards the potential audience. In appraising the efforts of the young British Broadcasting Company in 1923, the Sykes Committee noted that "much of the broadcast matter is of considerable educative value and may awaken new interests among listeners of all classes . . . and it is obviously of importance that a high standard should be maintained."[49]

Yet it was recognised at an early stage that broadcasting is, ultimately, a service and the needs of the audience cannot be subsumed by the tastes of the broadcaster. The Crawford Committee noted astutely in 1925 that the listener was entitled to some latitude in the content of broadcasts, and that the transmission of much highbrow material would be unwise if it was more than the licensee was prepared to accept. Many years later, in 1949, the Beveridge Committee was to reiterate the point: broadcasters who were only responsible to their own consciences would be better described as irresponsible — "broadcasting without listeners has no purpose at all."[50] At the same time, it was asserted that every effort had to be made to raise standards of style and performance. The general ethos which was established early on, therefore, was that the broadcaster should gently introduce the audience to a range of better quality products in the expectation that levels of communal taste would gradually be raised as listeners' habits became more educated.[51]

---

[48] See Sykes, above, n. 4, paras 6 and 7.
[49] *ibid.*, para. 9.
[50] Above, n. 8, para. 235.
[51] In particular, the BBC was given from the start, and accepted, the role of upholding music as art in broadcasting. See (Ullswater) Broadcasting Committee, *Report* (1935) Cmd. 5091, paras 95–96.

These themes have continued to set the parameters of discussion about programming in public service broadcasting and they received their most extensive official airing in the Pilkington Committee's report in 1962. There, the object of broadcasting was seen as the duty "to bring to public awareness the whole range of worthwhile, significant activity and experience."[52] Yet the Committee felt unable to stipulate what good broadcasting was, following both the Chairman of the BBC's Governors and the Director-General of the ITA; instead, an empirical approach was preferred, in which good standards are recognised as and when encountered. The difficulty with this eclectic method, however, is that it rather tends to invite the use of broadcasters' preconceived notions of taste as the criteria for identifying good standards whilst obviating the need to articulate or justify them. Furthermore, it does not relieve broadcasting of its central dilemma, described so well by Anthony Smith:

> "When it finds a level of taste at which it can successfully aggregate its audience, it becomes culturally valueless; when it occupies a higher ground in a spirit of dedicated intellectual exclusiveness, it fails in its purpose of serving the entire society."[53]

Pilkington's solution to the dilemma was to attempt to reconcile the wishes of some broadcasters to adopt a more elitist approach to programming with the inclination of audiences to accept a more popularised content. Thus, the Committee did not associate good taste with the taste of the audience as a whole; to accept that approach would be to see the public as a mass and to adopt a patronising and arrogant attitude to particular individuals under the guise of democratic principle. Only by being given a wide range of subject-matters would individuals have sufficient freedom to choose what to watch. On the other hand, good broadcasting did not involve giving the public what is good for it; rather it involved giving a lead in choosing what the public should be able to select, in order to enlarge worthwhile experience. In explaining the problem in this way, implying that the public's cultural horizons were somewhat limited,[54] Pilkington was articulating a responsibility which had become

---

[52] Above, n. 9, para. 23.

[53] See A. Smith, *The Shadow in the Cave* (1973), p. 24. See also Trethowan quoted in Annan, above, n. 10, para. 16.37.

[54] J. Curran and J. Seaton, *Power Without Responsibility* (5th ed. 1997), pp. 177–178, are especially critical of this patronising attitude.

accepted by public service broadcasters to help in broadening and deepening public taste by being in touch with it, yet being slightly ahead of it.[55]

In this latter respect, Pilkington had considered that the ITA had been altogether too negative in seeing its role as the mirror of society's morals and values, and it accused the Authority of falling foul to "triviality . . . a natural vice of television", especially as manifested in its quiz games![56] Almost ten years later, the Annan Committee's concern was the opposite, that broadcasters were going too far in advancing cultural frontiers. By going beyond the raising of programme levels above triviality, they were challenging deeply-rooted sensibilities in areas which were not simply regarded as esoteric but central to the public's lifestyle, and they were not taking public objections seriously enough.[57] Annan's accent, therefore, was on broadcasters' being more aware of the possible offence that their programmes might be causing whilst recognising that the multiplicity of values in a "plural society" would inevitably increase the likelihood of causing offence to somebody at some time. Annan had no easy answer to the problems of "striking a balance between creative freedom and the sensibilities of the audience." No universally acceptable moral code was available, no single standard could be applied to all programmes and for the whole of the public. There was a case for tolerance and for the value of the artist's unravelling of the complexities of life — "But having said that society's codes of what is right and what is wrong are too simple, the broadcaster should not imply that right and wrong do not exist."[58]

Despite Annan's emphasis on diversity and the need to take a plurality of interests into account, the Committee continued the tradition of previous reports in suggesting that public service broadcasting required minimum standards and, indeed, endorsed the broadcasting authorities' guidelines and codes of practice as "unexceptionable".[59] But its proposals for a fourth channel did envisage some relaxation of those standards, in furtherance of the aim to encourage new productions which say something new in new ways. If Annan's report signalled a shift in emphasis in the regulation of broadcasting's quality, it was to remind broadcasters of many

---

[55] Above, n. 9, paras 48–50.
[56] *ibid.*, paras 98 ff.
[57] Above, n. 10, paras 16.4 and 16.36.
[58] *ibid.*, para. 16.37, quoting Trethowan. See also paras 16.38 to 16.39.
[59] *ibid.*, para. 16.18.

pluralistic features of British society. At the same time, it continued the tradition of acknowledging the broadcaster as being responsible for deciding how those features are to exert an influence.

It was the debate in the mid-1980s, at the time when the Peacock Committee was reviewing the status of the BBC, that signalled a shift in thinking about that responsibility. The development of technology which enabled audiences to behave like consumers and purchase the programming product which they were able to afford, raised questions about the need for common standards to be imposed on all media. Peacock's vision of a future with electronic publishing[60] challenged the idea that electronic media should be treated more severely than the unregulated publishing media.

Schematically, we can imagine different levels of media law and regulation which deal with quality. Some restrictions, in the criminal law and the law of torts, would deal with what is considered generally anti-social activity. Such laws would apply to everybody, not only the media; examples which are especially relevant to the media would be the laws of obscenity and of defamation. A higher level of restriction would comprise requirements which were considered necessary because of some special features of the media, for example, their capacity to cause harmful effects, or the nature of their audiences or readerships. Yet a higher set of restrictions would be directed at positively promoting certain values, such as good quality programming and journalism.

In public service broadcasting, all three levels of restriction are implicit in the remit. Indeed, in recognition of that, the provisions of the Obscene Publications Acts 1959 and 1964 did not apply to broadcasters before 1991.[61] For other media, however, the issue is whether they should be subject only to the general law or whether the second or third levels of restriction should be imposed on them. As discussed above, in the press, the case for imposing such additional levels has not been accepted, on the grounds that it would interfere with editorial autonomy and that the market process allows readers to self-censor if they so wish. For broadcasting, however, an opportunity to consider the merits of differentiating between different media was provided with the deregulation of commercial programming heralded by the 1990 Act. But caution proved to be a

---

[60] Above, n. 7.

[61] The exempting provision of the Obscene Publications Act 1959, s. 1(3), was repealed by the Broadcasting Act 1990, s. 162.

more desirable policy and the result was that the 1990 Act imposes a basic standard of programming on all electronic media. It only distinguishes between them in respect of the third level of restrictions and the level of positive quality which they must deliver.

One reason for this caution is continued uncertainty about the potentially harmful effects of the electronic media. It is claimed that television has an immediacy and emotional power which could damage members of the audience. The main focus of concern has been with the portrayal of violence, although the impact of nudity and sexual behaviour is also considered important. In addition, the possibility that more attenuated effects occur in relation to general levels of taste, morality and culture has been voiced. Where research has been conducted in order to test these hypotheses, however, the results have tended to be equivocal; at best, correlations between types of programme and supposed effects have not been strong and, in particular, it has not been easy to identify directions of cause and effect because so many intervening variables exist. Yet although the evidence, certainly for the moment, fails to satisfy the condition that harmful effects must be demonstrated before censorship can be justified,[62] there has been a paternalistic reluctance to ignore the possibility that some individuals may well be vulnerable to media influences.

Other reasons for caution are based on forms of moral disapproval. There is still some residual feeling for an earlier sentiment that "whatever is published is presumed to be in some way approved, or at least condoned, by the society which permits its publication", and that "the airwaves, unlike the printing presses, are licensed by Parliament."[63] More significant is a sensitivity to the possibility that members of the audience will be offended by programming. There has been a particular emphasis on the circumstances of family viewing, where private responses are overlaid with social sensitivities which may produce embarrassment. Both kinds of reasoning based on moral disapproval depend, however, on the existence of programming which is broadcast to a universal audience. Such

---

62 See G. Cumberbatch & D. Howitt, *A Measure of Uncertainty — The Effects of the Mass Media* (1989); S. Livingstone, "On the Continuing Problem of Media Effects" in *Mass Media and Society* (J. Curran and M. Gurevitch eds., 2nd ed. 1996). For elaboration of the harm condition, see J. S. Mill, *On Liberty* (1859); H.L.A. Hart, *Law, Liberty and Morality* (1963); Home Office (Williams), *Report of the Committee on Obscenity and Film Censorship* (1977) Cmnd. 7772, para. 7.2.

63 Annan, above, n. 10, para. 16.3.

universal programming must cater for as much of the audience as possible and that entails minimising the amount of offence which will be given to the majority. Even if public service fulfils its role of catering for a variety of tastes and moral standards — by providing a range of different material at different times, so that everybody receives a fair chance of seeing or hearing their preferred programmes — it is still available to all. Universal broadcasting does not allow the possibility of choosing which programmes will be available.

Where audiences are allowed to choose which segments of programming they wish to receive, the arguments for imposing a second level of basic restrictions are much weakened. If members of a potential audience can control effectively the material which reaches them, it becomes their responsibility to decide, rather than the broadcaster's or regulator's.[64] The logic of this view is that the amount of regulation for basic standards (the second level restrictions) should diminish in proportion to the segmentation of programming. Two conditions need to be satisfied, however. One is that segmentation should be effective. This implies that the programming is not free-to-air but is by subscription, and this may imply encryption (coding) of the material. The other condition is that there should be adequate information available to the audience to allow informed choices. In practice, this requires attention to be given to sufficient signposting and scheduling of material. Given those conditions, a graduated (or "scaleable") approach to quality regulation seems appropriate for programming, one which does not necessarily depend on the nature of the delivery system, but which looks to the character of the audience. As will become clear, however, media regulation in the United Kingdom has not yet proceeded far in that direction.

Basic Standards

The Broadcasting Act 1990 does, however, distinguish basic standards from more positive obligations, thereby significantly changing the regulation of commercial programming. Under section 2 of the

---

[64] See C. Munro, *Television, Censorship and the Law* (1979), making a similar point at p. 170.

repealed 1981 Act, the IBA had a duty to provide a public service and to ensure the maintenance of a high general standard in programmes in each area in all respects, particularly in respect of content and quality. It also had a duty to secure a wide showing or hearing for programmes of merit, maintaining a proper balance and wide range in their subject-matter, having regard to the programmes as a whole and the days and times of broadcasts. Under the current legislation, there are no such obligations that public service should be provided or that all programmes should meet those high standards. Instead, the ITC and Radio Authority have duties to secure that, "taken as a whole", that is, across the whole range, the services are of "high quality and offer a wide range of programmes calculated to appeal to a wide variety of interests."[65] Only Channel 4 retains a public service remit which continues to be modified to require a suitable proportion of matter calculated to appeal to tastes not generally catered for by ITV and to encourage innovation and experimentation.[66] The effect of these changes is that, for all but Channel 4 programmes, it will be permissible for low quality programming to be supplied, provided that there is sufficient high quality material available elsewhere. Much of the balance will be provided by Channel 4, but there is also a set of specific, positive obligations imposed on Channels 3 and 5, to reflect the character of their services as broadcasting which is universal, or near universal, although they do not amount to public service as such.

The provisions of the 1990 Act do not, however, follow through the logic of deregulating to take account of more segmented programming, where the audience has some control over the material received. Instead, it sets out a number of basic standards which the preceding White Paper had described as "consumer protection."[67] These are minimum requirements which go beyond the general law, but which are still considered necessary to govern the less regulated regime. Thus, the regulatory bodies must do all that they can to secure that "nothing is included in programmes which offends against good taste or decency or is likely to encourage or incite to crime or to lead to disorder or be offensive to public feeling." In

---

[65] Broadcasting Act 1990, ss. 2(2)(b) and 85(3)(a).

[66] Broadcasting Act 1990, s. 25. The former duties of the IBA were set out in the Broadcasting Act 1981, ss. 2 and 11. For transitional provisions, see the 1990 Act, Sched. 11.

[67] Home Office, *Broadcasting in the 90s: Competition, Choice and Quality* (1988) Cm. 517, para. 7.1.

addition, they have duties to draw up codes giving guidance in respect of programming standards and, specifically, the portrayal of violence.[68] The BBC has almost identical obligations under its Agreement[69] and it also elaborates their application in its own code.[70] To assist in these matters, the Broadcasting Standards Commission is required to publish a code of practice relating to violence, sex, taste and decency, and the broadcasters and regulators are obliged to ensure that their codes reflect its substance.[71]

Given the various and sometimes conflicting considerations which apply to the promotion of standards, however, it is not surprising that broadcasters and regulators have not felt able to offer any detailed guidance for decision-making. Although there are differences of emphasis, the basic approach in the BBC's *Producers' Guidelines* and *The ITC's Programme Code* is similar. They articulate the relevant factors as fully as possible and draw attention to certain dominant principles, but the general tone is discursive and reflects the complexity of deciding what are appropriate standards.

1. Good Taste, Decency and Offensiveness to Public Feeling

The requirement to satisfy these standards, so far as possible, applies to the whole of the programming media. The concepts involved tend to overlap and all depend upon some assessment of the values and attitudes which are held and approved by the general populace at the time the relevant programme is disseminated. In this respect, conceptions of what amounts to good taste, decency and inoffensiveness are likely to vary over time. Although good taste appears to have a more objective, or at least permanent, quality than offensiveness, neither the broadcasters nor the courts have attempted

---

[68] 1990 Act, ss. 6, 7, 90, 91.

[69] Department of National Heritage, *Copy of the Agreement Dated the 25th Day of January 1996 Between Her Majesty's Secretary of State for National Heritage and the British Broadcasting Corporation* (1996) Cm. 3152, (hereinafter "BBC Agreement"), clause 5.2(c).

[70] BBC, *Producers' Guidelines* (1996). The BBC's obligations used to be contained in the Resolution of the Board of Governors in 1981, reiterating Lord Normanbrook's assurances, and appended to the previous Licence and Agreement. The Corporation undertook a duty to maintain a high general standard and accepted that so far as possible programmes should not infringe what are were in effect the present minimum requirements in the 1990 Act. See BBC, *Producers' Guidelines* (1989), chaps. 12–16. See also BBC, *Annual Report and Accounts 1986–87* (1987) p. 63.

[71] Broadcasting Act 1996, s. 108. See BSC, *Code on Standards* (1998). This revised version has been published with the Commission's Code on Fairness and Privacy in *Codes of Guidance* (1998) pp. 19–37.

to offer definitions or draw distinctions about a subject which all agree to lack consensus. The Broadcasting Standards Commission (BSC) has continued the debate, but does not appear yet to have added to the general principles that have already been identified.[72]

It is possible to make some distinctions, of course. Taste has been described as "a matter of manners which reflect the prevailing sense of what is done or not done between individuals", perhaps implying a certain ephemeral quality.[73] Whether taste is good or bad involves aesthetic judgment.[74] Decency connotes more morally serious matters and has been the subject of much legal discussion which has not, however, served to illuminate its meaning. In *Knuller v. DPP*[75] Lord Reid maintained that "Indecency is not confined to sexual indecency; indeed it is difficult to find any limits short of saying that it includes anything which an ordinary decent man or woman would find to be shocking, disgusting or revolting."[76] Earlier, however, indecency had been described as "something that offends the ordinary modesty of the average man . . . offending against recognised standards of propriety at the lower end of the scale."[77] Here, the suggestion is that indecency involves the infringement of a moral standard.[78] This accords with the BSC's interpretation of decency as reflecting ideals which "acknowledge our shared values" and "enduring values of right and wrong" as opposed to the rapid changes of fashion in taste.[79] In turn, offensiveness has been described as that which upsets, distresses, disgusts, outrages or puts out members of the public in relation to what is and is not appropriate for public as opposed to private consumption.[80] This view was advanced in the context of sexual matters, but it would appear to apply to other areas, for example, blasphemy, abusive language, or violence and the invasion of privacy itself. In addition, it appears to have overtones of mere disgust or annoyance.

Transmissions which are in bad taste, offensive to public feeling or indecent span a range of unacceptable practices, therefore, involving

---

[72] BSC, *Code on Standards.*

[73] General Advisory Council to the BBC, *Tastes and Standards in BBC Programmes* (1973), p. 2.

[74] See Home Office, (Williams), above, n. 62, para. 7.2.

[75] [1973] A.C. 435.

[76] *ibid.* at 458.

[77] *R. v. Stanley* [1965] 1 All E.R. 1035 at p. 1038, *per* Lord Parker C.J.

[78] *cf.* A. Ellis, "Offense and the Liberal Conception of the Law" (1984) 13 *Philosophy and Public Affairs* 3–23.

[79] BSC, *Code on Standards*, para. 1.

[80] Home Office (Williams), above, n. 62, paras 7.4, 7.12.

matters of little more than etiquette at one extreme, through aesthetic judgment and inconsistent lifestyle to moral disagreement at the other extreme, and there is a tendency not to dwell on the nuances which separate them.[81] This allows the broadcasters and regulatory bodies considerable scope for implementing their duty to regulate the content of programmes so that they contain "nothing" of that nature. A number of considerations serve to preserve broadcasters' and programme providers' discretion, however. There is much scope for reasonable argument about what constitutes taste and what would be regarded as offensive or indecent, and it may be doubted whether any recognised standards do persist. In addition, the circumstances in which the material in question is experienced are crucial. The anticipated audience, the time of transmission and the overall objective of the programme maker are all factors which will influence judgments about its propriety.[82]

A related factor, the weight and contexts of different parts of the programme has been the subject of judicial comment, in *Att.-Gen. v. IBA*.[83] The case involved an attempt to stop the showing of an allegedly indecent programme about the artist, Andy Warhol. Lord Denning maintained that the words "nothing is included" in section 4(1)(a) of the 1981 Act "showed that the programme is to be judged, not as a whole, but in its several parts, piece by piece." But Lawton L.J. preferred to consider the programme as a whole and noted that "whether an incident is indecent must depend on all the circumstances, including the context in which the alleged indecent matter occurred."[84] However, the courts would not interfere in an attempt to enforce the minimum requirements of section 4(1)(a) unless the regulatory bodies misdirect themselves or come to an unreasonable conclusion — "They are the censors."[85] The point was repeated in *ex p. Whitehouse*,[86] a case which involved an attempt to prevent the screening of the film, *Scum*, which depicted scenes of violence and abuse in a Borstal. It was held that the IBA's duty to be satisfied about compliance with section 4(1)(a) was a "best endeavours" obligation. It would be fulfilled if it adopted an

---

[81] The courts have treated them in a unitary manner. See *R. v. IBA, ex p. Whitehouse* (1985) *The Times*, April 4.
[82] See generally, G. Robertson, *Obscenity* (1979); Home Office (Williams), above, n. 62.
[83] *Attorney-General (on the relation of McWhirter) v. IBA* [1973] 1 All E.R. 689.
[84] *ibid.* at pp. 706a and 707a.
[85] *ibid.* at p. 704.
[86] Above, n. 81.

appropriate system for the purpose, one which allowed for effective supervision of programming by IBA staff and the possibility of referring difficult issues to Members of the Authority. Furthermore, the system need not be foolproof: failure to meet the requirements of section 4(1) on a particular occasion would not constitute a breach of that duty in itself, although the regulators might be reasonably expected to react to the failure by modifying their system.

This reasoning may be taken to apply to the current, and identical, provisions of sections 6(1)(a) and 90(1)(a) of the 1990 Act. In regulating quality, therefore, the broadcasters and regulatory bodies have been allowed considerable leeway in interpreting and implementing their duties. In considering good taste, decency and offensiveness, the ITC has identified a number of areas of particular concern. In relation to bad language, it requires it to be defensible in terms of context and authenticity, and suggests that offensiveness occurs when it is used to excess and without justification. The portrayal of sex and nudity must be defensible in context and presented with tact and discretion — "the aim should be to move, not to offend", which does not preclude the writer's intention to shock or disturb. Jokes based upon physical disability or race must be treated with sensitivity. In addition, there is guidance on the invasion of privacy which is derived from the duty to prevent offence.

The BBC's approach is basically the same in seeking to stimulate but not shock, taking into account public opinion.

> "The basic pillars of decency rest on telling the truth about the human experience, including its darker side, but we do not set out to demean or brutalise through word or deed, or to celebrate cruelty . . . an item . . . must be justified by its purpose, and by the overall quality of the programme, and there must be due consideration of its context in the schedule . . ."[87]

These themes echo the words of Sir Hugh Greene, who maintained that "Relevance is the key — relevance to the audience and to the tide of opinion in society. Outrage is wrong. Shock may be good."[88] Yet there is a latent ambiguity in such firm advice which is itself open to differing opinions about its practical meaning. In two areas the need for more specific guidance has been considered more acute,

---

[87] BBC, *Producers' Guidelines* (1996), chap. 5, para. 1.
[88] Sir Hugh Greene, *The Conscience of the Programme Director* (1965).

namely children's viewing and the portrayal of violence. Even in these matters, however, the preferred method is to structure practical reasoning by emphasising what is relevant, rather than issue rigid directives.

2. Children's viewing

For some years, broadcasters have developed and subscribed to a "watershed"[89] or "family viewing"[90] policy whereby 9.00 p.m. is regarded as the time before which programmes unsuitable for children should not be scheduled. Progressively less suitable, more adult, material can be shown after this time, which is the point beyond which the broadcasters will not accept full responsibility for children's viewing. There is an awareness, however, of changes in children's viewing habits and the flexibility introduced by time-shifting with video recorders; it may be unrealistic to assume that all children's viewing is supervised, especially at weekends. Although there should be careful monitoring of films and serials which might appeal to children on late slots, there is also a resistance to the schedules being controlled by children's programming, especially in the BBC. It maintains that parental supervision and adequate signposting is the solution to any problems that might arise; otherwise, adult material would have to be screened far too late. Careful scheduling is very important: "A good rule of thumb is to avoid taking the audience by surprise." Little assistance is given on the nature of unsuitability, although the BBC mentions "common sense" and has considered, in the past, what "reasonable parents would agree about".[91] The ITC cites relevant factors as including violence, bad language, innuendo, blasphemy, explicit sexual behaviour and scenes of extreme distress. The fact that viewing takes place in the home, often in a family context, and that television creates a strong visual impact, justifies caution where these matters are concerned.[92] For the ITC, this caution extends to the regulation of more segmented programming in the cable and satellite sectors. The regulator has been prepared to make a minor concession in allowing the watershed to be brought forward to 8 p.m., but is clearly

---

[89] See BBC, above, n. 87, chap. 5, para. 2.
[90] ITC, *The ITC Programme Code* (1998), para. 1.2.
[91] See BBC, *Violence on Television. The Report of the Wyatt Committee* (1987).
[92] See General Advisory Council to the BBC, above, n. 73. This approach is endorsed by the Broadcasting Standards Commission; see *Code on Standards* (1998), paras 2–14.

wary that subscription to bouquets of programming will not prevent unlimited access to programming in the absence of consistent control through parental-lock devices. However, the ITC is conducting an experiment with pay-per-view channels whereby a dispensation from the watershed will be given to channels which can demonstrate an adequate security (PIN) system, with detailed subscription billing and full information about the content of programmes available. Should this experiment prove successful, the only basic standards which would need to be imposed on such segmented programming would be the requirements of the general law, although it is doubtful whether the ITC would agree and the present legislation would not allow it.

For all that, the regulatory trend is towards an acceptance of a more liberal stance, provided there can be adequate control of programming reception so as to allow responsible adults to make decisions about what their children watch. In the United States, the Telecommunications Act 1996[93] made provision for the Federal Communications Commission (FCC) to require manufacturers of television receivers to install a blocking device (the "V-chip") in sets of thirteen inches or greater. The V-chip is intended to operate in conjunction with a system of programme ratings which the statute encouraged the industry to devise voluntarily rather than have imposed by the FCC. Agreement was duly reached for a scheme which uses symbols to indicate appropriate age levels for viewing and, in early 1998, the FCC ordered manufacturers to start inserting the chip.[94]

In the European Broadcasting Directive, Article 22 makes provision for the protection of minors by making a distinction between an absolute ban on some sorts of programming and a conditional ban on others. There should be no broadcast of "any"[95] programme which "might seriously impair the physical, mental or moral development of minors, in particular programmes that involve pornography or gratuitous violence." The same is the case with such programmes which are "likely to impair" such development, "except where it is ensured, by selecting the time of the broadcast or by any technical measure, that minors in the area of transmission will not

---

93 ss. 551, 552 and 652. These provisions are within a part of the statute known as the "Communications Decency Act 1996."

94 FCC News Announcement, Report No. GN 98–3, March 12, 1998.

95 This word was added to the 1989 Directive in the revision of 1997.

normally hear or see such broadcasts." Furthermore, in a paragraph added in the revised version of the Directive, when such programmes are broadcasts in an unencoded form, they must be preceded by an acoustic warning or accompanied by a visual symbol. The revised Directive also requires a feasibility study to be conducted, within a year of publication, into V-chip technology, ratings systems and family viewing policies. One difficulty with the Directive's bans is that they are based on empirical criteria, albeit with low standards of proof, and the evidence for adverse effects from the media remains ambivalent. But it is likely that the new provisions will be seen as endorsement of a policy of prudence for free-to-air broadcasting, consistent with the basic requirements of the Broadcasting Act 1990, and encouragement for the more marginal types of programming to become fully segmented.

3. *The Portrayal of Violence*

This area is one of special sensitivity for broadcasters; it was initially highlighted by the Pilkington Committee,[96] was the subject of extended discussion by the Annan Committee[97] and is the subject of much public pressure.[98] Both the BBC and the ITC have published guidance on the issue and both adopt broadly the same approach.[99] Providing a code of absolute or universal rules is eschewed in favour of inviting the programme-maker to think about the particular content and style of his or her own programme and its likely effect on the audience. A discursive style is adopted, therefore, in which moral, artistic and empirical considerations are evaluated.

The broadcasters accept that violence is a fact of life and often an essential ingredient of drama, so to ignore it would be unrealistic and untrue. As the BBC has previously put it:

> "It cannot be overlooked that violent situations sometimes evoke qualities of courage and leadership which are admired by the majority of people. When producers make use of violence with integrity, their right to portray violence should be upheld."[1]

---

[96] Above, n. 9, paras 42ff.

[97] Above, n. 10, paras 16.1–16.51.

[98] This was given as one of the reasons for setting up the Broadcasting Standards Council: see chap 6.

[99] BBC, *Producers' Guidelines* (1996) chap. 6; BBC, *Guidelines for the Portrayal of Violence on BBC Television* (1993); ITC, *ITC Programme Code* (1998); BSC, *Code on Standards* (1998), paras 48–78.

[1] BBC, *Guidelines for the Portrayal of Violence on BBC Television* (1993).

In the ITC's words, "there can be no defence of violence shown solely for its own sake" and "the editor or producer must be sure that the degree of violence shown is essential to the integrity and completeness of his or her programme."

Note is also taken of the degree of public concern about violence in programmes, the BBC in particular drawing attention to the upset that violence causes to many people, and its potential to desensitise when used to excess — "Most audiences expect any violent scenes to serve a moral or social point." There is an emphasis on the standards of decency and acceptability held by the broadcasting audience. The most vulnerable members of the audience are not regarded as being able to exercise any veto on programming, but their existence places the onus on programme-makers to justify their decisions to show violence if any risk exists. In addition, the importance of advance notice of scheduling arrangements is emphasised.

What the guidelines do, then, is to identify possible risks and effects in the light of available research evidence. There is a commitment to review policies from time to time,[2] taking into account relevant research findings. These latter have continued to be ambiguous about the likely effects of violence on television.[3] The broadcasters' approach, however, has been to advocate care, sensitivity and caution. Consequently, the dangers to the young and the emotionally insecure are noted, as is the fear that violence portrayed on television may be imitated in real life. The cumulative effect of violence and its possible tendency to result in desensitisation are also recognised; a callous indifference to violence is identified as being of particular concern. Other matters which are mentioned include the counter-productive effect of sanitised violence and the effects of violence apparently remote in distance or time. The general message that emerges is that the programme-maker is expected to try to be aware of the susceptibilities of particular audiences at particular times, and to balance these against the necessary requirements of relevant and serious journalistic objectives in news and current affairs, on the one hand, and the valuable insights into human activity that artistic creativity may express through violence, on the other.

---

[2] For the ITC, see Broadcasting Act 1990, s. 7(1). This commitment is shared by the BBC.

[3] See above, n. 62. However, reports into television violence, jointly commissioned by the BBC and the regulators, by Sheffield University in 1996 and Adam Irving Associates in 1997, have led to reappraisals of the adequacy of the guidance available. See ITC New Release 106/96 and 105/97.

4. *Programmes Likely to Encourage Crime or Lead to Disorder.*

The duty not to broadcast these types of programme is contained in the BBC's Agreement and in section 6(1)(a) of the Broadcasting Act 1990, which is to be interpreted in the same manner as the other duties in that paragraph. The IBA took the view that "any programme item which on any reasonable judgment would be said to encourage or incite crime or to lead to disorder is unacceptable." That interpretation appears to be consistent with the judgment in *ex p. Whitehouse*.[4] What is reasonable will involve the probability that crime will be encouraged or that disorder will follow, taking into account the susceptibility of the audience, with the latter not necessarily depending on audience size. Both the BBC and the ITC provide more specific guidance in identifying a number of factors which are relevant to programming decisions in this area. Interviews with criminals are particularly sensitive especially when they are wanted by the police. So too are interviews with people who use or advocate violence or other criminal measures; in this context, the portrayal of para-military organisations, especially in Northern Ireland, is singled out for special caution, involving consultation with top management — a caution which has been reflected in actual decisions not to broadcast,[5] although the question of due impartiality also arises here. Other areas of concern are the treatment of hijacking and kidnapping reports, the demonstration of criminal techniques, and the presence of television cameras at demonstrations and scenes of public disturbance. In the latter case, the fear is that some individuals will "play to the gallery" or engage in "copycat" disorder. Included too are restrictions on the portrayal of drug-taking, solvent abuse, smoking and drinking, together with front seat passengers who are not wearing seat belts. In all cases, regulation is based on the belief that broadcasting is actually capable of having the effect that is sought to be prevented, or at the least that there is a risk that this might be so. That such beliefs are justified remains to be demonstrated, although that is not to say that a safe strategy may not be the appropriate one for public service broadcasting.

Positive Obligations

In recognition of the quasi-public service nature of Channels 3 and 5, they have certain obligations in addition to the basic standards which

---

[4] See above, n. 81.

[5] An example was the "Real Lives" affair in 1985. See the discussion in chap. 6.

all programming must satisfy. The obligations satisfy a variety of policy objectives. Generally, they recognise that the commercial channels have been providing such services free-to-air and that to deprive the audience of them would be a net loss to consumer welfare. In addition, the commercial supply of public service programming provides an element of healthy competition for the BBC and Channel 4. Thus, there is provision for schools programming and subtitling for the deaf, in sections 34 and 35 of the Broadcasting Act 1990, respectively. Arrangements for the financing and broadcasting of Gaelic programmes in Scotland is made in sections 183 to 184 of the 1990 Act. Not least, the Act requires Channels 3 and 5 to comply with a threshold of quality in programming, under sections 15 and 16, and there is provision for the supply of news in sections 31 and 32. These matters will be discussed in chapter four.

D. Regulating for Privacy

For over a quarter of a century, a perennial theme in deliberation about media standards has been the desirability of controlling journalists' and broadcasters' intrusions into privacy. Since the general law in Great Britain does not recognise a right to privacy as such, the broader debate has examined the arguments for providing a general remedy which could be exercised by all citizens against each other's invasions of privacy. However it has been the aims and transgressions of the media which have most shaped and stimulated discussion. In relation to this topic, therefore, there has been a reversal of the question of what standards additional to those applicable to all citizens should be imposed on the media. Instead, the issue has become that of deciding how far the interests of the media count against the introduction of a general law. On that point, the claims that the protection of privacy would infringe the media's freedom of communication, and that privacy cannot be adequately defined, are not convincing[6] and, if the judges do not succeed in creating a remedy at common law,[7] incorporation of the European

---

[6] See E. Barendt, "Privacy and the Press" 1 *Yearbook of Media and Entertainment Law* 23–41.

[7] See H. Fenwick & G. Phillipson, "Confidence and Privacy: A Re-examination" (1996) 55 *Cambridge Law Journal* 447–455.

Convention on Human Rights[8] will provide a basis for such general protection. To some extent, the case has been conceded by virtue of the regulatory schemes which already exist. They acknowledge, at least, the moral and ethical basis for guidance in this area, given that the media are most likely, by the nature of their activities, to infringe individuals' privacy. However, although the press has been prompted to adopt self-regulation as a defensive tactic in resisting legislation, the media's overall experience of privacy regulation shows that there will continue to be a need for special sensitivity to their concerns.

A major reason for such sensitivity is that the concept of privacy is not easy to elucidate and its priority in securing protection over other interests is not self-evident.[9] In general, it is a claim about the individual's right to restrict the availability of information about himself or herself. The justification for such restriction is typically couched in terms of a natural need for personal space, or control over the presentation of one's identity or self to the outside world.[10] Essentially, however, the claim is that individuals should not have to account for themselves in respect of certain information[11] and protection of privacy may be overridden by an appeal to a significant public interest in disclosure. Intrusions or deceptions, for example, in the form of snooping, surreptitious surveillance, trespassing, or intercepting letters and telephone conversations, may be justified if keeping the material relatively secret would adversely affect the public at large, notwithstanding the harm or distress which may be caused to the individuals concerned.

The difficulty, however, is to decide in which circumstances the information is sufficiently "other-regarding" for the public to have a justifiable claim, if not a right, to know about it. Some cases are reasonably clear: if facts about anti-social or harmful practices are private, that does not justify their continued secrecy; and facts which are relevant to politicians' ability to govern are required to be publicly known in the interest of participation in the democratic process. The media's role is organised around more mundane objectives, however,

---

[8] Human Rights Bill 1997.

[9] See R. Wacks, *Personal Information: Privacy and the Law* (1989); *The Protection of Privacy* (1980); (Younger) *Report of the Committee on Privacy* (1972) Cmnd. 5012; Lord Chancellor's Department and the Scottish Department, *Infringement of Privacy* (1993). On the more recent discussions of the Calcutt Inquiry, see chap. 5, below.

[10] For example, see R. Post, "The Social Foundations of Privacy: Community and Self in the Common Law Tort" (1989) 77 *California Law Review* 957–1010.

[11] For an elaboration of this point, see T. Gibbons, "Personality Rights: The Limits of Personal Accountability" (1997–98) 3 *Yearbook of Media and Entertainment Law* 53–74.

in the form of their news values, and those values provide a powerful incentive to provide information, not because it is *in* the public's interest to know it, but because it is simply *of* interest to them.[12]

As with other matters of quality in the media product, the distinction between the two meanings of interest has proved difficult to identify in practice. The Younger Committee considered that —

> "because it is impossible to devise any satisfactory yardstick by which to judge, in cases of doubt, whether the importance of a public story should override the privacy of the people and personal information involved, the decision on this point can be made only in the light of the circumstances of each case."[13]

Even where criteria have been specified for identifying "gratuitous publicity", they tend to shape thinking rather than provide solutions. Examples are: what is the nature of the public interest and how essential is publication of the person's identity, how public is the person concerned and the information involved, how was the information acquired, and how serious was the invasion of privacy.[14]

In the absence of a general right of privacy, however, a set of common themes has emerged as worthy of special attention when considering media behaviour. Partly, they are a response to public criticism of journalists and, partly, they are an expression of professional ethics. In broadcasting, there has generally been a willingness to articulate and comply with regulatory standards for dealing with intrusions into privacy, whereas, in the press, there has been some resistance to the acceptance — at all — of constraints on journalistic activity. Much debate has centred on questions about the appropriate regulatory approach, a matter which will be considered in chapter six, but this section will examine some of the key issues which both sectors of the media have attempted to tackle.

Guidance about protecting interests in privacy is contained in as many as five separate codes of practice. The press are governed by the PCC's code of practice.[15] Until then, the only guidance for the press was the Press Council's Declaration of Principle on Privacy,

---

[12] On this distinction, see Younger, above, n. 9, para 157. See also *Francome* v. *Mirror Group* [1984] 2 All E.R. 408.

[13] Above, n. 9, para. 187

[14] Wacks, above, n. 9, pp. 99–106.

[15] Press Complaints Commission, *Code of Practice* (1997). The Code can be accessed on the Commission's Web Site at http://www.pcc.org.uk/ .

published in 1976 which stated that "the justification for publication or inquiries which conflict with a claim to privacy must be a legitimate and proper public interest and not only a prurient or morbid curiosity", that is, when "the circumstances relating to the private life of an individual occupying a public position may be likely to affect the performance of his duties or public confidence in him or his office."[16] Deception and surreptitious surveillance or the causing of pain or humiliation to bereaved or distressed people could be justified where that was the only reasonably practicable method of obtaining information in the public interest. Such wide formulations allowed much leeway for the press to judge what would affect public duties, or what were reasonably practicable methods, and the Press Council was never able to enforce the Declaration effectively.

Until 1998, practical guidance for dealing with privacy issues in broadcasting was included only in the BBC's, the R.A.'s and the ITC's programming codes. Its provision was derived from the broadcasters' general duty not to allow programming which is offensive to public feeling. Given their common experience, they adopted a broadly similar approach, although the ITC's rules were more detailed. Under the 1990 Act, the former Broadcasting Complaints Commission (BCC) had a duty to investigate and adjudicate on complaints relating to privacy, but it had no duty to devise a code. Although it published its decisions on privacy complaints, it did not develop a systematic caselaw or readily accessible set of principles.[17] Under section 107(1)(b) of the Broadcasting Act 1996, its successor, the Broadcasting Standards Commission (BSC), has the same duty to adjudicate. But it has an additional obligation to draw up a code of guidance as to the principles to be observed and practices to be followed for the avoidance of "unwarranted infringement of privacy in, or in connection with the obtaining of material included in programmes" which are broadcast by the BBC or included in licensed services. The new *Code on Privacy and Fairness*,[18] which took effect from the beginning of 1998, is clearly based on the broadcasters' practices, but

---

[16] The Press Council, *The Press and the People* (1982–83), p. 291, (1985), p. 241.

[17] See T. Gibbons, "The Role of the Broadcasting Complaints Commission: Current Practice and Future Prospects" (1995) 1 *Yearbook of Media and Entertainment Law* 129–59.

[18] Broadcasting Standards Commission, *Code on Fairness and Privacy* (1998). This has been republished with the Commission's revised Code of Standards in *Codes of Guidance* (1998), pp. 9–17.

it is also an attempt to articulate the BCC's experience. In doing so, it incorporates provisions which reflect past differences of opinion with the BBC and the ITC and R.A., but which they are now obliged to incorporate into their own codes of practice.[19] Compared with the press, which has tended to favour the interests of the public, the broadcasters have sought to offer a more even balance, although the recent trend within the BSC appears to be oriented towards the privacy of the individual.[20] The following discussion examines some of the more important principles which are to be found in the different codes. They are necessarily couched in broad terms and, as with other provisions of the programmers' codes, what they do is to shape ways of thinking about the problems that media activities raise.

Privacy and Public Interest

As a preliminary point, the general style has been to avoid providing a definition of privacy, although the PCC's revised code does describe certain spheres of privacy as "private and family life, home, health and correspondence."[21] Instead, the emphasis is on the nature and scope of the public interest in obtaining information. These are supplemented with more detailed comments on the acceptability of, for example, using hidden microphones or cameras, doorstepping, showing suffering and distress, and dealing with children. The basic approach is illustrated by the BSC's code, which draws a distinction between the questions "has there been an infringement of privacy?" and "if so, was it justified?", and proceeds to deal only with the latter in the following terms:[22]

> "An infringement of privacy has to be justified by an overriding public interest in the disclosure of the information. This would include revealing or detecting crime or disreputable behaviour, protecting public health or safety, exposing misleading claims made by individuals or organisations, or disclosing significant incompetence in public office. Moreover, the means of obtaining the information must be proportionate to the matter under investigation."

---

[19] Under s. 107(2) of the 1996 Act. In fact, there are many elements of the BSC's code which draw on the ITC's and especially the BBC's guidelines.
[20] See Gibbons, above, n. 17.
[21] Press Complaints Commission, *Code of Practice* (1997), para. 4.
[22] Broadcasting Standards Commission, *Code on Fairness and Privacy* (1998) para. 14.

This phrasing, which has been adopted by the ITC,[23] may be contrasted with the PCC's code which states that the public interest test includes:

> (i) Detecting or exposing crime or a serious misdemeanour. (ii) Protecting public health and safety. (iii) Preventing the public from being misled by some statement or action of an individual or organisation";

but that, in cases involving children, an "exceptional" public interest must be demonstrated to override the "normally paramount" interests of the child. Yet a third formulation is used by BBC which variously describes the public interest as arising where crime or seriously anti-social behaviour is involved. However, its approach appears to be the same in substance, albeit couched in a more accessible style:

> "The BBC should respect the privacy of individuals, recognising that intrusions have to be justified by serving a greater good . . . programmes should confine themselves to relevant facts and avoid gossip. The information we broadcast should be important as well as true."[24]

All these versions of the test owe much to the recent debates about privacy reform which have produced a loose consensus about the kinds of issues that public interest involves.[25] However, the PCC's threshold does appear lower than that of the broadcasters, making it easier for the press to invoke public interest to justify intrusions into privacy. Indeed, in 1996, the Chairman of the PCC exhorted editors to adopt a stricter approach to its interpretation and posed a series of questions which should be asked to ensure that a "genuine" public interest was being invoked and that publication of a story or accompanying photographs was necessary.[26] His suggestions were not incorporated into the recent revision of the code, however, other than for the reporting of children.

The Requirement of Consent

There is general acceptance that the publication or broadcast of words or images should not take place without the individual's

---

[23] ITC, *The ITC Programme Code* (1998) para. 2.1.
[24] BBC, *Producer's Guidelines* (1996) chap. 4 generally.
[25] See chap. 5, below.
[26] Lord Wakeham, "Privacy and the Public Interest," speech delivered on November 21, 1996.

consent, unless the material is outside his or her private life but is sufficiently in the public domain.[27] This applies to events in private places, but also to events in "sensitive" places such as hospitals, prisons or police stations, and material recorded by closed-circuit television cameras.[28]

In dealing with public figures, the BSC makes the point that what interests the public is not the same as the public interest and that, "even when personal matters become the proper subject of enquiry, people in the public eye or their immediate family or friends do not forfeit the right to privacy . . ." Furthermore, reflecting the BBC's advice, mentioned above, "any information should be significant as well as true. The location of a person's home or family should not normally be revealed unless strictly relevant to the behaviour under investigation."[29] Particular attention should be given to individuals who have become incidentally associated with media reporting, simply because they happened to be near or in the background of a public event, or because their relatives or friends are involved. These cautions are implicit, but not articulated, in the PCC's much more brief statement of principle.

In relation to hidden microphones and cameras, the BSC states that "the use of secret recording should only be considered where it is necessary to the credibility and authenticity of the story . . .", so as to ensure fairness to the subject as well as the protection of his or her privacy. Normally, recording in a public place should not be secret except where it will "serve an overriding public interest" which justifies the decision to gather the material, the actual recording of that material and the broadcasting of it. Unattended microphones or cameras are not permitted on private property without the "full and informed consent" of the occupiers, unless seeking permission might frustrate the investigation of matters of an overriding public interest. Generally, the use of recording devices in respect of subjects on private property must be proportionate to the importance of the story and, when secretly recorded material is broadcast, care must be taken not to infringe the privacy of innocent bystanders. The code also makes clear that secret recording of material for entertainment purposes is, effectively, subject to a veto by the persons concerned;

---

[27] PCC Code, para. 3(i); BSC Code, para. 16; BBC code, chap. 4, para. 2; ITC code, para. 2.2.

[28] Para. 16.

[29] Para. 17.

their consent should be obtained and, if they request it to stop, the programme-makers should comply.[30] Again, these provisions are reflected in the advice of the BBC and the ITC,[31] who also require approval from senior management for surreptitious filming. The PCC's comparable requirement is succinct, but essentially sets out a similar principle: "The use of long-lens photography to take pictures of people in private places without their consent is unacceptable . . . private places are public or private property where there is a reasonable expectation of privacy."[32]

Doorstepping

There is also specific provision for doorstepping, whereby journalists attempt to obtain an interview or statement by waiting for and confronting an individual without prior appointment, at home or at a place of work. The BSC's code states that people who are currently in the news cannot reasonably object to being questioned and recorded by the media in public places. But even they "have the right to make no comment or to refuse to appear in a broadcast," although fairness may require in such a case that the fact of the individual's choice, and his or her explanation for it, are given in the programme. The code recognises that surprise can be a legitimate device to elicit truth, especially when there is an overriding public interest in investigation and disclosure. However, while doorstepping may be acceptable when there have been repeated refusals to grant an interview, the subsequent, repeated attempts to take pictures or obtain an interview may constitute an unwarranted infringement of privacy.[33] In the PCC's code, this issue is included in the clause on harassment: "Journalists and photographers must neither obtain nor seek to obtain information or pictures through intimidation, harassment or persistent pursuit."[34]

---

[30] Para 18.

[31] ITC, para. 2.4; BBC, chap. 4, para. 2.

[32] PCC, *ibid.*

[33] BSC, para. 25. See also ITC para. 2.9; BBC, chap. 4, para. 3.

[34] PCC, para 4(i). The phrase referring to persistent pursuit was included following the PCC's review of its code after the death of Diana, Princess of Wales and widespread public discussion of the problem of the *paparazzi*. See PCC Press Release of September 25, 1997, reporting a statement given at a press conference by its Chairman, Lord Wakeham.

There are detailed provisions which deal with people in suffering and distress. Broadcasters should not put pressure on such individuals to provide interviews and it is implied that they should not even be approached if that would add to their distress or infringe their privacy, unless an overriding public interest is served. Before revealing victims of accidents or crime, the next of kin should be informed, and prior consent should normally be obtained before filming in situations of stress, such as in hospitals or at funerals.[35] Here, the PCC version in relation to grief and distress is much weaker, referring only to the need for sympathy, discretion and sensitivity. In addition, in relation to hospitals, and unlike the broadcasters' guidance, it makes a distinction between public and non-public areas and only requires permission to enter the latter.[36] By contrast, the BBC's guidance takes a stricter approach to "media scrums" and the combined effect of attention by a large number of new organisations. It suggests that some form of pooling arrangement should be attempted but, if that fails, there will be times when the BBC should withdraw and "when we therefore miss material which other organisations gather and publish."[37]

Not least, the codes set out additional guidance for programming which involves children. Here, their vulnerability is a prime concern and their right to privacy is not to be forfeited because of their parents' fame or notoriety, or because of events in their school. Generally, care must be taken that their gullibility or trust is not abused and they should not be interviewed on matters of significance without consent unless the item is of overriding public interest and the child's appearance is absolutely necessary.

Revisiting Previous Material

Both the press and the broadcasting media resurrect previously used material from time to time, and this raises the problem of relative privacy. Generally, the press have proceeded on the basis that, once

---

[35] BSC Code, paras 28–30; BBC's code, chap. 4, para. 5; ITC code, para. 2.5.

[36] PCC, paras 5 and 9. Yet it was in the wake of Gordon Kaye's treatment by the *Sunday Sport* and his failure to secure legal redress (*Kaye v. Robertson* [1990] F.S.R. 62) that the Calcutt Committee was established.

[37] BBC code, chap. 4, para. 4. The ITC code states that reporters and media crews should leave media scrums unless there is a continuing public interest in their presence (para. 2.9).

information has been reported previously, it remains in the public domain and can be used without further justification. Although more sensitive to the distress that revisiting such material can cause, the broadcasters' practice was similar. In particular, it was not uncommon to use earlier footage to illustrate current material but, in the *Wade and Sandiford*[38] case, the BCC took the view that there were circumstances in which this could amount to an infringement of privacy and its approach was effectively endorsed by the Court of Appeal.

The issue arose from two programmes, broadcast by Granada Television, which incorporated material about deceased persons whose families had not been forewarned of the intention to use it. Mr. Wade complained that a programme, called "How Safe Are Our Children", which included a photograph of his daughter and footage from a previous film about her rape and murder, caused an unwarranted infringement of his privacy when he unexpectedly saw it in a crowded public house. Mr. and Mrs. Sandiford complained that a programme, called "The Allergy Business", similarly infringed their privacy by showing photographs and material relating to their anorexic daughter, diagnosed as having allergies, but who had died from pneumonia after severe dieting. The BCC upheld the complaints and Granada sought judicial review, claiming that the Commission had misdirected itself in applying an overly broad interpretation of privacy. Granada argued that the material was already in the public domain and that it did not refer to the complainants but to their daughters; for both reasons, there had been no infringement of the complainant's privacy. However the Court of Appeal rejected the application. Balcombe L.J., drawing on Prosser's work,[39] considered that, where matter had once been in the public domain, that would not prevent its resurrection some years later from giving rise to an infringement of privacy. Similarly, referring to Art. 8(1) of the European Convention on Human Rights, the French law of privacy, the Calcutt Committee's formulation and United States decisions, he held that it would be too narrow an interpretation to confine a complainant's privacy to the individual concerned without extending it to his or her family. In the absence of a

---

[38] *R. v. Broadcasting Complaints Commission ex p. Granada Television* [1995] 3 E.M.L.R. 163; [1995] C.O.D. 207, C.A. The judgment upheld the decision of Popplewell J., *The Times*, May 31, 1993.

[39] W. L. Prosser, "Privacy" (1960) 48 *California Law Review* 383.

definition of privacy in the 1990 Act, it had to be taken that Parliament had accepted that its elucidation was best left to a specialist body such as the BCC, whose members had experience of broadcasting. As a consequence, the BSC's code now contains restrictions on the repeated use of traumatic library material which identifies people who are still alive or have recently died, and goes further in requiring notice to be given to immediate relatives or surviving victims where programmes examine past events, even where the events have been in the public domain.

The BSC's rule requires only that relatives are notified where it is practicable to do so. Nevertheless, it is not entirely clear how far the programmers should defer to relatives' wishes that material should not be included at all. In the *Wade and Sandiford* case, both parties conceded, and the Court of Appeal did not disagree, that the absence of permission to show the programme would make any infringement unwarranted. If this is so, it goes too far in enabling relatives to hold an effective veto on programme content. Interestingly, the BBC does not concede as much in stating that material should be used against the objections of those concerned only if there is a clear public interest. More generally, it is a moot point whether publicity which is given to one person constitutes, in itself, an interference with his or her relatives' privacy.[40]

The Production Process

Reflecting judicial decisions about the BCC's jurisdiction, the BSC's code states that privacy can be infringed during the obtaining of material for a programme, even if none of it is broadcast, as well as in the way in which material is used within the programme.[41] As mentioned above, the 1996 Act does refer to the production process, in the phrase "in connection with the obtaining of material included in . . . programmes", and that repeats the terminology of the previous legislation which governed the BCC. In the *Lloyd* case,[42] however, the BBC challenged the BCC's interpretation of the words. It claimed that film obtained during a visit to Mr. Lloyd's home, but

[40] See Gibbons, above, n. 17.

[41] Broadcasting Standards Commission, *Code on Fairness and Privacy* (1998) para. 15.

[42] *R. v. Broadcasting Complaints Commission ex p. BBC* [1993] E.M.L.R. 419; [1993] C.O.D. 137.

which had been edited out, had not been obtained in connection with the gathering of the material which had been included in the programme which was subsequently broadcast. MacPherson J. rejected that argument and upheld the BCC's view, that the fact that the material shot at the Lloyd's house had not been shown did not mean there had been no obtaining of material which had been included in a programme. He said that, on a purposive construction of the statutory language, the BCC's function was to consider complaints about invasions of privacy during the preparation of programmes irrespective of whether the material itself was subsequently broadcast,[43] and it would be "verging on the absurd" if the editor's decision to include or exclude material were to determine the Commission's jurisdiction.

The decision in the *Lloyd* case was correct in terms of the purpose of the BCC as envisaged by Annan and the White Paper which preceded the early legislation,[44] although the statute itself was intended to reject such a remedy.[45] Yet it appeared to extend the BCC's jurisdiction to any preparatory research for a programme, including material gathered for a programme idea which becomes transformed into another. A more recent decision, however, made it clear that the BCC could not provide an avenue of redress for every invasion of privacy conducted under some programme-making pretext. In *ex p. Barclay*,[46] it was held that, there must be a broadcast for material to be connected to it and no remedy lies where an alleged invasion of privacy relates to material obtained for a programme yet to be broadcast. The decision has the effect of respecting producers' editorial discretion not to show infringing material, but it places great weight on the literal interpretation of the word "broadcast" rather than any principle for protecting privacy. Interestingly, neither the BBC's nor the ITC's codes make reference to the relationship between the production process and the broadcasting of programmes.

---

[43] Drawing on the recommendations of Annan.

[44] Home Office, *Broadcasting* (1978) Cmnd. 7294, paras 77–78.

[45] The Broadcasting Act 1981 used the phrase "in . . . programmes *actually* so broadcast", apparently because Parliament did not want to endorse Annan's recommendation.

[46] *R. v. Broadcasting Complaints Commission ex p. Barclay* [1997] E.M.L.R. 62, *The Times* October 11, 1996.

E. Impartiality and Pluralism

An important purpose of media content regulation has been the promotion of pluralism. The theoretical justifications for regulating the dissemination of information and opinion through the media are to ensure that it is presented accurately and without bias, and to protect the interests of the audience in obtaining all kinds of knowledge, whether scientific, social, moral or political. The underlying values are those which justify freedom in communication, that is, the prevention of dominance by any particular interests in the pursuit of knowledge and the facilitation of political participation in a democracy. The idea is to make sufficient evidence available to the audience for them to justify reasonable beliefs about the state of the world.[47] Although the media are unlikely to regard the pursuit of such values as their primary goal, there is a strong public interest in securing their protection because of the media's major contribution in supplying various types of information and in co-ordinating the way that knowledge is acquired.[48] The general aim is to limit any distorting influence of the media so that no conception of reality or an appropriate policy can be held out as authoritative simply because the media reproduce it. In promoting media pluralism however, the traditional approach to regulation has distinguished between the press and the programming sectors.

The Press

Apart from the law's general constraints on publishing material which is, for example, defamatory, obscene, in contempt of court or officially secret, there are no formal standards which require the press to maintain a commitment to accuracy and the avoiding of bias in disseminating information and opinion. On the contrary, the practice of the press rests on the assumption that everybody is in the same position as itself in enjoying the negative liberty to meet untrue or unacceptable claims by publishing a more persuasive rebuttal.

---

[47] See above, chap. 2; see also T. Gibbons, "Impartiality in the Media" (1986) *Archiv fur Rechts-und Sozialphilosophie* Beiheft Nr. 28, pp. 71–81.

[48] See D. McPhail, *Mass Communication Theory: An Introduction* (3rd ed., 1994), chap. 3.

Nevertheless, the press does formally subscribe to the pursuit of full and fair reporting, and to the presentation of correct and balanced accounts in the course of publishing news and matters of interest to its readership.[49] But the status of the press as a principal source of information, discussion and advocacy[50] often takes second place to strong commercial motives to improve circulation figures by satisfying readers' other interests. The former Press Council had amongst its objectives the somewhat ambivalent one of maintaining the character of the British press in accordance with the highest professional and commercial standards.[51] In practice, it had little effect and the Press Complaints Commission's aspirations are less ambitious, being confined to the handling of complaints about inaccuracy, intrusions into privacy and journalists' methods of obtaining stories. Any standards which do prevail can be attributed more to good journalistic practice.[52]

In acknowledging pluralistic aims, the press has reflected a free market approach in which it has been assumed that the absence of restrictions on the way in which material is gathered and published is most likely to avoid unacceptable domination by sectional interests and groups.[53] In so doing, it has rather under-emphasised the economic and social constraints which act on entering the market-place of ideas, a consideration which has been accepted as crucial in the broadcasting and other programming media. There, a broad conception of the scarcity rationale has required that, in the absence of actual opportunities for testing or challenging the veracity of media output, the medium itself should ensure that pluralism prevails.[54] For many years, the press has been under increasing pressure to adopt a similar approach but so far it has conceded little, if anything, to the proponents of regulation in this sphere. By contrast, all the programming media, not only broadcasting, operate within a relatively tightly controlled framework.

---

[49] Royal Commission on the Press, *Report* (1949) Cmd. 7700, paras 361 *et seq.*; Royal Commission on the Press, *Final Report* (1977) Cmnd. 6810, paras 2.3, 15.2.

[50] Reflecting the words of the Royal Commission in 1949, above, n. 49, para. 377.

[51] Press Council's Constitution, para. 48(ii), reproduced in G. Robertson, *People Against the Press* (1983), pp. 19, 36.

[52] See generally, McQuail, above, n. 48, pp. 121–132.

[53] See Royal Commission on the Press, *Final Report* (1977) Cmnd. 6810, para. 2.4.

[54] See (Sykes) Broadcasting Committee, *Final Report* (1923) Cmd. 1951, paras 6 and 7; (Annan) *Report of the Committee on the Future of Broadcasting* (1977) Cmnd. 6753, para. 2.4; and see the discussion in chap. 2, above.

Programming

In broadcasting, as discussed earlier, politicians' anxieties about the power of the medium led the BBC to accept the self-denying ordinance, subsequently applied to all programming media, that news and controversial material should be treated in an impartial manner and that the Corporation should not provide editorial comment. While Reith may have been able to square this with an idealistic view of broadcasting as the purveyor of knowledge, the real concern was about risking a concentration of editorial power in a single, powerful means of communication.[55] Although it imposes constraints on journalists' choices, the criterion of impartiality is intended to prevent the impression being fostered that there is one, or one correct, point of view about the nature of important facts or issues. As such, it may be rationalised as a constitutional standard for media practice, given abiding assent to the regulation of political aspects of broadcasting and given the external influence that government can exert. However, in political terms, its justification depends on the continued existence of a few dominant sources of broadcasting power and, should the media become fully diversified, the threat of an individual medium's political partiality would be considerably diminished. Yet in terms of democratic principles, the duty of impartiality may have a more enduring role in protecting pluralism because it positively requires a diversity of viewpoints to compliment any provision the market may make.

The BBC's obligations are now set out in its Agreement with the Secretary of State.[56] This Agreement formalises the previous informal arrangements whereby the Corporation recognised a duty to provide "a properly balanced service which displays a wide range of subject matter", and affirmed that controversial subjects had always been treated "with due impartiality" and that this practice would continue both in news services and in the general field of programmes about public policy.[57] The phrasing of the Agreement reflects the

---

[55] For example, Sykes, above, n. 54.

[56] BBC Agreement, clause 5.1(c).

[57] They were affirmed in a Resolution of the Board of Governors and contained in an Annex to the Licence and Agreement. The resolution renewed in substance certain assurances given to the Postmaster-General by Lord Normanbrook, Chairman of the Board in 1964. Lord Normanbrook's undertaking was, in fact, given in the face of pressure from Reginald Bevins, the then Postmaster-General, to place the BBC's obligations on a statutory footing. See C. Curran, *A Seamless Robe* (1979), p. 71.

obligations which were imposed on commercial licensees under the 1990 Act. All programmes must "treat controversial subjects with due accuracy and impartiality, both in . . . news services and in the more general field of programmes dealing with matters of public policy or of political or industrial controversy." For this purpose, a series of programmes may be treated as a whole. Although it may be regarded as implicit in this duty,[58] there is also a requirement that the BBC should not provide editorial comment, except in relation to broadcasting policy. As a positive obligation, the Agreement continues to require that the Corporation should transmit "an impartial account day by day prepared by professional reporters of the proceedings in both Houses of Parliament."[59] Generally, the BBC is required to draw up a code which deals with impartiality of treatment.[60]

When commercial broadcasting was first established, the approach adopted by the BBC had been incorporated into the legislation, and it continues to be an important part of the so-called "consumer protection" elements of the Broadcasting Act 1990. In relation to television programming, the ITC must do all that it can to ensure that its licensees comply with the requirement that all news given (in whatever form) in their programmes is presented with "due accuracy and impartiality." In addition, the ITC must ensure that "due impartiality is preserved on the part of the person providing the service as respects matters of political or industrial controversy or relating to current public policy" — again, a series of programmes may be considered as a whole. In relation to religious programmes, there is a slightly less onerous requirement that "due responsibility" be exercised; in particular, viewers' susceptibilities must not be exploited, nor must there be abusive treatment of particular beliefs.[61] There is also a restriction on editorialising which is phrased differently from that imposed on the BBC and is arguably a little more liberal in not extending to current affairs generally: the ITC must also secure the exclusion of the views of persons providing the service on matters (other than the provision of programme services) which relate to current political or industrial controversy, or to current public policy.[62] There is also a requirement to draw up a code

[58] See E. Barendt, *Broadcasting Law: A Comparative Study* (1993), pp. 100–101.
[59] BBC Agreement, clause 3.3.
[60] It forms chap. 2 of BBC, *Producers' Guidelines* (1996).
[61] Broadcasting Act 1990, s. 6(1)(b), (c) and (d).
[62] *ibid.*, s. 6(4).

to elaborate these matters.[63] One interesting point of comparison is that the BBC's constraints are not confined to "current" public policy; the implication is that the Corporation has a more onerous duty to satisfy when dealing with matters of historical interest.[64]

In relation to radio services, the potential for greater diversity in programmes and for more specialised access to the medium is reflected in the slightly more relaxed standards which the Radio Authority is required to enforce. Thus, although news must continue to be presented with due accuracy and impartiality in national licensed services, matters of religion, current political or industrial controversy, or current public policy in a local radio service need not be presented impartially, but only so that "undue prominence is not given in the programmes to the views of particular persons or bodies." The restriction on editorialising still applies, however.[65]

In devising these constraints on programming, the central concern has been to ensure that the programme-makers should distance themselves from the content of the programmes in order to prevent their powerful influence from becoming associated with any particular point of view. At the same time, pluralism requires that programming should be distributed so that no particular point of view gains a disproportionate advantage from use of a medium which is pervasive and relatively limited in the variety of channels that it can provide. Notwithstanding the growth in cable programming, however, similar considerations are currently applied to that medium also. Formerly, under the repealed Cable and Broadcasting Act 1984, the fact that cable offered greater opportunities for diversity, and therefore greater choice for the viewer, was used to justify a more relaxed approach. Broad application of the "no undue prominence" standard enabled channels to develop limited emphases on some points of view. Under the 1990 Act, however, it has been accepted that the diet of programming offered by cable is not, as yet, substantially different from broadcasting. The same principles which apply to the latter are also applied to cable, therefore, except that the ITC may substitute the "due responsibility" test in place of "due impartiality", if it considers that this is appropriate, where a licensable programme service will cater for a particular area or locality.[66]

---

[63] ITC, *The ITC Programme Code* (1998), s.3.

[64] This appears to be implicitly accepted in the *Producers' Guidelines*, chap. 2.

[65] Broadcasting Act 1990, s. 89.

[66] Broadcasting Act 1990, ss. 47(4) and (5). *cf.* Cable and Broadcasting Act 1984, s. 11(3)(a), and see (Hunt) Inquiry, *Cable Expansion and Broadcasting Policy* (1982) Cmnd. 8679, paras 9–13.

Interpreting Requirements of Accuracy and Impartiality in Programming

Although the requirements to be duly accurate and impartial are couched in mandatory terms, they allow considerable flexibility to the regulatory bodies to determine their meanings as everyday standards. The regulatory framework and practice essentially reflect an aspect of public service broadcasting that had been developed by the BBC and applied to the independent sector by the IBA. The approach has been continually discussed and broadly endorsed by a series of Broadcasting Committees and by Parliament. There has been relatively little judicial commentary, and it is the BBC's and the regulators' guidelines which articulate what accuracy and due impartiality entail.

1. Accuracy

The BBC has always stressed the importance of accuracy.[67] Its current guidelines require accuracy unconditionally, insisting that producers must be prepared to check constantly to preserve the BBC's reputation.[68] This continues to reflect Schlesinger's observation, in his study of BBC news production,[69] that caution appeared to be the watchword for the BBC's journalism, with reliability and accuracy being more important than the more usual imperative of speed; if a doubt existed and could not be checked, an item was to be excluded rather than have a wrong version of the facts presented. Although the IBA adopted the basic approach of the BBC, they did not give accuracy such emphasis, and that is also the case with the ITC and the R.A., who repeat the statutory requirement with little elaboration.[70]

While there is an assumption that accuracy can be achieved, the various guidelines do not attempt a definition of the term, although the IBA had suggested it to mean, in a circular way, the absence of mistakes. In practice, it is not some absolute conception of accuracy

---

[67] See BBC, *General Survey of the Broadcasting Service* (1949) in Memoranda submitted to the (Beveridge) *Report of the Broadcasting Committee 1949* (1951) Cmd. 8117, p. 12.

[68] BBC, *Producers' Guidelines* (1996), chap. 2, part 2.

[69] P. Schlesinger, *Putting "Reality" Together: BBC News* (2nd ed., 1987), pp. 90 and 135 *et seq.*; see also BBC, *Annual Report and Handbook 1986* (1985), p. 23.

[70] ITC, *The ITC Programme Code* (1998), section 3; R.A., *News and Current Affairs Code*, section 1.

which is applied, even if that could be envisaged at all, but one which depends on professional judgments about the information which can be relied upon as being correct or not. The emphasis is on producing a version of accuracy which is the product of honest and sincere aspirations towards finding and presenting facts, manifested in procedures which are accepted as establishing veracity for practical purposes.[71] These procedures include attributing news to authoritative sources, and an emphasis on facts and verifiability.[72] The BBC highlights the distinction between primary and secondary sources, the need to weigh facts to arrive at "the truth", the need to use accurate language and the need for care in reporting statistics. It also recommends that material obtained from one news agency should be substantiated by material from another agency. Another issue which the BBC discusses, and which is also mentioned in the ITC and the R.A. guidelines, is the problem of reconstructions of factual events; here the aim is to construct the programme and label its components so as not to mislead the viewer. All these attempts at guidance suggest that "due" accuracy is, in practice, taken to mean the absence of a deliberate creation of falsehood, but further questions about the capacity of observers to perceive and describe events as true are not considered. This more difficult question will be taken up later, in relation to impartiality.

2. *The Concept of Impartiality*

Impartiality is concerned with the placing of particular information or opinions in a wider context. In the press and publishing, the task of seeking that context is left to the reader. What distinguishes programming, and especially broadcasting, is that responsibility for situating material in context is imposed on the service provider. It represents a restraint on broadcasting editors' personal freedom to communicate, but underpins the institution's freedom to promote media pluralism.[73] The nature of the duty of impartiality has been articulated by broadcasters over a number of years and the current formulations, in the BBC's and the regulators' codes, represent a consolidation of their views. The BBC's thinking has, naturally, been very influential. Impartiality has been said to entail that a public body

---

[71] See P. Golding and P. Elliott, *Making the News* (1979), p. 208.
[72] See McQuail, above, n. 48, chap. 8.
[73] See Barendt, above, n. 58, chap. 2.

should not promote particular views sponsored by individual sections of the community and, for the BBC, this has meant that every view likely to infringe on public opinion should be reflected at some time in BBC programmes, with the responsibility for judging the validity of such opinions to be left to the public itself.[74] As the BBC's General Advisory Council once put it, the aim should be to provide the maximum amount of information for the public which is consistent with the fair representation of conflicting interests.[75] More recently, the BBC has described the essence of impartiality as seeking to ensure that a proper range of all significant activities and trends are featured and reported, and that all views are accorded due weight.[76]

The IBA's approach was very similar, the essence of impartiality being interpreted as an aspect of "fair dealing." More specifically, "the programme should not be slanted by the concealment of relevant facts, or by misleading emphasis; nor should investigation turn into a case for the prosecution or defence, or into a form of trial by television."[77] The latter expression was adopted by the R.A., who also describe impartiality as providing "an appropriate range of views . . ."[78] When the ITC drew up its code, it used different language to make the same point: "the obligations of fairness and a respect for the truth [are] two qualities which lie at the heart of impartial broadcasting."[79] This phrasing has, in turn, been embraced by the BBC in its current Producers' Guidelines: due impartiality is regarded as a "core value" which "requires programme makers to show open-mindedness, fairness and a respect for truth." Furthermore, the idea of impartiality appears to have become more assimilated with diversity, and it is stipulated that, across the whole range of programme genres, "No significant strand of thought should go unreflected or unrepresented on the BBC."[80]

It is clear that the theoretical foundation of impartiality rests on a conception of fairness. In the context of gaining knowledge, it means the absence of bias and the allowing of all opinions to be fully

---

[74] Cited in Annan, above, n. 54, para. 17.7.

[75] General Advisory Council to the BBC, *Tastes and Standards in BBC Programmes* (1973), p. 6. See also (Crawford) Broadcasting Committee, *Report* (1925) Cmd. 2599, p. 12.

[76] BBC, *Producers' Guidelines* (1989), para. 4.1.

[77] I.B.A., *Television Programme Guidelines* (1985) para. 6.3.

[78] Radio Authority, *News and Current Affairs Code*, paras 1.1 and 1.2.

[79] ITC, *The ITC Programme Code* (1998), section 3.1.

[80] BBC, *Producers' Guidelines* (1996), chap. 2, part 1.

presented. No opinion can be ruled out as unworthy of consideration; instead, its validity should be tested in reasoned discourse.[81] For opinions to be treated fairly, the presenter must be neutral towards them. However, where a range of views is offered by broadcasters in this manner, and is accepted as a fair reflection of all the information available, the broadcast assumes an authoritative status which lends a semblance of objectivity to its contents. In turn, broadcasters have recognised that, if they wish to be trusted and believed, they must not be seen to be "beholden" to anyone,[82] and that implies the protection of editorial independence from pressure to favour particular interests. The idea of fairness in impartiality, therefore, implies a value-free service which can be relied upon to provide objective accounts of life and society.

Yet, as Golding and Elliott have noted,[83] objectivity and impartiality are not the same: while the former connotes "a complete and unrefracted capture of the world", the latter suggests a narrower achievement in "a disinterested approach to news [or indeed other information] lacking in motivation to shape or select material according to a particular view or opinion." In seeking to maintain credibility and authority, broadcasters tend to adopt the more passive role in avoiding bias by maintaining an attitude of neutrality towards the most basic assumptions held within our culture.[84] The commitment to fairness in achieving knowledge through impartiality, therefore, is one qualified by the values that the broadcaster introduces, both wittingly in the case of democratic aims, reflected in the meaning ascribed to "due" impartiality, and perhaps unwittingly[85] in the case of other biases. For that reason, the amount of independence that broadcasters enjoy may be regarded as relatively superficial, although the irony is that it is sufficient to lend an air of authority to the reality that broadcasters portray.

In attempting to achieve impartiality, different considerations apply in respect of programmes on particular occasions and the general effect of programmes over a period of time. In the short term, the emphasis need only be upon balancing different views to produce a

---

[81] This is not necessarily the same as a market-place of ideas leading to truth. See chap. 2, above.
[82] Sir Michael Swann, *The Autonomy of Broadcasters* (1974) p. 5.
[83] P. Golding & P. Elliott, *Making the News* (1979) p. 207.
[84] P. Elliott, "Production in the Political Context of Broadcasting" in *Politics and the Media* (M. J. Clark ed., 1979).
[85] *ibid.*

fair account of the relevant arguments and their relationship with each other, either within a single programme or a suitably co-ordinated series.[86] To a large extent, the BBC's and the regulators' guidelines are concerned with the details of such arrangements. In the longer term, greater problems of general bias arise.

In order for views to be balanced, they must be selected for inclusion in the media's output, but the criteria for selection have tended to be elusive, or where identified, controversial. The more extended interpretations of impartiality, which will be described below, do give some assistance in this process of selection. To publicise as wide a range of views as possible prevents particular perspectives from dominating and gives many opinions an opportunity to reach the audience. Nevertheless, with limited access to the medium, choices have to be made about what is to constitute the boundaries of a range of views and about which views are to be included as a fair, representative account of the range. It is here that choices are likely to be influenced by the background expectations that broadcasters share.

In the collection of news, information is considered to be essentially factual and is selected by reference to what journalists consider to be topical, easily communicated and of immediate interest.[87] In the latter case, traditional news values are pursued in concentrating on personal conflict and other events which consist of dramatic intrusions on routine living.[88] Here, broadcasting does not create its own priorities; rather, it follows the press.[89] In doing so, it refrains from imposing its own version of reality on the facts, which are taken as given. In dealing with current affairs, which involves a broader discussion of opinion and public issues, judgments have to be made about the significance of events depicted in the news and of the public response, and some sense is required of what is relevant to society's needs and aspirations, and what is an appropriate agenda for public debate. Again, broadcasting does not have its own version of what that involves, other than identifying the prevailing public opinion amongst its mass audience. In doing so, it can do little more than reflect a consensual view of the social order, even if it does not

---

86 Annan, above, n. 54, para. 17.9.

87 See R. V. Ericson *et al., Visualizing Deviance: A Study of News Organization* (1987) chap. 1; McQuail, above, n. 48; R. Negrine, *Politics and the Media in Britain* (2nd ed. 1994), chap. 4.

88 See Golding and Elliott, above, n. 83, pp. 209–210.

89 See Schlesinger, above, n. 69, pp. 163 *et seq.*

actively support the dominant values in society,[90] although it may expose it to extended, specialist treatment.[91]

In relation to both news and current affairs, then, the work of the journalist as "gatekeeper"[92] in selecting and presenting information, complicates the assumption that impartiality can be achieved. In both areas, broadcasting relies on the effective denial of a selection problem as a guarantee of fair dealing; indeed, in evidence to the Annan Committee, both BBC and ITV journalists were "bewildered" by analyses of their activities as "agenda-setting", seeing the news as being "selected fairly but without artificial balancing and without political motive or editorial colouring by trained journalists", or "a plain unvarnished account of happenings, as free as humanly possible of bias . . ."[93] While the Annan Committee took a more realistic view of gatekeeping — "News cannot be some sort of objectively established entity"[94] — it did not regard its existence as inconsistent with impartiality; any difficulties could be resolved by diversifying the choice of programmes and improving the training of journalists. Whether such an approach would in itself go far enough in eliminating a natural tendency to incorporate contemporary ideology may be doubted, however.[95] While a working consensus about the present state of knowledge is probably indispensable,[96] a more active role on the part of broadcasters in seeking out and disseminating alternative views may be needed to forestall the impression that the media account is authoritative.[97] Such a role would, however, create considerable tension in the special relationship which currently exists between the State and the broadcasting media. In particular, it would require a withdrawal of the medium's commitment, to be discussed later, to advance democratic values.

---

[90] See Golding and Elliott, above, n. 83, p. 209; Glasgow Media Group, *Bad News* (1976).

[91] See R. Wallis & S. Baran, *The Known World of Broadcast News: International News and the Electronic Media* (1990), chap. 3, discussing the impact of the "Birt-Jay" approach to specialist news treatment in the BBC.

[92] See Annan, above, n. 54, para. 17.26.

[93] Annan, above, n. 54, para. 17.28. In this context, see the criticisms of the Glasgow Media Group's work in M. Harrison *T.V. News: Whose Bias?* (1985).

[94] Annan, above, n. 54, para. 17.29.

[95] See M. Schudson, "The Sociology of News Production Revisited" In J. Curran & M. Gurevitch (eds.), *Mass Media and Society* (2nd ed. 1996).

[96] See J. Lichtenberg, "In Defence of Objectivity Revisited" In J. Curran & M. Gurevitch (eds.), *Mass Media and Society* (2nd ed. 1996).

[97] See P. Hughes, *British Broadcasting: Programmes and Power* (1981). See also J. Curran and J. Seaton, *Power Without Responsibility* (5th ed. 1997), pp. 310–312.

IMPARTIALITY IN PRACTICE

In implementing the duty of impartiality, the broadcasters have long recognised,[98] as did Annan,[99] that impartiality is not synonymous with mathematical balance. The Broadcasting Act 1981 had acknowledged that there could be a broad approach to impartiality, by allowing the criterion to be applied over a series of programmes. Furthermore, it is worth noting that the BBC's and the regulators' current obligations relate to impartiality in the provision of the whole service, not separate programmes. In the past, the IBA used to permit impartiality to be assessed over a relatively long period, provided the context was made clear, and the BBC similarly recognised that it was not necessary or desirable to cover all issues in one programme if justice was to be done to the range of issues that needed to be explored. Much scope was thus allowed to editorial judgment in determining whether issues needed to be considered in a single programme or could be explored over a length of time. Relevant considerations would include the degree to which issues were currently controversial, the likelihood that they would be revisited and the extent to which the audience would realise that an extended treatment had been planned. The present guidelines adopt this earlier advice, stressing the importance of planning and of highlighting the nature of a series for the audience.

Unfortunately, at a late stage in the passage of the 1990 Bill, a number of objections were voiced in the House of Lords. It was said that that the television broadcasters had been abusing their position in showing programmes that dealt with issues in an unacceptably partial way. Although the objections had little substance, especially in the context of the broadcasters' existing approach to impartiality over time, the Government faced strong pressure to require each individual programme to be impartial. It therefore produced a compromise in the shape of section 6(5) and (6) of the 1990 Act.[1] These supplement section 6(2), which states that, in applying the provisions relating to due impartiality, "a series of programmes may be considered as a whole." Under section 6(5), however, when drawing up its Code, the ITC is required to ensure that licensees

[98] BBC, *Producers' Guidelines* (1996), section 2, part 1; ITC, *The ITC Programme Code* (1998), section 3.1; Radio Authority, *News and Current Affairs Code*, para. 1.3.
[99] Above, n. 54, para.17.9.
[1] There is no comparable duty placed on the Radio Authority in s. 90 of the Act.

preserve impartiality in the treatment of "major matters falling within subsection (1)(c) [which deals with matters of political or industrial controversy or relating to current public policy] as well as matters falling within that provision taken as a whole." It is not easy to make sense of these duties, not only because "major matters" is so inherently vague, but also because it is unclear what is involved in taking the other matters in the subsection "as a whole." In fact, it appears that section 6(5) does not actually exclude what it was thought to, that is, the treatment of major matters over a series of programmes. The ITC has attempted to make sense of these provisions by noting the importance of context in interpreting "major matters" and stressing the period in which the relevant issue is active: "if the matter became a live issue of debate between the political parties in Parliament, or the subject of imminent government action, due impartiality would be required within a more limited timescale."[2] The BBC mentions issues of national or regional "significance".[3] In the absence of clarity in the legislation, they have reiterated what has been the previous practice of the broadcasters.

Similarly, the ITC's response to section 6(6) of the 1990 Act, which requires its code to deal with the question of timescale in some detail, has been to articulate what had always been the IBA's approach. The Commission has accordingly set out requirements for the audience to be given sufficient information to demonstrate the link between individually partial treatments of the same issue, and to provide sufficient opportunities for a reasonable balance of views to be obtained within the series. Under its new Agreement, the BBC has been subjected to virtually identical provisions[4] and the effect has been similar. While the Corporation had been slow to articulate the practicalities of ensuring due impartiality,[5] the defect was remedied in the first edition of its Producers' Guidelines and its current guidance hardly differs from that of the ITC.[6]

Related to the question of impartiality and in-depth treatment of issues in single programmes is the matter of so-called "personal view" programmes. The current approach endorses the traditional practice of allowing individuals to express their arguments in a single programme, to bring unorthodox views to the audience, convey a

---

[2] ITC, above, n. 98, section 3.

[3] BBC, *Producers' Guidelines* (1996) chap. 2, s. 2.6.

[4] BBC's Agreement, cl. 5, paras 4 and 5.

[5] The *News and Current Affairs Index* (3rd ed., 1987) did not deal with the issue.

[6] BBC, *Producers' Guidelines* (1996), chap. 2, part 1, paras 2.3 and 2.6.

sense of conviction about strong beliefs or share personal experience. The broadcast of such programmes, however, has been conditional on the imposition of special requirements to ensure an overall sense of impartiality. Thus, it must be made clear that only one view amongst many is being expressed and, if the programme is one of a series, the series should provide a range of views across a wide social and political spectrum within a reasonable period of time. In addition, such programmes have to be accurate and fair, that is, not misrepresent opposing viewpoints, and there has to be an opportunity for a response, for example, in a right to reply programme or a pre-arranged discussion programme.

Other provisions of the BBC's and the regulators' guidelines deal with such issues as impartiality in drama and drama-documentary, and the conduct of interviews, especially with politicians. All the relevant provisions of the guidelines show what the Annan Committee emphasised[7]: that being impartial often embraces rather complex considerations. Certainly, the concept is not synonymous with either balance or neutrality.[8] Not only is it important that the widest possible range of views and opinions be expressed but, when countered, they should be allowed to be discussed in different terms from those in which they were originally posed. In addition, the weight of opinion which holds each view has to be taken into account, although broadcasters must recognise that both the range of views and their weight are constantly changing. Given this flux, however, and as Annan recognised, the requirement of impartiality can be a spur to innovation rather than a passive restraint on dealing with controversial subjects at all.[9]

Nevertheless, there is one feature of the impartiality requirement which confirms that its principal rationale is to advance, not freedom in communication, but the control of the programming media by politicians. While the notion of impartiality demands an even-handed approach in general, the qualification, "due", enables it to be weighted in appropriate circumstances. It has been consistently interpreted to authorise the favouring of certain beliefs and values which are held to be fundamental. Thus the BBC was able to say that it regarded impartiality as involving, "not absolute neutrality or

---

[7] Above, n. 54, para. 17.10.

[8] This has long been the BBC's view. See BBC, *Fairness and Impartiality in Broadcasting* (1987), especially at pp. 8–9.

[9] *cf.* Barendt, above, n. 58, who thinks the options are more stark.

detachment from those basic moral or constitutional beliefs upon which the nation's life rests. For example, the BBC does not feel obliged to be neutral as between truth and untruth, justice and injustice, freedom and slavery, compassion and cruelty, tolerance and intolerance."[10] This view had been elaborated in evidence to the Annan Committee: being a "constitutional creation" of Parliament and part of the nation, the BBC could not be impartial towards the maintenance or dissolution of the nation, nor towards behaviour which Parliament had decided was unacceptable and made it illegal.[11]

The IBA interpreted "due" impartiality slightly differently, perceiving themselves to be, not the guardians of a certain attitude towards life and politics, but a reflector of the social mood. Hence, it considered itself as "not required to secure impartiality on matters such as drug-trafficking, cruelty and racial intolerance, for example, on which society, even today, is virtually unanimous."[12] Yet "it seems clear that the old consensus view of what should be broadcast is weaker than it was", and it hinted[13] that it regarded the interests of their viewers and of freedom of information as its touchstones. Although it may be a matter of emphasis, this more flexible approach seems to be more characteristic of independent broadcasting. Hargreaves had argued, for example, that impartiality should not preclude the questioning of basic standards, nor deny a hearing to dissidents in the interests of upholding democracy and the rule of law; impartiality is directed towards the search for truth facilitated by journalistic scrutiny.[14] Similarly, the ITN view advanced before Annan, albeit more cautious, was that ITN would reflect all differences within Parliament, although "[we] would not go outside as it were and bring in ideas that we like better."[15] This reflects the ITC's present description of due impartiality as "the fair treatment of contentious issues in the arena of democratic debate."[16]

Annan's view was much closer to the BBC's. It noted that broadcasters are working within a system of parliamentary democracy and must share its assumptions:

---

[10] BBC, *Annual Report and Handbook 1986* (1985), p. 196.

[11] Annan, above, n. 54, para. 17.7.

[12] IBA, above, n. 77, para. 6.1; ITC, (Annan) *Report of the Committee on the Future of Broadcasting* (1977) Cmnd. 6753, para. 3.2.

[13] IBA, *Television Programme Guidelines* (1985); *Annual Report and Accounts 1982–83* (1983) p. 24.

[14] P. Hargreaves, "Television and Current Affairs" in *Politics and the Media* (M. J. Clark ed., 1979). Hargreaves was a writer for independent television at the time.

[15] Annan, above, n. 54, para. 17.7.

[16] ITC, *The ITC Programme Code* (1998).

> "They should not be expected to give equal weight or show an impartiality which cannot be due to those who seek to destroy it by violent, unparliamentary or illegal means . . . While it is right that the accepted orthodoxies should be challenged, equally it is essential that the established view should be fully and clearly put and that the status and implications of the challenge should be made clear."[17]

These sentiments are now incorporated into section 6(6) of the 1990 Act and clause 5.3 of the BBC's Agreement which both state that "due impartiality does not require absolute neutrality on every issue or detachment from fundamental democratic principles."

One of the most significant aspects of the impartiality requirement, therefore, is its relationship with parliamentary democracy. The obligation of "due" impartiality is an important symbol that programmers, and especially broadcasters, are regarded as being part of the constitutional structure. This development, amounting to a partial sequestration of programmers by the State, has been consolidated independently of any obligation to provide public service broadcasting. It has the effect of denying the facility to present any deeply critical accounts of the political system which supports that structure.[18] Instead, the values and beliefs of the system form a base-line which implies certain attitudes towards issues such as the rule of law, the use of direct action industrial disputes[19] or the complex problems of Northern Ireland;[20] radical analysis of society and political objectives tends to be avoided. None of this is surprising in itself, for it reflects a resolution of the traditional dilemma which besets liberal democracy of deciding how far the undemocratic can be tolerated. Broadcasting performs the function of consolidating a constitutional consensus by using its authority to treat some themes as sacred, even if it appears to be rather cautious in its reliance on parliamentary debate as its touchstone. What this means, however, is that both the free speech principle, and regulation of the media based on freedom in communication are severely compromised; broadcasting journalists have substantive constraints on the content of their programming, and regulating for openness and diversity of

---

[17] Annan, above, n. 12, paras 17.9, 17.10.

[18] See P. Hughes, *British Broadcasting: Programmes and Power* (1981).

[19] Glasgow Media Group, above, n. 90.

[20] Golding and Elliott, above, n. 83, pp. 62–63, 217; Annan, above, n. 54, paras 17.11 *et seq.*; Munro, *Television, Censorship and the Law* (1979) pp. 146 *et seq.*; Schlesinger, above, n. 69, chap. 8; B. Rolson, (ed.) *The Media and Northern Ireland* (1991).

viewpoint cannot be achieved when the State's interest dominates the context of debate. Broadcasting, therefore, is neither as independent nor as fair as might be inferred from the standard of impartiality.

A second aspect of democratic influence on broadcasters may also be noted. There is a belief that, while due impartiality is satisfied where as broad a range of opinion as possible is allowed expression, some account must be taken of the weight of that opinion. The problem is that, if impartiality is concerned with issues and not people, how far need the broadcasters heed popular endorsement of points of view? If the aim is to act as an extension of the democratic forum, opinion should be reflected in a representative manner. But where the aim is to identify qualitatively significant perspectives, their status cannot depend on public opinion except where that is relevant to the credibility of beliefs which are held to be true. The issue is of practical importance to those who hold extremist or maverick views and who wish to have them reflected in mainstream programming. In suggesting that new ideas must always be presented in the context of established beliefs,[21] the Annan Committee's approach on this issue was not clear, perhaps reflecting the ambivalence in the broadcaster's role. A sense of continuity is important, not only in developing knowledge, but also in maintaining stability in society. While the rationale for the regulation of information and opinion is directed towards the ideal acquisition of knowledge, its practical function is to provide a service that appeals to the common fund of experience held by a general audience. In doing so, the status quo is consolidated or, at least, made more difficult to challenge. In this way too, then, broadcasting can be seen to be performing a significant role at a constitutional level.

Impartiality and Politicians

In addition to the general requirement of due impartiality, the treatment of party political discussion has been subject to more elaborate regulation which has evolved from consultations between the broadcasting authorities and the main political parties as members of the unofficial Committee on Party Political Broadcasting. The existence of the Committee may be interpreted as an attempt by the

---

[21] Annan, above, n. 54, paras 17.10 and 17.15.

politicians to maintain control over political broadcasting, but its role has diminished in recent years. At one time, it was all but conceded by the broadcasters that they would propose a distribution of broadcasting time to the various parties but that the Committee would actually allocate it unless, as happened in 1983, it could not reach agreement.[22] However, the Committee has not met since 1983, its work having been administered through the Government Chief Whip. Furthermore, the BBC and the ITC have concluded that it would not be lawful for them to delegate their responsibilities to the Committee and their published practice now makes it clear that it is they who determine the allocation of political broadcasts.[23] Obviously there is a delicate balance to be struck here: the programmers should be able to make independent judgments about the political parties' demands, but they should not be expected to set the ground rules for canvassing. In the event, the BBC and the ITC adopted broadly similar guidelines and these were accepted by the Committee. In a further move to distance themselves from the politicians, however, the BBC, ITC, R.A. and S4C have issued a consultation paper[24] in which they proposed that party political broadcasting should be considerably reformed. Before considering those proposals, the existing arrangements will be reviewed.

The BBC allocates time for political broadcasting as part of its general remit to provide public service broadcasting. In the commercial sector, a similar obligation is imposed on Channels 3, 4 and 5, and on independent national radio, as a licence condition. The power to include such a condition is provided by sections 36 and 107 of the Broadcasting Act 1990, which allow the ITC and the R.A., respectively, to determine the precise arrangements.

Outside election periods, there are annual series of party political broadcasts which are allocated by a formula which allows one broadcast for every 2,000,000 votes polled by each U.K. party at the previous general election. In Scotland, the Scottish National Party is entitled to one broadcast for every 200,000 votes and, in Wales, Plaid

---

[22] See, for example, BBC, *Producers' Guidelines* (1987) section 6, para. 3; *cf.* ITC, *The ITC Programme Code*, section 4.

[23] See BBC, *Producers' Guidelines* (1996); ITC, *Draft Amendments to the ITC Programme Code* (1997). See also *R. v. BBC and ITC ex p. Referendum Party*, *The Times*, April 29, 1997 (and Lexis transcript). The Radio Authority's *News and Current Affairs Code* (1994), para. 3.3 did not concede any power to the Committee.

[24] BBC, ITC, R.A. and S4C, *Consultation Paper on the Reform of Party Political Broadcasting* (1998).

Cymru is entitled to one broadcast for every 100,000 votes. The maximum number of broadcasts in the annual series is five. During an election, any party which fields 50 or more candidates is entitled to one party election broadcast on television of five minutes' duration. Otherwise, the parties' allocation is agreed by reference to their electoral support at the previous general election, their performance in elections since then, an assessment of their current electoral support and the number of candidates fielded by them. In respect of the major parties during the 1997 general election, for example, the allocation was five television slots of ten minutes for the Conservative Party and the Labour Party, and four for the Liberal Democrats. The BBC and the R.A. arranged a similar proportion of slots on radio. For Scotland and Wales, there are additional arrangements to reflect the different political complexions of those countries. Supplementary requirements are stipulated, for programmes which occur pending a parliamentary or local government election, by section 93 of the Representation of the People Act 1983. In those cases, broadcasts about a constituency or electoral area may not include a candidate at the election unless the other candidates consent. The guidelines warn of the special care needed to ensure that discussion of general issues does not stray into constituency matters, noting that, in any event, appearances in programmes not about the election would be likely to enhance the candidate's standing and thereby breach the requirement of impartiality.[25] Editorial control of party political and party election broadcasts rests with the relevant parties, but they must satisfy the general requirements of the BBC's Agreement and the Broadcasting Act 1990. That includes the duty not to include material which offends against good taste and decency and, in this context as generally, the broadcasters have a degree of discretion in deciding what that means. Thus, the BBC were entitled to require the removal of a sequence of shots of aborted foetuses from a party election broadcast to be shown by the Pro-Life Alliance Party.[26]

The remaining special arrangements which exist in the context of political speech concern the "Aide-Memoire", which resulted from an agreement between the main political parties and the BBC made in 1947 and revised in 1969, and which provided for the broadcast of

---

[25] See BBC, *Producers' Guidelines* (1996), section 19; ITC, *The ITC Programme Code*, appendix 2.

[26] *R. v. BBC ex p. Pro-Alliance Party* (1997) March 24; Lexis.

ministerial statements. In it, the BBC recognised the executive responsibilities of government and its right to explain events or seek public co-operation through the medium of broadcasting.[27] One category of such broadcasts related to non-contentious explanations of legislation or administrative policies. The other related to matters of "prime national or international importance" and provided for a right of reply to be accorded to the Opposition with a general discussion to follow those announcements. The IBA were not a party to the arrangement, but agreed to transmit the BBC's broadcasts in the second category.[28] The ITC makes no provision for such ministerial broadcasts. In practice, apart from Budget broadcasts and Opposition replies to them (first introduced in 1928), they have fallen into disuse as the political parties have become more sophisticated in public relations and news management. The staging of "media events", together with a steady flow of press releases and press conferences, are more than adequate substitutes for direct ministerial broadcasting. When the BBC's new Agreement was settled in 1996, there was no reference to the Aide-Memoire.

In recognition of the sensitive relationship between broadcasters and politicians, the programme codes contain detailed guidance for ensuring impartial treatment. There is discussion, for example, about the problems of using present and former politicians as interviewers or presenters or in non-political roles; there is a need to avoid politicians' gaining unfair advantages by either participation or mere appearances in programmes. There is also guidance about the conduct of interviews with politicians and the need to prevent them, or their spin-doctors, from controlling the agenda. The ITC's code actually invites licensees to consider whether negotiations about the parameters of interviews should be made known to viewers, but there is little evidence of any such transparency. Indeed, because the programmer has to ensure impartiality notwithstanding conditional appearances, late withdrawals from programmes or simple refusals to appear, viewers will generally not be aware of the pressures which politicians' demands may place on editorial integrity.

---

[27] BBC, *Producers Guidelines* (1989), chap. 6; *cf. Producers' Guidelines* (1996), chap. 18 para. 2.4. See (Beveridge) *Report of the Broadcasting Committee 1949* (1951), Cmd. 8117, appendix H; the Consultation Paper, appendix 1.

[28] The IBA did not transmit the BBC's discussion but made their own arrangements instead. With the exception of a statement about the Prevention of Terrorism Act in 1974, the IBA did not transmit broadcasts in the non-contentious category and would not do so as a matter of course.

The changing nature of politicians' relationship with the media was the prompt for the suggestions for reform made in the broadcasters' consultation paper. This points to the expansion in news and current affairs coverage of politics and the nature of party political broadcasts as being more like advertisements than public service announcements. In those circumstances, it recommends that the annual series should cease and be replaced by more broadcasts at election times. The proposed new pattern would result in a reduction of broadcasts for the main political parties, from five to four slots of five minutes, but there would be an increase for the Welsh and Scottish parties to reflect what is now considered to be a four party system. For parties not currently represented in Parliament, a new threshold is proposed to reflect potential electoral support better and to prevent the use of political broadcasts as free advertising, the proposal is that there should be entitlement to a broadcast if at least one sixth of parliamentary seats is being contested by the party.

The creation of special guidelines for ensuring impartiality in respect of political broadcasting reflected the programmers' continued concern about politicians' disapproval of their activities. Since more detailed guidelines bring a degree of specificity to editorial judgments, they also helped to forestall complaints that access to the media is being allocated unfairly. However, the politicians retain a keen appreciation of the fairness of their treatment and some have been increasingly willing to challenge the programmers' decisions in the courts. This has forced the broadcasters to rely more on their constitutional and statutory mandates rather than accommodations with politicians. Nevertheless, the courts have refused to impose a numerical balancing exercise on them, acknowledging what is apparent from the earlier discussion, that complex judgments are involved in determining what is impartial treatment. This acknowledgement of their legal responsibilities to take independent decisions has led programmers to gain a new confidence in their ability to deal with rather subtle judgments about political impartiality in programmes generally, as the issuing of the consultation paper demonstrates.

Although legal challenges are not uncommon before constitutional courts in other jurisdictions,[29] until recently, it has been relatively unusual in Great Britain and Northern Ireland for aggrieved politicians to seek redress from the courts. One source of grievance

---

[29] See Barendt, above n. 58, pp. 174–87.

concerns the general treatment afforded political parties in allowing them direct access to the media. An early example was the *Lynch* case,[30] where a political party objected to being excluded from participation in election programming (a general discussion and a phone-in). The BBC had refused it access because it had neither fielded candidates in at least five constituencies nor secured a sufficiently high percentage of the vote in a previous election. Hutton J. held that, even if the BBC's duty of impartiality was legally enforceable — which he doubted, since it was not contained in the then Licence and Agreement — the Corporation's rules were reasonable measures to secure impartiality which did not require equal access for all parties. Similarly, in *Wilson v. IBA (No. 2)*,[31] the IBA's allocation to the Scottish National Party (SNP) was challenged on the grounds that the party had been given proportionately fewer slots compared with the major British parties (two instead of five). The court held that, since two of the major parties' allocation would be broadcast exclusively in Scotland, the SNP had been given the same number in respect of Scottish issues, whilst reflecting the context of Scottish politics in the United Kingdom more broadly. However, in a case dealing with the Scottish referendum on devolution in 1979, the distribution of access to broadcasting was held to be in breach of the duty to show impartiality because it adhered too rigorously to party political affiliation. Where a question such as devolution was to be answered either positively or negatively, impartiality required equal treatment to be given to advocates of each side of the issue. The IBA's allocation of equal time to the four main political parties, three of which supported devolution and one of which opposed it, was consequently held to be unlawful and an interdict was issued to prohibit the series of programmes from being shown.[32]

Nevertheless, in the *Referendum Party* case,[33] and drawing on the Scottish precedents, the English Divisional Court has confirmed that the BBC and the ITC have a broad margin of discretion in determining what is impartial treatment. The Referendum Party had complained that it was unfair that, prior to the General Election of 1997, it had been allocated only one party election broadcast by each

---

[30] *Lynch v. BBC* [1983] N.I. 193.

[31] 1988 S.L.T. 276.

[32] *Wilson v. IBA* 1979 S.C. 351.

[33] *R. v. BBC ex p. Referendum Party*, *The Times*, April 29, 1997, and Lexis.

of the broadcasters, compared with five each for the Conservatives and Labour and four for the Liberal Democrats. The BBC and ITC had based their allocation on an assessment of each party's standing and support in the country, but the Referendum Party considered that they had given excessive weight to past electoral support (which a new party could not demonstrate) and that they had given insufficient weight to the number of candidates which they were fielding (about 85 per cent of constituencies). However, Auld L.J. noted that:

> "Impartiality in this context is not to be equated with parity or balance as between political parties of different strengths, popular support and appeal . . . It means fairness of allocation having regard to those factors, yet making allowance for any significant current changes in the political arena and for the potential effect of the medium of television itself in advancing or hindering such changes."

The court considered that the BBC and ITC had not given exclusive weight to electoral support, but had used it as only one of a number of indications of support, such as opinion polls and the significance of the number of candidates fielded. Such a subjective and contentious exercise had been left to the broadcasters by Parliament and they had not acted irrationally in exercising their judgment.

Another set of cases has dealt with the related but wider issue of broadcasters' treatment of political parties generally. One decision addressed the BBC's coverage of party political conferences and, in particular, the reduced time devoted to minority parties. The SNP complained that to allow five hours to them in programmes broadcast to Scotland, compared with eighteen to Labour, seventeen to the Conservatives and thirteen to the Liberal Democrats, was unfair. However, the BBC argued that its duty was to provide impartial coverage across the whole of the United Kingdom and that its view of the SNP's significance, based on electoral support and opinion polls, was reasonable. The court agreed and refused an order to restrain the extended broadcasting of the other parties' conferences in Scotland.[34] The context of Scottish politics also featured in the SNP's challenge to the Scottish Channel 3 companies' indications that they would exclude the party's leader from a series of televised

---

[34] *Scottish National Party v. BBC* (1996). The case is reported and discussed in C. Munro, *Scottish National Party v. BBC — Round Two* (1996) 146 *New Law Journal* 1433–1434.

"head-to-head" debates prior to the General Election of 1997. It applied for an interdict to prevent such programmes from being shown in Scotland before the election. The application was refused, however, on the technical grounds that, in objecting to as yet hypothetical programmes, it was premature. But the court confirmed that the obligations of impartiality under section 6 of the Broadcasting Act 1990 were directed at the provision of programming as a whole, both in terms of geographical coverage and time-scale. It would only intervene if the discretion in applying the rules was *Wednesbury* unreasonable.[35]

This structural dimension to impartiality is underlined by a decision of the Divisional Court about the relationship between impartiality and fairness to individuals. A complaint was made to the Broadcasting Complaints Commission (BCC), by Dr David Owen, that the Alliance between his Social Democratic Party and the Liberal Party was not being given sufficient exposure and publicity in news and current affairs programmes, despite having received a similar proportion of votes (if not Parliamentary seats) as the Labour Party in the preceding General Election. The BCC rejected the complaint on jurisdictional grounds, one of which was its opinion that it had been set up to consider personal types of complaint rather than broad issues of broadcasting policy. The court agreed,[36] although it was not prepared to hold that the relevant statute actually precluded such a broad interpretation. However, the BCC had a general discretion to decline jurisdiction "if it appears to them for any other reason inappropriate for them to entertain, or proceed with the consideration of, the complaint"[37] and the court held that it had acted reasonably, in the *Wednesbury* sense,[38] in concluding that it was being asked to formulate a criterion for determining whether a political party was a major political force in the country, and that it was inappropriate for it to do so. The court noted that the essence of Dr Owen's complaint was political and that the broadcasters' editorial policy would have to be assessed by reference to the fundamental and controversial issue of electoral reform. This problem of securing

---

[35] *Scottish National Party v. Scottish Television and Grampian Television* (1997). The case is reported and discussed in C. Munro, "Party Politics and the Broadcasters — Round Three" (1997) 147 *New Law Journal* 528, 533.

[36] *R. v. Broadcasting Complaints Commission ex p. Owen* [1985] 2 All E.R. 522.

[37] Broadcasting Act 1981, s. 55(4)(d), now replaced in the same terms by the Broadcasting Act 1990, s. 144(4).

[38] *Associated Provincial Picture Houses Ltd v. Wednesbury Corporation* [1948] 1 K.B. 223.

impartiality was not within the remit of a tribunal intended to deal with complaints about the fairness of individuals' treatment by the media.[39]

All these cases demonstrate a judicial reluctance to intervene in the details of decisions about impartiality. The exception is the Scottish courts' willingness to prevent the screening, in Scotland, of an interview with the Prime Minister in a BBC *Panorama* programme, three days before Scottish local elections. A local election candidate had objected that the interview would have given an unfair advantage to the Prime Minister's party, because the views of other national leaders would not have been given a similar opportunity to have been aired before the polling day. An interim interdict was issued on the grounds that an arguable case had been made out that the BBC had not made sufficient provision for balanced coverage leading up to the election.[40] While there was some urgency about the matter, the decision did appear precipitous[41] because the broadcaster was not given an adequate opportunity to remedy the problem. The prospect of the courts exercising actual control over what is broadcast is not appealing, not least because of the subtlety of expert judgment that is required in cases of impartiality. However, one aim of judicial review is to render decision making more transparent and justifiable. The *Panorama* case does raise a difficult issue which has not yet been fully considered, either by the courts or the broadcasters. In the contemporary political environment of devolved politics, it will not be adequate to rely on the formal remit to provide impartial treatment across the United Kingdom programming stream as a whole. It should be recalled that impartiality is dependent on context; the broadcasters' consultation document's shift of focus to the election period will not avoid the issue.

Impartiality and Personal Access

Beyond politicians' preferential access to the media lie more general issues. Some have claimed that, as a public resource, broadcasting

---

[39] See A. Boyle, "Political Broadcasting, Fairness and Administrative Law" [1986] *Public Law* 562; E. Barendt, *Broadcasting Law* (1992), chap. 8. See also H. Rawlings, "Impartiality in Television Coverage of Politics" (1985) 48 M.L.R. 584–589.

[40] *Houston v. BBC* (1995). The case is reported and discussed in C. Munro, "The Banned Broadcasting Corporation" (1995) 145 *New Law Journal* 518–520.

[41] See Munro, above, n. 35.

facilities should be available to all instead of being the preserve of professionals. As a response, there has been a certain amount of experimentation with access programmes in which individuals or groups have been allowed to make their own programmes with full editorial and often considerable technical control. The Annan Committee was sceptical about the general benefits of such programmes, however: "Mere multiplication of different viewpoints will not help our society to understand itself, or to understand why people hold different opinions [. . .] To let everybody say anything they like produces Babel."[42] There is much force in this objection and it raises questions about the appropriate way of reconciling the claims of those who demand access with the importance of using broadcasting as an efficient method of communication.

One way of achieving that would be to adopt a common carrier model whereby access to the media is open to all who are prepared to pay for it. Where programming is directed at segmented, rather than universal, audiences, that may be an attractive solution (subject to fair price regulation). Yet given that there is only a finite amount of time available for an audience to receive programming, a common carrier model does not fully satisfy the goal of media pluralism to enable a diversity of programmes and audiences to engage with each other. Another option would be for at least public service broadcasters to shift the emphasis away from a passive role in processing information and opinion, and to concentrate on encouraging fair access instead. This would involve a more active role for editors in accepting individual claims much more sympathetically and ensuring that all substantial messages of differing points of view should be aired. The aim would be to demonstrate to the audience the prevalent diversity of opinion and belief. It would be a positive role requiring that no point of view be allowed to dominate, in order to prevent disproportionate influence by the medium itself, and entailing the active seeking out of unorthodox and innovative views as alternative agendas for programming.

The task of the public service broadcaster goes further, however. Although Annan was perhaps too confident about the broadcasters' public service skills in responsibly mediating ideas, their role is precisely to do that — to choose what is significant and to present it to a more or less universal audience in an intelligible way. That responsibility may be more important than individual access.

---

[42] Above, n. 12, para. 18.11.

Broadcasters can no longer be expected to produce a consensus from a variety of opinions and hold it out as a balanced and impartial product. Yet without some commitment to connecting differing perspectives it may become increasingly difficult, in a fragmented society, to identify constitutional values and establish the basis for democratic compromise. The tensions in broadcasting only reflect the deeper strains that this broader enterprise creates, but it reinforces the belief that impartial public service broadcasting will continue to be needed to complement fully commercial provision.

Fairness

Related to the requirement of impartiality, but distinct from it,[43] is the claim that the media should treat individuals fairly when dealing with them, including reporting or commenting on them. In broadcasting regulation, there is an active expectation that programmers will promote fairness. In the press, by contrast, there is little more than a grudging acknowledgement that some right of reply might be conceded when requested.

In the press, there has long been a strain between the ideals that that are considered appropriate for the industry and editors' claims to absolute control over what they print. The Press Council advanced the general principle that any person or organisation identifiably attacked in the columns of a newspaper or periodical is morally entitled to, and should be given, an opportunity to make a reasonable reply.[44] In practice, the "right" was hedged about with qualifications which tended to deny readers a fair presentation of both sides of an argument where controversy existed. As Robertson noted,[45] replies were denied where respondents were not themselves the subject of an explicit attack, where there was the possibility of a libel action, or where the reply was not confined to the bare details of the original piece. In addition, if the attack was thought to be "fair" or simply reflected the newspaper's right to be partisan about particular moral or political beliefs, no reply was conceded or, at least in the latter case, the editor was allowed a rejoinder. The effect of this attitude

---

[43] See *R. v. BBC, ex p. Owen* [1985] 2 All E.R. 522. See above, n.36. The decision is also discussed below, in chap. 6

[44] The Press Council, *The Press and the People* (1978), p. 3.

[45] G. Robertson, *People Against the Press* (1983), pp. 78–88.

was to prevent affected parties from influencing the parameters of discussion in the press. Instead, the readership's interests, which are not necessarily the same, were considered to be of sufficient concern and the Press Council consistently refrained from either advancing or enforcing arguments to the contrary.

Of course there are many difficulties involved in developing arguments for fairness into a workable right of reply. The press is a commercial enterprise whose sense of public responsibility will, realistically, be tempered by financial constraints[46] There are practical questions about the scope of the right, the appropriate length of replies, the amount of advance notice required, what might constitute an excessive number of demands for access, and the establishing of machinery to enforce it. All have financial implications as well as testing the principle involved in fair access. Nevertheless, they only present insurmountable problems if the right of reply is interpreted as a mechanical exercise in allocating column inches. If, instead, the underlying principle is recognised to be that of avoiding the unjustifiably authoritative dissemination of information and opinion, then the thrust of the press's "moral" responsibility is sincerely to alert the reader to the fact that other points of view do exist. This would go some way towards fair dealing without necessarily entailing the duty actually to present those other views, as the public service broadcasting model requires.

The prevailing opinion in the press, however, which the Calcutt Committee endorsed,[47] is that a right of reply is unworkable and an interference in editorial autonomy. The PCC's *Code of Practice* requires only that "A fair opportunity for reply to inaccuracies must be given to individuals or organisations when reasonably called for." This is related to the requirement that "inaccurate, misleading or distorted material should not be published."[48] In practice, the same problems persist for complainants.[49] Editors have the discretion to determine what is inaccurate and what is reasonable. There is no guarantee or likelihood that, if a reply is allowed, it will reflect fully

---

[46] See Royal Commission of 1949, above, n. 49, paras 140 *et seq.* and Royal Commission of 1977, above, n. 49, para. 2.4. In the United States, the nature of the press as private enterprise has been regarded as a reason for denying access: *Miami Herald Publishing v. Tornillo* 418 U.S. 241 (1974).

[47] Home Office, *Report of the Committee on Privacy and Related Matters* (1990), Cm. 1102. See chap. 6, below.

[48] Clauses 2 and 1, respectively.

[49] L. Blom-Cooper & L. R. Pruitt, "Privacy Jurisprudence of the Press Complaints Commission" [1994] *Anglo-American Law Review* 133.

the complainant's grievance or that it will receive the same prominence in the newspaper as the offending original piece. The PCC claims, however, that editors have changed their attitudes and are responding more favourably and speedily to complaints. It maintains that complaints rarely reach the PCC because the newspaper concerned has dealt with them informally and where they do go further, they are typically reached without the need for a formal adjudication.[50] That is not the same as offering a right to reply, however, and the complainants' apparent satisfaction should not be taken as an indication that they have been fairly treated.

In broadcasting, as in the case of intrusions into privacy, the former BCC had a duty to consider and adjudicate on complaints of "unjust or unfair treatment" in BBC programmes and those included in licensed services. As with privacy, this duty has been passed to the BSC, under section 107(1)(a) of the Broadcasting Act 1996, and extended to include drawing up a code of practice to remedy the BCC's failure to articulate a principled approach.[51] The basic obligation, which is also set out in the BBC's,[52] ITC's[53] and R.A.'s codes, is that broadcasters should avoid unfairness especially through the use of inaccurate information or distortion, such as juxtaposition of material taken out of context. They should also avoid misleading the audience about what it is being shown if that would be unfair to those taking part in the programme.[54]

More specifically, the BSC's code has a detailed set of rules for clarifying the expectations of significant contributors to programmes. These rules reflect the approach of the BCC, which was widely regarded as being unsympathetic to broadcasters' needs and interests in making current affairs and investigative programmes. Thus, potential contributors must be told about the nature of the programme and its purpose. Actual contributors must be told what the programme is about, why they were contacted, what kind of contribution is expected from them and whether the programme is live or recorded. They must not be coached or induced into saying anything untrue. More controversially, they must be informed about

---

[50] PCC, *Annual Review 1997: Serving the Public* (1998).

[51] See T. Gibbons, "The Role of the Broadcasting Complaints Commission: Current Practice and Failure Prospects" (1995) 1 *Yearbook of Media and Entertainment Law*, 129–159.

[52] BBC, *Producers; Guidelines* (1996), chap. 3

[53] ITC, *The ITC Programme Code* (1998), paras 3.7, 3.8.

[54] Broadcasting Standards Commission, *Code on Fairness and Privacy* (1998), para. 2.

areas of questioning and, wherever possible, the nature of other likely contributions. They must also, where appropriate, be made aware of any significant changes to the programme as it develops which might reasonably affect their original consent to participate and cause material unfairness. This latter requirement is not contained in the BBC's and the ITC's guidance and this is not surprising.[55] Many of these requirements impose unacceptably strict constraints on editorial autonomy and fail to take account of the practicalities of programme-making, which tends to be dynamic and organic rather than pre-planned. The rules also suggest that standards of fairness which are appropriate to the criminal justice system are necessary to investigative journalism, again imposing too strict a threshold.

The BSC's code also deals with accuracy; all material facts have to be considered before transmission and fairly presented.[56] Here, there may be a signal that the BSC is moving away from one line of decisions by the BCC in which it failed to distinguish between material and trivial facts, with the result that complaints were upheld in respect of minor and inadvertent inaccuracies. The effect was to highlight minor instances of unfairness and to give a distorted view of the overall worth of the programme, the justification being that the BCC's remit was not to judge the merits of a programme but to satisfy complainants' grievances. However, in another line of decisions, greater emphasis was placed on the impact of an item on the programme as a whole and the BSC's current formulation appears to endorse that approach, which is also reflected in that of the ITC. A related feature of the BCC's practice, which is not specifically mentioned in the new code, is the need to convey an accurate impression of scientific or specialist evidence to the audience. For programmes containing such information, the materiality of facts is determined by reference to the assumed knowledge of the audience and the consensus of expert opinion which exists. One aspect of accuracy which has not been handled so sensibly in the past is the factual basis of contemporary drama. The code requires that the drama should not distort the verifiable facts or give an unfair impression of the characters on whom it is based. But there seemed to be some loss of perspective when, following the depiction of fictional Brownies in a soap drama as under-age drinkers and

[55] However, the former BCC's power to impose such a restriction was upheld in *R. v. BCC ex p. Channel 4 Television Corporation and Another* (1995) March 28, Lexis.

[56] Above, n. 54, paras 7–9.

shoplifters, the BCC upheld the Guide Association's complaint that it treated real Brownies unfairly.[57]

Finally, two differences of emphasis between the BSC and the programmers may be noted. Neither the BBC's nor the ITC's codes contain the provision of the BSC's code that an unfair broadcast should be corrected promptly and with due prominence, where the complainant so wishes, unless there are compelling legal reasons for not doing so. The latter may well account for the omission, as a matter of prudence. The other omission is better explained as an assertion of editorial autonomy. The BSC's code states that, where a programme alleges wrong-doing or incompetence, or contains a damaging critique of an individual or organisation, those criticised should normally be given an opportunity to respond to or comment on the arguments and evidence in the programme. However, the BBC specifically states that, for legal reasons and to maintain editorial independence, it will not agree to showing contributors a copy of the finished programme.[58]

---

[57] BCC *Annual Report* 1990 (1989–90) H.C. 507, 90/93.
[58] BBC, chap. 3, para. 2, *cf.* ITC, para. 3.8.

Chapter Four

Market Structure

Protecting a public interest in communication has been an important influence in shaping economic arrangements for the media. Although different types of organisations developed whenever media activity expanded and diversified, so that various methods have been used to finance it and regulate its commercial operation, a constant theme has been the need to reconcile market forces, entailing competition and efficiency, with the constraints that are demanded by arguments for a free but responsible media. The press has been least affected by those arguments, the general assumption being that economic independence provides sufficient safeguards for opportunities to publish. Only competition policy and a minimal demand for journalistic standards modify this basic approach. By contrast, the BBC has represented the greatest commitment to regulation in the public interest. Together with its own particular cultural ethos, it has retained many features of the structure which Reith considered to be so essential for the consolidation of the then new medium: "assured sources of funding, the brute force of monopoly, [. . .] and national coverage."[1] Between these two extremes lie the various components of the commercial or "independent" sector, including the satellite and cable industries, and radio. Economic arrangements in those cases reflect variations in the mix between free market and fully regulated approaches. Partly, these have developed from challenges to the view that total isolation from competition is a prerequisite for maintaining editorial independence and quality. In addition, there has

---

[1] R. Negrine, "Great Britain: The End of the Public Service Tradition?" in *The Politics of Broadcasting* (R. Kuhn ed., 1985), p. 18.

been a more recent questioning of the belief that public service is a necessary goal for all programming media, prompted to some extent by a greater awareness of the potential for diversity which the newer technologies provide. This trend has also been encouraged by the trend away from mass communication that is enabled by such technologies, especially digital transmission, and their capacity to reconstitute relationships between producers and consumers of programmes.

A. Market Sectors

The Press

The press operates in an environment which is virtually free from regulation. It is, of course, subject to the general law but, apart from some special provisions for newspaper mergers and cross-ownership with the electronic media, discussed in the following chapter, there are no particular constraints on its economic activity. Two sectors may be identified, the national and the regional. The British press is unusual in having a large number of nationally distributed titles. Currently, there are eleven daily newspapers (five broadsheets or "quality" papers, two mid-market and four tabloids or "popular" papers) and 10 Sunday newspapers (four broadsheets, two mid-market and four tabloids). The regional press is buoyant, but ownership tends to be concentrated and, with exceptions, it uses much syndicated material and maintains a high ratio of advertising to editorial content. There is also a large circulation of "free-sheet" advertising, much of it connected with regional papers.

Public Service Broadcasting

1. The BBC and the Early Monopoly

Although broadcasting owed its beginnings to private enterprise,[2] its public dimension was identified at a very early stage and had a

---

[2] The following historical account is based on T. Burns, *The BBC: Public Institution and Private World* (1977), chap. 1; A. Briggs, *The History of Broadcasting in the U.K.*, Vol. I *The Birth of Broadcasting* (1961); R. Coase, *British Broadcasting: A Study in Monopoly* (1950); P. Scannell and D. Cardiff, *A Social History of British Broadcasting*, Vol. I *1922–1939 Serving the Nation* (1991).

profound influence in shaping the industry's organisation and financial base. It seemed a natural progression to extend the State's interest in communication from the written, in regulating the Royal Mail, to the electro-magnetic, in prohibiting all radio transmission and reception without a licence issued by the Post Office.[3] Following the First World War, when this medium was controlled by the Armed Services, there was much pressure to develop its potential for the civilian population. Manufacturers of radio receivers wished to stimulate demand for their products by establishing a system of organised transmissions. At the same time, there was an enthusiastic and vocal body of radio amateurs who wished to see an increase in the number of transmissions authorised by the Post Office. The latter had taken a very cautious approach, influenced by military advice, initially allowing only experimental broadcasts of 15 minutes each week and later designating only one waveband to be shared by all who wished to transmit!

The Post Office, however, was concerned about the potential chaos that would be caused if the airwaves were allowed to become crowded, as had happened in the United States. It was also concerned about the position of the Marconi Company and unwilling to allow it to use its dominance in the new industry to gain a monopoly over transmissions. Reluctant to allow competition, therefore, it encouraged the manufacturers to find a co-operative solution in the shape of the British Broadcasting Company, which was formed in 1922 with shareholding being limited to British manufacturers of radio receivers.[4] From the outset, the Company was never intended to be a fully commercial venture;[5] broadcasting was regarded as something of a burden which had to be endured by the manufacturers to facilitate the sale of their equipment and it was here that they looked for their full profit. To this end, the only ready-built sets which the Post Office licensed for reception, at a fee of ten shillings, were ones marked as BBC-approved. The Company's income was derived from half the proceeds of this fee, together with a royalty levied on the sale of the receivers. The objects of the venture were that transmissions would be co-ordinated, the continuance of the receiver market would be protected for home producers and, by giving a monopoly to the Company, the Post

---

[3] Under the Wireless Telegraphy Act 1904.

[4] See Burns, above, n. 2, pp. 8–9

[5] See Briggs, above, n. 2, p. 120.

Office could avert the threat from Marconi. It was not long before widespread evasion proved to be a problem, one which was exacerbated by some confusion over the status of those who built their own sets from parts not approved by the BBC. The Company, fearing for the consequent loss of revenue, complained to the Post Office and, eventually, the first Broadcasting Committee was appointed in 1923. The Committee, chaired by Sir Frederick Sykes,[6] considered that there was a strong public interest in the "public property" which the wavebands comprised, but that the BBC's wish to control the market for equipment could not be justified. As a way out of the dilemma, it indicated an end to the BBC's dependence on the commercial success of the industry by recommending that there should be only one licence, whether for ready-built, home-made or experimental receivers, with three quarters of the fee to be passed on to the Company, the proportion to increase as the sale of sets increased. That fee would be the sole source of the Company's revenue. The system of royalties, which had provided little income and which tended to dampen demand by inflating the price of sets, was to be discontinued.[7] The possible alternative approach to finance, through advertising, was considered but rejected on the ground that it would affect the quality of broadcasting. These recommendations were implemented in due course[8] and have formed the basis for the BBC's financing ever since.

Once these arrangements had been established, the BBC assumed the position of a *de facto* monopoly in broadcasting. Despite the fact that its share ownership was extended to include over 1,600 manufacturers and 80 wireless dealers, and that the Post Office retained the option to license transmissions by other companies, in practice broadcasting was concentrated in one institution. Yet there was widespread agreement at the time that the alternative to monopoly would be "confusion [. . .] and the debasement of an influence far too permeating to be allowed to be vulgarised."[9] In fact, the company's activities had already become virtually isolated from the commercial pressures of the radio industry. It was almost inevitable, then, that the second Committee on Broadcasting, chaired by Lord Crawford, recommended that broadcasting should no longer

---

[6] (Sykes) Broadcasting Committee, *Report* (1923) Cmd. 1951.

[7] In return, Reith managed to secure agreement that the Post Office would enforce payments of the licence fee: Briggs, above, n. 2, p. 195.

[8] Wireless Telegraphy (Explanation) Act 1925.

[9] *The Times*, November 15, 1924.

be organised as a private enterprise, but should be reconstituted as "a Public Commission operating in the National Interest."[10] Ever since, the British Broadcasting Corporation has enjoyed a protected status.

2. *Protection from the Market*

Whilst acknowledging the contribution that the BBC's status made to broadly good programming in this country, the Peacock Committee was critical of the way it was supported.[11] Successive government policies established and maintained a "comfortable duopoly" which restricted entry to the market and segmented the sources of finance available to the BBC and the independent sector. When the latter was introduced in 1954, with its finance based on advertising, it had been felt that the two services should be complimentary and not in competition with each other. The aim was to prevent a lowering of the quality and range of programmes to the detriment of public service broadcasting. The effect, however, was to isolate consumers from determining the amount and nature of programming, because they did not pay directly for the transmissions they received and the choice of service was in any event limited. As a consequence, consumer interests had to be protected by some means other than market forces. Although regulation by the government was one avenue, there was a tendency for grievances to focus on the necessity and amount of the licence fee, and that became manifested in political dissatisfaction.

In addition to these negative features of the duopoly, the Peacock Committee summarised as follows a number of arguments against its retention.[12] A duopoly restricts free entry to programming. In addition, it provides no impetus to maximise the volume of the audiences on each side because financial stability is not seriously affected by reductions in audience ratings. Furthermore, a duopoly tends to encourage broadcasters to measure the worth of their work by reference to their own professional standards, and to enhance their reputations in that respect by winning awards, without deferring to consumers' perceptions of good broadcasting. Last, but not least, a duopoly militates against cost-consciousness in so far as it provides too secure a financial base for operations.

Ranged against these points are a set of arguments in favour of a duopoly.[13] Having a secure source of income is regarded as important

---

[10] (Crawford), Broadcasting Committee, *Report* (1925) Cmd. 2599, para. 5.
[11] (Peacock) *Committee on Financing the BBC* (1986) Cmnd. 9824, chap. 4.
[12] *ibid.*, para. 197.
[13] *ibid.*, para. 196.

because it allows for opportunities to plan programming in the long term. It minimises political interference and enables risks to be taken in programming policy in the interests of public service. In addition, it is thought that public service in promoting regional diversity in culture and taste will be protected. As for the problem of remoteness from the audience, it is maintained that, in the long run, a duopoly extends audience taste and thereby provides them with greater satisfaction than if they had been confined to a fare of currently popular programmes. In any case, it is said, competition does exist but in the form of encouraging new initiatives in programme design, and amongst producers.

However, economic realities have changed the nature of this debate. The onset of cable, satellite and digital programming has already broken the duopoly. The arguments are really about the regulatory framework which will best protect public service broadcasting,[14] and it seems clear that many choices cannot be made appropriately in a market context. If public finance is considered appropriate for some kinds of programming, it is usually because the market is reluctant to provide it. From the market's perspective, the prospect of competing with a publicly funded service is not attractive because that service may enjoy an unfair advantage. Furthermore, as Peacock conceded, where the commercial finance is based on advertising, there may not be sufficient moneys available to support both sectors. However, too much should not be made of the financial aspects of the duopoly. Much more significant is the fact that a regulatory space was created for the existence of public service broadcasting. As the success of Channel 4 demonstrates, public service can be privately financed, but it is a regulatory scheme which sets up (that is, constitutes) the market for it and which allows it to flourish. Similarly, the somewhat reduced public service obligations placed on Channels 3 and 5 are commercially viable because of the regulatory framework for the sector. Ultimately, then, the preservation of public service values depends on some isolation from the full impact of market forces.

3. *The Fourth Channel*

Channel 4 and the Welsh Authority are responsible for providing television programmes as a public service in the independent sector.

---

[14] For the case against giving it priority, see D. Sawers, "The Future of Public Service Broadcasting" in M. E. Beesley (ed.) *Markets and the Media* (1996).

They were established in 1980, following discussion by the Annan Committee.[15] Under the Broadcasting Act 1990, their remit was retained while the rest of the sector was deregulated. When the channels were first established, an interesting innovation was that they did not make their own programmes, a practice which has continued. Instead, they commission, purchase and edit programmes and films from independent producers. Programmes on Channel 4 are required to give it its own distinctive character and supplement the material offered on Channel 3, continuing an obligation which existed in respect of the previous ITV, while the Welsh Authority's programming (S4C) has a distinctly Welsh emphasis.

In 1993, Channel 4 became a statutory corporation like the Welsh Authority. Before then, it had been a subsidiary of the IBA and the ITC.[16] Whereas Channel 4's services are licensed by the ITC, the Welsh Authority has remained a broadcaster in its own right. Under the pre-1993 arrangements, each channel was financed from subscriptions raised from the ITV companies, in return for which the companies were allowed to sell advertising on the channel. While S4C continues to need to be subsidised, Channel 4 steadily increased its audience appeal and by the time of the 1990 legislation, it appeared to be in a position where it could meet its expenditure from advertising revenue.[17] Consequently, its funding was changed and from 1993 it became responsible for selling its own advertising.

Commercial Television

Regulation of commercial, or "independent", television is the responsibility of the ITC. In keeping with the aim of the Broadcasting Act 1990 to facilitate diversity and competition, the ITC has a duty to discharge its regulatory and licensing functions in the manner in which it considers is best calculated to ensure: first, that there is a wide range of television programme services available throughout the United Kingdom; secondly, that there is "fair and

---

[15] (Annan), *Report of the Committee on the Future of Broadcasting* (1977) Cmnd. 6753, had recommended that an Open Broadcasting Authority should administer the fourth channel, however; see chap. 15.

[16] Broadcasting Act 1990, ss. 23–27 and Sched. 11, Pt. II, para. 3. Chap. VI of the 1990 Act governs the Welsh Authority.

[17] Peacock, above, n. 11, para. 73; Home Office, *Broadcasting in the 1990s: Competition, Choice and Quality* (1988) Cm. 517 (White Paper), para. 6.24.

effective competition" in providing them and services connected with them; and, thirdly, that the services are, taken as a whole, of high quality and offer a wide range of programmes calculated to appeal to a variety of tastes and interests.[18] In relation to the newer forms of service, such as satellite, the Commission has considerable scope to decide how those objectives are to be achieved. In the case of terrestrial services, the legislation is more restrictive, although it thereby provides a base in terms of which the diversity of the overall structure has to be measured.[19]

1. Channel 3

The pattern for terrestrial services builds on the practice which already existed in independent television. The principal service is Channel 3, which replaces ITV but retains its character as "a nationwide system [. . .] to be structured on a regional basis".[20] The system was originally created by the Independent Television Authority (ITA), which had been deliberately given complete freedom by Parliament to determine the matters relevant to the allocation of contracts through what Lord Clark, the first chairman of the ITA, had described as "creative legal thinking and skilful negotiations."[21] The first proposals offered to the ITA did in fact contain other options such as providing particular types of programme intended for the whole country, or making a variety of programmes to be shown at particular times of the day. These were rejected in favour of a regional dispersal of power which was intended to encourage competition and prevent the development of a centralised, monopolistic institution like the BBC.[22] Only relatively recently did these early ideas surface again, with the introduction of breakfast-time television, for which the 1990 Act makes continued provision in allowing the Commission to designate a national Channel 3 service to be offered at particular times of the day.[23]

---

[18] Broadcasting Act 1990, s. 2(2)(a).
[19] Although the regulatory bodies have enjoyed fairly wide discretion, Parliament has always taken a close interest in the broad shape of the services to be offered. By contrast, in the United States, for example, the Federal Communications Commission has greater power to organise the structure of the industry, but in conjunction with the requirement to hold public hearings. See D. Ginsberg, *Regulation of Broadcasting* (1979) pp. 75 *et seq.*
[20] Broadcasting Act 1990, s. 14(1) and (2).
[21] A. Briggs and J. Spicer, *The Franchise Affair* (1986), p. 12.
[22] Annan, above, n. 15, para. 13.16.
[23] Broadcasting Act 1990, s. 14(5) and (6).

For all that regionalism has been established, however, it has never been a comfortable arrangement and the 1990 Act has not changed that. One element of the "quality threshold" in section 16 is the requirement that a sufficient amount of time is given to a suitable range of programmes that are of particular interest to persons living within the area for which the service is provided. There was a similar provision in the earlier legislation,[24] suggesting that some relationship exists between regions, as defined by their cultural and traditional characteristics, and centres of broadcasting activity. In fact, from the beginning, technical constraints, such as the frequencies available and the location of transmitters, determined the boundaries of programme contractors' areas.[25] Initially, the main aim was to extend the coverage of independent broadcasting as quickly as possible, with the award of early franchises proceeding on completion of the necessary technical arrangements. By the time the contracts were being considered for renewal in 1982, the Independent Broadcasting Authority (IBA), the successor to the ITA, felt unable to make major changes to the regional pattern despite anomalies such as the boundaries along the Pennines, the Welsh border and the Scottish border. Another difficulty has been the conflating of geographically different areas into single programme areas — for example, the south of England or the Midlands — but the IBA experimented with the creation of sub-regions to resolve it and there is provision to continue that approach in section 14(3) of the 1990 Act.

Regionalism is obviously inspired by the public service aim to cater for the particular needs of diverse audiences, but it has had to be imposed by regulation to counter the constant pressure of commercial interests against it. Their influence on the size of area tends to inhibit any movement towards smaller and culturally more meaningful regions. The viability of programme companies is determined by the buoyancy of the advertising market, which must be large enough to pay for the service provided, as indeed the IBA recognised.[26] That has led to a different perspective on regionalism, characterising it more in terms of marketing criteria than cultural identity, with advertisers researching and creating area profiles in order to maximise sales.[27] Nevertheless, the IBA sought to protect

---

[24] Section 4(1)(d) of the Broadcasting Act 1981.

[25] Briggs and Spicer, above, n. 21, p. 12, citing the Postmaster-General's Television Advisory Committee which reported in 1952.

[26] *ibid.*, pp. 19, 56–61.

[27] See J. Curran & J. Seaton, *Power Without Responsibility* (5th ed. 1997), pp. 173–180.

local interests proper by insisting on a minimum number of hours of regional programming, and it also required regional representation in company management and shareholding. The latter is no longer required under the 1990 Act but, in practice, it did little to consolidate a regional approach, for the most important influence on the shape of the system turned out to be the competitive framework that was allowed to develop, in particular the arrangements for networking programmes across the country. Under earlier legislation, both the ITA and the IBA had had to secure "adequate competition to supply programmes between a number of programme contractors independent of each other both as to finance and as to control."[28] In devising a suitable means of implementing that obligation, the ITA had at first envisaged that there should be at least two companies competing with each other in each programme area, but this never happened, despite the possibility that the market could have sustained the additional competition given the early high profitability of the industry. In order to introduce diversity, the early framework was split between weekday and weekend contracts, but that arrangement was generally discontinued in 1968 and has only been retained for the London area.[29]

What emerged, as a method of satisfying the requirement for competition without disturbing the local monopolies of the contractors, was the other major characteristic of ITV, and now Channel 3, a system of limited competition between programmes — the national network. Sir Robert Fraser, the first Director-General of the ITA, told the Annan Committee that the structure was modelled on the organisation of the national and local press.[30] The idea was originally for four companies to be responsible for the bulk of programme production, but to be linked to each other and to smaller companies by "a network connection technically capable of giving an unlimited introduction of programmes from any one region into any other and the stations to be in full competition in selling to each other."[31] In fact, a rather different arrangement developed. The "Big Four" contractors, Rediffusion, ATV, ABC and Granada, created a system of national programming whereby they would use each others' programmes in their own schedules and sell them to the ten

[28] For example, the Broadcasting Act 1981, s. 20(2)(b).

[29] Provision for this arrangement continues in the Broadcasting Act 1990, s. 15(1)(b).

[30] Annan, above, n. 15, para. 13.16; see also C. Munro, *Television, Censorship and the Law* (1979), p. 31.

[31] Fraser, quoted in Briggs and Spicer, above, n. 21, p. 13.

regional companies for an amount which included a proportion of their advertising revenue. By the time that the major contractors had become the "Big Five" network companies, with the establishment of Yorkshire TV, the ITA had accepted the system, having refrained from interference on the remarkable ground that the operation of the companies' business was their own affair.[32]

As the Pilkington Committee noted, the effect was for the companies to re-assemble the Authority's allocation of the franchises, since any basis for choosing a particular contractor to produce programmes could be neutralised in the network. Furthermore, the supply of programmes was restricted, with the ten regional companies experiencing some difficulty in gaining the transmission of their programmes nationwide. Some attempt to meet these problems resulted in the formation of what is now the ITV Association (the ITVA, formerly the ITCA) in 1971 as a joint body to promote the industry's interests and to provide less acrimonious arrangements for planning schedules. As a more direct response to the unease expressed by the Pilkington Committee, the ITA were given responsibility for supervising the network in the hope that greater flexibility might be introduced in the public interest.

That task was then given to the IBA, who were empowered[33] to give directions requiring the supply of one contractor's programmes for inclusion in another's schedule with a reciprocal obligation on the latter to purchase. There was also provision for approving the financial and other arrangements involved, and any voluntary networking agreements. It is doubtful whether the introduction of a statutory responsibility made much difference, however. It seems that the IBA accepted the existing arrangements as suitable for approval without change. They retained formal control but, in practice, it was the ITVA which settled the Live Network Agreement whereby the use of programmes was allocated. Although the IBA had a place on the network programme committee and may have secured a wider showing for some regional programmes, its influence was generally minimal. The network was explained rather than defended before the Annan Committee, which considered it worked well, although it expressed some concern that diversity of editorial control was lacking in regional television.[34] When information was being circulated to

---

[32] ITA, *Annual Report and Accounts 1961–62* (1962).
[33] Under s. 24 of the 1981 Act.
[34] Annan, above, n. 15, paras 13.3, 13.15, 13.30.

prospective contractors at the time of reallocation of franchises prior to 1982, the IBA gave no indication of its intention to alter the arrangements which had existed for so long. It was only more recent pressure to increase competition which led to the Big Five giving up a slight amount of their guaranteed time on the network — but by that time they were no longer the biggest five.

The principal objection to the network concerned the side-effects of the near monopoly situation that resulted. The market for programmes had been restricted by reducing the opportunities for transmission and by setting prices so as to favour the Big Five. As a result, there were fewer sources of programmes and there was little incentive for regional companies to produce programmes for a wide audience. Not only was this undesirable from the perspective of competition policy, but it was also inconsistent with programming objectives to extend knowledge by disseminating as wide a range of material as possible. The problems experienced by TVS, a regional contractor which replaced Southern TV in 1982, serve to highlight the commercial disadvantage which could occur. Where a company had an audience which was not interested in network programmes, in this case because the subject-matter was alleged to be too "northern" in orientation, its viewing was likely to fall, with a consequent reduction in advertising revenue. Yet the company was prevented from selling its own type of programme to the wider market because it had only limited time under the network agreement. For its part, the IBA maintained that a network brought many benefits. It enabled the costs of production to be spread over the whole system in proportion to each licensee's advertising revenue. It also had the overall effect of continuity and stability, with companies being able to predict the likelihood of national coverage for the programmes that they made as well as knowing what programmes were available for them to buy. Without that certainty, there was a danger that smaller companies might overreach themselves and make commitments which they could not fulfil. In its commentary on the passage of the 1990 Bill, the IBA stressed these commercial advantages of the network, especially for the process of applying for licences, in enabling realistic proposals and business plans to be made. Previously, a different theme had been more apparent, namely the protection that the network could provide for public service. It was felt that the larger, generally more secure companies could use their guaranteed time on the network to distribute the "flagship" programmes that may not otherwise have obtained wide audiences.

Although a network clearly has a role in serving the broader interests of distributing knowledge, that argument did not carry much weight. It may have been that some were suspicious that ITV companies were using the IBA's defence of public service to shield their positions. Prior to 1990, then, the IBA began to emphasise the importance of the network for securing both diversity and high quality programming, regardless of the size and resources of the local companies.

In discussion leading to the Broadcasting Act 1990, there was general agreement amongst politicians and regulators that the regional character of the ITV system should be retained in the new Channel 3 service, and it was on that basis that the competitive tendering process was designed. However, the original policy reflected in the 1990 Bill was that no provision should be made for a network; it would be left to the companies themselves to judge whether one was commercially desirable. There was no doubt that the companies did see the advantages of a network and, indeed, prior to 1990, a new agreement had been negotiated whereby companies opted to become predominately makers or buyers of programmes. The ITC's role was envisaged as supervising it to ensure "fair and effective competition",[35] to eliminate restrictive practices and to secure wider and easier access to the national market in programmes at realistic prices. Given the expectation that Channel 3 would evolve from ITV, however, it was recognised that networking arrangements would have to be incorporated into the competitive tendering process for new licences. Even if market forces would ultimately determine arrangements for the exchange of programmes, some co-ordination of intentions was required to prevent the devising of licence specifications and the costing of bids from disintegrating, for no progress can be made where the parties' participation in a process is contingent upon everybody else's. To meet this point, the IBA suggested that provision should be made for a "transitional" network during the licensing round and a short period thereafter, and that was incorporated into section 39 of the 1990 Act.[36] As it has transpired, the new networking arrangements have acquired a pivotal role in the

---

[35] A more rigorous requirement than the "adequate competition" in the 1981 Act, and making it less easy for the Commission to adopt the IBA's passive approach.

[36] For discussion of the current networking arrangements, see below, chap. 5. For the importance of calculating the impact of network arrangements on the tender, see the discussion in *R. v. Independent Television Commission ex p. TSW Broadcasting Ltd.* [1996] E.M.L.R. 291, *The Times*, March 30, 1992.

operation of Channel 3. The establishment of a Network Centre, with primary responsibility for scheduling on behalf of all the regional licensees, has consolidated it as a national channel rather than a regional system. In addition, considerable power has passed to the professional programmers at the Centre. Together with the consolidation of ownership in Channel 3, this development calls into question the continued need for the channel to be constituted and regulated under a regional framework. Both issues will be considered further in the following chapter.

2. *Channel 5*

Channel 5 is a new service which was established under section 28 of the 1990 Act. It cannot reach the whole of the United Kingdom, but it is required to be able to reach a minimum area as stipulated by the ITC. This minimum was determined by the government by making more effective use of the available terrestrial frequencies, many of which were reallocated for the purpose. In practice, Channel 5 will have a coverage area approaching about 80 per cent of the United Kingdom, although there is no requirement that it should be available to everybody within that area.[37] The major limitations on the new channel are technical. More extensive coverage would involve interference with existing (non-television) services or with other uses of the frequencies on the north-west coast of Europe. As it is, some recipients will have had to purchase different aerials and many home video recorders, which used the same frequency, have had to be retuned, albeit at the expense of the Channel 5 licensee.[38]

Apart from these constraints, the channel has to satisfy broadly the same standards as Channel 3, apart from those pertaining to regional programming.[39] Otherwise, the intention behind the 1990 Act was to let the market determine the nature of the new service. The ITC was given a broad discretion to decide whether there would be more than one licensee, providing different parts of the service at different times

---

[37] Broadcasting Act 1990, s. 28(4); *Hansard* Standing Committee F, February 15, 1990, cols. 773–776. Following the Government's allocation of a major frequency to digital terrestrial broadcasting in 1994, the maximum possible coverage had been revised to around 50 per cent, but further reorganisation of a number of transmitters enabled the original estimate of 70 per cent to be achieved by the time the tendering process had been completed towards the end of 1995, and the channel's coverage will eventually approach 80 per cent.

[38] Under the Broadcasting Act 1990, s. 30.

[39] Broadcasting Act 1990, s. 29.

of the day or week but, from the beginning, the shadow ITC indicated that it would prefer a single licensee, probably based in the north, although it had no firm view as to whether the licensee should produce programmes itself (on the Channel 3 model) or be a publisher (as with Channel 4).[40] Contrary to speculation in the industry, the legislation did not allow the ITC to advertise for locally based services, for example, transmitting only to a particular conurbation. Initially, there was little enthusiasm for another terrestrial channel and two rounds of tendering were required before the licence was awarded. A major problem for the industry was to settle a distinctive character for the channel, both to meet the requirement of diversity and to attract financial support, and there remain doubts as to whether it will be able to attract sufficient viewers, and advertising, to make it successful. That challenge lies with Channel 5 Broadcasting who were awarded the licence in 1996 and commenced broadcasting in the spring of 1997.

3. *Satellite Services*

Five channels for direct broadcasting by satellite (DBS) were allocated to the United Kingdom in 1977 and the first moves to exploit them were contained in the now repealed Cable and Broadcasting Act 1984.[41] Around 1984, the BBC had been encouraged to lead the way in DBS but it had had reservations on grounds of cost. At the government's instigation, a consortium was formed, comprising the BBC, the ITV programme contractors and private enterprise, to be regulated by a Satellite Broadcasting Board, under the 1984 Act. That project failed to get off the ground, so the IBA took up residual powers to award franchises to British Satellite Broadcasting. After some delay, it started transmissions (for reception by its controversial "squaerials") in 1990. By the end of that year, financial difficulties had led to a merger with Sky Television, to form BSkyB, albeit without the regulator's permission. Its contract was therefore revoked, but the IBA was left embarrassed and without a franchise holder. Notwithstanding a power to do so under the 1990

[40] IBA Background Paper No. 15, February 13, 1990.

[41] The Home Office had conducted a Departmental study which reported in 1981 (*Direct Broadcasting by Satellite*) favouring development of the medium and that was followed by the report of the Advisory Panel on Technical Transmission Standards (*Direct Broadcasting by Satellite*) in 1982. See also R. Negrine (ed.), *Satellite Broadcasting* (1988). On satellite law generally, see S. White, S. Bate and T. Johnson, *Satellite Communication in Europe: Law and Regulation* (1994).

Act the ITC did not attempt to revive the DBS project, the commercial realities having overtaken the regulatory scheme.

BSkyB has been the most successful of a number of initiatives using medium powered satellites employing less sophisticated technology, such as Astra, instead of the advanced but expensive DBS. Such satellite services are regulated by section 45 of the 1990 Act, which enables the award of what is essentially a nominal licence for satellite television services, so that minimum standards of taste, decency and so on can be enforced. Apart from supervising such standards, the regulatory regime has not attempted to influence the content of what are highly segmented services operating in a Europe-wide market. However, the 1990 Act did allow the ITC to licence satellite broadcasters who were not based in the United Kingdom but who simply uplinked their programming from there. Because of this, and partly reflecting also the status of London as a European centre of programme production, many satellite broadcasters chose to conduct their operations under British licences. This gave rise to complaints that such licences overlapped with the regulatory jurisdiction of other E.C. countries and did not reflect the principle of mutual recognition underlying the Broadcasting Directive. In due course, the European Court of Justice ruled that satellite services should only be licensed by the United Kingdom where the person providing the service is "established" there. The ruling was incorporated into the revised Broadcasting Directive and is reflected in revisions made to the 1990 Act in 1997.[42] The effect is that the ITC can continue to license operators whose principal place of business is in the United Kingdom or who control editorial decisions about the service. It can still license operators who use United Kingdom allocated frequencies, satellite capacity or transmission bases, but only if they are not established in states which are members of the European Economic Area.

---

[42] See *Commission of the European Communities (France intervening) v. United Kingdom* Case 222/94 [1996] 3 C.M.L.R. 793; Council Directive (89/552/EEC) of October 3, 1989 and Directive 97/36/EC of the European Parliament and of the Council (Consolidated Version 1997) ("the Broadcasting Directive"). The Satellite Television Service Regulations 1997 (S.I. 1997 No. 1682), reg. 2, Sched, paras 3–5, amended the original sections 43 and 45 of the 1990 Act. They also repealed section 44 which had empowered the ITC to issue licences for DBS. The overall effect was to abolish the previous distinction between "domestic" and "non-domestic" satellite services. This enables conformity to the E.C. requirement that all such services should be regulated on a similar basis. But it also recognises the failure of the DBS project.

4. Local Delivery Services

Local delivery services are typically not concerned with making, editing and co-ordinating programmes as is the case with television and radio. The service that they provide is often described as cable television, but it is really characterised by the use of telecommunications systems, rather than broadcasting, to distribute programmes obtained from various sources, such as terrestrial television or radio, satellite or, possibly, purpose-made tapes. The systems used might include cable, optical fibre, microwave or some combination of these, perhaps connected to a satellite receiving dish.[43] Responsibility for structuring this sector of the industry was given to the former Cable Authority, under the Cable and Broadcasting Act 1984, and has now been taken over by the ITC.[44] The regulatory system is "dual key", however, in requiring providers to obtain separate telecommunications or wireless telegraphy licences (or both) in addition to the ITC's licence. To complicate the matter further, where a local delivery service operator provides a programme which has not already been licensed, for example, as a satellite or terrestrial television programme, it must also be licensed as a licensable programme service.[45] Such licensable programme services might include, for example, home shopping, information or link services provided by local delivery licensees, and relays of large screen presentations such as football or boxing matches. The statutory definition also appears to include "webcasting" on the Internet. The essential point is that the service is conveyed by means of a telecommunications system for reception in two or more dwelling houses in the United Kingdom, whether simultaneously or in response to separate requests by different users. Although normal Internet use involves interactivity, which is excluded by the definition, the use of "push" technology to allow Internet providers to supply what is really programming material will mean that such services should be licensed by the ITC. More generally, although the regulatory framework is extremely flexible, if unnecessarily complex,

---

[43] See the report by the Information Technology Advisory Panel, *Cable Systems* (1982). It resulted in the setting up of an inquiry, chaired by Lord Hunt of Tamworth, which reported within six months: *Cable Expansion and Broadcasting Policy* Cmnd. 8679.

[44] Broadcasting Act 1990, Part II. The telecommunications system itself must be licensed separately, either under the Wireless Telegraphy Act 1949 or the Telecommunications Act 1984, Part II. Both sets of licensing authorities are required to consult with each other; see the 1990 Act, s. 75(2), the Telecommunications Act 1984, s. 3.

[45] Broadcasting Act 1990, ss. 46–47.

there has been little opportunity to develop any coherent policy because the industry is still relatively immature and the underlying thrust of the legislation has been to allow the market to determine the shape and rate of progress. So far, investment in cable and related services has been much slower than anticipated because of the high capital outlay involved and doubts that the audience will be large enough to make the enterprise financially worthwhile. It has been difficult to encourage them to start at all, let alone impose a structure on them.

Initially, it was envisaged that the cable industry would lay the foundation for a revolution in information technology.[46] It was accepted that cable companies would want to develop entertainment as the main source of returns on their investment, but it was hoped that they would therefore have the incentive to lay cable networks across the country and thereby facilitate the growth of "interactive services". These were to include home shopping, banking, betting, information services, data-processing and other computing and business transactions, both at home and abroad. The aim was to encourage commercial enterprise to create a cable infrastructure. In order to achieve that, it would be necessary to take advantage of the new technology in the form of "wideband" (or "broadband") cable systems that were capable of carrying more than 16 television channels.[47] Accordingly, those systems were designated as the "prescribed diffusion services" which the Cable Authority had a duty to promote under the 1984 Act. Indeed, even before the Act took effect, in order to capitalise on the entrepreneurial enthusiasm which had greeted the announcement of the decision to move away from broadcasting as the major type of electronic media, the government established a procedure for granting interim franchises for wideband services.[48]

Although the original expectation was that all new developments would involve wideband systems, the lack of investment caused that to be revised.[49] In addition, the Cable Authority recognised a case for

---

[46] See the White Paper, *The Development of Cable Systems and Services* (1983) Cmnd. 8866.

[47] See Cable Authority, *Annual Report and Accounts* (1986) para. 13.

[48] There were eleven "pilot" projects which were granted licences by the Home Office and the Department of Trade and Industry in 1983 under the Post Office Act 1969, s. 89. See Cable Authority, above, n. 47, paras 14 and 30 and appendix.

[49] See R. Negrine, "Cable Television in Great Britain" in *Cable Television and the Future of Broadcasting* (R. Negrine ed., 1985).

filling gaps between large systems with smaller ones on a transitional basis and it felt that any increase in the number of systems would increase the viability of programme provision. As a result, there was a shift in policy, enabling another type of ordinary diffusion service to be licensed, one which involved distribution through Satellite Master Antenna Television (SMATV). That type of service was considered suitable for systems passing up to 10,000 homes, in areas where they would not compete with wideband systems. They were not expected to provide interactive services, but were given only relatively short licences in order regularly to review the possibility of upgrading to wideband.

Under the 1990 Act, there was a further shift in policy as optimism about the pace of change diminished. The general effect has been to allow fragmentation of the market to encourage greater competition, but also to enable investment to take place on a smaller, less costly and possibly less risky scale. Thus, it is no longer expected that new cable operators will have to achieve 100 per cent coverage of their areas; instead, it will be for them to assess a realistic proportion and timescale, and to incorporate that into their proposals when bidding for a licence. Existing prescribed diffusion licence operators have been allowed to convert their licences to local delivery service licences. Although the Act imposes a framework for licensing, it does not promote any policy for local delivery, other than the minimum of intervention to prevent chaos.[50]

Considerable interest in local delivery services has been expressed by telecommunications companies who are seeking to expand not only cable television, but telephone services. In order to encourage these companies to invest in the business, and to prevent British Telecom (BT) from dominating the market, a restriction was imposed on BT's ability to reciprocate by providing competing services along its cable system. Under the provisions of its telecommunications licence,[51] BT has not been allowed to convey entertainment services locally in its own right until 2001. There has also been a restriction on the provision of entertainment services nationally in its own right. However, BT has not been excluded entirely from competing in the television market. The restriction on

---

[50] By contrast, other European systems have attempted to integrate cable into a media policy: see Negrine, above, n. 49.

[51] Issued by OFTEL under the Telecommunications Act 1984. The restriction also applies to other national public telecommunication operators and to Kingston Communications.

conveyance applies to the conveyance of local delivery services, but it does not extend to "video-on-demand" since that strictly consists of a service specifically requested by telephone and not available simultaneously to another household.[52]

However, faced with uncertainty about its plans in a rapidly converging market, the new Labour administration has used a review which had been previously planned for 1998 to announce a change in government policy. From 1998, BT and the other public telecommunications operators will be given the option of competing immediately in the provision of broadcasting entertainment to the minority of United Kingdom homes (17 per cent) which are currently outside local delivery licence areas. From 2001, they will be allowed to compete throughout the whole country.[53] The latter change will require primary legislation to take efect. In the meantime, the ITC has changed its own policy on the issuing of local delivery licences and that will be considered later in this chapter. For a time, the superiority of broadband cable meant that this new conpetition would have posed little threat to the cable companies, but the development of optical fibre networks means that BT is now well positioned to provide an alternative to local delivery services.

5. Digital Terrestrial Television

Another sector where an extensive regulatory framework has been established, but without knowing how the industry will develop, is digital broadcasting. European-wide research into the technology has proceeded for more than a decade and it is already being used in some satellite transmission. Part I of the Broadcasting Act 1996 anticipates its practical implementation in terrestrial broadcasting by introducing a setting which is intended to encourage competition and investment in new services. In due course, it is anticipated that there

---

[52] On the Conservative government's policy, see Department of Trade and Industry, *Competition and Choice: Telecommunications Policy for the 1990s* (1991) Cm. 1461 (White Paper). The policy was reaffirmed in Department of Trade and Industry, *Creating the Superhighways of the Future: Developing Broadband Communications in the UK* (1994) Cm. 2734. In respect of the video-on-demand exception, see M. Rhodes, "Cable and Satellite Broadcasting and other Transmissions" in C. Long, *Telecommunications Law and Practice* (1995).

[53] Department of Trade and Industry and Department of Culture, Media and Sport, *Broadband Britain: A Fresh Look at the Broadcast Entertainment Restrictions* (1998).

will be a complete switch to digital terrestrial transmission, with analogue transmission ceasing and its frequencies being allocated to other uses.[54]

Digital broadcasting enables the programme provision to be separated from transmission. A particular frequency need no longer be associated with a particular television or radio channel. Instead, by converting images and sound into binary digits and coding their relationship to each other, it is possible send material for many programmes and sources of information along a single frequency. At the receiving end, the code can be deciphered and the appropriate bits of information can be reassembled to provide separate programmes. Digital compression enables a relatively small amount of data to be sent when pictures are of low quality or almost still (only the changes from frame to frame need be transmitted), and enables more enhanced data to be sent to provide high-definition or wide-screen programming. There is considerable flexibility, therefore, as to the way that the frequency can be shared between programmes and services.

The process of compressing and combining digital signals and allocating the use of available frequencies to ensure that the electronic information is efficiently and accurately directed to the correct recipients, is known as "multiplexing". It is one part of a wider process of obtaining marketing and transmitting programmes. It will be possible, for example, for a package of services to be brought together to meet the needs of the various audiences which will have access to the frequency. A range of programme types and data services may be offered in differing permutations, possibly by reference to particular themes or "bouquets". In theory, all these functions could be undertaken by one operator, as is the case with some digital satellite provision, and is likely to be the case with the BBC. However, the government's policy in respect of commercial terrestrial transmission was to separate the operators to encourage investment, especially by non-media sources, and competition generally. Multiplex services will operate, then, to co-ordinate and manage the terrestrial broadcasting of programmes and information in digital form — they may be regarded as digital wholesalers in the marketing chain — and programme provision will be treated separately.

---

[54] See generally, Department of National Heritage, *Digital Terrestrial Broadcasting* (1995) Cm. 2946.

Unlike the case with local delivery services, but following the pattern established for broadcasting generally, the government set the parameters for the development of the new enterprise through its control of spectrum allocation.[55] Six frequencies were made available for digital terrestrial broadcasting. Three are expected to provide around 90 per cent coverage of the United Kingdom, and others will provide, respectively, 85, 75 and 70 per cent. The one with most extensive coverage was allocated to the BBC and the remaining five were assigned for use by multiplex services to be licensed by the ITC under the 1996 Act. A separate licence will be required for a new concept, the digital programme service, which covers programming (other than that provided by the BBC) whose only dissemination by terrestrial means is in digital form. However, digital programming which is also provided in analogue, but otherwise identical, form on Channels 3, 4 and 5 is defined as a "qualifying service"[56] and does not need another licence. To encourage the development of digital terrestrial television, the existing commercial analogue broadcasters have been guaranteed capacity on multiplex frequencies provided that they provide such qualifying services.[57] The BBC is fully committed to digital services[58] and licences for all the other multiplexes were awarded in the middle of 1997. The process of developing a consumer base, initially involving the manufacture and marketing of new receiver equipment, is the next stage in the initiative.

Commercial Radio

1. *Local Radio and National Radio*

Commercial radio was introduced by the Sound Broadcasting Act 1972. The aim was to establish a series of local services as public services, each of which would cater for the needs of the audience receiving its transmissions. Thus it would complement the national

---

[55] Broadcasting Act 1996, s. 6.

[56] Broadcasting Act 1996, s. 2.

[57] Special arrangements have been made for the Welsh language S4C, however, because the Welsh Authority broadcasts Channel 4 programmes at the times of the day when S4C is not scheduled. The Welsh Authority are required to simulcast only that Welsh language service and not duplicate Channel 4 provision, which is likely to be available to Welsh viewers through Channel 4's own multiplex.

[58] See BBC, *Extending Choice in the Digital Age* (1996).

and regional services of the BBC in a way which would be consistent with the traditional model for radio represented (and advocated) by the Corporation.[59] It was for the IBA to create a structure for services within those constraints, but the legislation did not provide any guidance about the characteristics of an area that might constitute a "locality" and no clear policy emerged. Instead, radio stations were based in major conurbations in the hope that they could sustain advertising revenue. That expectation was not always borne out, with the result that financially weak stations had to reduce their (more expensive) public service programming. There was considerable financial restructuring as a result, and the development of the sector virtually ceased some years ago.

Opinion in the industry was that the IBA had adopted too restrictive a policy for the needs of the more flexible radio market. Its transmission rentals were too expensive, and restrictions on programming and advertising were too paternalistic and limiting. Around 1983–1984, the sector was in crisis and the IBA was forced to respond by reducing rentals, in many cases to zero, relaxing rules on sponsorship and allowing radio stations to be bought and sold more easily. An important turning point was the subsequent acceptance by the government that spectrum scarcity was not as significant a constraint in radio as it was in television, and that opened up the possibility that a realistic market could be developed.

A parallel development was the growth of the community radio movement, which aimed to use radio as a public resource and to reflect cultural diversity in localised communities. Although the government initially proposed to allow an experiment with community stations in 1985, it cancelled the plan prior to a general election. Following the publication of the White Paper in 1988,[60] the IBA announced a compromise in the shape of the proposal to award 26 "incremental" contracts, involving new stations within existing independent local radio areas. It was intended to diversify existing programming, in some cases with an ethnic emphasis. Many of these new stations were to experience severe financial problems, however. The general picture that emerged from the state of commercial radio in the 1980s, then, was one of confusion and difficulty. The IBA did

---

[59] See T. Jones, "The Regulation of Commercial Radio Broadcasting in the United Kingdom" (1989) 14 *North Carolina Journal of International Law and Commercial Regulation* 255–278 at 262 *et seq.*

[60] Above, n. 17. The White Paper incorporated most of the ideas that had been advanced in the Green Paper, *Radio: Choices and Opportunities* (1987) Cm. 92.

not produce a distinctive policy, being driven rather by economic pressures, and the government had vacillated.

The Broadcasting Act 1990 offered an opportunity to make a fresh start. A more realistic approach was taken to the more precarious state of the radio market. At the same time, provision was made for expanding the market where possible; in particular, the Act enabled the rather belated introduction of national commercial radio. A significant change, therefore, was the removal of any requirement that independent radio should be provided as a public service. A new regulatory body was established, the Radio Authority, with the general duty to do all that it can to secure the provision in the United Kingdom of "a diversity of national services each catering for tastes and interests different from those catered for by the others", together with "a range and diversity of local services" which may include community services.[61]

Generally, the R.A. must do its best to secure a wide range of programmes calculated to appeal to a variety of tastes and interests, and to ensure fair and effective competition in the provision of services. In terms of structure, then, the R.A. has a clearer remit than that of the IBA, enabling it to balance the pattern of national, local and community services. Essentially, however, its function has been to respond to market initiatives and co-ordinate them, having gauged feelings about the way radio should be developed. If there is a gap in this scheme, however, it is the failure to take sufficient account of community radio as a major impetus for change. The assumption in the legislation is that such stations can be embraced within the wider local radio structure. Yet if community radio is envisaged as a non-profit making venture, as is more usually the case, it seems unlikely that it could survive in the commercial sector without fundamentally altering its character.

The radio sector now appears to have developed into a fairly vibrant industry. Three national licences have been awarded, and there has been a flexible approach to the advertising of new local radio licences. The latter total more than 180 and, in addition to a diversity of urban-based stations, they include a number of regional services for which invitations were issued in 1995.

---

[61] Broadcasting Act 1990, s. 85(2)(a) and (b).

2. *Digital Sound Broadcasting*

Digital terrestrial sound broadcasting, or digital audio broadcasting (DAB), will be regulated similarly to digital terrestrial television,[62] but there is less opportunity for expanding it. The government has allocated two multiplexes for national radio, one to the BBC and the other for independent broadcasters. There will be a further five multiplexes allocated for local radio services. Existing independent radio licensees under the 1990 Act will be given reserved capacity on the second national multiplex if they are prepared to provide a digital version of their service. However, since the available frequencies are limited compared to television and there will be pressure on that reserved space to developing new programming, they will not be required to provide a fully simultaneous broadcast of their analogue programming.[63] The exact amount of capacity will be determined in the light of the broadcasters' needs and the amount of frequencies available, but it is anticipated that the three independent national broadcasters will be allocated, between them, about one sixth of the capacity available on the second multiplex. If they want to develop new digital services, they will have to purchase some of the remaining capacity. One interesting feature of the scheme for local radio is that the BBC will have to compete for digital capacity at this level with commercial operators.

Additional and Other Services

Additional services consist of telecommunications services which use the spare capacity that exists on radio and broadcasting frequencies. Their best known use is the provision of teletext, the BBC version being Ceefax and the current independent contractor being Teletext (which replaced Oracle). Other facilities that may be provided are subtitling, automatic video programming, automatic radio tuning, stereo sound, and enhanced picture quality. In addition, spare capacity can be used for purposes such as subscription data services, data transfer and remote control of machinery. These have greater

---

[62] Broadcasting Act 1996, ss. 40–72.

[63] Under s. 41 of the 1996 Act, a "simulcast radio service" is analogous to a qualifying service in digital television. It differs, however, in applying only to national radio and in providing what is actually less simulcasting, by s. 48.

commercial potential and the 1990 Act makes provision for that to be exploited. The ITC and the RA are required to do all that they can to secure that spare capacity is actually used, by granting licences by competitive tender for the purpose.[64] They are able to determine the number of licences and how the capacity is to be divided but, generally, the purpose of any service will be for the market to decide. In order to protect public teletext, however, which might be squeezed out by services with a higher commercial return, the ITC has a duty to secure a public teletext service on Channels 3 and 4.[65] Digitally broadcast additional services, such as teletext or data services, are regulated separately.[66]

Under section 86 of the Broadcasting Act 1996, new provision was made for the award of restricted television service licences. They enable advantage to be taken of spare analogue frequencies for broadcasting to particular establishments or for particular events, such as a festival. Similar provisions in respect of radio were included in section 84(2) of the 1990 Act.

B. Licensing

Franchising: The General Approach

After the Second World War, the public ownership of broadcasting and the monopoly of the BBC came under increasing scrutiny. As an institution, the BBC was commonly regarded as bureaucratic, complacent and insufficiently responsive to audience preferences.[67] This made it particularly vulnerable to the pressure exerted by a vigorous political lobby which gained prominence after the Conservative administration took office in 1951. Wishing to see an expansion of the market for consumer goods, it favoured the introduction of free enterprise to television broadcasting.[68] It was felt

---

[64] Broadcasting Act 1990, ss. 48–55, 114–120.

[65] Teletext services are subject to the ITC's programming and advertising codes, but there is a supplementary code, *The Code for Text Services* (1998), which provides additional guidance.

[66] Broadcasting Act 1996, ss. 24–27, 63–66; there is no competitive tendering for these licences.

[67] (Beveridge) *Report of the Broadcasting Committee 1949* (1951) Cmd. 8116, paras 182–186.

[68] See A. Briggs, *The History of Broadcasting in the United Kingdom;* Vol. IV *Sound and Vision* (1979), pp. 427 *et seq.* See also B. Sendall, *Independent Television in Britain: 1 Origin and Foundations 1946–62* (1982).

that an injection of competition would stimulate new thinking about broadcasting and it was also envisaged, of course, that the use of alternative means of finance, in particular the sale of advertising space, would turn out to be reasonably profitable.

The framework for the independent sector in television was established by the Television Act 1954. The Act adopted a form of franchising for the allocation of broadcasting resources. This was preferred because it provided a means of dealing with the monopolistic tendency that might be expected when, given the scarcity of available broadcasting frequencies, there would be constraints on full competition for advertising revenue amongst broadcasters. The approach was extended to sound broadcasting in 1972 and it was adopted again, in 1984, when the expansion of cable was heralded.[69] Most recently, the Broadcasting Act 1990 has sought to introduce a purer form of franchising for independent services generally, by reducing public service requirements and allowing the increased use of new methods of transmission.

Whichever approach is adopted, franchising has operated in a much modified way in practice, so far. This has been especially so in relation to independent television where, before the 1990 Act, public interest considerations were given a priority that allowed the market only a limited role in determining the framework of the service. By contrast, the reduced emphasis on public service in cable, satellite and independent radio broadcasting, with correspondingly greater weight given to mere financial ability to provide the desired service, allowed franchising greater scope to work in those areas. This was enhanced by the Broadcasting Act 1990, which introduced considerable diversity into the economic arrangements for providing television and radio services. This was both a response to new developments in technology and a reflection of the Conservative administration's commitment to free enterprise and competition.[70] The object was to dismantle the vertical structure that characterised the operations of the IBA and to incorporate the "lighter" approach to regulation that the Cable Authority had begun. Unlike the IBA, the ITC and the R.A. are not broadcasters, with ultimate responsibility for the programmes that are disseminated. Nor do they own and manage the

---

[69] Sound Broadcasting Act 1972; Cable and Broadcasting Act 1984.

[70] It was part of a broader trend in Europe; see V. Porter, "The Re-Regulation of Television: Pluralism, Constitutionality and the Free Market in the USA, West Germany, France and the U.K." (1989) 11 *Media, Culture and Society* 5–27.

equipment for transmitting television and sound broadcasts; those operations have been privatised.[71] In addition, it is no longer assumed that a programme service and the programmes that it contains have to be supplied by the same organisation. Thus, the large television companies have to provide opportunities for independent producers, and cable has been redesignated as local delivery services in the expectation that they will draw their programming from a wide variety of sources. Where spare capacity exists in broadcasting and in cable, a similar approach has been taken to the provision of additional services, such as teletext, view-data or interactive facilities like home shopping. In regulating all these activities, the Independent Television Commission and the Radio Authority have a broadly strategic role in moulding the structure of the industry, but within the parameters of the legislative scheme.

Discretionary Allocation by Repute

Of all the IBA's functions, it was the process of allocating programme contracts that presented the greatest difficulties. The reason lay mainly in the nature of the task. As the Pilkington Committee noted, the Authority had to select a contractor who had financial stability but who could also be trusted to provide a public service in broadcasting.[72] The latter concept is fluid, even amorphous, and cannot be easily rendered into hard criteria. It may be identifiable only through a sense of shared understandings between broadcasters, and the IBA seemed to recognise this in the weight that it gave to the personalities and the broadcasting repute of those that were involved in broadcasting ventures.[73] The emphasis on public service did, however, place a considerable burden on applicants for contracts, who found it hard to quantify the costs involved and the revenue that might result. From the beginning, it was maintained that there was no natural connection between the qualifications that a contractor would be expected to possess and the amount of money that they might offer.[74]

---

[71] Broadcasting Act 1990, Part IV. The privatised company is called "National Transcommunications".

[72] (Pilkington), *Report of the Committee on Broadcasting 1960* (1962) Cmnd. 1753, para. 556; see generally paras 552–567.

[73] See Briggs and Spicer, above, n. 21, pp. 30–31.

[74] *ibid.*, quoting Sir Robert Fraser, first Director-General of the ITA.

Nevertheless, some indications of the type of criteria that were used by the Authority did emerge over the years, although it must be remembered that its membership changed and there were shifts in policy. Information about the characteristics of acceptable contractors could be gleaned from the invitations for applications which were issued when new contracts were to be awarded, and from comments in the Authority's annual reports. For the most part, however, the information was only generalised without offering much detailed or useful guidance, and no reasons were given for choosing one company rather than another. One of the attractions of a franchising approach is that it does enable new ideas to be floated and justified, and it may not be appropriate to impose rigorous constraints rather than to set a broad agenda and allow innovatory ideas to be discussed and negotiated. That should not have ruled out all expectations that the choice would fit into a broader pattern of reasoning, however. Against the consideration of flexibility must be set the facts that a tradition of public service and professional standards does exist, that financial and technical competence can be assessed on fairly objective criteria, and that the results of experience are an important factor in long term planning.

In 1955, the ITA's only indication of their thinking was provided in a request that applicants give a "broad picture of the type of programme they would provide, their proposals for network or local broadcasting of their programmes, some indication of their financial resources, and the length of contract they would desire."[75] By the time of the round in 1967–1968, a greater amount of information was required, with set questions about the applicant's "group composition, its financial structure, interests represented outside television, programme policy intentions, details of studio facilities and arrangements, and its operational timetable."[76] How this information was supplied by the applicants and how it was assessed by the Authority is not known, despite its use in a major and traumatic reorganisation of the franchises.[77] It did emerge that the ability to provide a high quality programme service was a major concern,[78] but the general impression which the Authority's

---

[75] Invitation to contractors issued in August, 1955, quoted in Briggs and Spicer, above, n. 21, p. 14.

[76] Briggs and Spicer, above, n. 21, p. 29.

[77] See B. Sendall, *Independent Television in Britain 2. Expansion and Change, 1958–68* (1983); N. Lewis, "The IBA Contract Awards" [1975] *Public Law* 317–340 at 319–326. See also Lord Hill, *Behind the Screen* (1974).

[78] ITA, *Annual Report and Accounts* (1967–68), pp. 5–6.

deliberations gave was that "they had sought earnestly to provide the best results without being able to convince that their methods were likely to achieve them."[79] This is not surprising in view of what Lord Hill, then Chairman of the Authority, told the Annan Committee, that its greatest difficulty had been in judging between promise and performance.[80]

By the time that the franchises came to be allocated prior to 1982, a number of changes had been introduced to the procedures adopted by the IBA in response to a wealth of criticism,[81] and the effect was to provide much more information about the sort of contractors that the Authority was seeking. That information was contained in detailed particulars which accompanied invitations to submit applications.[82] To a great extent, these appeared simply to explain the statutory position, but they also offered some guidance about the IBA's interpretation of its role. On the composition of the companies, it was stated that IBA policy was to prefer diversity of ownership and an appropriate degree of local ownership, although is not clear how the latter could actually influence programming.[83] On finance, the companies had to demonstrate that their funding, management and personnel resources were adequate to produce the programmes offered. On programme production itself, details had to be given of the amount of network and regional material anticipated to be supplied; here, the Authority did give some guidance about the desired proportions in relation to each particular area, together with the amount of new programming to be originated, whilst placing a strong emphasis the importance of local material. In general, however, the Authority's main policy was described in its yearbook at the time as seeking to provide a broad balance of interests within the system as a whole and to ensure that the "control and ownership of each company forms an identity and character likely to provide a balanced and high-quality service and genuinely reflect the area served." The Authority was concerned with marginal changes to consolidate the regional character of the existing framework, therefore, rather than the encouragement of major innovation.

---

[79] N. Lewis above, n. 77, p. 321

[80] Above, n. 15, para. 13.22.

[81] e.g. *Second Report of the Select Committee on Nationalised Industries* (1971–72) H.C. 465; Annan, above, n. 15. For reactions from the industry, see Briggs and Spicer, above, n. 21, chap. 2.

[82] These are documented in Briggs and Spicer, above, n. 21, pp. 61 *et seq.*

[83] Similar doubts have been expressed about the criteria for selecting local sound contractors; see R. Baldwin, M. Cave and T. Jones, *The Regulation of Independent Local Radio and its Reform* (1986).

Many felt that the IBA's financial judgment was their major failing. It was said to have demonstrated an unrealistic view of the financing of broadcasting when imposing conditions about programming on contractors.[84] In particular, during its final round of television franchising, it was thought that it was too preoccupied with securing regional finance for regional contracts for the good of programming. Instead of requiring that a solid financial base existed whatever its source, it assumed that an element of local ownership would somehow ensure that local community interests would be reflected in programming. Apart from the absence of any mechanism for such influence over editorial decisions, the sophisticated structure of corporate finance seemed to have been overlooked.[85] It is not very clear, however, that local finance actually featured as a significant variable in the choice of contractors, despite its emphasis in the criteria which were made public. A statistical study of the franchising process for independent local radio, conducted by Baldwin, Cave and Jones, used regression analysis to examine the possible influence of characteristics such as local involvement, financial factors, broadcasting experience and operations, and concentration of ownership upon the securing of a franchise. They were not able "to establish a correlation between probability of success and particular characteristics of the applicant, or to identify any significant difference between applicants which were successful and those which failed. The closest to a statistically significant result is the observation that winners tended to have a higher proportion of capital already acquired at application than losers."[86] But, as the authors suggest, the implication of this result is not necessarily that decision-making is arbitrary or capricious, but that it is consistent with the exercise of expert judgment which cannot, however, be articulated because of the complexity of the issues involved. In particular, the IBA had to form an assessment of the prospective contractor's commitment to public service broadcasting in the future, together with the likelihood that it would be implemented efficiently.

---

[84] Pilkington, above, n. 72, para. 572.

[85] The point applied equally to local radio; see Baldwin, Cave and Jones, above, n. 83, p. 16.

[86] *ibid.*, p. 20. See also J. Porter, *Independent Television in Britain,* Vol. 4 *Companies and Programmes 1968–80* (1990).

Competitive Tendering

One of the fears of those who resist the regulation of the media is that it enables the State to become too closely involved in its activities.[87] In relation to media ownership, regulation may be justified in order to control monopoly power over both the commercial enterprise itself and the communication of material.[88] One advantage of franchising by competitive tendering is that, in theory, it avoids the problem of State interference by allocating property rights in a way which substitutes competition for government decision. It achieves this by recognising that particular services need to be associated with particular frequencies or other channels of transmission for a stable period, rather than being subject to everyday fluctuations in the market. As a result, it enables temporary monopoly rights to be conferred on the provider of a service, but this can occur only after that person has competed with others in the first place for the right to enter the market as sole supplier. Competition *for* the market, then, is seen as a substitute for competition *in* the market.[89]

A number of other advantages in theory are claimed for franchising as an allocative mechanism. First, it increases market contestability; that is, it provides opportunities for new programming to enter the market. It does this by allowing contractors to offer to supply the market before they have committed their resources, thereby reducing their costs of entry, especially sunken costs (such as transmission equipment) which cannot be easily recovered if the venture is unsuccessful. Secondly, franchising provides the regulator with information about the competitiveness of potential suppliers, increasing the chance that the most efficient will be chosen. Thirdly,

---

[87] See D. Tucker, *Law, Liberalism and Free Speech* (1985), chap. 6; E. Barendt, *Freedom of Speech* (1985), pp. 98–107.

[88] See A. I. Ogus, *Regulation: Legal Form and Economic Theory* (1994) chap. 15; S. Breyer, *Regulation and Its Reform* (1982), chap. 4. Of course, the relative scarcity of frequencies is controlled by government but, even if they were willing to allow a free market in frequencies as property rights, there would be strong reasons of public interest for regulating their use, as Peacock conceded; see the discussion in Peacock, above, n. 11, paras 134 *et seq.*

[89] The discussion of franchising theory draws on S. Domberger, "Economic Regulation through Franchise Contracts" in *Privatisation and Regulation: The U.K. Experience* (J. Kay *et al.* eds., 1986). See also Ogus, above, n. 88; C. Veljanovski, "Cable Television: Agency Franchising and Economics" in *Regulation and Public Law* (R. Baldwin and C. McCrudden eds. 1987)

it provides the possibility of contract termination as a sanction on poor performance. Finally, it is relatively cheap as a method of allocating property rights, provided that decisions are based on the franchisee's willingness to pay and not some less tangible standard.[90]

This latter condition is crucial to the successful implementation of franchising theory. Two basic approaches are possible. In one, the bidder who offers to pay most for securing the franchise may be deemed the winner. Here, the amount bid will be determined by the profits which are anticipated to accrue during the contract period but, although that amount will be paid to the State, there can be no guarantee that the franchisee will not accumulate excessive monopoly rents. There is an alternative, whereby the franchise is awarded to the bidder who offers to charge the lowest price to consumers or who offers what the regulatory body considers the best combination of price and quality, the intention being to bring prices down to levels which come close to expected unit costs of production. However, this approach has not been implemented in practice.[91]

The general principle in the 1990 Act, therefore, is that franchises should be awarded by competitive tender to the highest bidder. Depending on the type of service being offered, however, there are a number of modifications to the basic scheme, and less tangible criteria have been given a major role in the regulatory bodies' decision-making. The four main stages in the process are the invitation to apply for a licence, the application itself, the elimination of persons who do not pass a threshold of minimum requirements and the award of the licence to the person submitting the highest cash bid, which is payable in instalments. In the cases of satellite, licensable programme services and local radio, however, tendering is dispensed with altogether.[92]

The invitation to apply is issued after the ITC and the R.A. have established the structure of the service, taking into account their own duties and the licensees' obligations that are imposed by the 1990 Act.

---

[90] See R. Baldwin, M. Cave and T. Jones, above, n. 83, p. 29. See also R. Baldwin *et al.*, "The Regulation of Independent Radio and its Reform" (1987) *International Review of Law and Economics* 177–191.

[91] Ogus describes the first approach as "monopoly price bidding" and the second (which is also known as a Chadwick/Demsetz auction) as "consumer price bidding." He suggests that the former may be more attractive to governments because they receive payments from the bidders. See A.I. Ogus, above, n. 88, p. 326.

[92] Provision for competitive tendering is set out in the Broadcasting Act 1990, ss. 15–17, 28 (Channels 3 and 5), 73–76 (local delivery services), 51–52 and 116–117 (additional services), and 98–100 (national radio).

It specifies the fee payable, as a contribution to the operating costs of the regulatory body, together with other financial commitments that the licensee will have to make. For Channels 3 and 5, the ITC is also required to give general guidance about the sort of programmes that it would want included in an acceptable service. When the invitation to apply was published, as expected, it was ITV programming prior to the 1990 Act which was the model.[93]

Applications have to include standard types of information, unlike those for satellite and licensable programme services where the procedure is informal. The aim is to provide a common basis for comparison when selecting licensees. Thus, applicants have to set out their proposals for meeting the specification for the service, their cash bid, their financial position and any other information that may reasonably be required to consider the application. In relation to radio, local delivery and additional services, the technical plan for implementing the service is a further consideration. For Channels 3 and 5 however, the substance of the service matters much more and the application must show how the so-called "quality threshold" will be reached.

Passing the threshold of minimum requirements is the most crucial stage in the whole process of tendering. The legislation makes it clear that applicants can only go forward to the next stage, when the size of the cash bid determines the outcome, if the ITC or R.A. are satisfied that the requirements have been met. The first criterion is that the proposal meets the specifications for the service in question. By implication, that includes conditions of general application such as those relating to ownership and good taste or impartiality. In addition, with local delivery and additional services, it means that the service is technically feasible and meets with the approval of OFTEL. In the case of radio, it means that the service must have the appropriate national characteristics. For Channels 3 and 5 there must be a "proper proportion" of European programmes and independent producers must be able to contribute at least 25 per cent of programmes. For the terrestrial channels, there must also be a commitment to providing a sufficient amount of diverse and quality programming, with a regional character in the case of regional Channel 3. Indeed, for Channel 3, the requirements are only a "notch down" from those of public service, and they demand the

---

[93] See ITC, *Invitation to Apply for Regional Channel 3 Licences* (1991). See also *Hansard* Standing Committee F, Broadcasting Bill, February 1, 1990, col. 496.

same types of expert judgment that the IBA had to exercise under the former franchise system. The greater the stipulation of positive, substantive programming, then, the greater is the discretion that is given to the regulatory bodies and the less important is the cash bid. Clearly, much depends upon the way that the minimum is defined and the Channel 3 round of bidding showed that the hurdle was set fairly high.

The regulators' influence is reinforced by the second criterion to be met, that the service can be maintained during the licence period. This requires the applicant's business plan to be examined in the light of the information supplied to the ITC or R.A. The cash bid is included in this information and the applicant's ability to pay the instalments on it, together with the levy (discussed later), provide an important basis for assessing the resources available for the proposed service. At this stage, therefore, an application containing a high bid will not outweigh one with a lower bid but which is more realistically attainable. Only if applications have satisfied the threshold, be it technical or quality, will they proceed to the final stage.

At that stage, the licence is awarded to the person submitting the highest cash bid. There is power to award it to another applicant in "exceptional circumstances", but that is not defined.[94] One such instance, specifically mentioned in the Act, is that the source of funds for a bid would make it against the public interest to award a licence. Otherwise, the government maintained, an exceptional case could include a situation where a lower bid offered much better value for money in terms of the quality of service offered. However, there were justifiable doubts that the courts would agree with that view. As a result, in relation to Channels 3 and 5, exceptional circumstances are stated to include bids where the "quality" of service to be provided is "exceptionally high" and "substantially higher" than that proposed by the highest bidder.[95] In relation to local delivery services, exceptional circumstances include situations where the technical plan indicates coverage "substantially greater" than that offered by the highest bidder.[96] Assuming that these expressions can be defined with

---

[94] Broadcasting Act 1990, s. 17(3), also applied under ss. 29(1) and 44(3)(a). See for example also s. 76(3) (local delivery services) and s. 100(3) (national radio). Both the government and the ITC refused to be drawn on what "exceptional circumstances" might be. For television broadcasting, there is limited guidance in s. 17(4): see text below.

[95] Broadcasting Act 1990, s. 17(4).

[96] Broadcasting Act 1990, s. 76(4).

any precision, these provisions suggest that bidders may have an incentive to pitch their proposals some way above the quality threshold, although diminishing marginal returns would make it difficult for one to be so much better that it would override the cash price. In fact, the exceptional circumstances provisions have not been used when awarding licences.

The aim of a tendering scheme is to promote competition and to enable choices to be made on supposedly more objective market criteria. It is not without its problems, however. As Domberger notes, bidding may be ineffective, it may be discouraged by sunken costs and it may be limited by the transaction costs involved.[97] Bidding may be ineffective if there is an insufficient number of bids or if they are insufficiently dispersed; in those cases, in theory, collusion may occur, thereby reducing competition. In the case of broadcasting, the difficulty arose not because of collusion, however, but because the IBA's scheme required bidders to opt for particular contract areas and was not flexible enough to enable bids to be diverted to other areas where competition was lacking.[98] As a means of overcoming this problem, it has been suggested that the award of contracts should be staggered in order to increase the pool of bidders for a limited number of areas at any one time.[99] This would make it more difficult for the ITC and R.A. to take a strategic view of the independent sector's structure, however, and it would introduce a great deal of instability. As an alternative, it might be possible to encourage bidding in the form of flexible packages which could include alternative options tailored for particular regions as part of a general proposal. That would increase the cost of constructing a bid, but it would also increase the chances of success, and the cost does not appear to deter applicants where the chances of success are probably slimmer. Under the 1990 Act, the absence of any constraints on multiple bidding was considered an incentive to more effective bidding, although the IBA was unhappy about this because they thought that the ITV companies would be encouraged to bid for each other's areas and that would affect their working relationships in Channel 3. In fact, this was not a particular problem. More disappointing was the lack of competition in some areas, a gap which

---

[97] The following section draws on Domberger, above, n. 89. See also M. Waterson, "Issues in the Regulation of Cable TV" (1984) 4 *International Review of Law and Economics* 67–82.

[98] See Briggs and Spicer, above, n. 21, p. 187.

[99] By Lord Thompson, cited in Briggs and Spicer, above, n. 21, p. 193.

exposed the regulator's failure to set realistic reserve prices on the auction.

Sunken costs may discourage bidding because of the difficulty in estimating the value of initially costly and virtually fixed assets. For that reason, the incumbent may be seen to have an advantage over the new bidder. This problem does not occur to such an extent where the franchise is an operating contract rather than an owning contract. There, the contractor does not acquire ownership of certain fixed assets, but uses them for a rent. The problem then, however, is that there is less incentive for the contractor to minimise costs in respect of those assets and the owner, usually a public body, is left with the responsibility for maintenance and renewal. In the independent sector, a midway position used to exist whereby the IBA owned the transmission network, with the programme companies having to provide studio and production assets. Under the 1990 Act, transmission and associated engineering were privatised. It was still possible, as happened in the past, for a new Channel 3 licensee to buy the production assets of the outgoing contractor, but some of the previous incumbents separated their production and delivery operations so that they could re-establish themselves as programme providers in the event of their failing to secure a licence. Their assets were not for sale, therefore, and new bidders would have had to take that into account when costing their bid. As for Channel 5, the prospect of bearing the cost of retuning video recorders was bound to depress interest in the venture, at least in the short term, until other changes in the system settled in.

The other main limitation on the potential for franchising to create effective competition is the transaction costs involved. Some broadcasters have voiced the complaint that the process diverts resources and energy from the main objective of making programmes. In addition, there are difficulties in specifying the precise nature of the service to be provided. That makes it difficult in turn for bidders to quantify the costs that they are likely to incur.[1] Under the 1990 Act, the ITC is required to provide bidders with examples of the kind of programmes that might feature in the Channel 3 and 5 services for which they invite applications,[2] but those will not be easily quantifiable. As Domberger observes, "Clearly franchising is likely to be most effective where the product

---

[1] See Baldwin, Cave and Jones, above, n. 83, pp. 29 *et seq.*

[2] Broadcasting Act 1990, s. 15(2).

or service to be supplied can be defined with relative precision."[3] The matter was complicated by the IBA's interest in maintaining the structure of the independent sector as a whole, including the networking arrangements which placed constraints on bids for regional contracts and imposed additional burdens on network contractors. Despite the change in emphasis in the 1990 Act, these were important concerns in the new tendering process.

THE LEVY

An important element to be considered in the tendering process was provision for extracting a levy or "additional payments" from the licensee. Since 1964, programme contractors were subject to this special tax on the returns from their services. It was intended to give the public a share in the monopoly exploitation of their asset, the airwaves.[4] Under the previous legislation, the levy was calculated on the basis of the companies' profits, latterly 45 per cent on U.K. profits and 22.5 per cent on overseas profits.[5] Under the 1990 Act, the levy is calculated on its original basis, the companies' revenue. That may be thought to increase efficiency, since the incentive will be to increase the proportion of profits to revenue, rather than decrease it, as used to be the case. On the other hand, there will be less reason to use profits to increase investment and, partly for that reason, there is provision in the 1990 Act for encouraging training in the industry.[6] Under the competitive tendering process, the levy is calculated as a percentage of "qualifying revenue", essentially that attributable to the supply of programmes, and it is included in the invitations to apply for the relevant licences. In relation to Channel 3, the percentages varied according to the income it was predicted that the licence area would generate. For the national breakfast time service, it was 15 per cent; for the East, West and South Midlands, London Weekly, London Weekend, North West and South and South East areas, it was 11 per cent; for the East and Yorkshire areas, the figure was 7 per cent; for Central Scotland, the North East, Wales and the West Country it was 2 per cent; and for the Borders, the

---

[3] Above, n. 89, p. 277.
[4] See Peacock, above, n. 11, paras. 68–70.
[5] Under the Broadcasting Act 1981, ss. 32–35.
[6] Broadcasting Act 1990, s. 15(3)(c).

Channel Isles, the North of Scotland, Northern Ireland and South West England, the figure was 0. Inevitably, a bidder's ability to sustain payment of a proportion of its revenue is a crucial factor, both in a bidder's choosing whether to bid and in the regulators' judgment as to whether the quality threshold has been crossed. In practice, it is as significant as the size of the cash bid. For that reason, the percentage set for local delivery services has initially been 0, to encourage investement in cable television.

Franchise Allocations

1. Channel 3

As a competitive exercise, the franchise round in 1993 was reasonably successful. There was a total of 27 bids for 16 franchises. Of those, there were four bids submitted in each of two licence regions and three bids in each of seven more regions. However, there were only two bidders in each of four regions and, remarkably, only one bid was submitted in as many as three regions. There was no obvious association between the number of bids submitted and the size or potential market of a region. A major surprise, however, was Central's sole bid of a minimal £2,000 for the lucrative East, West and South Midlands region.

As an exercise in tendering, the franchise round tended to confirm the difficulties predicted by franchise theory. The bids were wildly at variance with each other, both within licence regions and across different regions. The highest, albeit unsuccessful, bid was £59.7 million for the South and South-East region by the incumbent TVS. Within that region, Carlton bid £18 million and CPV-TV bid £22.1 million, but the successful bid was that of Meridian at £36.5 million. Some bids were within a few million pounds of each other but, in most regions, the variance was between 4 and 19 million pounds. Whilst a lack of comparability across regions might be expected, since each region was taken to have its own peculiar characteristics which were to be costed into the bid, the variation within regions shows how difficult it was for the applicants to agree the value of the licences they sought. This should not have been too surprising, though, because construction of the tenders necessarily involved major exercises in speculation. For the duration of the licence — 10 years — the costs and the value of different strands of programming had to be estimated, together with the income that they would generate from advertising and sponsorship. This required assumptions to be made about the buoyancy of not only the advertising market, but also the national economy, and indeed the international economy, during the licence period. There was much scope for reasonable differences of opinion, therefore, about the appropriate factors to be taken into account.

These difficulties were compounded by the most significant feature of the competitive tendering process for Channel 3 and mentioned earlier; that is, the discretion given to the ITC by the inclusion of the various thresholds. Of these, the "quality" threshold was the most important because it defined the very product that was the subject of the tendering, but the ITC's assessment of the business plan also turned out to be crucial. Of the 27 applicants for the 16 franchises, 13 failed to pass the quality threshold. In most of those cases, the cash bid had been greater than that of the successful applicant.[7] In three cases, the applicants satisfied the quality threshold but were unable to satisfy the ITC that they could sustain the service during the period of the licence. Ironically, one of those was TVS's bid for the South and South-East region; it had played a major role in promoting the case for changing the allocation of licences. It was another applicant, however, who decided to challenge the ITC's decision.

TSW was the incumbent applicant for the South-West licence. It submitted a bid of £16.1 million, but the licence was awarded to Westcountry Television, who offered £7.8 million.[8] The ITC decided that TSW's case was one of overbidding. TSW had relied on profit forecasts which were derived from an optimistic view of the growth in national advertising revenue during the licence period. At best, the company would be working on such minimum costs that it would be unable to make further reductions without sacrificing quality and, if advertising revenue were to grow at a more realistic rate (albeit only 1.3 per cent less), the bid could not be sustained. The Commission based its conclusions on a variety of sources. All bids had been required to comply with "sensitivity" tests to illustrate their viability under different economic circumstances. External consultants were employed to provide information and clarification. In addition, its

[7] Thereby confirming the political rhetoric that licences could not be "bought" by the applicant with the most money.

[8] A third applicant, TeleWest, failed to meet the quality threshold.

staff produced a series of briefing papers on the applications and their compliance with the thresholds. TSW sought judicial review of the ITC's decision, but their claim was rejected by the House of Lords[9] on the grounds that it disclosed no illegality, irrationality or procedural impropriety.[10] The court disapproved TSW's attempt to analyse the assessments made in the ITC's staff briefing papers to discover whether they contained any mistakes, finding that Members of the Commission had established an appropriate procedure for testing the applicants' financial estimates and had come to their conclusions independently after taking all relevant considerations into account.[11] Following this strong endorsement of the judicial process as one of review and not appeal, other unsuccessful applicants who had wished to challenge the ITC's decisions on the quality thresholds decided not to proceed.

Interestingly, the court proceedings demonstrate what was already apparent from the ITC's invitation to apply for a licence, which is that the Commission felt that it had to reach an independently based judgment about the premises on which the different bids were made. In this respect, the advantage claimed by franchising theory, that the costs of tendering are passed to the applicants, was not borne out. The point of the business threshold was to ensure that services could be sustained, and the ITC would not have been acting in the public interest if they had relied on the applicants' information base alone and simply allowed them to succeed or fail in the market. On that basis, it would have been possible for the tendering to have been arranged so that the ITC determined the business criteria in advance; what the competition contributed was a broader set of materials for them to consider.

As with the earlier franchise awards by the IBA, the Channel 3 award prompted many criticisms within the industry. Not all of these came from the losers. Many regretted the loss of respected incumbents, such as Thames, although Thames did have the foresight to reconstitute itself as a production company. The transaction costs of the exercise for each applicant, amounting to many hundreds of thousands of pounds, was widely regarded as

---

[9] *R. v. Independent Television Commission ex p. TSW Broadcasting Ltd.* [1996] E.M.L.R. 291, *The Times*, March 30, 1992. See the note by T. Prosser, "The House of Lords and Channel 3 Licences: The *TSW* Decision" (1992) 3 *Utilities Law Review* 47–50.

[10] Following *Council of Civil Service Unions v. Minister for Civil Service* [1985] A.C. 374, and *Associated Provincial Picture Houses Ltd v. Wednesbury Corporation* [1948] 1 K.B. 223.

[11] For further discussion, see below, chap. 6.

wasteful. The absence of a reserve price or a guide price for each licence area enabled some companies to gamble that they would have no opposition and they thereby gained a disproportionate benefit. Other companies clearly overbid, committing more resources than they could comfortably afford, to secure their licences. A guide price would have further compromised the theoretical advantages of franchising, of course, but most of them had already been sacrificed and, in retrospect, it was clear that the ITC was committed to undertaking the research which would have been necessary.

Since the Channel 3 franchising process is unlikely to be repeated unless, as will not be the case, the whole sector were to be reorganised by the ITC,[12] the lessons of the 1990 round are of a general nature. The advantages of the process were that it introduced a degree of openness and transparency that had not previously characterised television licensing; it represented a break from the past. It also encouraged new entrants. Generally, it provided a fairer means of allocating lucrative streams of revenue, despite the criticisms (with hindsight) of the disparities in tender prices. In the overall allocation, however, the size of the cash bid only determined five awards (where it served as tie-breaker between applicants who had met the threshold requirements). The process had the semblance of objectivity but, in reality, the legislative scheme was an elaborate way of achieving a combination of quality and value for money. It would have been possible for a regulator to achieve the same objectives through a process of full discretionary allocation, albeit one better justified and based on more explicit criteria than that operated by the IBA. The main point is that, once non-market considerations become the central focus of organising a programming service, the expert's judgment, credentials and accountability should be given due prominence and not hidden behind a veneer of allocative efficiency. It is interesting to note that one effect of the Channel 3 round turned out to be the creation of a service which was not too different from ITV in terms of quality, but which was better than the legislation demanded. A combination of the IBA's indications of acceptable quality, together with the wish of many bidders to outbid each other in terms of quality, enabled the ITC to incorporate the tender promises as conditions of the licences.[13] Unless licences are

---

[12] See the discussion of franchise renewals, below.

[13] Broadcasting Act 1990, s. 33. The section also applies to Channel 5.

renegotiated downwards in terms of quality, many elements of the old system have become entrenched in the new.[14]

2. Channel 5

The invitation to apply for the Channel 5 licence was made first in 1992, but there was only one bidder on that occasion, Channel Five Holdings. However, the ITC decided not to award the licence because it was not satisfied with the business plan and the company's capacity to sustain the service during the 10-year licence period. A second invitation was then issued in 1994.

As already indicated, the service is required to include programming which meets the statutory quality threshold, but the invitation offered a fairly generous timetable for reaching the full level of provision. For example, only 30 minutes of news and only three and a half hours of children's programmes need be included each weekday in the first year of service, rising to 50 minutes and seven hours, respectively, after five years. Similarly, the service is not required to achieve full coverage of the minimum area until the fifth year. These concessions were obviously a recognition of the greater risks involved in an immediate high investment in the new service.

In the second tendering exercise, the ITC received four bids. One was for £36.3 million, from UKTV, and another was for £2 million pounds, from NCTV. Interestingly, the remaining two, from Virgin and from Channel 5 Broadcasting (C5B), were for exactly the same amount: £22,002,000. The ITC indicated that, if it discovered collusion between applicants, it would not grant a licence to them on the grounds that they would not be fit and proper persons to hold a licence.[15] However, the regulator secured undertakings that there had been no collusion and proceeded to consider the merits of the bids.

In the ITC's view, all the applicants submitted acceptable business plans, but both UKTV and Virgin failed the programming limb of the quality threshold. The licence was therefore awarded to C5B as the highest remaining bidder. Virgin then sought judicial review of that decision on the grounds that the ITC had acted irrationally, in the sense of *Wednesbury* reasonableness,[16] in coming to its decision.

---

14 See P. Goodwin, "Did the ITC save British Public Service Broadcasting?" (1992) 14 *Media, Culture and Society* 653–661.

15 See ITC, News Release: "Channel 5 Statement", (1995) 38/95. The relevant provision of the Broadcasting Act 1990 is s. 3(3)(a).

16 See above, n. 10.

However, the Court of Appeal held that the challenge must fail.[17] Reiterating the House of Lords' stance in *ex p. TSW,* it noted that the 1990 Act had entrusted the ITC to exercise expert judgment when assessing whether applicants had crossed the quality threshold, and that the Commission had adopted a "meticulous" approach to its task and evaluated the evidence with "model care". The ITC concluded that Virgin's bid had not proposed sufficient staff or editorial supervision to provide a high quality news service, and did not indicate a range of programme suppliers or of innovative programmes, nor sufficient staff to demonstrate an ability to provide sufficient programming of high quality. The Commission also felt the bid contained insufficient diversity, with too many repeats. Given the Commission's skills and experience, and the careful procedure which it had adopted, the court was not prepared to allow itself to become a forum for appealing against the licensing decision.

3. National Radio

Under the 1990 Act, provision was made for the establishment of three national services, one on FM and the others on AM. To forestall the possibility that diversity would be interpreted within the genre of popular music, which is likely to be the most profitable market, it was specified that one service must cater for spoken material and another for "music other than pop music."[18] These national licences were awarded by competitive tendering which followed a similar pattern to that established for Channel 3. However, there was a modified quality threshold which consisted of a requirement for diversity and an adequate business plan to ensure continuation of the service during the period of the licence. There was no requirement that the services should provide full national coverage, only that they should make the best use of frequencies.

The first licence to be awarded was the non-pop music service. It was granted to Classic FM who bid £0.67 million, the second highest.

---

[17] *R. v. Independent Television Commission ex p. Virgin* [1996] E.M.L.R. 318. See C. Marsden, "Judicial Review of the Channel 5 TV Licence Award" (1996) 5 *Nottingham Law Journal* 86–91.

[18] Broadcasting Act 1990, s. 85(2)(a)(ii). Pop music is defined in s. 85(6) as including "rock music and other kinds of modern popular music which are characterised by a strong rhythmic element and a reliance on electronic amplification for their performance", regardless of their popularity in terms of sales. See *Hansard*, H.C. Deb. Vol. 172, cols. 327–330 (May 9, 1990). The Act imposes a regime which has some semblance of external pluralism.

A greater amount was bid by Showcase Radio, but it failed to provide guarantees of finance within six weeks of the award. The service went on air in 1992. The second national licence, one of the AM frequencies, was granted to Virgin Radio, which went on air in 1993. The bid was for £1.8 million, again, the second highest. INBC had offered more, but were considered to be unable to sustain the service. Finally, Talk Radio secured the remaining AM frequency with a highest bid of £3 million and started broadcasting in 1995. Generally, the tendering rounds were not as controversial as those for terrestrial television. This may be because the licence conditions were less onerous and the regulator had less discretion, with the result that the tenders were easier to quantify.

4. *Local Delivery Services*

Of all the sectors subject to competitive tendering under the 1990 Act, local delivery services appear to satisfy best the theoretical requirements for tendering. However, the sector is also one of the more precarious in the programming media. This is because the market is extremely competitive, with challenges from terrestrial television, satellite and the home video industry. In recognition of the large investment entailed by laying a cable infrastructure, and the prospect of low returns in the early part of a licence period, the ITC's practice has been to set the qualifying revenue at a variable percentage under 74(2) of the 1990 Act. Typically, it is set at 0 per cent for the first one to three years, rising to 1 to 3 per cent up to the tenth year, and 4 to 8 per cent for the final years. Although there has been some competition between applicants for franchises, a considerable number have been awarded to single bidders,[19] most of whom bid very low amounts.

However, the lifting of the restrictions on the provision of broadcast entertainment by public telecommunications operators, discussed earlier, means that the whole basis of local delivery licensing is no longer viable. The point of awarding a franchise is to give the operator the exclusive right to provide services in the relevant area but under the new policy, competition from the public telecommunications operators will undermine that exclusivity. Recognising this difficulty, the ITC has changed its own policy to

---

[19] Only the Milton Keynes franchise attracted a real competition between four applicants. The licence was awarded in 1997 to a British Telecom subsidiary who had offered £4.5 million.

reflect the new situation.[20] From 1998, in those parts of the country where there are currently no local delivery licences (17 per cent), new licences will be awarded on a non-exclusive basis. In relation to existing, new licences, the operators may apply to the ITC to issue them with non-exclusive licences. Since non-exclusive licences do not enjoy the privileges of local monopolies, there is no longer any justification for imposing a levy on qualifying revenue, and it will be set at 0 per cent. Although the ITC does not make it clear, there is also no longer any sense in holding an auction and awarding licences to the highest cash bidder under the new policy. This is because anybody who applies and who meets the relevant technical and business thresholds can have a licence. However, to comply with the existing statutory scheme, the formalities of the auction process will have to be continued until new primary legislation can be introduced. In the meantime, therefore, it appears that applicants for new local delivery licences will be asked to make only nominal bids. In the one sector where competitive tendering seemed most likely to work, it is no longer needed.

Discretionary Allocation by Criteria

1. Local radio

Under the 1990 Act, the major exception to the competitive tendering process relates to local radio.[21] It is considered unnecessary because the radio spectrum is wide enough to allow hundreds of stations to compete with each other. At the same time, radio lends itself to catering for highly segmented audiences, including those representing specialist tastes or community interests. In allocating local radio licences, then, considerable weight is to be given to the substantive character of the services being offered. While the R.A. has to be satisfied that the service will be financially viable, the ways in which the service will cater for the tastes and interests of persons in the locality that it serves, and broaden the range of programmes available to them, are intended be principal determining factors. There will be costs with this form of allocation, however, unless firmer criteria for

---

[20] ITC, *News Release:* "ITC Announces New Local Delivery Licensing Policy" (1998) April 28, 43/98.

[21] Provision for local radio is made in the Broadcasting Act 1990, ss. 103–104.

making these judgments are provided by the R.A. There has been intermittent criticism that the granting of local licences has been less than transparent, but it is difficult to force the R.A. to articulate their reasoning. Judicial review was sought by one incumbent who failed to secure a renewal of a licence, but the criterion of *Wednesbury* reasonableness was inadequate to provide a remedy, given that the R.A.'s discretion had been granted "in the widest terms."[22]

2. *Digital Terrestrial Television*

The Broadcasting Act 1996 sets out an elaborate scheme for licensing multiplex services through a competitive — but not tendering — process. The process was modified in respect of the analogue broadcasters, however, once they confirmed their intention to take up their guaranteed places. The second multiplex was then reserved for the exclusive use of the Channel 3 companies and Channel 4, together with the public teletext provider (currently, Teletext Ltd). The ITC did not advertise the licence, but invited an application from the companies setting out their proposals. The application was required to satisfy the ITC that the service would comply with its technical requirements, that the service would be sustained throughout the licence period and that there would be no charge imposed for the digital transmission of the analogue service. In due course, the licence was awarded to the companies' subsidiary, Channel 3 and 4 Limited. The third multiplex was reserved half for Channel 5 and half for S4C in Wales or for Gaelic programming in Scotland. It was advertised in accordance with the competitive process, but subject to the licensee's obligation to provide the reserved capacity and was granted to SDN in 1998. Obviously, the opportunities for new digital services on that multiplex will be much reduced.

The remaining three multiplexes were to be licensed in accordance with sections 7 to 17 of the 1996 Act. In issuing the invitation to apply, the ITC did not stipulate any levy (additional payments) in order to encourage the development of the new services, and in recognition of the high levels of investment that would be required. Applicants were required to set out their technical plan, proposals for programming and other services, proposals for access to the services by viewers and business plan. The technical plan covered the extent

[22] *Re Trax FM Ltd* (1996) March 21, Lexis, *per* Beldam L.J.

of coverage and the timetable for achieving it, together with proposals for transmission and digitalisation in respect of which the ITC published guidance.[23] The programming proposals were required to give details of the various digital programme services and additional digital services which were envisaged. The access proposals were of some importance because they contained indications of the kinds of decoding equipment that will be needed by viewers to receive the programmes and the kinds of incentive, such as the gift of set-top boxes or financial discounts, that might be offered to viewers to encourage them to buy receiving equipment. From the consumer's perspective, there are clear attractions in having a single set-top box which can provide access and decryption for all multiplex services in the area. Multiplex licence applicants would have had to consider, therefore, the relationship between their own and others' proposed systems.[24] Finally, the applicant's business plan had to demonstrate that the service could be maintained throughout the licence period, initially twelve years. The legislation makes provision for some public consultation on the applications and for that consultation to be taken into account in awarding licences.

In awarding the multiplex licences, the dominant criterion for the ITC is "the development of digital television broadcasting in the United Kingdom otherwise than by satellite". Apart from this, the only requirement is a diversity of services appealing to a wide variety of tastes and interests. There is no requirement as to quality. The ITC is empowered to include a number of specific conditions in multiplex service licences, however: applicants' undertakings can be incorporated into their licence, they must ensure that their programmes are duly licensed and they must not show undue discrimination in contracting for digital services. Furthermore, multiplex providers are not allowed to restrict the potential that digital broadcasting allows to vary the amount of frequency made available for different kinds of broadcasting. It may be desirable, for example, for a programme provider to buy extra capacity, to show a

[23] The requirement in s. 7(3)(a) of the 1996 Act that they should publish guidance about technical equipment meant that the ITC were able to encourage the development of an industry standard.

[24] The general policy has been to allow the market to develop a standard for a common set-top box. The terrestrial digital broadcasters (the Digital Multiplex Group, or DMUX) agreed a specification at the end of 1997; see BBC *News Release* 4.11.97, issued on behalf of DMUX.

high-definition film, from a news provider, at a time when the latter is conducting a studio interview which has less demands on picture quality; programme providers cannot insist on making contractual arrangements which interfere with the very basis of the multiplex service itself, however.

In the middle of 1997, the ITC awarded the licences for all three of the fully commercial multiplexes to one company, British Digital Broadcasting (BDB), which is jointly owned by Carlton and Granada Television. The decision was accompanied by a list of reasons why the application had been preferred to its rival, Digital Television Network. One was BDB's better, more cautious business plan. Another was its more realistic proposed expenditure on promoting the new technology and offering subsidies to viewers. The ITC thought that BDB's audience appeal was actually less innovative, but it nevertheless satisfied the requirement of diversity. However, BDB would not have been awarded the licence if it had not restructured its ownership following the ITC's expression of concern that BSkyB was a shareholder in the company, given that the provision of BSkyB programming was a core element of the proposed service. It was also a condition of the award that Granada, which had a significant interest (over 5 per cent) in BSkyB, could not acquire control of BDB from Carlton. Curiously, the ITC's concern, that the arrangement would be anti-competitive, did not extend to the supply of such programming in itself. It can hardly be insignificant that Sky programmes will not only dominate satellite provision, but will also be a major component of the principal alternative platform for subscription viewing.[25] Furthermore, the ITC's decision to award all three licences to one company does not appear to encourage competition, let alone media pluralism. The underlying rationale for the decision, however, is a strong desire to see the new venture develop successfully and to avoid risk. The ITC emphasised the value of secure funding, broadcasting experience and programming with proven audience appeal. Unfortunately, it has committed itself to a

---

[25] The decision was strongly criticised by OFTEL as raising "substantial concerns" in the pay-tv and conditional access markets: *OFTEL's Submission To The ITC On Competition Issues Arising From The Award Of Digital Terrestrial Television Multiplex Licences* (1997). Although the ITC consulted with other regulators and with the European Commission, the outcome is apparently being challenged in Europe. OFTEL's interest arose because it has a duty, under s. 3 of the Telecommunications Act 1984, to maintain and promote effective competition between persons engaged in commercial activities connected with telecommunications in the U.K.

less than adventurous diet for digital terrestrial broadcasting. Additional variety will have to be supplied by the BBC and the other traditional programmers.

The procedure for licensing digital programme services (the material disseminated through multiplex services) is relatively informal. Licences will be issued, essentially, on demand.[26] However, they attract the general conditions relating to licensed services, under section 6 of the 1990 Act, together with the application of the Programme Standards and Advertising Codes. In addition, the ITC's duty to monitor programming and to conduct audience research applies to digital programme services.

3. *Channel 3 News Contract*

Under the Broadcasting Act 1981, news in the ITV sector was provided by one company, ITN, which was owned collectively by the ITV companies. In the interests of diversification, but retaining the idea of a news service particularly associated with Channel 3, the 1990 Act gave the ITC power to nominate any company which could provide high quality news as a provider. The expectation was that there would be more than one company supplying news to the channel. Channel 3 companies were not allowed collectively to own more than 49 per cent of any nominated provider.[27] In fact, only one company was nominated, ITN, and the 1996 Act has altered the position so that news provision on the channel in the future will again be restricted to one provider.[28] The reason for the change is that it was considered desirable to encourage a single provider to offer a counterbalance to the BBC's news provision. However, the role of the ITC has been limited to nominating potential candidates to a pool and it is the Channel 3 companies who will select the next provider.

4. *Restricted Services*

Restricted services licences are intended to be awarded flexibly to cater for particular needs. Examples are hospital or school radio

---

[26] Under s. 18, Broadcasting Act 1996. The only limitation on issue is that the licensee is a fit and proper person, under s. 3(3)(a), Broadcasting Act 1990, and is not restricted from holding licences, under s. 5(1).

[27] Broadcasting Act 1990, s. 32.

[28] Broadcasting Act 1996, ss. 74–77.

services and student or ethnic television services. The ITC's policy is award on a short-term basis, for not more than two years in general and not more than 56 days for festivals. As with the R.A.'s awards, the aim is to add to the provision of services in the locality.

Duration and Exchange

Determining the optimal length of licences for the purposes of maximising competition is not an exact matter. As Domberger explains, there is a trade-off:

> "Shorter contracts increase the likelihood that the number of bidders will fall to levels which threaten the viability of the contest [because costs are likely to exceed revenue in the short term]. Longer contracts make it more likely that incumbents will benefit from important informational and other advantages which impair competition at the bidding stage."[29]

Under the 1981 Act, terrestrial television and radio contracts lasted for eight years. When cable was introduced, an initial period of 15 years was chosen, to reflect the high investment costs to be incurred, with subsequent periods being eight years. Similarly, in order to compensate for their participation in the development of direct broadcasting, the television companies' contracts were extended by statute in 1984.[30] Under the 1990 Act, the basic balance has been struck at 10 years for television services and eight years for radio. The exception is 15 years for local delivery services. Under the 1996 Act, multiplex service licences will last for 12 years.

In practice, the length of a licence will not be so important as the provisions for its renewal and the likelihood that the same licensee can hold it for an extended period of time. From the bidder's viewpoint, when a franchise falls to be renewed, the incumbent may enjoy an advantage in respect of the information which is needed in order to make a successful bid. Where the criteria for success are not publicly articulated and depend on shared understandings between the regulatory body and incumbent contractors, newcomers may not

---

[29] Above, n. 89, p. 277.

[30] Cable and Broadcasting Act 1984, s. 46.

get a fair chance to compete. From the regulator's perspective, long-term capital investment in the form of equipment and buildings and the job security of employees are just two examples of reasons for extending franchises to present incumbents and, indeed, before the Pilkington Committee's Report, the ITA had incorporated extension options into their contracts. Pilkington emphasised, though, that contracts should not last too long because there was a need to provide a sanction against companies that do not fulfil the terms of their agreement with the Authority,[31] a point that was endorsed by the Select Committee on Nationalised Industries in its report in 1972.[32]

The argument is one which has recurred throughout the history of independent broadcasting. Following the "brutal exercise"[33] of reorganising the franchises in 1968, the Annan Committee received much evidence of the disruptive effects of losing a contract. The favourite solution canvassed before it was the rolling contract, in which a company would have a relatively short contract but would normally expect to have it extended for three years at a time unless a shorter period was justified where its performance was not up to the mark. The IBA were not happy with this proposal, however, because it restricted its scope for changing contract areas or the terms of a franchise and for allowing opportunities for new companies to bid. The Committee rejected the rolling contract idea, mainly on the grounds that this would not make independent television sufficiently accountable to Parliament. Although it recognised that loss of franchise was "inevitably a crude and inflexible method of control" and should be accompanied by a system of due warning, it considered that to deny any provision for it would turn the IBA into an "ineffective finger-wagger".[34]

Under section 20 of the 1990 Act, special provision is made for the renewal of licences for Channel 3 television services.[35] A licensee may apply for renewal after six years of the licence have elapsed. If the ITC is not satisfied that the service would continue to meet licence requirements throughout the period of the renewed licence, or if it proposes to restructure the system by altering the licence areas or the

---

[31] (Pilkington) Broadcasting Committee, *Report* (1962) Cmnd. 1753, paras. 552–597.
[32] Above, n. 81.
[33] (Annan) *Report of the Committee on the Future of Broadcasting* (1977) Cmnd. 6753, para. 13.17.
[34] *ibid.*, para. 13.20.
[35] The procedure for Channel 3 in s. 20 applies to Channel 5 by s. 28.

times and days for which the service is provided, it must put the new licence out to tender in the usual way. Otherwise, the application must be considered at the latest by the time a fresh licence would have to be advertised and the incumbent is entitled to have it renewed. The new licence will take effect from the date of renewal and may itself be renewed under the same procedure in due course. This means that the arrangement is effectively, given the time taken to administer the renewal, an eight-year rolling licence. This is all the more so because the ITC does not have power to seek new programming proposals from the licensee. It is required to set a notional cash bid, however, and it has a discretion to set a new figure for the levy.

The ITC has now started this process for Channel 3.[36] Taking audience research into account, it has decided not to alter the Channel 3 structure. It does not propose to issue new licences, therefore, unless an incumbent is unwilling to continue. Since the current licences expire at the end of 2002, the first date that renewed licences can come into force is the beginning of 1999 and licensees have been asked to apply for renewal at the latest by the end of 2000. In exercising its discretion in respect of the levy (the additional payments), the ITC has proposed what is a radical change to Channel 3's financial arrangements. Instead of mimicking an auction, the value for the licence during its 10 year period will be calculated to decide the total amount of moneys which have to be paid in respect of the cash bid and qualifying revenue (the levy). Only 25 per cent will then be attributed to the cash bid, which will be a fixed sum, and the remainder will be obtained through the qualifying revenue by setting an appropriate percentage amount. The aim is to enable the levy to be used to adjust each company's payments so as to correct the distorting effect of the disparate bids that were tendered during the 1993 round. It will also allow companies' total payments for their franchises to be more directly related to their revenue. The effect of this proposal, which must (and probably will) be agreed by the licensees, is to render the 1993 round even less relevant. However, the tendering exercise did have an important result, namely, the securing of the licensees' programme undertakings, and they will not be altered. Although licence ownership is contestable, the basic features of Channel 3 have been consolidated.

---

[36] ITC, *Consultation Paper on Channel 3 Licence Renewals* (1997).

Since licence renewal is normally desirable, it offers an attractive incentive to co-operate when it occurs on favourable terms. The ITV programme contracts were extended in the 1980s to encourage the companies to invest in satellite. It is interesting to note that, under the Broadcasting Act 1996,[37] favourable conditions for renewal are given to radio licensees who invest in digital transmission.

[37] ss. 92 and 94.

Chapter Five

Finance and Concentrations of Power

Regulation plays an important role in shaping the structure of media markets, but equally important as a reason for regulating the media has been a desire to control their economic influence. There are three aspects to this concern. One is that sources of finance may interfere with editorial independence. A second is that concentrations of ownership may reduce media pluralism, and the third is that anti-competitive practices may reduce the choice and quality of service available to readers and audiences. These worries have not been diminished with the general trend away from mass media towards greater diversity of output, with broader bases for finance and a less restrictive approach to media control. However, scrutiny of the BBC's finances, in recent years, has provided an opportunity to re-examine the regulatory approach to media power. The most recent major review of the Corporation's finances, by the Peacock Committee, applied the logic of the general trend to the whole industry and offered a number of sweeping proposals to reduce regulation in favour of market processes. Many of those recommendations were incorporated into the Broadcasting Act 1990 and the BBC's revised Charter and Agreement, and they are likely to have far-reaching implications.

A. Finance

Public Ownership

Although the BBC is no longer a monopolist broadcaster in either radio or television, it remains in public ownership and arrangements for financing it are very similar to those that were established in 1926. Under clause 10 of its present Agreement, the government pays a grant to the BBC in respect of its Home Service. Foreign broadcasts are financed separately, by the Foreign Office. The grant is paid on an annual basis, although in monthly instalments, and presently represents almost all of the BBC's income. Its source, as in the Corporation's earliest days, has been the revenue obtained from the fees payable for broadcasting reception licences. At present, licences are issued and the fees are set by the government, under sections 1 and 2 of the Wireless Telegraphy Act 1949.[1] Formerly, the money did not pass through the BBC but was collected by the Post Office on behalf of the Home Office and paid into the Consolidated Fund. The grant was then made to the BBC, having been approved by Parliament, for an amount which equalled the revenue from the licence fees after the deduction of collection and administrative costs. Now, the Corporation is itself responsible for fee collection on the grounds that it has the greatest interest in the fee's efficiency and acceptability, although it will not normally bear the loss of revenue from defaults in payment.[2] Some minor, secondary income is derived from marketing BBC products, such as publications and videos or programmes. This is likely to increase significantly, however, with the expansion of the BBC's commercial operations, discussed below.

The rationale for a continuing dependence on the licence fee has been that it enables the BBC to remain free from any commitment "to pursue any objective whatsoever other than the full realisation of the purposes of broadcasting."[3] The aim has been to isolate public service broadcasting from economic influences, this being consonant with the idea that commercial forces would lower standards and allow the medium to become controlled by sources of financial power. Given that aim, some way of providing public finance is required and a predictable source of income tied to the licence fee has been regarded as superior to the alternative of financing the BBC directly out of taxation. The latter has been thought to be constitutionally unsound because it would interfere with the BBC's political independence and the two Committees, Annan and Peacock, which have examined the BBC's finances in recent years have both

---

[1] For an account of the system and its enforcement, see (Peacock), *Committee on Financing the B.B.C.* (1986) Cmnd. 9824, paras 4341.

[2] Broadcasting Act 1990, s. 180.

[3] (Pilkington), *Report of the Committee on Broadcasting 1960* (1962) Cmnd. 1753, para 495.

accepted this point.[4] Finance from taxation would entail general parliamentary supervision and that would involve government in detailed scrutiny of programming policy, including matters of cost and content, with the danger that improper pressure would be brought to bear. The licence fee system is a method, therefore, of creating a constitutional distance between broadcasters and politicians.

It is a method which brings its problems, however. The effect of inflation has been to make it a less secure source of income. For a time, the expansion of the market for colour television, which attracted a higher receiving licence fee, was able to hide the effect of increased costs in broadcasting. But the demand for colour has now flattened out and this has placed the resources of the BBC under increasing stress. As a consequence, the BBC has made ever more frequent requests for an increase in the fee and, as the Annan Committee observed two decades ago —

> "The public has not liked this. The licence fee is criticised as inflexible — it has to be paid annually and refunds are permissible only in limited circumstances. It is also criticised as a poll tax and as a regressive tax: users of television, except those with colour sets, have to pay the same fee whether they are rich or poor."[5]

Inevitably, such objections place the setting of the fee firmly in the political arena and the Peacock Committee depicted the choice for the Home Secretary as being one of balancing the needs of the BBC with the interests of licence fee payers.[6] Once that type of balancing occurs, however, it becomes difficult to separate broadcasting policy from political objectives. The fact that there should be no interference with the way the BBC spends the block of money which is allocated to it may be of no avail in countering the temptation for governments to exert political pressure. Furthermore, the very possibility of such pressure could inhibit plans for innovatory and critical programming if a conflict with government policy was anticipated. Certainly, in recent years, there have been many fears expressed that the BBC had become compliant in just this way.[7]

---

[4] (Annan), *Report of the Committee on the Future of Broadcasting* (1977) Cmnd. 6153, paras 10.6–10.13, 10.22; Peacock, above, n. 1, para. 59.

[5] Annan, above, n. 4, para. 10.3.

[6] Peacock, above, n. 1, para. 57.

[7] See, *e.g.* P. Whitehead, "Reconstructing Broadcasting" in *Bending Reality* (J. Curran *et al.* eds. 1986).

Insofar as these problems result from the need to renegotiate the fee on a regular basis, the Peacock Committee recommended that it should be indexed to take account of inflation as a means of placing at arms length what it described as the paymaster and piper relationship. It suggested indexation by reference to the Retail Price Index, despite the BBC's view that broadcasting costs increase more rapidly, as a means of instilling economic discipline. In the longer term, however, the Peacock Committee envisaged a more radical change as a means of dealing with BBC finance, and it sketched a vision of an age of electronic publishing in which technology had developed sufficiently for programmers and audiences to have a market nexus. Services would continue to be financed by advertising but the main alternative would be subscription, whereby consumers could pay-as-they-viewed for the particular, encrypted programmes that they chose to receive. Anticipating that demand for public service programming might reduce, the Committee suggested that a Public Service Broadcasting Council should be established to finance public service provision.[8]

Although the age of electronic publishing remains a long term possibility, a number of short and medium term steps have already been taken towards its realisation. Transferring responsibility for the licence fee was one, indexing it another. In addition, in an approach that was also intended to make the Corporation more competitive and reduce its vertical organisation (whereby all the processes of programme-making, editing, production and transmission are arranged within a single hierarchical structure), it has been required to fund a considerable proportion of programming from external sources. In fact, the BBC had been engaged in co-production for some years, in order to spread high production costs. But, at a "seminar" at Downing Street in October 1987, the BBC, and also the ITV companies, agreed to work towards taking a 25 per cent quota of "independent productions." The arrangement was subsequently underpinned by the 1990 Act and power was given to the Director-General of Fair Trading to police it.[9] One effect may be to make the Corporation's output less distinctively that of the traditional BBC, which has to be seen in the context of the proposal that it should progressively replace income obtained through the licence fee with finance from other sources.

---

[8] Peacock, above, n. 1, paras 621–25, 682–699. *cf.* Annan, above, n. 4, para. 10.25.

[9] Broadcasting Act 1990, ss. 186–187. A similar requirement is imposed on the independent sector by s. 16(2)(h) of the Act.

The White Paper which followed the Peacock report endorsed the broad thrust of the Committee's preference for financing broadcasting through subscription. It did not support an immediate switch to that method for the BBC, however, since it would result in a loss of consumer welfare: some viewers would not subscribe to services currently available to them "free." It also rejected the mandatory fitting of "peritelevision" sockets to receivers (that is, the technology to facilitate subscription), preferring the market to respond in due course. Nevertheless, government policy was to provide the BBC with incentives to move towards subscription by authorising it to encrypt more of its services (it has experimented with providing night-time subscription services to certain professions) and by agreeing "licence fee increases of less than the RPI increase in a way which takes account of the BBC's capacity to generate income from subscription."[10]

The effect of this policy was to place increased financial pressure on the Corporation and, in due course, it responded with a fundamental review of its economic structure.[11] The outcome was a major re-organisation of the BBC's financial management in an effort to reduce costs by significant amounts. The main change has been the development of an internal market within the Corporation — "producer choice".[12] It has led to rigorous budgeting, with internal departments buying and selling their skills within the organisation. It has also been accompanied by a greater use of services provided by individuals or companies outside the BBC where that proves to be more efficient.

Even as these changes were taking place, the government appeared to soften its policy towards the BBC. It announced in 1993 that the Corporation would be given an increase in the licence fee that was linked to inflation, in recognition of the savings that had been made. But this reward for compliance with the government's expectations has had its own price.[13] Many employees of the BBC appear to be concerned about the effect that cost-cutting is having on the quality of programming and the public service ethos which underpins the

---

[10] Home Office, *Broadcasting in the 90s: Competition, Choice and Quality* (1988) (White Paper) Cm. 517, para. 3.11.

[11] See BBC, *Extending Choice. The BBC's Role in the New Broadcasting Age* (1992).

[12] This is explained in BBC, *Responding to the Green Paper* (1993). (The Green Paper is *The Future of the BBC* (1993) Cm. 2029).

[13] See J. Seaton, "Broadcasting in the age of market ideology: is it possible to underestimate the public taste?" (1994) 65 *Political Quarterly* 11–19.

BBC.[14] The latest process of renewing the Corporation's Charter tends to confirm these fears. The government envisaged that the BBC's traditional remit would continue, but alongside new developments in the commercial sector. The Corporation's transmission system has been privatised.[15] The licence fee will remain the principal source of income for public services for at least five years, but there must be continued cost-effectiveness.[16] In 1996, the fee was settled until 2002 by being linked to the Retail Price Index, at first positively but then negatively.[17] Significantly, the new Charter — for the first time — allows the BBC to provide "commercial services" funded by advertisements, subscription, sponsorship, pay-per-view, or other alternatives, whether free-to-air or encrypted.[18] The new Agreement prohibits licence fee moneys from being used to subsidise such commercial services but there is provision for reviewing the contribution of commercial income to the Home Services after 2001.[19]

The unresolved question is whether the BBC's commercial activities will in fact be expected to subsidise public services in the medium term. At present, in the form of BBC Worldwide and BBC Resources,[20] their income must be kept completely separate from licence fees, but they are being encouraged to expand considerably. This idea of keeping the commercial activities distinct has the appearance of guaranteeing public finances, but the Corporation's very success in selling its (public service) products will eventually

---

[14] See, for example, J. Tusa, "Implications of recent changes at the BBC" (1994) 65 *Political Quarterly* 6–10.

[15] Broadcasting Act 1996, ss. 131–135. The network was sold in 1997 to Castle Transmissions International Ltd for a ten year period.

[16] Department of National Heritage, *The Future of the BBC: Serving the Nation, Competing World-Wide* (1994) Cm. 2621, paras 1.11–1.18.

[17] For 1997–98, the fee is directly linked to the Retail Price Index (RPI). For subsequent years, the relationship is: 1998–99, RPI +3%; 1999–2000, RPI +0.5%; 2000–01, RPI –1%; 2001–02, RPI –2.5%: Department of National Heritage, *Press Notice* No. 408/96.

[18] Department of National Heritage, *Copy of the Royal Charter for the Continuance of the British Broadcasting Corporation* (1996) Cm. 3248 (hereinafter "BBC Charter"), art. 3(c).

[19] Department of National Heritage, *Copy of the Agreement Dated the 25th Day of January 1996 Between Her Majesty's Secretary of State for National Heritage and the British Broadcasting Corporation* (1996) Cm. 3152 (hereinafter, "BBC Agreement"), Clause 10.1(b), 10.2.

[20] See generally, http://www.bbcworldwide.com . The creation of BBC Resources Ltd, as a wholly owned subsidiary of the BBC, was approved by the Governors at the beginning of 1998. It will enable the BBC to sell its production skills to the outside (and internal BBC) market without being directly funded by the licence fee: BBC *Press Release* 20.02.98.

undermine the legitimacy of its public functions. It will be questioned whether public funding is needed at all to sustain public service and commercial operators will come to regard it as a unfairly subsidised product which enjoys a competitive advantage in the marketplace.[21] Although the licence fee will remain the principal source of income for the BBC in the short term, the general trend, then, is to push the BBC away from public service as an organisational aspiration to public service as a programming genre.

Advertising and Sponsorship Finance

While subscription will be developed in the medium term, advertising and, to a lesser extent, sponsorship are the main source of finance in the independent sector and are likely to remain so for many years. At present, the more common form is the insertion of short "spot" advertisements between programmes or at intervals during them. The rates charged vary according to the size of the target audience, with the more popular, networked programmes commanding the greatest amounts. Until recently, sponsorship, whereby some contribution is made to the costs of production in return for publicity, was restricted as an outlet for advertisers, but the 1990 Act marked a change in attitude that has provided for a rapid expansion of this kind of finance.

The Peacock Committee conducted an extensive review of the scope for advertising in the media in its discussion of the financing of the BBC.[22] Whilst it was cautious about predicting changes in the overall size of the market, it was generally optimistic that the demand for advertising would grow and that it could be extended to finance more media services, albeit at the cost of lower revenue as supply expanded in the short term. The Committee's main emphasis, however, was on the effect that advertising can have on the range and quality of programming and the welfare of viewers and listeners. As the report put it, "The main defect of a system based upon

---

[21] For a survey of developments in the European Community, see R. Craufurd Smith, "Getting the Measure of Public Services: Community Competition Rules and Public Service Broadcasting" (1997–98) *3 Yearbook of Media and Entertainment Law* 147–175.

[22] Peacock, above, n. 1. See also, J. Curran & J. Seaton, *Power Without Responsibility* (5th ed., 1997), pp. 187–194. For an historical survey, see B. Henry, (ed.), *British Television Advertising: The First 30 Years* (1986).

advertising finance is that channel owners do not sell programmes to audiences, but audiences to advertisers."[23] From an efficiency perspective, the audience can only indicate its preference for a programme by watching or not watching it. From the advertiser's view, support for the programme will only be viable if the audience is sufficiently large and that means that it will need to appeal to the lowest common denominator amongst audience tastes.[24] It is unlikely that advertisers would generally want to appeal to diverse audiences, subject to two exceptions: "niche" advertising can be sustained on specialist channels, as Channel 4 has demonstrated and, in addition, a highly saturated market may encourage attempts to find new audience outlets for advertisements.[25]

For these reasons, advertising poses a considerable threat to the maintenance of diversity in programming. Indeed, as Peacock noted, advertisers have an interest in programme content and "There would certainly be a risk that controversial drama, critical consumer programmes, current affairs programmes and satirical programmes which challenge conventional attitudes and prejudice would not be supported by them."[26] As already noted, in the absence of a fully developed market in media services, with a multiplicity of channels offering wide consumer choice, the Committee concluded that it would actually diminish welfare if the BBC were to be financed by advertising in competition with the independent sector.

The Fourth Channel

There is no reason in principle why public service broadcasting should not be financed by advertising or sponsorship. The former ITV sector and Channel 4 were such services, but only the latter now fulfils the remit. However, when Channel 4 was established as a public corporation which would sell its own advertising and sponsorship, under the 1990 Act, its position was considered to be somewhat precarious. In the interests of preserving an element of public service broadcasting in the independent sector, a safety net was created for it.

---

[23] Peacock, above, n. 1, para. 617.
[24] *ibid.*, para. 421.
[25] The general convergence to the middle is known as "Hotelling's effect." See R. Collins & C. Murroni, *New Media, New Politics* (1996) pp. 62–63.
[26] Above, n. 1, para. 315.

In 1993, therefore, a minimum income was set for Channel 4 at 14 per cent of all revenues from the provision of terrestrial television services. That percentage could be altered by the Secretary of State, but not before 1998. Where the Corporation's actual income was greater than that figure, half the surplus was to be paid into a reserve fund and half was to be distributed by the ITC to the Channel 3 companies. If Channel 4's income were to fall below the 14 per cent mark and there were insufficient funds in the reserve, the ITC would be able to levy the companies for a maximum of 2 per cent of total television revenues.[27] Many commentators were sceptical about the capacity of this scheme to succeed in protecting Channel 4's remit.[28] There was concern that the channel's fortunes would depend on the buoyancy of the advertising market at a time when the development of other initiatives in the commercial sector would create more competition for advertising budgets. The worry was that, if Channel 4 found that it was unable to sell its own slots, its losses would cause the television companies to bring pressure to reduce its minimum income, and the service would necessarily be curtailed.

In fact, Channel 4 has confounded the sceptics and has been very successful. It has found itself, therefore, paying large sums of money (£89.9 million in 1998) to the Channel 3 companies (who are wealthy in their own right and are Channel 4's competitors) and a similar amount into the reserve fund. In the past, the government has resisted requests by Channel 4 to change the arrangements and remove the safety net, possibly sharing the view that Channel 4 are being premature in believing that they can compete with the new cable and satellite services. However, the Broadcasting Act 1996, section 83, amended the rules, enabling variations to be made to the percentages payable by Channel 4 and the Channel 3 companies to each other, and making it possible to alter the amount of Channel 4 revenue which is paid into the statutory reserve fund. Recent policy was to cap that reserve fund at what was considered an appropriate amount and, while it remained at that level, to allow Channel 4 to retain the relevant income. In 1997, therefore, Channel 4 was allowed to keep around £87.1 million to meet current expenditure. The ITC indicated,[29] however, that it no longer believed there was a

---

[27] Broadcasting Act 1990, ss. 26 and 27.
[28] Including myself, in the first edition of this book!
[29] ITC, News Release: "Channel 4 Funding Formula" (1997) July 1, 51/97, being the text of a letter sent to the new Labour Administration's Secretary of State.

case for retaining the safety net. It proposed that it should be phased out, to cushion the depletion in Channel 3's income and to allow Channel 4 to develop plans to devote the increase in its resources to new, especially digital, programming. The Secretary of State agreed to make that change, but subject to Channel 4's improving the quality of its public service and investment in programme production.[30] For 1997, therefore, the proportion of surplus income that Channel 4 was required to pay to Channel 3 was 50 per cent, but in 1998 it will be 33.3 per cent, and zero for 1999 and subsequent years.

The success of Channel 4 does not mean, however, that the BBC could be financed by advertising and sponsorship. Channel 4 caters for a minority audience which attracts "niche" advertising. Most importantly, however, it operates within a regulated market structure, that is, the preservation of some features of the duopoly together with its own statutory underpinning.

Standards for Advertising and Sponsorship Generally

Whatever the aims of programming, there is a continued need for advertising to be regulated in the independent sector. One justifying principle is that the range and quality of programming should be protected, so that financial pressures do not compromise editorial integrity or distort freedom in communication. The other principle is one of economic efficiency, to ensure that consumers can make informed choices without being exploited, and that advertisers can compete with each other on fair terms. Under the Broadcasting Act 1981, the context for regulation was that of public service. Consequently, advertising was not allowed to compromise editorial independence, adversely affect consumer interests or generally intrude on the content of programmes. To further these aims, there were tight restrictions on presentation and timing, and sponsorship

---

[30] Department of Culture, Media and Sport, Press Release 14/97, July 28, 1997. Channel 4's licence was duly revised at the beginning of 1998 and contains new commitments which include increases in specially commissioned works, production outside London, multicultural programming and innovative film. There is also a lower limit on repeats, a greater commitment to training and new requirements for peak-time diversity generally. In April 1998, the ITC announced that it would no longer require Channels 3 and 4 to cross-promote each other's programmes under s.37 of the 1990 Act.

was virtually prohibited. Those constraints remained until 1993 but, while the new legislation allowed some scope for the previous regime to become more relaxed, the ITC and R.A. have been fairly cautious in departing from previous practice.

The 1990 Act reflects many provisions of earlier legislation in delegating extensive powers to the ITC and R.A. to draw up advertising codes and issue directions about acceptable advertising. Sections 8 and 92, however, contain a limited number of specific rules which are considered essential, regardless of the content of the codes. They may be justified as restrictions on expression which are needed to achieve a broader freedom in communication. With the exception of party political broadcasts, a licensed service must not include advertisements inserted by or on behalf of a body whose objects are wholly or mainly of a political character, nor advertisements which are directed towards any political end, nor advertisements related to any industrial dispute (other than a public service advertisement inserted by government).[31] These requirements are consistent with the general duty to preserve impartiality, which applies to advertisements in any event; it should not be possible to use financial power to secure political advantage. Yet, somewhat inconsistently, religious advertisements are no longer expressly excluded.[32] It is also provided that there must be no unreasonable discrimination in respect of advertisers, and licensed services must not include sponsorship from anybody who makes or supplies products whose advertising is prohibited. In addition to these rules, the general requirements as to good taste and decency and the prohibition on subliminal programming also apply.[33]

These requirements have been incorporated into the regulators' codes and have generally been applied without controversy. However, in 1994, the British Section of Amnesty International was prohibited by the R.A. from advertising the plight of refugees in Rwanda and Burundi on the grounds that it was a body promoting political objectives. Amnesty sought judicial review of the Authority's decision but the Court of Appeal held that the regulator had not misinterpreted the provisions of section 92, and nor had it acted unreasonably in applying the section.[34] On the interpretation of

---

[31] Broadcasting Act 1990, ss. 8(2)(a), 8(3), 91(2)(a) and 91(3). Provision is made for party political broadcasts in ss. 35 and 107.

[32] Broadcasting Act 1981, Sched. 2, para. 8.

[33] Broadcasting Act 1990, ss. 6 and 89.

[34] *R. v. Radio Authority ex p. Bull* [1997] 2 All E.R. 561.

"political", the Court held that it was permissible for the R.A. to adopt the approach used in determining whether a trust was constituted for political purposes, that is, where the direct and principal purpose is to further the interests of a political party or to procure changes or reversals in laws, government policies or government decisions, in this country or a foreign country.[35] On this view, the morality of the political objectives is irrelevant. It was for the R.A. to be satisfied, however, that the objects of the body in question were indeed "wholly or mainly" of a political nature. On that point, the court adopted the approach used in the *Derbyshire* case,[36] that the common law offers the same protection to freedom of speech as does Article 10 of the European Convention on Human Rights. Since the relevant provisions of section 92 — directed at the status of the body rather than the content of the proposed advertisement — applied a blanket ban on freedom of speech, they had to be interpreted restrictively: the body's objects had to be substantially or primarily political, meaning at least 75 per cent of them. Nevertheless, in coming to its conclusion that such a threshold had been crossed, the Authority was allowed some latitude in judging the complicated nature of Amnesty's constitutional arrangements and the court was not prepared to interfere with its decision. The result is rather unsatisfactory, however, because the court's restraint is due to the non-interventionist basis of *Wednesbury* reasonableness.[37] The judgments make it clear that, had it understood the real nature of Amnesty's organisation, the Authority might equally have found grounds for believing that its objectives were primarily directed to education and research. Furthermore, there are clear hints that, if Amnesty made a new application to the Authority, advertisements which focused on its humanitarian and educational work should succeed.

In some ways, the R.A. is to be commended for its concern that broadcasting may be used to promote political propaganda. Yet its stance illustrates an underlying distrust of the audience's ability to interpret the material transmitted to them. Of greater concern than the overt political message may be the more subtle relationship between advertisers' interests and the content of the programmes

---

[35] Adopting the test in *McGovern v. Attorney-General* [1981] 3 All E.R. 493.

[36] *Derbyshire C.C. v. Times Newspapers Ltd.* [1993] A.C. 534.

[37] *Council of Civil Service Unions v. Minister for Civil Service* [1985] A.C. 374; *Associated Provincial Picture Houses Ltd v. Wednesbury Corporation* [1948] 1 K.B. 223.

they finance, although the tradition of advertising regulation has been to inhibit interference with editorial decision-making as far as possible.

Apart from the specific statutory requirements, it is the codes published by the regulatory bodies which are the principal source of regulation of advertising and sponsorship in programming.[38] Each regulator's code is required to be drawn up after consultation with interested parties, including the other regulatory body, the licensees, representatives of the audience, advertisers and professional organisations who can advise about products. The codes govern standards and practice, and prescribe the types and methods of advertising and sponsorship which are prohibited. In respect of the latter, and unusually, compared to the general pattern of media regulation, the regulators must consult the Secretary of State from time to time and take account of any directions that he or she may issue. In practice, this has involved taking notice of and incorporating the requirements of more general consumer legislation at the domestic and European Community levels. Advertising and sponsorship do present media regulators with a disproportionate share of problems. This is because most restrictions will be directly inimical to companies' commercial interests. New forms of advertising, such as teleshopping and innovative kinds of sponsorship, have also posed new challenges because of the way that they blur the distinction between programme content and marketing. But the regulators have taken a fairly robust approach in placing the onus on advertisers to show that they are not compromising editorial independence.

One significant change in the 1990 legislation is that there is no longer any power to pre-vet advertising scripts although, towards the end of 1988, the IBA had already decided not to use it for all but the more sensitive cases, such as advertisements for alcohol or financial services. Outside the legal framework, however, a system of what may be called "co-operative regulation" has emerged from the earlier arrangements. In the television sector, the ITV Association used to offer advice and scrutiny in conjunction with the IBA, and when the new Channel 3 was established in 1993, it set up a new division, the British Advertising Clearance Centre (BACC), to continue that service. Some system of advance clearance is obviously to the

---

38 For general discussion of the earlier provisions, see C. Munro, *Television, Censorship and the Law* (1979), chap. 4.

advertising companies' advantage because the filming and editing that is needed to correct breaches of the advertising and sponsorship codes can be very expensive. Formally, the process is only advisory; the advertiser submits a script or preliminary video to the BACC, but there is no contractual relationship between them. In practice, however, the BACC's view is conclusive. When it has made a decision, it notifies the television companies and, although they are free to accept or reject advertisements, they are guided by the BACC. The ITC is, of course, not bound by the BACC's decisions but it appears to work closely with it. It will not issue rulings about the acceptability of specific proposed advertisements, but it does indicate whether it approves of the BACC's guidance[39] and ITC staff may offer informal advice to advertisers. In the radio sector, a similar approach has been adopted, with the important difference that the system of copy clearance operated by the Radio Advertising Clearance Centre (RACC) is built into the Radio Authority's code. "Special categories" of advertisement are required to receive central clearance by the RACC before they can be broadcast. These include material relating to betting and gaming, medical or financial services, children, alcohol and food. There is also a system for national and regional clearance, but local advertisements are approved or disapproved by the station which is being asked to broadcast them.[40] In radio, some means of achieving consistency over a large number of stations is important, but the clearance system in that sector makes clear what is only less apparent in the television sector, that the regulatory bodies have co-opted the industry into regulating itself in anticipation of formal enforcement. This has the advantage of securing legitimacy for the basic regulatory approach, but it also avoids the need for the regulators to use resources (which they cannot afford) in *ex post facto* scrutiny of the vast amount of advertising and sponsorship which is broadcast.

---

[39] The ITC's formal position is set out in the forward to *The ITC Code of Advertising Standards and Practice* (1995). Interestingly, in *R. v. The British Advertising Clearance Centre ex p. Swiftcall* (1995, unreported), Carnworth J. suggested that, in practice, the ITC are guided by the BACC's decisions. That case involved a unsuccessful challenge, based on legitimate expectation, to the BACC's request that Swiftcall's advertisement, which it had cleared, should be suspended pending investigation of a complaint that it was misleading.

[40] See Radio Authority, *Advertising and Sponsorship Code* (1996) p. 3.

Advertising Standards in Television

In this section, the rules applicable to television advertising will be examined in more detail. The issues are more complex than those in radio and they are also governed by European Community obligations. The R.A.'s guidance is considerably shorter but, in the context of radio, adheres to the same principles that are applied to television. For that sector, the ITC has drawn up a code in three separate parts. The first is *The ITC Code of Advertising Standards and Practice* (the "Advertising Code"). This is supplemented by the *ITC Rules on Advertising Breaks* (the "Breaks Code"). Thirdly, there is *The ITC Code of Programme Sponsorship* (the "Sponsorship Code"), which covers the most rapidly developing sector of the industry and which was re-issued in a revised form in the early part of 1997. From time to time, the ITC issues notes of guidance about the application of these Codes and they are binding on licensees. In devising the regulatory provisions, the ITC is assisted by a consultative body, the Advertising Advisory Committee, which also provides specialist expertise on such topics as medicines and foodstuffs. The three advertising-related codes are complemented by provisions in the *ITC Programme Code* which are intended to maintain the separation of programming from advertising and sponsorship. The codes have the effect of transposing the requirements of the European Broadcasting Directive,[41] which the ITC is required to take into account under section 9(9) of the 1990 Act, and in many cases they impose stricter obligations.[42] Enforcement is effected through the normal arrangements for supervising licensees. Importantly, the ITC discourages a legalistic approach to interpreting its codes, all of which contain the introductory remark that "The detailed rules set out below are intended to be applied in the spirit as well as the letter."

1. General Advertising

Advertising consists of material which is disseminated by television in order to promote the supply of goods and services in return for

---

[41] The consolidated Council Directive (89/552/EEC) of October 3, 1989 and Directive 97/36/EC of the European Parliament and of the Council of June 19, 1997 [1989] O.J. L298/23 and [1997] O.J. L202/60 respectively (hereinafter, "Broadcasting Directive"). See also http://europa.eu.int/en/comm/dg10/avpolicy/twf/tvconse.htm/ .

[42] These are justified by Art. 3, which allows such requirements in respect of broadcasting exclusively within a member country's jurisdiction.

payment. It may be contrasted with sponsorship, which consists of contributions made to programme production with a view to promoting the image, activities or products of the sponsor.[43] In general, advertising should be "legal, decent, honest and truthful", the same principle that is promoted by the Advertising Standards Authority. The Advertising Code goes much further, however. A major requirement, from both an editorial and a consumer perspective, is that "Advertisements must be clearly distinguishable as such and recognisably separate from the programme."[44] The test is whether the distinction is clear to viewers and the aim is to avoid what the European Broadcasting Directive describes as "surreptitious advertising" in Article 10.4. The Code sets out a wide range of situations where the audience may not appreciate that items are not strictly programmes.[45] For example, "situations, performances and styles reminiscent of programmes must not be used in such a way as to risk confusing viewers as to whether they are watching a programme or an advertisement". In cases of doubt, it is for the broadcaster to demonstrate that an item really is an advertisement. Direct imitations of specific programmes are not permitted at all, but it is recognised that the success of some advertising depends on its humorous treatment of existing programme styles, and parodies are acceptable provided that they use different performers from those who appear in the programme itself and that it is readily apparent that the advertisement is no more than a parody. To clarify the latter point, such advertisements must not be shown adjacent to the programme that inspired the parody.[46] More generally, advertisements may not refer to themselves as programmes and must not refer to the use or appearance of any product or service in any programme. There are also prohibitions on associating advertising with news and current affairs in order to lend it greater authority or credibility. Expressions such as "News Flash" are not acceptable in advertisements and extracts from recent or current programme material are not allowed unless they involve books, videos or audio

---

[43] This distinction is the one adopted in the Broadcasting Directive.

[44] r.5. This rule was amended in January 1997 to provide greater clarity but without altering the essence of an earlier version.

[45] This reflects the definition of surreptitious advertising in Art. 1(d) of the Directive. There is also a prohibition on subliminal advertising, in Art. 10.3, and that is incorporated into r. 7 of the Advertising Code. This actually reflects a more comprehensive prohibition on all kinds of subliminal material in s. 6(1)(e) of the Broadcasting Act 1990.

[46] More detailed provision is found in r. 4.2.16 of the Advertising Breaks Code.

tapes of material directly connected with the programme. Extracts from broadcasts of Parliamentary proceedings are also not acceptable. Complementary provisions are found in Rule 6, which prohibits the regular presenters of news or current affairs programmes from featuring in advertisements, and leading performers in programmes from appearing in adjacent advertisements. In this context, the codes make additional provision for "long advertisements": any advertisement which lasts longer than one minute must be carefully assessed to ensure that it will not be confused with programming material, and regular reminders of its advertising nature must be issued every minute.[47]

The Breaks Code deals with matters of scheduling and presentation of advertisements in close detail. It reflects and sometimes exceeds the requirements of Article 11 of the Broadcasting Directive, which establishes the general principle that advertisements should be inserted between and not during programmes, but then allows breaks within programmes where exceptional conditions are met. The Code imposes various prohibitions on the inclusion of advertisements within specific types of programme, for example, the religious and devotional, those covering Royal ceremonies or appearances, those designed and broadcast for school reception, and those which the ITC designates on the grounds that they are, for example, of a particularly harrowing or sensitive nature.[48] News or current affairs programmes, documentaries, religious programmes and children's programmes, may not have advertising breaks if they are scheduled for less than half an hour. In addition to these categories, which are specifically mentioned in the Directive, the prohibition is extended generally to live Parliamentary proceedings of half an hour or less and, for Channel 3 and Channel 4 (in recognition of their public service obligations), to children's programmes, news and current affairs programmes, and single plays of the same length. Also, any kind of programme of twenty minutes or less scheduled duration is prohibited from carrying advertising. Furthermore, in relation to religious and Royal ceremonies, a buffer of thirty seconds must be inserted between the programme and an advertisement.

In relation to advertising during programmes, the Breaks Code requires that not only should advertisements be inserted at natural

---

47 r. 7.1 of the Breaks Code.

48 rr. 5 and 6 of the Breaks Code. Apart from the broadcasting of a religious service, these prohibitions are stricter than the exceptions permitted by Art. 11.5.

breaks which do not damage the integrity or value of the relevant programme, but that such "centre breaks" are taken "only at a point where some interruption in continuity would, in any case, occur (even if there were no advertising)."[49] By way of examples, a break in a drama may be taken only where there is "a clearly marked and dramatically significant lapse of time in the action" or "a complete change of scene" or an interval in the original version of a play. For documentaries and discussion programmes, the break should occur when there is a change of topic or where filmed inserts terminate or where new participants in a discussion are introduced. Detailed provision is also made for musical programmes and for sport. In the case of the latter, breaks may occur at natural intermissions or where the focus of live coverage of a long event shifts. The impression must not be given in edited highlights that the editing has occurred to accommodate advertising. For foreign sports programmes, however, the break pattern of the originator is used and that may, of course, entail the acceptance of sporting events which are organised to accommodate advertising (for example, ice hockey).

Other provisions of the Breaks Code set out precise periods of time for determining the frequency and length of advertisements. Since the advertising market in broadcasting is based on precise timing, such detail has become necessary to create a "level playing field" on which broadcasters and advertisers may compete with each other in the general context of a regulatory scheme that attempts to preserve programme integrity. Thus feature films and films made for television should have no break if they are scheduled at 45 minutes or less, but longer films may be interrupted once for each complete period of 45 minutes.[50] For programmes other than magazine, sporting or similarly structured material, a period of at least twenty minutes should normally elapse between each successive advertising break during the programme unless a break at a shorter interval would better serve the interests of viewers, for example, if that fitted better with a natural break in continuity. For Channels 3 and 4,

---

[49] In this respect, it is stricter than the Directive.

[50] To illustrate the detail of the Code's provisions, a further break is allowed if the duration of the film is at least 20 minutes longer than two or more complete periods of 45 minutes. For Channels 3 and 4, however, the maximum period of any such break is three-and-a-half minutes (r. 5.7(A)), a difference which the United Kingdom justifies by Art. 20 of the Directive. That article allows Member States to lay down different rules in respect of broadcasts intended for the national territory and not capable of being received in another Member State.

breaks should not exceed three to three-and-a-half minutes, depending on programme length and, by implication, longer advertisements may only be broadcast in between whole programmes. Generally, long advertisements (more than one minute) must be flagged as such.[51] There are also detailed provisions about the total amounts of advertising which are permitted. They are expressed as a percentage of one hour's broadcasting.[52] For example, there is a general 15 per cent limit on advertising, an average of nine minutes per hour, with no more than 12 minutes per hour (20 per cent) for spot advertising (as opposed to longer advertising features). However, for Channels 3 and 4, the total amount of advertising in one day must not exceed seven minutes per hour, which is 11.6 per cent. During peak viewing, that limit is permitted to increase to seven-and-a-half minutes per hour (12.5 per cent).[53]

The revised Broadcasting Directive makes new provision for "teleshopping", that is, making direct offers to the audience for the supply of goods or services in return for payment (and also known as home shopping, infomercials or advertorials).[54] Teleshopping spots are subject to the same rules as for advertisements. But there is additional provision for teleshopping "windows" to be made available on channels not exclusively devoted to teleshopping for a minimum uninterrupted duration of 15 minutes. The maximum number of such windows per day is eight and they must not exceed a total of three hours. The aim is not to make provision for extended teleshopping, which benefits from additional time in any event, but to make it distinct from teleshopping spots and thereby further separate it from programming. The revised Directive also makes new provision for exclusive teleshopping and self-promotion channels.

The Advertising Code also imposes a variety of restrictions on the content of advertisements. Some represent an affirmation of some basic values but others reflect an enduring caution about the susceptibility of viewers to the influence of television. One group of rules[55] deals with various personality interests and the protection of the environment, broadly incorporating the provisions of Article 12 of the Broadcasting Directive, but also imposing stricter requirements. Thus, advertisements should not be offensive to public

---

[51] Again, these differences are justified by Art. 20 of the Directive.
[52] Art. 18, subject to Art. 20,
[53] These stricter rules are justified under Art. 19.
[54] Under Art. 18a. The provisions are incorporated into the Breaks Code, s. 8.
[55] rr. 13–15 and 20–22.

feeling or prejudice respect for human dignity, but neither should they offend against good taste or decency or exploit a living person's privacy. Advertisements should also comply with U.K. and E.C. law relating to discrimination, and they should not encourage behaviour prejudicial to health and safety or to the protection of the environment. These restrictions may be regarded as unexceptionable, subject to reservations about imposing taste and decency. However, the ITC's approach to "unacceptable" products and services is much stricter than the requirements of the Directive, which only prohibits advertising for cigarette and other tobacco products, again reflecting a mixture of concerns about consumer protection and moral paternalism. In addition to the ban on tobacco then, advertisements should not deal with breath-testing devices, the occult, betting tips, betting and gaming, private investigation agencies, personal or consumer advice services, guns and gun clubs, or pornography.[56] There are also stricter approaches to the advertising of medicinal products[57] and alcoholic beverages.[58] In respect of the latter, for example, advertisements must not be directed at children and participating actors must be clearly adult.[59] Alcohol consumption must not be linked to enhanced physical performance, driving, social or sexual success, or therapeutic qualities, and the encouragement of immoderate drinking and an emphasis on high alcoholic content of a drink are also prohibited. The use of humour is allowed, albeit not to circumvent the rules; however, that is an area where advertisers do appear to be willing to push the Code to its limits.

Advertising directed at children is of particular concern, both at the European and domestic levels. Article 16 of the Directive requires that advertising shall not cause moral or physical detriment to minors and sets out certain criteria for their protection. The ITC's Advertising Code responds with a whole appendix devoted to advertising and children, elaborating the basic principle that:

---

[56] r. 18. The Directive's ban on tobacco products is found in Art. 13.

[57] Art. 14 of the Directive deals with medicinal products but imposes only minimal obligations on the advertising of such products, being confined to prescription products. The Advertising Code has a whole appendix (appendix 3) devoted to such advertising and Art. 14 is reflected in its r. 7. Appendix 3 also reflects the requirements of E.C. Council Directive 92/28/EEC which have been transposed into U.K. law by The Medicines (Advertising) Regulations 1994 (S.I. 1994 No. 1932) and the Medicines (Monitoring of Advertisements) Regulations 1994 (S.I. 1994 No. 1933).

[58] Art. 40 of the Directive; r. 40 of the Advertising Code.

[59] The rule requires a real and apparent 18 year old for drinks containing 1.2% alcohol by volume or less, and a real or apparent 25 year old for volumes above that limit.

> "At times when large numbers of children are likely to be viewing, no product or service may be advertised, and no method of advertising may be used which might result in harm to them physically, mentally or morally, and no method of advertising may be employed which takes advantage of the natural credulity and sense of loyalty of children."[60]

There are detailed provisions relating to misleading images, exhortation to buy by exploiting inexperience, exhortation to parents to buy, and depiction in dangerous situations, together with the scheduling of potentially unsuitable material.[61]

Other provisions of the Advertising Code may be mentioned more briefly, to illustrate the range of material which they cover. Thus, advantage should not be taken of individuals' private lives, their fears must not be played on "without justifiable reason", and their superstitions must not be exploited. Advertisements must comply with the provisions of the Trade Descriptions Act and they should not make unfair comparisons with, or denigrate, other advertisers or products. Testimonials must be genuine, as must guarantees, and there are restrictions on the use of the word "free" and on unacceptable reproduction techniques (for example, using glass or plastic to simulate the effects of polishes). There are also appendices which deal with financial advertising, charity advertising and religious advertising.

Generally, the aim of advertising controls is to maintain editorial integrity so far as possible and to protect consumers. The detail of the ITC's Codes and the attention which is given to the topic in the European Directive are indications of the commercial importance of setting clear and predictable rules for competition. Much more troublesome is the regulation of television sponsorship.

2. *Programme Sponsorship*

The IBA's relaxation of a complete ban on sponsorship had been prompted by increasing pressure in an industry which was eager to develop new forms of promotional activity, and by the recognition that sponsorship was already being widely introduced in other

---

[60] Advertising Code, appendix 1, r. 1. For a review commissioned by the ITC, see B. Young, *Emulation, Fears and Understanding: A Review of Recent Research on Children and Television Advertising* (1998).

[61] Remarkably, r. 15 of appendix 1 states that, "Children in advertisements should be reasonably well-mannered and well-behaved"!

European jurisdictions and was about to be regulated by the European Broadcasting Directive. The Broadcasting Act 1990 endorsed the trend at the political level and paved the way for a fuller development of sponsorship simply by not including the prohibition contained in the 1981 Act.

A single provision of the European Directive, Article 17, deals with sponsored television programmes, but the ITC's approach has been much more elaborate and cautious. It has been anxious to protect the interests of viewers and the editorial integrity of programme-makers, notwithstanding considerable pressure from the industry to expand an additional source of revenue and commercial opportunity. The ITC's view is that the expansion of new forms of media, such as cable and satellite, does not yet justify a reduction of public interest regulation for the free-to-air channels. Nevertheless, some relaxation of regulation has occurred with some differential requirements in respect of terrestrial analogue broadcasting and other kinds of delivery. In its general approach to sponsorship regulation, the ITC maintains that its principal objective is "to ensure that the development of this source of revenue and programme finance does not alter the character of programme services in such a way that they become adversely influenced by commercial considerations".[62] In keeping with its developmental approach to this area, the Sponsorship Code was revised in 1994, following an extensive review, and the same process has been repeated in 1997.

Two main principles underlie the ITC's approach. The one which is first mentioned in the Code is "maintaining the distinction between advertising and sponsor credits, in order to ensure that credits are not used as a means of extending allowable advertising minutage."[63] Here, it will be recalled that precise regulation of advertising time is essential to constructing a competitive environment for advertisers. The other principle appears later and relates to sponsor influence: "A core principle of this Code is the preservation of programme integrity by not allowing programme agendas to be distorted for commercial purposes."[64]

In maintaining the first of these principles, the ITC has been required to respond to the ingenuity of advertisers in creating

---

[62] ITC, *Review of ITC Code of Programme Sponsorship: Explanatory Memorandum* (1996) para. 5.

[63] Sponsorship Code, r. 2.1.

[64] Sponsorship Code, r. 9.1.

different ways of financing programme production. For the purposes of the Code, a programme is deemed to be sponsored if "any part of its costs of production or transmission is met by an advertiser with a view to promoting its own or another's name, trade mark, image, activities and products or other direct or indirect commercial interests". Elaborating this definition, the rule stipulates that "advertiser-supplied" programmes will be deemed to be sponsored if the programme funders have contributed to the programme for promotional rather than investment purposes. Conversely, a barter arrangement, whereby a programme is provided in exchange for airtime, does not in itself make the programme sponsored. Similarly, merchandising or licensing arrangements based on characters or elements of a programme (such as the sale of toy figures or any objects carrying representations of the programme's characters or scenes) are not deemed to be sponsorship, provided the programme or its transmission are not funded "in any way whatsoever" by the manufacturer or licensee. Some of these distinctions are, of course, very fine. Where children's programmes are created, for example, in order to maximise the potential for merchandising, the success or failure of the merchandiser's business, and hence the royalty payments received by the programme-maker, are dependent on the programme's content.

Editorial independence is rightly regarded as crucial; the rule is simply that "No sponsor is permitted any influence on either the content or the scheduling of a programme in such a way as to affect the editorial independence and responsibility of the broadcaster". The ITC has been troubled by advertiser-supplied programmes, but it has adopted a more relaxed approach to consumer advice programmes by allowing sponsorship of programmes offering general advice in the sponsor's field of interest, provided they do not actually advise what to buy.

The coverage of events and locations also raises particular difficulties of sponsor influence, but the test is what can be clearly justified by the editorial needs of the programme itself. To determine whether an event has *bona fide* non-television status, television coverage must not be the principal purpose of the event and the event must be open to members of the public irrespective of whether or not it is televised. In respect of tobacco sponsorship and branding, there is a requirement that licensees should comply with the voluntary agreement reached between the Minister for Sport and the

Tobacco Manufacturers' Association.[65] This imposes limits on the location of event advertising in relation to television camera sight-lines, prevents tobacco advertisements on participants and officials, and prevents arena design and colouring from resembling the sponsor's corporate identity.

It is an important requirement that sponsors be identified, but problems have been created with the use of "straplines" (corporate slogans) which often function as advertising slogans. They are permitted in vision only. Advertising messages, as such, continue to be forbidden and the absence of sound in straplines is considered to assist in maintaining the distinction between advertising and sponsorship.[66] To that end, there are detailed rules about sponsor credits. The credit must identify the sponsor and explain the sponsor's connection with the programme, for example, "sponsored by" or "in association with", but it may not give the impression that the programme has been made by the sponsor, for example, "brought to you by". While credits may indicate the general connection between a sponsor and a brand or the nature of the sponsor's business, it may not show the sponsor's product or service and may not contain promotional material. For Channels 3 and 4, there are limits on the length of credits.

Maintaining the distinction between advertising and sponsorship, rule 10 of the Sponsorship Code deals with promotional references: "it is unlikely that any reference at all [. . .] to the sponsor will be editorially justified", and the same is likely to be true of any product or service. The issue is closely related to "product placement", which is prohibited by rule 12 of the Sponsorship Code and defined as "the inclusion of, or a reference to, a product or service within a programme in return for payment or any other valuable consideration to the programme maker or ITC licensee (or any representative or associate of either)." But where a product or service is an essential element within a programme, the programme-maker may acquire it at no cost, or less than full cost, in exceptional circumstances; in that case, it is not product placement provided no undue prominence is given to the product or service in question. Obviously, production teams will be keen to trim their budgets by obtaining such donated goods and services, and the companies who

---

[65] On January 31, 1995.

[66] The ability to register such straplines as trademarks, under the Trademarks Act 1994, has complicated this problem.

donate the items will be hoping for some promotional benefit. There may be a fine line between pure generosity and encouraging a programme-maker to find room for the item in the programme. The Code attempts to deal with this problem by emphasising editorial independence and stressing that there should be "no additional inducement nor negotiation or agreement circumscribing the nature of references to the product or service or their manner of appearance". More generally, and in addition, the ITC's Programme Standards Code, rule 10.6, prohibits undue prominence for commercial goods and services in programmes of any kind, whether sponsored or not. There has been some pressure on the ITC to allow "masthead programming", whereby programming is made or funded by a publisher, incorporates the name of the publisher's product — for example, a magazine — and includes similar editorial content. Initially, the Commission was only prepared to relax its approach in respect of channels other than Channels 3, 4 and 5 but masthead programming will be allowed on all channels from the autumn of 1998. However, the sponsorship rules will be revised to ensure that the distinction between editorial content and advertising is maintained.

Finally, some sponsorship is absolutely banned and this reflects the provisions of Article 17 of the Broadcasting Directive. "Sponsorship is allowed only for whole programme or substantive programme strands. [. . .] No other element of the television service may be sponsored, including items of station presentation or continuity, or viewers' competitions" (rule 5). However, "showcases" (themed programme blocks) and "seamless" channels (without distinct programmes) may be sponsored, provided other prohibitions do not apply. Sponsorship is also prohibited for those who manufacture or provide either tobacco products or pharmaceutical products available only on prescription (rule 4). But the Code goes further than the Directive in preventing any body whose objects are wholly or mainly of a political nature from sponsoring programmes, together with any manufacturer or supplier of any product or service which is prohibited from being advertised under the Advertising Code. Importantly, the sponsorship of news and current affairs is also not allowed (rule 8). News includes items ranging from local to international coverage, together with business and financial reports which contain interpretation and comment. The rule makes some concession for what are described as "specialist news reports", however, provided they are presented outside the context of general news programmes. These consist of reports about matters such as the weather, cultural matters, sports, traffic, and travel.

As with advertising, the guiding principles for sponsorship regulation are based on a combination of public service, consumer protection and market fairness. The latter has had a particularly strong influence on the elaborate scheme which has emerged to provide a "level playing field." The partitioning of advertising and sponsorship, on the one hand, and programming, on the other, is crucial to media independence. But equally, the regulator is under strong pressure from the industry to maintain strict control of advertising time and to sustain the distinction between product selling and promotional publicity.

B. Ownership

Concern about the nature of ownership and control in the media has been voiced almost since the development of modern mass media.[67] The principal reasons have been summarised as the need "to keep the market open for newcomers and to prevent any tendency towards editorial uniformity or domination by a few groups."[68] The first reason refers to competition regulation in general, the second to pluralism as an element of freedom in communication. In addition, reasons of economic or cultural protectionism have been advanced to explain restrictions on foreign ownership of domestic media companies.

As a subject of competition regulation, the media industry raises the same kinds of problems that are experienced in other industries. The aim of regulation is to prevent single firms from controlling too much of the market. The justification for doing so is that, unless the tendency to monopoly power is restrained, excessive prices will be

---

[67] For a contemporary survey, see G. Williams, *Britain's Media: How They Are Related* (2nd ed. 1996). This section draws on research being undertaken by the Manchester Media Project, directed by myself, Peter Humphreys and David Young, which is investigating "Regulating for Media Pluralism: Issues in Competition and Ownership". The project examines developments in the United Kingdom, Germany and the European Community and is funded by the Economic and Social Research Council as part of its Media Economics and Media Culture Programme (award No. L126251009). The project's results are due to be reported in 1999.

[68] Home Office, *Broadcasting in the 90s: Competition, Choice and Quality* (1988) (White Paper) Cm. 517, para. 6.48.

charged to the consumer and there will be no incentive to produce a wide range of products. The result will be a loss of general welfare from the lack of choice and the failure fully to exploit resources. In principle, the problems of regulation are no different for the media industry: the regulator needs to identify the relevant market, determine the extent of market power which the firm enjoys and judge whether that is being abused or otherwise inhibits full competition.[69]

Whether competition regulation is adequate to deal with problems in the media industry depends on the way that is characterised. If media companies are regarded as supplying a particular kind of consumer product — broadly entertainment — there is no case for treating them in a special way, but if the media's association with free communication is considered significant, the economic criteria for competition may be insufficient to allow a diversity of viewpoints to reach the readership or audience.[70] In economic theory, the idea of "market contestability" has underpinned the orthodox approach to competition: whether a monopoly may be said to exist depends on the extent to which it is possible for competitors to enter a market. In Veljanovski's words:

> "Consider the newspaper industry [. . .] while some media companies have many interests and are relatively large, they are not dominant. Newcomers can and do challenge established newspapers, which must compete both with those new entrants and with other established titles."[71]

If this view appears technical and unreal, it is because, for the consumer, the *experience* of diversity does not coincide with its mere possibility. In practice, a 25 per cent share of national newspaper circulation may well be thought to constitute effective dominance; it is rather expensive to start a newspaper.

This latter sentiment reflects the basis for the intuitive approach to controlling media ownership which has developed in regulatory practice. The aim has been to counter the fear that a large portion of media output will be dominated by one or a few powerful voices. It is intuitive, however, because there is a certain amount of ambiguity about the way media enterprises are controlled and the precise

---

[69] See generally, R. Whish, *Competition Law* (3rd ed. 1993).

[70] See D. Glencross, "Television Ownership and Editorial Control" (1996) 2 *Yearbook of Media and Entertainment Law* 3–19.

[71] C. Veljanovski, *The Media in Britain Today* (1990), p. 18.

location of the power that is exercised over them. In the era of the press "barons", there was less difficulty in identifying sources of control. Although interference in editorial policy was rarely admitted, there was often a pervasive proprietorial interest in what was published.[72] The situation is less clear today as modern communications tend to be shaped by the much more diffuse power of large companies. Furthermore, the trend towards conglomeration, whereby a large company will hold stakes in a range of market sectors, has made it even more difficult to trace the impact of ownership on the final media product. While some corporations have grown by concentrating on media matters, others have adopted a much more general strategy whereby media interests form only a small part of the overall enterprise.

Murdock has highlighted a number of distinctions which have to be made in order to describe the nature of control that may be exercised. Thus, "allocative control" refers to the formulation of overall policy, including the distribution of financial resources. "Operational control" is concerned with the effective use of the resources allocated and the way that shapes the range and content of the media product.[73] Furthermore, it is possible to describe control in instrumental terms, emphasising the power wielded by particular individuals and groups, or in structural terms, stressing the general political and economic environment and its influence on decisions. Any resulting analysis will be extremely complex and it may become difficult to separate causality from correlation in examining the precise relationship between corporate power and media content. In the absence of firm knowledge about its effects, however, it has appeared reasonable to adopt a cautious approach and to follow the feeling that an excessive concentration of corporate power in the media enterprise, especially in the programming media, will have a deleterious effect on the quality of knowledge that it provides.[74]

The other set of concerns about concentration of power in the media applies not so much to combinations of media ownership as to

---

[72] See S. Koss, *The Rise and Fall of the Political Press in Britain* (1990).

[73] See generally, G. Murdock, "Large Corporations and the Control of the Communications Industries" in *Culture, Society and the Media* (M. Gurevitch *et al.* 1982).

[74] The assumption that there is a fairly direct relationship between ownership and content has also been made in United States regulation, but there is little evidence that diversity in one has produced plurality in the other. See M. Price & J. Weinberg, "The Telecommunications Act of 1996" (1996) 2 *Yearbook of Media and Entertainment Law* 99–110.

the infiltration of external sources of power that can use the media to enhance that power. Thus, there have long been restrictions on ownership and control by foreign investors on the simply protectionist grounds that the interests of British broadcasting or business would be adversely affected. The point is related to arguments in favour of quotas for British and European programming. So, too, in the interests of media independence, it is considered desirable that political organisations and government should not be able to invest in television and radio. Although similar considerations appear to apply to control by religious organisations, the principle has recently been relaxed in relation to radio. In the same vein, other organisations involved in communication may have too much influence to justify their ownership or control of other media ventures.[75]

The Press

Traditionally, economic arrangements for the press have involved a minimum of intervention by the State. To own a newspaper has been regarded as the commercial manifestation of the liberty to speak. The press has operated in the context of the market and, for the most part, the only regulatory constraints that it endures are those that exist generally to constitute the market. While this freedom of commercial operation is regarded as a means of safeguarding newspapers from interference by government, it has been recognised, especially since the Second World War, that broader interests in freedom of communication will not be served by unrestrained private ownership if the effect is to introduce distortions in the way knowledge is distributed.

One issue relating to press ownership is the use of proprietorial power.[76] Generally, the law does not distinguish between the owners of newspapers and their editors and journalists. The latter are regarded as professional mouthpieces for the proprietor, but without any independent claim to protection for their own freedom of expression. Proprietorial influence is more diffuse in the modern press, with individual control[77] having been replaced by corporate

---

[75] (Sadler), *Enquiry into Standards of Cross-Media Promotion* (1991) Cm. 1436.
[76] See, generally, T. Gibbons, "Freedom of the Press: Ownership and Editorial Values" [1992] *Public Law* 279–299.
[77] See J. Curran & J. Seaton, *Power Without Responsibility* (5th ed. 1997) chap. 7.

ownership by a relatively few large companies, some specialising in media matters but others regarding the media as a further diversification of already widespread interests.[78] Although patterns of ownership can be documented,[79] the influence of owners' views on editorial decisions is less easy to quantify because the nature of corporate ownership (discussed above) often makes it difficult to locate the source of any influence. Nevertheless, there is evidence of proprietorial intervention in editorial matters[80] and this raises concerns that media power is not being used to further democratic interests.

Such concerns do not carry much weight in a market environment where a newspaper is no more than a property right, rather than a public service. Editors and journalists are the employees of proprietors, so the principal way to protect them is by contract, assuming the proprietor is willing to bargain away his or her interests. An interesting device for creating institutional constraints on the relationship between editors and proprietors is illustrated in the ownership of *The Guardian* and *The Observer*. The papers are owned by The Guardian and Manchester Evening News plc which is owned, in turn, by The Scott Trust. Editors are employed so that the papers "shall be carried on as nearly as may be upon the same principles as they have heretofore been conducted."[81] Since the Trust selects its own members, it perpetuates its own values which it advances in selecting its editors. However, once the editors are chosen, the trustees do not intervene in editorial policy, whether or not it will affect circulation figures. Indeed, the Trust is used to subsidise the newspapers in times of economic hardship. Apart from the policy of the Scott Trust, the Press Complaints Commission has encouraged newspapers to write guarantees of independence into editorial contracts,[82] but their efficacy is uncertain.

Another approach to limiting proprietorial influence on editorial decisions has been the appointment of independent directors to safeguard editorial values in cases of newspaper mergers. Example

---

[78] Murdock, above, n. 73.

[79] See G. Williams, above, n. 67. See also C. Veljanovski, *The Media in Britain* (1990). Formerly, the Annual Reports of the Press Council provided details of newspaper ownership.

[80] For example, Koss, above, n. 72. See also, J. Curran & J. Seaton, above, n. 77; particular examples are H. Evans, *Good Times, Bad Times* (1983) and F. Giles, *Sundry Times* (1986).

[81] See P. Schlesinger, *The Scott Trust* (1986, reprinted 1991) p. 7.

[82] PCC, *Annual Report and Accounts* (1997).

were the purchases of *The Times*, first by Thomson and later by News International, and Lonrho's takeover of *The Observer*. The Monopolies Commission rightly regarded such appointments as little more than symbolic,[83] since the directors cannot effectively control the newspaper's policy and can only resort to publicising their disagreements with the company.

Where direct regulation of proprietors' behaviour is not possible, the application of competition policy enables the risks of concentrated media ownership to be at least reduced. The first Royal Commission on the Press, noting the way ownership of the press was becoming increasingly concentrated, drew attention to the possible dangers of monopoly power for the media. The ability to select news, determine its presentation and subject it to analysis could cause the monopolist to exercise a strong influence on public opinion. Even if it were not consciously abused, there might not be sufficient competition to encourage accuracy and efficiency.[84] Although there is no regulation of press content in the United Kingdom, therefore, the economic activities of newspaper companies are governed by general competition law and its aim to reduce monopolistic concentrations of ownership.

However, the law makes special provision for newspaper mergers, in recognition of the press' contribution to freedom of speech. Newspaper transfers and mergers are governed by the Fair Trading Act 1973. Under section 58, a newspaper may not be transferred to a proprietor whose newspapers would have an average circulation of 500,000 copies per day (including the paper to be acquired) unless the relevant minister, the Secretary of State for Trade and Industry, gives consent (conditionally or unconditionally). Normally, that consent cannot be given until a report has been obtained from the Monopolies and Mergers Commission. The exceptions are where the minister is "satisfied that the newspaper concerned in the transfer is not economic as a going concern and as a separate newspaper." In that case, if also satisfied that if the newspaper is to continue as a separate concern, the case is one of urgency, the minister may give her consent without a report. If satisfied that the newspaper is not intended to continue as a separate newspaper, the minister must give consent unconditionally and without a report. In addition, where the

---

[83] Monopolies Commission, *The Times and Sunday Times* (1966–67) H.C. 273.

[84] Royal Commission on the Press, *Report* (1949) Cmd. 7700, para. 274. See also Royal Commission on the Press, *Final Report* (1977) Cmnd. 6810, chap. 14.

paper to be merged has a circulation of 50,000 or less, the minister may also give consent without such a report. This latter provision represents a relaxation of the former threshold of 25,000 and allows companies to undertake more acquisitions in the regional markets without regulatory intervention.[85] Under section 59 of the Fair Trading Act 1973, the Monopolies and Mergers Commission has to consider whether the transfer may be expected to operate against the public interest, taking into account all relevant interests and, "in particular, the need for accurate presentation of news and free expression of opinion."

Generally, the legislation is invoked in respect of local newspaper transfers or mergers. Transfers of national newspapers have proved more controversial because they show the relative weakness of the regulatory arrangements in the face of strong commercial pressure, especially in response to loss-making ventures such as quality newspapers. *The Times* was not commercially successful when it was bought by the Thomson organisation (which had extensive television and publishing interests including *The Sunday Times*) in 1966. The then Monopolies Commission was concerned that the paper's editorial identity would be subsumed by the larger group. However, it was faced with the stark choice between allowing the paper to fold and accepting assurances that editorial autonomy would be respected.[86] More worrying, when the same paper was subsequently bought by News International, the matter was not referred to the Commission by the minister. The grounds appeared to be that the paper's survival was at stake, despite the fact that *The Sunday Times* was included in the deal and remained a going concern and that News International owned two major tabloids, *The Sun* and *The News of the World*. Although the details could not be explored by the Commission, some attempt to allay concerns about editorial independent was made by attaching conditions to the minister's consent. The company's articles of association were amended so that the editors could not be removed without the approval of six independent directors appointed by the minister. A similar approach was adopted by the Monopolies Commission itself, in an effort to prevent proprietorial interference, when it approved Lonhro's bid to

---

[85] See Fair Trading Act (Amendment) (Newspaper Mergers) Order 1995, S.I. 1995 No. 1351; Department Of National Heritage, *Media Ownership: The Government's Proposals* (1995) Cm. 2872, para. 6.42.

[86] Monopolies Commission, *The Times and Sunday Times* (1966–67) H.C. 273.

purchase *The Observer* when the paper was experiencing financial difficulties.[87]

The United Kingdom's competition law is currently being revised to bring it into line with the European Community's approach to such regulation. The Competition Bill 1997 does not alter the merger provisions relating to newspapers, however. The reason given by the government is that a special regime for such mergers continues to be required because of their impact on freedom and variety of expression of opinion.[88] This is true of the Monopolies and Mergers Commission's role (which will operate as part of a broader Competition Commission when the Bill becomes law) but the explanation ignores the effect of the wide discretion given to ministers and the fact that, in the past, such discretion has not noticeably been used to further media pluralism. There is too much scope for political pressure to be exerted and insufficient scrutiny of the parties' economic positions before the political decisions are taken. It would be better if the competition authorities had an independent brief to examine transfers of ownership in the press which came to their attention. Furthermore, there is still much to recommend the suggestion of the third Royal Commission on the Press that, unlike the present position where there is virtually a presumption that a proposed merger or transfer should go ahead, the onus should be placed on its supporters to show that it would serve the public interest.[89] There is limited provision for such a test to be applied in relation to cross-holdings between the press and the programming media, and that will be discussed below.

Commercial Programming

The public ownership of the public service broadcasters was discussed earlier. The main focus of ownership regulation in the programming media concerns the commercial sector. In the past, the legislative approach was to provide a broad framework for dealing with ownership and control, with the IBA filling in the detail where

---

[87] Monopolies Commission, *The Observer and George Outram & Co.* (1981–82) H.C. 378.

[88] Department of Trade and Industry, *A Prohibition Approach to Anti-Competitive Agreements and Abuse of Dominant Position* (1997).

[89] Above, n. 84, paras 14.25 *et seq.*

necessary. It adopted a rather strict interpretation of its duty to secure adequate competition between programme contractors as to finance and control,[90] and had a rule that a body holding over 5 per cent in one ITV company would not normally be allowed to hold more than 1 per cent in another ITV company.[91] For other ownership patterns, the approach provided flexibility, but it also brought some uncertainty about the standards being applied and the need to rely on the discretion of an agency that did not always find it easy to resist commercial pressures — for example, in relation to cross-ownership, discussed later.

An alternative approach was introduced by sections 5 and 83 and Schedule 2 of the Broadcasting Act 1990, which contain detailed rules for the ITC and R.A. to enforce. They are required to secure that disqualified persons do not become licence holders and that other restrictions on the holding of licences are complied with. In its original version, Schedule 2 was very complex in an attempt to be all-inclusive and to trace corporate ownership to the controlling interest so far as possible. Predictability was obtained, but at the expense of excessive rigidity and the need to anticipate all difficulties in advance in order to avoid loopholes.[92] Despite the inevitable loss of responsibility, however, in a deregulatory Act that replaced the general duty to provide public service with one of promoting competition, the ITC and R.A. appeared content to have their discretion curtailed in exchange for clear authority to restrain financial and commercial judgments. Under the Broadcasting Act 1996, however, a new Schedule 2 was substituted in the 1990 Act and, although it retains and compounds many of the intricacies of the original, it returns a considerable amount of discretion to the regulators to implement a new scheme for ownership control.

Before considering that scheme, some general constraints may be noted. In Part I of Schedule 2, as substituted, there is an all-embracing definition of "control". It includes the holding or beneficial entitlement to more than 50 per cent of the equity in a company or possessing more than 50 per cent of its voting power. But it also allows the regulators to look through technical arrangements and attribute control to the person who effectively

---

90 Broadcasting Act 1981, s. 20(2)(b).

91 IBA, *Background Paper* (1990) No. 5.

92 See I. Ehrlich and R. Posner, "An economic analysis of legal rulemaking" (1974) 3 *J. Legal Studies* 257–286.

determines corporate policy and decisions, that is, the person able "by whatever means and whether directly or indirectly, to achieve the result that the affairs of the body are conducted in accordance with his wishes". In addition, control is attributed to a person who holds or possesses only 50 per cent of equity or voting power, but who has made an arrangement with another person as to the manner in which voting power will be exercised. These latter provisions were inserted by the 1996 Act to close loopholes which became apparent under the original provisions. "Warehousing" arrangements had been set up, whereby interests were held in excess of what might legally be held by one company, by creating corporate structures that were technically acceptable. In addition, "deadlocking" arrangements, whereby two shareholders have equal holdings or voting power so that neither of them is able to control the company on its own, enabled evasion of the spirit, if not the letter, of the law.[93]

1. Disqualifications

Under section 5(1) and section 83(1) of the 1990 Act, the regulators must do all that they can to ensure that a "disqualified person" does not become or remain the holder of a licence. The list of such disqualified persons is contained in Schedule 2, as amended by the 1996 Act, and reflects a variety of policy issues. First, there are individuals who do not have an appropriate connection with the United Kingdom because they are neither European Community (E.C.) nationals who are ordinarily resident within the Community nor persons ordinarily resident in the United Kingdom. Similarly, corporate bodies are disqualified unless they are formed under the law of a Member state and have their registered office or principal place of business there.[94] Secondly, and in accordance with the traditional principle of political impartiality in broadcasting, bodies with political connections are disqualified. This includes a local authority or its officers, a body whose objects are wholly or mainly of a political nature or its officers or affiliates, companies that are associates of local authorities or political bodies, and companies in which local authorities, political bodies, their affiliates or associated companies have more than a 5 per cent interest, or any bodies that they control. Reaching further back, the list continues with any body

---

[93] See *R. v. Radio Authority ex p. Bull* [1997] 2 All E.R. 561.

[94] Ordinary residence or incorporation in the Isle of Man or the Channel Islands counts for this purpose.

which is controlled by a non-E.C. person together with any body that is controlled by one of the foregoing politically connected bodies and any company in which it has more than a 5 per cent interest.

The requirement of an E.C. connection does not apply to local delivery services nor to the new digital services. The aim appears to have been to encourage overseas, especially North American, investment to establish the services. The same provision is made for satellite services and this has been controversial because it has been objected that it gives an unfair advantage to programming that is channelled via the medium-powered Astra satellites. In practice, that means the BSkyB services owned by News International. During the passage of the 1990 Bill, however, the government suggested that the case for protectionism depended on the scarcity of British frequencies but, since Astra satellites operate from Luxembourg, they would be unaffected by British regulation. Furthermore, the government argued that investment in Astra was already established and was unlikely to be affected by British policy; the effect of denying licences would be to remove finance and employment from the United Kingdom, and with no obvious advantage. Those arguments have much force, recognising that British investment in cable and satellite has been slow, but they avoid the reason why the issue was raised at all, namely that the Schedule does not deal with the extent to which interests in Astra services and the British national press should be allowed to coincide.[95] Currently, BSkyB has a *de facto* monopoly over British satellite broadcasting and its parent company, News International, owns *The Times* and *The Sun*, whose combined national daily circulation is over 30 per cent, together with *The Sunday Times* and the *News of the World* whose combined Sunday circulation is over 35 per cent. Even if there is no concentration of editorial policy, and it is difficult to demonstrate that one way or the other, there is obviously commercial pressure to cross-promote the two media.

Another area of controversy concerns the amount of influence that religious bodies should have on various services. It might be thought that religious beliefs are likely to be as strongly held and as influential as political beliefs, so that religious bodies should also be disqualified persons. A strong religious lobby ensured, however, that religious organisations can own radio stations and, while they cannot own

---

[95] See *Hansard* Standing Committee F, Broadcasting Bill, January 25 to January 30, 1990, cols. 294–392.

television services, a discretion has been vested in the ITC to exempt satellite services and programme services specially made for cable. Any dangers that may arise from exploitation, in relation to fund-raising, the manipulation of religious feeling or "American-style" evangelism, should be contained by the ITC's control of ownership and the regulation of programme content. Since these dangers are related to the exclusivity of the audience, one anomaly under this regime is the, perhaps remote, possibility that a national radio service could be controlled by a religious organisation.[96]

Other disqualifications may be mentioned more briefly. Any body that receives more than half its finance from public funds[97] is not allowed to own or control a radio service. This reflects the view that commercial enterprises should not have public subsidies although, in doing so, it glosses over the distinction between local and community radio. Disqualification can also arise where a local authority or a body already disqualified because of their political connections is, in the opinion of the ITC or R.A., exerting an influence over a licensee in a manner adverse to the public interest. In addition, the BBC and the Welsh Authority are disqualified, as are advertising agencies and their associates. However, unlike the previous position, companies connected with the music industry are not precluded from ownership or control of radio stations, despite their already strong associations with them.

2. Accumulations

The next part of Schedule 2 deals with restrictions to prevent accumulations of interests within and between licensed services. In the original version, a complicated method was set out for establishing concentrations of ownership through "cascading" layers of corporate control, and further detail was provided in secondary legislation.[98] In brief, and to give a flavour of the approach, any one person could hold only the following licences: one in the case of services provided on national Channel 3, Channel 5, and national radio; two in the case of regional Channel 3; and thirty-five in the case of local radio services. Special provision was made for regional Channel 3, national Channel 3 and Channel 5, so that a licensee for

---

[96] See *Hansard* H.C.Deb. Vol. 172, cols. 154–168 (May 8, 1990).
[97] Other than a local authority, the BBC or the Welsh Authority.
[98] Broadcasting (Restrictions on the Holding of Licences) Order 1991 (S.I. 1991 No. 1176, as amended by S.I. 1993 No. 3199 and S.I. 1995 No. 1924).

one of those services could not hold or have an interest of more than 20 per cent in one of the others. Nor could holders of any of those licences, taken as a whole, and holders of domestic satellite or national radio licences have more than a 20 per cent interest in one of the others. In regional Channel 3, it had only been possible, originally, for a licence for a "large" region to be held together with a licence for one of the six smaller regions, but that restriction was removed in 1993. The two London licences could not be held by the same person, however. Furthermore, where two such regional Channel 3 licences were held by one person, any interest in a third licence was limited to 20 per cent and any further interest was limited to 5 per cent. The 20 per cent rule also applied to cross-holdings between Channels 3 and 5, national radio services and, broadly, different types of satellite service. It also applied where the areas served by regional Channel 3, local radio and local delivery services coincided to a significant extent. Furthermore, all these restrictions applied to companies which controlled licensees. For the radio sector, the basic method was applied through a "points" system which was introduced through delegated legislation.[99]

It will be clear that this approach to accumulations was extremely complicated and the use of delegated legislation to lend it some flexibility (three statutory instruments in the five years that it operated) did not assist. It also promoted a rather mechanical way of quantifying media power and the cascading figures of 20 per cent or 5 per cent represented only estimates of the holdings that are needed to give effective control.[1] These considerations, together with strong industry pressure to relax the rules further,[2] prompted a search for different ways of regulating media ownership. Similar issues were being discussed at the European Commission[3] and in Germany[4]

---

[99] *ibid.*

[1] Under previous legislation, the IBA used to interpret control in a very liberal manner, to mean a voting interest of more than 50 per cent, this being the strictly legal minimum.

[2] A lobbying body, the British Media Industry Group, was formed for the purpose. See G. Williams, above, n. 67.

[3] European Commission, *Pluralism and Media Concentration in the Internal Market* (1992) COM(92) 480. See L. P. Hitchens, "Media Ownership and Controls: A European Approach" (1994) 57 *Modern Law Review* 585–601; A.J. Harcourt, "Regulating for Media Concentration: The Emerging Policy of the European Union" (1996) *Utilities Law Review* 202–210. M. Feintuck, "Good News for the Media? Developments in the Regulation of Media Ownership in Britain and Europe" (1995) 1 *European Public Law* 549–562.

[4] See P. Humphreys, *Media and Media Policy in Germany* (2nd ed. 1996).

during the mid-1990s, and the theme which emerged as a likely basis for legislation was the notion of "market share" as a means of measuring media power.

The basic idea which underlies the market share approach is that media power should be assessed by reference to the influence that it has on its readership and audience. Rather than regulating crudely in terms of individual media sectors (newspapers, radio, television), there should be an attempt to quantify the relative impact of different kinds of media on the individuals who use them. Different genres within each medium and their relative impact on pluralism should, ideally, be fundamental to such an assessment; competition issues aside, extensive control over news and current affairs output might be expected to raise greater concern than dominance in comedy or entertainment. Furthermore, if influence on audience or readers' opinion is the purpose of regulation, the relationship between radio and television companies and the wider media market (books, magazines, cinema, video, theatre) should be included in the measure.[5] Obviously, the problem is how to devise a suitable measure. One approach is to use revenue as an indication of economic power and, therefore, ability to attract readerships and audiences. A money measure provides a common denominator across different media and genres, indicating the relative value which is credited to them. However, the precise relationship between revenue and influence is indirect, may be insensitive to multiple-genre services, may vary depending on the investment policy of the medium, and would not reflect publicly owned media, although it would be possible to introduce weightings to correct those problems. The alternative approach to revenue measures is to concentrate on the audience. An easy method is to measure audience share (receivers tuned to a channel) and readership (copies of newspaper sold), but it is crude in not taking into account both the relative influence of different media sectors and the nature of different audiences and readerships. Even simpler as a measure is the concept of audience or readership "reach": the number of people who view a programme or read a newspaper as a proportion of the total number of people in the market. This appears to capture the idea of media influence most closely and offers a common denominator between media, but it only

---

[5] For further discussion of these issues, see B. Robinson, "Market Share as a Measure of Media Concentration" in T. Congdon *et al.*, *The Cross Media Revolution: Ownership and Control* (1995). The following outline draws upon his analysis.

provides an aggregate figure, does not show intensity of consumption and, crucially, it is difficult to survey in practice.

Notwithstanding the theoretical reservations about market share, the idea was the centrepiece of the consultation paper, *Media Ownership: The Government's Proposals*.[6] It duly explored the possibility of an exchange rate which reflected each kind of media's relative ownership of the total media market, but there was little consideration of the way media markets should be defined and the relationship between markets and media influence was not explored. In the end, devising a suitable exchange rate proved too difficult for the legislators and a modified scheme was introduced to quantify market share. The legislation was implemented in advance of the conclusions of the European Commission's discussions on media ownership and the draft E.C. directive which had initially been expected during 1996. Furthermore, some aspects of the previous ownership scheme have been incorporated into the new one. There is, indeed, an experimental quality about the revised scheme.

The main idea is to calculate and regulate media ownership on the basis of the share of the market that the media acquire. The new scheme uses a method of approximating market share by adopting the measurement of audience share in television and radio, and circulation figures for newspapers. However, the general effect will be to liberalise the market and to reduce restrictions on media ownership, and this was considered desirable because it was assumed that large conglomerations in the United Kingdom would be needed to provide adequate competition against foreign, especially North American, companies. At the same time, the government insisted that its policy was to enhance diversity and plurality in the media and to prevent concentrations of ownership which might be considered against the public interest. In theory, the market share approach should have resulted in a legislative scheme that was much less complex than the one it replaced. But, in practice, the substituted Schedule 2 combines audience and readership share with various fixed limits on ownership relations and, for some purposes, combines the previous cascading of different percentage interests in different media services.

The basic rules are as follows. For television services, no person with more than a 15 per cent share of total audience time may do any of the following:

---

[6] (1995) Cm. 2872.

(a) hold two or more licences for Channels 3 and 5, satellite television, licensable programme or digital programme services; or

(b) have more than a 20 per cent interest in two or more licensees for such services; or

(c) hold one licence and have a 20 per cent interest in another such licensee; or

(d) provide a foreign satellite service (that is, established outside the U.K. but directed to U.K. audiences) and hold such a licence or have a 20 per cent interest in such a licence; or

(e) hold a digital programme services licence providing two or more of those services.

For these purposes, and to prevent accretion of interests, half the audience time which counts for a service in which a person has a 20 per cent interest is attributed to his or her primary audience share.[7] For television, audience time will be calculated on the basis of total audience time in respect of all television services capable of being received in the British Isles, using figures supplied by the Broadcasting Audience Research Board but subject to the ITC's discretion to determine their relevance. There are absolute limits on the holding of a Channel 3 licences (no national licence to be held with a Channel 5 licence, and no overlapping regional licences) and multiplex services (no more than three). There are also restrictions on overlapping digital and analogue services and a points system is introduced in respect of digital programme services. In relation to radio services, the 15 per cent threshold is again adopted but in conjunction with the points system that has already been established for radio audiences. This divides services so that 25 points are attributed to national radio or digital sound programme services. Thereafter, 15 points are attributed to other services in Category A (which covers a population exceeding 4.5 million), eight points to Category B (1 to 4.5 million), three points to Category C (400,000 to 1 million), and one point to Category D (less than 400,000). No

[7] This approach is similar to that which had already been adopted in respect of radio licences. In relation to Channel 3, however, the Conservative Government's intention in due course had been to alter the threshold, by order, so that the secondary audience time would be attributed on a 15 per cent interest.

person may hold more than 15 per cent of the total number of points attributable to all radio licences awarded. An absolute limit is placed on holding a national radio service (only one) or providing a national digital sound programme service (only one). There are also restrictions on holding overlapping local radio licences, but they are liberalising in allowing three licences (being no more than two FM or AM) to be held. However, such overlapping interests are subject to a potentially strict public interest test. It is based on the likely reduction in plurality of ownership, the effects on the range of independent radio services available in the local area, the effects on the diversity of sources of information available generally in the area, and the effects on the diversity of opinion on local radio in the area.

3. *Cross-media holdings*

For all the concern about accumulations, the principal anxiety about media concentration relates to cross-media interests. Cross-media holdings exist where the same people own or control combinations of the press, television and radio. It was noted by the Pilkington Committee that many felt that democracy would be threatened by such "an excessive concentration of power to influence and persuade public opinion" which might be used to present "a one-sided presentation of affairs of public concern."[8] For the most part, discussion of these issues centred round the relationship between broadcasting and the press, although they also led to restrictions being imposed on the sharing of interests across radio and television.[9] One result of Pilkington's deliberations, however, and its worries about the commercialisation of independent television at the expense of public service, was the creation of a power to prohibit newspaper shareholdings in programme contractor companies where that would be contrary to the public interest.[10]

The difficulties that a regulatory body can experience, when faced with the strong commercial pressures generated in cross-holdings, were illustrated in the early 1970s, when London Weekend Television was suffering financial and managerial problems. Criticising the ITA, the Annan Committee noted that it had encouraged the press to invest in television in order to offset the

[8] Above, n. 3, para. 627. The committee felt that, although the risk to democracy might be low, some limits had to be set: para. 632.
[9] Broadcasting Act 1981, s. 20(3).
[10] Latterly exercised by the IBA under s. 23 of the 1981 Act.

reduction in revenue that it was anticipated to suffer as advertising switched to the new medium. The Authority had been too lax in the case of LWT, however, in not properly controlling the extent of those interests. It allowed Rupert Murdoch, the newspaper proprietor, to hold a controlling part of LWT's equity (only 7.5 per cent) in order to assist the company in its moment of crisis and, indeed, to become a director for short while. At the same time, he had also acquired a large holding in an independent radio company which covered part of the franchise area. The IBA eventually intervened but not before much public disquiet, which the Committee reiterated, that he had gained unacceptably substantial power; "clearly there is an editorial danger if the same men own both the main media for news and political expression."[11] The Committee regarded the maximum acceptable holding of voting shares by a newspaper in a programme company should be 10 per cent, notwithstanding Murdoch's lower holding in LWT, and the total press interest in any such company should not exceed 25 per cent.

More recent trends in the industry have favoured an increasing relaxation of rules about cross-holdings. Companies have been eager to develop interests in different sectors of the media and, at the international level, large consolidations of corporate power have become regarded as a precondition of competitive success. The Broadcasting Act 1990 responded to this trend by protecting the position of the quasi-public service channels but liberalising cross-holdings more generally. Proprietors of national newspapers could not have more than a 20 per cent interest in a Channel 3 or 5 or national radio service and a 5 per cent interest in any second holding. Local proprietors were not restricted in this way, other than a 20 per cent interest in a regional Channel 3 service that served significantly the same area as the local newspaper. But local proprietors were not allowed more than a 20 per cent interest in a local radio or delivery service. In respect of all these services, there were broadly reciprocal restrictions on licensees' interests in newspapers. A notable omission, however, was the relationship between newspapers and satellite services. It is well known that two national proprietors have major interests in Astra services, indicating an undue concentration of media power. The government argued, however, that to impose restrictions would result in the curtailing of investment or that, in any event, there is such diversity in Astra services that the newspaper

[11] Annan, above, n. 4, para. 13.32.

proprietors would be unable to secure a dominant position for their own channels.[12] This disingenuously ignored the danger that a common corporate policy is likely to create pressure for more homogenised editorial positions or, as has occurred, cross-media promotion.

Under the changes effected by the Broadcasting Act 1996, the substituted Schedule calculates the market share of the press by reference to newspaper circulation, with national and local levels being distinguished. A national newspaper proprietor with a market share of 20 per cent or more may not hold a Channel 3 or 5 licence or a national or local radio licence, and a regional Channel 3 licence may not be held by a proprietor of a local newspaper with a local market share of more than 20 per cent in its coverage area. There are also restrictions, of 20 per cent, on participating interests. The effect is to remove many of the previous upper limits on cross-ownership. Local radio cross-holdings are also restricted; a local radio licence may not be held by a person with a local market share of 50 per cent or more unless the service is shared and he or she does not hold another such licence. In any event, and importantly, the new Schedule provides for a public interest test to be applied in relation to certain cross-holdings. A licence may not be granted for Channel 3, Channel 5, national radio or national digital sound programme services to a company which is, or is connected with, a national or local newspaper proprietor, if the regulator determines that under all the circumstances the holding could be expected to operate against the public interest. An existing licensee for one of those services may not become, or become connected with, such a proprietor, if the regulator makes a similar public interest determination within a one-off, three month period. This public interest test is not invoked, however, where the existing licensee is already a newspaper proprietor or connected with one. There are similar conditions imposed on the awards of Channel 3 and local radio licences, and digital programme services, in relation to national proprietors and local proprietors whose newspapers serve an area which is to a significant extent the same as the programming coverage area. The criteria for operating the public interest test are found in paragraph 13. The first is the desirability of promoting plurality of ownership in the broadcasting and newspaper industries, and diversity in the

[12] See *Hansard* Standing Committee F, Broadcasting Bill, January 25 to January 30, 1990, cols. 294–392.

sources of information available to the public and in the opinions expressed on television or radio or in newspapers. The second criterion is any economic benefits of concentration, such as technical development or an increase in employment or in the value of goods or services exported, and which could be attributed to that particular holding. The final criterion is the effect of the holding of the licence on the proper operation of the market in the broadcasting or newspaper industries or any part of them.

4. Assessment

A number of questions may be raised about the new scheme, although it is too early to assess its full impact.[13] One is the choice of 15 per cent as the threshold figure for television and radio services. It appears to have materialised as the intuitively correct indication of diversity in radio, but without a rational base.[14] Given that public broadcasters account for around 55 per cent of audience share, the threshold effectively means that a commercial licensee cannot acquire more than one third of the remaining audience. Putting it differently, it is considered that media pluralism can be secured by ensuring that the internal pluralism offered by the public broadcasters is complimented by at least three "players" in the commercial sector. The reasons for a 20 per cent threshold for newspaper cross-holdings are equally obscure, although it has had the effect of excluding the two largest current press interests, News International and the Mirror Group, from owning quasi-public service licences.

By contrast, in a similarly sweeping adoption of audience share as the basis of media ownership regulation in Germany, the figure of 30 per cent (equally unjustified) has been adopted as the maximum amount of total audience share which can be held by a broadcasting station. Above that limit, it is presumed that the owner has a dominant position in the market and exerts a prevailing influence on public opinion. Further, any station with a market share of 10 per cent or more will be obliged to provide "windows" of opportunity for smaller stations.[15] In discussion of a draft directive on media

---

[13] This, however, is one of objects of the Manchester Media Project: see above, n. 67.

[14] Originally, no more than six local radio licences could be held by one person and, later, no person could hold a combination of national, local or restricted licences whose total number of points exceeded 15 per cent of the total number of points attributable to all current radio licences.

[15] See P. Humphreys and M. Lang, "Regulating for Media Pluralism and the Pitfalls of *Standortpolitik*: A Study of the Re-regulation of German Broadcasting Ownership Rules" (1998) 7 *German Politics* (August).

concentration in the European Commission,[16] audience share has also been used but in a different way. The proposal has centred round the idea that there should be a 30 per cent upper limit on "monomedia" ownership, that is, ownership in one of the television or radio sectors, in respect of the relevant transmission areas. But this has been supplemented with a further upper limit of 10 per cent on total media ownership (including newspapers) in respect of the market in which the company is operating. The Commission's proposal is intended to be sensitive to the real influence that the media may exert by making the thresholds relative to actual markets. However, the proposal has yet to find agreement as the basis for a European-wide ownership law. One reason is that it does not differentiate between national and regional providers, so that local dominance of a market will be prohibited in the same way as the national dominance of a large multimedia corporation. In terms of media pluralism, this may not be a problem in theory but, in practice, it does not cater for unusual arrangements such as those of Channel 3. The Channel 3 companies have lobbied hard against the Commission's proposals because their local dominance is typically more than 30 per cent in their regions, but their individual national share is typically less than 5 per cent. However, the combined Channel 3 audience share is approaching 30 per cent and the issue turns, in that case, on the significance which is attributed to the networking agreement.

Another issue is the decision to include public service broadcasting in the total audience used as the basis for calculating the share reached by each programme service. This has the effect of depressing the audience share (and apparent market power) of other, commercial operators. Whether that is justified depends on whether there is an identifiable market for television and radio programming as a whole. If some commercial sectors are thought to constitute a separate market, for example, pay-t.v., the inclusion of public service broadcasters in the base may conceal the possible dominance of relatively small companies in such a market.[17] Since the public service

---

[16] See G. Doyle, "From 'Pluralism' to 'Ownership': Europe's Emergent Policy on Media Concentrations Navigates the Doldrums" 3 *The Journal Of Information Law And Technology* (*JILT*) <http://elj.warwick.ac.uk/jilt/commsreg/97—3doyl/>.

[17] According to the figures for January 1998, BBC 1 had 30.8 per cent of the audience share, BBC 2 had 11.5 per cent , Channel 3 combined had 29.1 per cent and Channel 4 had 10.1 per cent. By contrast, the Sky channels together accounted for 5.53 per cent. Of the cable and satellite channels, only Sky One (1.3 per cent) and Sky Sports (1.1 per cent) had a share of greater than one per cent. See ITC, News Release: "Television Audience Share Figures" (1998) 13/98.

broadcasters already cater for internal pluralism, there is a case for focusing entirely on the commercial sector when determining thresholds of concentration.

Other points to note about the new British regime are the greater discretion which has been given to the regulators, both in determining audience share and deciding matters of public interest, although it is not an increase in power that they appear to welcome. However, the one-off application of the cross-ownership test appears half-hearted and leaves no redress where ownership patterns change subsequently. More generally, there are doubts as to whether continued regulation of the structure of the industry can really deliver pluralism of information and opinion.[18] Diversity of ownership may not provide such pluralism if the tendency in the market is for most companies to compete to provide essentially the same kind of product.[19] Yet again, as the media markets converge, the detailed regulation of the terrestrial broadcasting sector may become less significant compared to the relatively unregulated cable and satellite sectors. As it happens, current regulation of television and radio does not depend on a structural approach to achieve its aims. Greater reliance is placed on designating the attributes of each service through licence conditions. It would appear to be possible, then, to dispense with ownership regulation in those sectors altogether, provided the regulators could be trusted to maintain programming standards. Indeed, to assist the ITC in that task, it have been given additional powers to ensure that the quality of service in Channel 3 does not deteriorate when changes of ownership occur.[20] However, although there is relative freedom to transfer ownership, the logic of that path has not been pursued. There is a feeling — basically caution — that an imposed pluralism is not a substitute for a diversity of creative sources and that commercial pressure by a limited number of powerful companies might be too much for the regulators to resist.

Whether cross-ownership between newspapers and electronic media will lead to more homogenised editorial positions or not, a more immediate issue has been that of cross-media promotion. This

---

18 For an earlier discussion of this question, see T. Gibbons, "Freedom of the Press: Ownership and Editorial Values" [1992] *Public Law* 279–299. A similar approach is recently to be found in R. Collins and C. Murroni, *New Media, New Policies* (1996) pp. 73–74.

19 See E. Barendt, "Structural and Content Regulation of the Media" (1997–98) *3 Yearbook of Media and Entertainment Law* 75–95.

20 Under s. 21A of the 1990 Act, inserted by s. 78 of the 1996 Act.

involves the advertising of one media product in another owned by the same company. The main ground for concern is that, in many cases, the promotion may be indirect; for example, the owner's newspaper may report the activities of his satellite service as if it were a news item. The Sadler Enquiry was set up to examine the issue and found that it was not a major problem, but suggested that it could be remedied by self-regulation. An informal code was recommended, to encourage transparency of ownership, to enable readers to make up their own minds about the weight to be given to editorial pronouncements and to guarantee independent editorial judgment. It was envisaged that newspapers would include regular statements, in a prominent position, about the commercial interests associated with them. They would also be expected to allow free access to rivals' advertising and to preserve professional standards of journalism.[21] There has been a complete lack of enthusiasm to implement the recommendation, however, both within the industry and on the part of government. The existence of cross-media promotion remains as a minor, but significant, example of proprietorial interference in editorial decision-making.

Transfers of Ownership

It will be recalled that, before the 1990, the IBA actively discouraged transfers of ownership of programme contractors.[22] The policy underlying the 1990 Act was quite different. Although the ITC and R.A. each have a duty to monitor ownership,[23] that is not intended to prevent takeovers or other changes of ownership in companies holding licences. One reason is that the relationship between the regulators and the progrmme providers has changed and is no longer defined by shared values of public service broadcasting. More generally, there has been a move to deregulation and an expectation that the ITC and R.A. should adopt a lighter touch.

Although it is not obvious on the face of the statute, the legislative aim was to use the competitive tendering process to start to

[21] .(Sadler) *Enquiry into Standards of Cross-Media Promotion* (1991) Cm. 1436.

[22] See *R. v. I.B.A. ex p. Rank Organisation* (1986), *The Times*, March 14.

[23] Although the Broadcasting Act 1990, ss. 3(6) and 86(7), requiring respectively that the ITC's and R.A.'s written consent to transfers reflect a similar provision in the 1981 Act.

restructure the finance and ownership of the broadcasting industry, especially the former ITV sector. For the latter, as indicated in the previous chapter, it was not envisaged that the elaborate procedure contained in the legislation would be invoked again when the first licences expired. Instead, the expectation was that the further changes in ownership and finance would take place through the market process. In anticipation of the newer approach, the ITC showed a more relaxed attitude to Thorn-EMI's proposal to take full control of Thames Television, early in 1991. However, Channel 3 was considered to be a special case, because of its quasi-public service character, and to provide a period of stability at the beginning of the licence period, section 21 of the 1990 Act gave the ITC power to impose a moratorium on transfers of ownership in that sector. The aim was to prevent resources from being used to fight takeover bids rather than being devoted to programming. The moratorium lasted, effectively, for two years, from the award of the licence to the end of the first year of broadcasting.

Financial pressures quickly forced a change in that policy, however. The difficulties which were being experienced by Tyne-Tees Television persuaded the ITC to permit a change of ownership to take place before the end of the moratorium. The company was taken over by Yorkshire Television (although it was technically a merger). Nevertheless, the two companies' licences remained independent of each other. This is a significant feature of the new regime: licences do not alter when different owners assume responsibility for them. They retain their original conditions and the new owner is required to implement the requirements of each licence separately.

The ITC's moratorium expired in 1993. At the same time, in response to demands within the industry for a more liberal approach to ownership, the government revoked the rule preventing two "large" regional licences to be held together. These two developments resulted in a flurry of merger activity and three acquisitions were made in 1994. Carlton took over Central, Granada took over LWT, and MAI group, which owned Anglia, bought Meridian. By the end of that year, those three groupings, together with Yorkshire, accounted for 82 per cent of Channel 3's advertising revenue.[24] In terms of audience share, however, the current figures are less alarming: at the beginning of 1998, Carlton and Central

[24] ITC, *Annual Report and Accounts 1994* (1995), p. 21.

accounted for 7.9 per cent, Granada and LWT accounted for 5.9 per cent and Anglia and Meridian accounted for only 4.6 per cent.

There has been further consolidation of the Channel 3 sector following the further deregulation introduced by the 1996 Act. At the end of 1996, MAI (who had earlier taken over the Anglia and Meridian licences) merged with United News and Media, a large publishing group which owned three national newspapers, *The Express, The Express on Sunday* and the *Daily Star,* together with a number of local newspapers and freesheets. Because the merger took place immediately before the 1996 Act came into effect, under transitional provisions the ITC was obliged to examine it against the public interest test. It concluded, however, that the merger would not have an adverse effect. At the end of 1997, United News and Media made further inroads into Channel 3 by taking over the HTV Group which held the licence for Wales and the West of England. Again, the ITC consulted interested parties on the public interest criteria but, in a rather brief determination, it announced that the takeover would not be expected to operate against the public interest. At the beginning of 1998, the United News and Media group had an audience share of 7.1 per cent.

Potentially more interesting issues have been raised by the consolidation which has taken place in the Scottish media since 1996. At the end of that year, the ITC decided that Scottish Television should be permitted to acquire Caledonian Publishing, a group which owned two Scottish local newspapers in Scottish Television's licence area. One reason was that the newspapers satisfied the cross-ownership criteria in not having a local market share of more than 20 per cent. The other reason was that public interest criteria were satisfied. In deciding whether or not the acquisition would operate against the public interest, the ITC examined the potential effect of the new ownership on the editorial independence of the Caledonian newspapers. It also scrutinised the fact that the Mirror Group owned under 20 per cent of Scottish Television and owned two newspapers in its licence area. However, it concluded that the Mirror Group's influence would not have sufficient effects for the acquisition to fail the test. The ITC also noted the strength and diversity of the Scottish newspaper market, together with the support that it received, in its consultation with the public, for retaining Caledonian Publishing in Scottish ownership as part of a new Scottish Media Group.[25] A few

---

[25] ITC, *News Release:* "Scottish Television plc", (1996) 77/96.

months later, the new group merged with the other Scottish Channel 3 licensee, Grampian Television. A public interest test was not applied because the ITC considered that the Caledonian newspapers did not serve the franchise area, which is the north of Scotland. As with the other changes in ownership, however, Grampian's exclusive licence conditions continue to apply. In terms of the ownership rules in the 1996 legislation, the changes in ownership do not appear significant: the two licensees' audience share at the beginning of 1998 was only 2.7 per cent. However, that figure is based on the total U.K. television audience. In Scotland, the fact is that one group owns much of the country's independent media. That situation is an interesting example of the need to operate ownership rules based on audience share at a local level. It also suggests that the ITC is taking full advantage of the public interest criteria to make decisions based, not on media pluralism, but on what is essentially industrial policy.

However, the latter conclusion must be treated with caution. One difficulty with the ITC's determinations about the public interest is that they provide little detail about the reasoning used to apply the public interest criteria and their relative weight. The ITC has published guidance on the test but it basically repeats the statutory language and imposes a procedure for supplying information.[26] So far, the R.A. has been more open about the way it exercises its discretion.[27] Possibly, there is some reluctance to give reasons which might provide hostages for judicial review. Given the clear trend towards greater concentration in the industry and the possible dangers for media pluralism, however, it is important that the regulatory provide good reasons for allowing such consolidation to take place.

C. Competition

In broadcasting, the Independent Television Commission and the Radio Authority have a major responsibility for promoting competition between programme providers.[28] Where that has

---

[26] ITC, *News Release:* "I.T.C. . . . Guidance on . . . Public Interest Test", (1996) 69/96.

[27] Radio Authority, "Proposed Acquisition of Leicester Sound Ltd by DMG Radio" (1997); this is a detailed account of application of the "radio specific" public interest test for overlapping local frequencies.

[28] Broadcasting Act 1990, ss. 2(2)(a)(ii) and 85(3)(b).

involved more than organising the structure of services, however, they have increasingly been obliged to work in partnership with the principal competition authorities, the Director-General of Fair Trading and the Office of Telecommunications. In many cases, the obligation has been self-imposed, in recognition of the relative lack of experience and expertise in competition regulation. But there are a number of specific areas where the legislation has required the ITC or R.A. to consult or defer to the other regulators.

Channel 3 Networking Arrangements

Originally, the aim of the ITV network agreement was that programmes could be introduced from a particular region to a national audience, with programme-makers in full competition in selling to each other. It developed, however, into a system in which a few large companies were responsible for the majority of programme production and the other, smaller companies had only limited opportunities to supply the network themselves. In addition, the pricing structure tended to favour the larger programme-makers.

Section 39 of the Broadcasting Act 1990 was introduced to restructure the network so as to eliminate the guaranteed quota arrangements which previously existed and to provide a more open, competitive framework. The ITC was empowered to publish guidance about the type of networking arrangements it would find acceptable, prior to the competitive tendering round, and, although it did not prove to be necessary, it could also impose an agreement if one did not emerge voluntarily. In either case, the test to be applied was whether the network enabled Channel 3 to compete effectively with other television services. More generally, the ITC is required to consult with the Director-General of Fair Trading and, once it has settled networking arrangements, refer them to him and inform him about subsequent modifications. For his part, the Director-General is required to report on any referral and determine whether they meet the two limbs of the competition test set out in the 1990 Act. First, the arrangements must not have the actual or intended effect of restricting, distorting or preventing competition in connection with business activity in the United Kingdom.[29] Secondly, if there is such

---

[29] Broadcasting Act 1990, s. 39(2)(a), (3)(a) and (12) and Sched. 4, para. 2(1).

an adverse effect, it must be justified by some countervailing economic benefit.[30] If the Director-General finds against the arrangements, the ITC or the Channel 3 licensees may refer the matter to the Monopolies and Mergers Commission, whose determination is binding.

The new networking arrangements which emerged for Channel 3 represented a major reorganisation. The ITVA agreed a budget for the commissioning and rights acquisition of programmes for network transmission on behalf of all the licensees, and it also set up a Network Centre to administer the budget and organise the Channel's programming schedules. The Network Centre selects proposals from licensees, who maintain responsibility for complying with their licence requirements, and contract with them to include the programme in the network schedule. However, the Director-General of Fair Trading considered that two elements of this agreement were anti-competitive, the requirement for independent producers to contract through licensees rather than directly with the Network Centre, and the practice of acquiring network rights in commissioned programmes for ten years. In terms of the second limb of the competition test, the Director-General considered that the arrangements contributed to improving the production of television services, and that viewers received a fair share of the benefit. But the two anti-competitive elements were not indispensable, so the arrangements failed the test.[31] The ITC and the licensees referred the report to the Monopolies and Mergers Commission, but they agreed with the Director-General[32] and a revised Networking Agreement was duly published in 1993. Independent producers now negotiate directly with the Network Centre and programme rights are not acquired for more than five years.[33]

Generally, the new networking arrangements are a distinct improvement on the old agreement which operated prior to the 1990

---

[30] Broadcasting Act 1990, Sched. 4, para. 2(2); this is based on Art. 85(3) of the Treaty of Rome.

[31] Director-General of Fair Trading, *Channel 3 Networking Arrangements* (1992) December 3.

[32] Monopolies and Mergers Commission, *Channel 3 Networking Arrangements* (1993) April 6.

[33] The Network Centre, *Code of Practice* (1993). There have been subsequent minor modifications to the agreement in 1994 and 1995, the latter increasing the smaller licensees' relative contributions to the network budget, and 1998, modifying the contribution formula.

Act. They provide much wider opportunities for a diversity of programming to reach a national audience, and on a much more competitive basis. However, if the arrangements are tested against the principle of freedom in communication, the benefits are not so obvious. The need to satisfy the Network Centre's schedulers means that the programmes which succeed are those which maximise audience figures during peak viewing times, and that will not necessarily provide a plurality of material. There is a deep tension in the networking arrangements, however. The licensees and the ITC tend to justify them with arguments about regionalism and the traditions of the independent television sector. But the tendency of the current arrangements is to undermine that tradition and, interestingly, the Director-General of Fair Trading did not appear to be convinced about its continued relevance.[34] The major advantage of the agreement, of course, is commercial; it enables companies which are relatively small, by international standards, to share costs, and it strengthens their position against the larger organisations which are tending to dominate the market.

Independent Productions and European Quotas

One of the aims of the Broadcasting Act 1990 was to reduce vertical integration in the media industry, whereby the same company undertook all aspects of the production process from the creative idea to transmission. This policy coincided with lobbying in the European Community for increased opportunities for competition at the European level, in the discussions preceding the European Broadcasting Directive (Television Without Frontiers). The result was a measure which has been retained in current Broadcasting Directive,[35] the requirement in Article 5 that "broadcasters reserve at least 10 per cent of their transmission time, excluding the time appointed to news, sports events, games, advertising, teletext services and teleshopping [. . .] for European works created by producers who are independent of broadcasters." At the Member States' discretion, a programme budget quote of 10 per cent may be substituted instead. The quota may be achieved progressively but it

---

[34] See Director-General of Fair Trading, *Channel 3 Networking Arrangements* (1992) December 3, paras 11.49–11.55.
[35] See above, n. 41.

must include recent works, that is, ones transmitted within five years of their production.

The 1990 Act has imposed a stricter requirement than this, however, in respect of the terrestrial licensed services and the BBC.[36] They are obliged to ensure that at least 25 per cent of their programming is provided by means of a range of independent productions, to be measured by reference the cost of acquisition as well as programme content.[37] In the case of the BBC, the Director-General of Fair Trading has a duty to monitor the Corporation's practice. Although it fell just short of the target initially, it has more recently surpassed it.[38] The quota was imposed on a voluntary basis in 1987, adopting a recommendation of the Peacock Committee. Together with the creation of Channel 4, it has provided a valuable underpinning for a vibrant independent production industry in the United Kingdom.

A related quota, but with quite different aims, deals with the European origin programmes. It was included in the European Broadcasting Directive as a counterbalance to the more economically liberal measures which Television Without Frontiers represented.[39] Championed by France, but opposed by the United Kingdom and Germany, it was partly intended to protect the European broadcasting industry from overseas and especially North American domination, but it is also an attempt to conserve a sense of European cultural identity. Although there was a concerted effort to strengthen the provision in the European Parliament debates prior to issuing the revised Broadcasting Directive, they were not successful[40] and the present Article 4 is virtually identical to the original. It requires Member States to ensure, where practicable, that broadcasters reserve "a majority proportion of their transmission time" for European works except for news, sports events, games, advertising, teletext services and teleshopping. The details of the requirement are remarkably vague, however. There is much scope for working around the definition of European works, which is based on

---

[36] Broadcasting Act 1990, s. 16(2)(h) and ss. 186–187.

[37] Broadcasting (Independent Productions) Order 1991, S.I. 1991 No. 1408; Broadcasting (Independent Productions) (Amendment) Order 1995, S.I. 1995 No. 1925.

[38] Office of Fair Trading, *Independent Productions Transmitted by the BBC* (1995) First Report; subsequent reports have been published on an annual basis.

[39] See R. Collins, *Broadcasting and Audio-Visual Policy in the Single European Market* (1994).

[40] See P. Keller, "The New Television Without Frontiers Directive" (1997–98) 3 *Yearbook of Media and Entertainment Law* 177–195.

European connections with sources of finance and with the production process, rather than any requirement as to quality or European culture. There are also no requirements as to scheduling European works at peak viewing times. The European Commission's scrutiny of Member States' practices shows that, while the public service broadcasters more than comply with the majority quota, the commercial companies — especially cable and satellite — do not.[41] Under the Broadcasting Act 1990, licensees for Channels 3, 4 and 5 must ensure that "a proper proportion" of matter included in programmes is of European origin.[42] There is a similar obligation imposed on the BBC.[43] In practice, the proportion is excess of 60 per cent, and easily complies with the Directive. Whether the quota requirement will make a significant contribution to the preservation of European culture must be doubted. Apart from uncertainty about the nature of "European-ness" in itself, the measure is imprecise and unfocused in its aims. Furthermore, it is not obvious that television is the appropriate tool for fostering cultural identity. Contemporary television programming is characterised as much by language and genre as by national, let alone continental, identity, and the aim should be to encourage access to the medium by a diversity of actual cultural forms rather than mandating one version of what is considered important.[44]

Conditional Access

The introduction of digital technology enables new methods of controlling the distribution of programming. Companies which can,

---

[41] See B. de Witte, "The European Content Requirement in the E.C. Television Directive — Five Years After" (1995)1 *Yearbook of Media and Entertainment Law* 101–127. A report by the European Commission for 1993 and 1994 was issued in 1996: COM(96) 302 final; a report on the following two years is expected in 1998. It may be noted that the Broadcasting Act 1990 does not impose European quotas on the cable and satellite companies.

[42] Broadcasting Act 1990, ss. 16(2)(g), 25(2)(e) and 29(2)(b) respectively.

[43] Agreement, clause 4.4(f).

[44] For a study of Canada's failure to protect "Canadian" broadcasting, see R. Collins, *Culture, Communication and National Identity: The Case of Canadian Television* (1990). For a more recent appraisal, see L.P. Hitchens, "Preparing for the Information Society: Lessons from Canada" (1997–98) 3 *Yearbook of Media and Entertainment Law* 97–146. On the theme of cultural identity, see more generally, M. E. Price, *Television, the Public Sphere and National Identity* (1996).

in turn, control that process are very important "gatekeepers" for the whole digital broadcasting industry. They are the companies which will manufacture and sell the "set-top boxes" which receive the "smart cards" that enable digital coding and decoding to take place. Such gatekeeping is described as "conditional access": access to digital services can be made conditional, in the sense of being restricted on the basis of technology and subscription. Such restrictions can be imposed on various aspects of the service. Customer management services involve the processing of orders for programming and the sending of bills. Subscriber management deals with the issue of smart cards and entitlements to different services. Subscriber authorisation is separate again and allows the programme to be received by the person entitled to it by sending messages within the digital transmission. A final dimension to conditional access is the encryption, that is, the coding and decoding or "scrambling and descrambling" of the digital signals so that they can be exclusively transmitted and received. For each of these services, there is a public interest in ensuring that providers do not gain complete control over access. The basis of that interest is not only competition policy but also the importance of maintaining media pluralism.[45]

During the passage of the Broadcasting Act 1996, the problem of conditional access was considered by many to be so closely associated with the issue of media ownership that it should be an integral part of the legislation. However, the government thought that it did not raise a major issue relating to plurality of information and that the main problem was one of competition. Since the technology was closely related to the telecommunications sector, responsibility for regulating conditional access was allotted to OFTEL.

The decision to give the responsibility to OFTEL was not technologically determined, however, and was not, therefore, policy neutral. OFTEL's statutory remit and its general ethos is to concentrate on competition and technical issues but not on content. In devising a regulatory regime, OFTEL was obliged to draw on a

---

[45] The *de facto* standard for European digital decoders has been the Videocrypt system which is wholly owned by News Datacom, a subsidiary of News International. The latter company has a 40 per cent share in BSkyB. BSkyB, in turn, has an agreement with News Datacom, giving it the exclusive right to market and supply the Videocrypt system. Whether this control remains significant will depend on which digital delivery system, terrestrial or satellite, secures a lead in selling its set-top boxes. Digital terrestrial operators are currently developing their own system. However, both systems will have to be compatible with each other in due course, to comply with the conditional access regulations.

European Community Directive intended to encourage the development of a common standard for digital transmission.[46] Its aim is to stimulate the industry and to benefit consumers by preventing monopoly and enabling widespread access to the technology. However, the measure does not mandate a set of common specifications for an access system but, instead, seeks to prevent anti-competitive practices which would allow any one system to dominate and exclude others. Whether that policy is sufficiently robust is a matter of debate. Generally, without some common standard for conditional access, there is the possibility that manufacturers may create a series of different systems catering for different services. That raises the prospect of consumers having to buy more than one kind of set-top box if they wish to receive all the available services. However, the outcome would not improve consumer welfare because it is likely that only small and fragmented markets would become established, with consumers tending to buy only one product. The general effect would be less choice for the consumers and reduced opportunities for the service providers to supply their programmes.[47] It is uncertain, however, whether the market, largely left to its own devices but with some regulatory support, can provide a common platform. An alternative approach would be to enforce a common technical standard for all conditional access systems. That has been rejected, however, on the grounds that it is too inflexible in a rapidly developing industry in which predictions about technological and commercial success are, at best, risky.

The current arrangements for regulating conditional access therefore incorporate the European Directive[48] through the issue of a class licence under the Telecommunications Act 1984, the Conditional Access Services Class Licence. This licence applies to anybody who provides conditional access services and is enforced by the Director-General of Telecommunications in accordance with the general policy set out in OFTEL's Guidelines.[49] These guidelines apply to all digital television services, whether distributed by satellite,

---

[46] *Directive of the European Parliament and the Council of October 24, 1995 on the Use of Standards for the Transmission of Television Signals*, O.J. No. L281 (95/47/EC).

[47] See A. Graham, "Exchange Rates and Gatekeepers" in T. Congdon *et al., The Cross Media Revolution: Ownership and Control* (1995).

[48] The Conditional Access Services Class Licence and the Advanced Television Services Regulations 1996 (S.I. 1996 No. 3151, as amended by S.I. 1996 No. 3197).

[49] Office of Telecommunications, *The Regulation of Conditional Access for Digital Television* Services (1997).

terrestrially or by cable. Despite fears to the contrary in the industry, they do go a long way towards preventing a single operator from gaining control of the new technology.

The key provision of the licence is Condition 1 which requires that the provision of technical conditional access services should be offered on a "fair, reasonable and non-discriminatory" basis. Condition 3 imposes OFTEL's fair trading requirement: applying the European Community's competition tests, acts or omissions are prohibited which prevent, restrict or distort competition through an abuse of a dominant position or an anti-competitive agreement. Other conditions in the licence prohibit "linked sales" (whereby the sale of one service is conditional on purchasing another) and undue interference or discrimination. There are also requirements to publish information about the terms of supply of conditional access services, to keep separate accounts in relation to such services, and to ensure that data which is obtained from a broadcaster, to enable conditional access to be provided, is kept securely and not passed on to another (possibly rival) business. The latter condition is significant because it meets some objections from the industry that regulating for shared access would compromise commercially sensitive information, such as subscriber lists. In addition to these negative restrictions, the Director-General is also given positive powers to insist on the provision of a common interface to allow different conditional access systems to inter-operate, presumably to be used if the market fails to provide a solution. He can also impose compulsory licensing of intellectual property rights where they are being used to prevent services being offered on reasonable terms or at all. Another key provision is Condition 2 which deals with "transcontrol", whereby cable operators must be allowed sufficient access and information about a conditional access system to allow them to transcontrol and retransmit programmes using their own conditional access system.

OFTEL's policy in enforcing the class licence is contained in the more detailed discussion to be found in its guidelines. For example, a broadcaster would be considered to be put at a competitive disadvantage if it were denied essential information about the conditional access system or be forced to make contracts for programming or information supply in return for access. Similar considerations apply to pricing and costs: there should be flexible terms which allow easy entry to, and withdrawal from, the access system. For example, it should not be necessary to have to apply for special transmission capacity to supply pay-per-view events. Nor should broadcasters be expected to underwrite any subsidies which are likely to be offered by conditional access providers as an incentive for consumers to purchase their set-top boxes. Generally, OFTEL's approach follows that adopted in domestic competition regulation and the practice of the European Commission. Although the Directive on Television Standards applies only to digital television, the logic is to extend the general principles of fair access at least to all digital services.[50]

Electronic Programme Guides

From the audience's perspective, conditional access will increasingly be manifested in the availability of Electronic Programme Guides (EPGs). These are analogous to programme listings, but they will do much more. Still in the process of development, they will consist of menus which show viewers what programmes are available and allow them to select what to watch. But, rather like a Web-style interface, it may be that choosing an item on the menu activates a connection to the service and may also enable automatic payment by electronic subscription. This means that most EPGs are likely to be conditional access systems. There are obviously many opportunities for unfair and anti-competitive practices to develop. For example, the order in which programmes are listed, the prominence given to brands or logos, the information supplied about programmes and the way that menus may be layered into different sub-menus are all capable of affecting the viewers' choice and of marginalising some programming. Where the EPG provider is also a programme provider, there is clear potential for conflicts of interest to arise. OFTEL's approach is to ensure that the consumers' needs should be given first priority and that the operation of the EPG does not restrict, distort or prevent competition. One requirement of the 1996 Regulations is that all set-top boxes must have the capacity to receive and display free-to-air broadcasts, such as those of the BBC or Channels 3 and 4. This means that EPGs must display such broadcasts in their menus in an easily accessible form.

---

[50] Joint OFTEL and DTI Notice and Consultation, July 1997, anticipating its implementation by 1999. On the approach to competition generally, see Whish, above, n. 69.

EPGs provide a good example of convergence between programming and delivery systems. EPGs will comprise material which is essentially programming and that invokes the ITC's interest, under its general duty to secure a wide range of services together with fair and effective competition.[51] Unless the EPG is not part of a conditional access system, this is will entail an overlapping jurisdiction with OFTEL. The EPG will need to be licensed by the ITC, and it will be concerned with the way the material is packaged and scheduled. It has therefore issued a code of practice[52] which sets out its approach. It focuses on the programming aspects of EPGs and universal programming in particular. It requires that EPG providers should not discriminate between free-to-air and pay television services. Due prominence should be given to public service channels, access to which should be no more difficult than other channels. Viewers should be able to obtain them without additional equipment or agreements and without being routed through pages containing details of pay services. However, where the EPG provider is also a broadcaster, no undue prominence should be given to that company's services at the expense of others. Generally, there is a duty to make agreements for EPG services on fair, reasonable and non-discriminatory terms, and the ITC guidance is consistent with that of OFTEL. In due course, it is anticipated that both regulators' codes will be merged.

Listed Events

The success of satellite providers has been largely due to their sports coverage. They have been able to invest large sums of money in acquiring exclusive rights to show sports events on a subscription basis. This has presented problems for public service broadcasters, however, because they have smaller finances and often cannot afford the high prices which sporting organisations now realise they can charge for television rights. Under previous legislation,[53] some protection had been provided for the public service broadcasters by giving them a right of first refusal for certain "listed events" and prohibiting them from being shown on a pay-per-view basis. The

---

[51] Broadcasting Act 1990, s. 2(2).
[52] ITC, *Code of Conduct on Electronic Programme Guides* (1997).
[53] The repealed Cable and Broadcasting Act 1984, s. 14.

1990 Act reduced that protection by abolishing the right of first refusal. However, there continued to be pressure from the industry to secure wider opportunities for exclusive coverage. In addition, there was increasing concern that the public service broadcasters would be unable to secure coverage of important events, even on a non-pay-per-view basis. The Broadcasting Act 1996 therefore introduced yet another set of arrangements to deal with the problem by enabling live coverage of sporting and other events of national interest by the public service terrestrial broadcasters.[54]

The aim is to provide an opportunity for live events to be covered, but the legislation does not require or guarantee such coverage. The basic scheme is that television services are divided into two categories, those provided universally by the BBC, Channel 3 and Channel 4, and all other services which do not have universal reach. There must be separate contracts to provide coverage of a listed event for each of these categories of service. There can be no exclusive live coverage of a listed event by one category of service unless the other category has also acquired the right to show the event at the same time, or unless the ITC gives permission. In giving permission, the ITC will have regard to the genuine opportunities which each category enjoyed to purchase the broadcasting rights. In particular, it will be concerned to ensure that public service broadcasters are not being excluded because the price of the rights is too high. In exercising its discretion under this part of the Act, the ITC must have regard to the criteria in its code of practice,[55] namely, the previous fees for such events, the time of day for live coverage, the audience potential, the period for which rights are offered and the competition in the market place. These provisions will certainly provide a cushion for the public service broadcasters, especially while there are high audience expectations that the listed events will be provided free. However, once subscription services attract a large share of the market, the "fair and reasonable" price for such events will rise and the public service broadcasters may be unable to compete.

The revised European Broadcasting Directive has more recently made provision for a more flexible yet more onerous approach to listed events. It allows Member States to take measures to ensure that broadcasters under their jurisdiction "do not broadcast on an

---

[54] Broadcasting Act 1996, ss. 97–105.

[55] ITC, *ITC Code on Sports and other Listed Events* (1997), required under s. 104 of the 1996 Act. A revised version of the Code will be issued in mid-1998.

exclusive basis events which are regarded by that Member State as being of major importance for society in such a way as to deprive a substantial proportion of the public in that Member State of the possibility of following such events via live coverage or deferred coverage on free television."[56] This provision has been incorporated into the 1996 Act's scheme by dividing the listed events into two categories. Group A events cannot be covered live on an exclusive basis unless the criteria mentioned above are satisfied. Group B events will only be given permision by the ICT for exclusive live broadcasting if provision is made for secondary coverage, such as delayed scheduling, edited highlights, or radio commentary.[57]

Premium Channel Bundling

Another issue which demonstrates the power of strong media companies is the practice of premium channel bundling, whereby a basic satellite or cable package of channels is supplemented with additional channels which attract an additional payment, or premium. A cable operator in the United Kingdom has complained that it is not able to acquire the Disney Channel from the satellite provider, BSkyB, without also receiving two other channels. The complaint is that it should be available on an individual basis where the complete package is not wanted. In July 1996, the Director-General of Fair Trading (who has general responsibilities for competition regulation) completed an investigation and extracted undertakings from BSkyB not to continue the practice of bundling at the wholesale (distribution) level.[58] The Independent Television Commission is

---

[56] Council Directive (89/552/EEC) of October 3, 1989 and Directive 97/36/EC of the European Parliament and of the Council (Consolidated Version, 1997), Art. 3a(1).

[57] An assessment of the previous list was completed in 1998 by the (Gordon) Advisory Group on Listed Events set up by the Department of Culture, Media and Sport. The Secretary of State accepted the general principles that it recommended and revised the list as follows. Group A events are: the Olympic Games, the FIFA World Cup Finals, the FA Cup Final, The Scottish Cup Finald (in Scotland), the Grand National, the Derby, the Wimbledon Tennis Finals, the European Football Championship Finals, the Rugby League Cup Final and the Rugby Cup Final. The latter three were not on the previous list. Group B events are: Cricket Test matches played in England (which used to be on the previous list), non-finals play in the Wimbledon Tennis Tournament, other Rugby Cup Finals matches, Five Nations Rugby matches involving home countries, the Commonwealth Games, the World Athletics Championship, significant matches in the Cricket World Cup, the Ryder Cup and the Open Golf Championship. See DCMS, *Press Notices* Nos 48/98 and 135/98.

[58] Office of Fair Trading, *The Director General's Review of BSkyB's Position in the Wholesale Pay TV Market* (1996). See M. Williams, "Sky Wars: The OFT Review of Pay-TV" (1997) 4 *European Competition Law Review* 214–229.

also investigating the matter in respect of the impact of bundling at the retail level. The ITC has a general obligation to secure competition between services in the television sector and it is concerned about the possible impact of bundling on the price, quality, choice and availability of the services in question. Until recently, it has not given high priority to such issues, but it now appears to be shifting its policy. In 1998, it adopted a series of sweeping measures which are intended to widen consumer choice over programming. Minimum carriage arrangements (whereby cable companies have to supply a minimum audience with the supplier's basic package) will be prohibited except in relation to channels using a single platform for delivery and newly established channels. Bundling arrangements will be minimised. Significantly, the ITC proposes to adopt a strict approach to enforcing these new practices arguing that it is serving the viewers' interests by doing so. In fact, as delivery platforms converge, its role in regulating the supply of programmes will increase because, in the newer media, the organisations with the greatest power will be those who control media content.

Chapter Six

Regulatory Process

This chapter considers various regulatory processes which are adopted to enhance the relationship between the media and their audience or readership. The theme is accountability: where an important public interest is being served by a limited number of institutions, there is a constitutional need for the bodies in question to give a good account of themselves and to demonstrate that their activities are justified. This is especially so where the body claims to be promoting the public's preferences or to be acting in the best interests of the public, had they reflected sufficiently on the matter. The latter tendency is especially associated with a professional approach to tasks, where being professional signifies that there is a body of expertise to which the decision-maker has special access and that it will be promoted responsibly. The concern of regulation, then, is to ensure that there are adequate mechanisms for supervision and for satisfying the public's grievances about media practice.

A. Political Supervision: the BBC

External Relations

It will be recalled that the BBC started life as a commercial enterprise but, following the report of the Crawford Committee, was reconstituted as a public corporation in 1926. The method that the Committee recommended was incorporation under the Companies Act, but the Postmaster-General preferred to proceed by way of

Royal Charter instead, because that was thought to lend a greater air of status and dignity. In addition, a Royal Charter would allow the Corporation to do anything lawful and not prohibited by the terms of the Charter, whereas a company's memorandum and articles would be likely to be much more limiting. The other alternative, incorporation by a special statute, was seen as compromising the new Corporation's independence "by investing it in the mind of the public with the idea that in some way it is a creature of Parliament and connected with political activity".[1] Today, the use of legislation does not carry such significance but, in the 1920s, the BBC was just beginning to establish a reputation for impartiality in public service that the Charter was intended to consolidate.

Under the terms of the Charter, the BBC is a corporation of 12 members, the Governors, who are appointed by the Queen in Council for a normal period of five years.[2] Apart from a Chairman and Vice-Chairman, the Governors must include persons designated as National Governors for each of Scotland, Wales and Northern Ireland. It is the Governors, as the Corporation, who are responsible for securing the objects laid down in the Charter. The Charter gives the BBC authority to provide its services, conduct commercial transactions and hold property, publish and maintain libraries, collect news across the world and, interestingly, to organise and subsidise concerts and other entertainments in connection with its broadcasting activities. There is also provision for the establishment of general and regional advisory councils, which the BBC consults about general issues of policy. These have no effective power but derive some influence from the BBC's tradition of taking consultation seriously.[3] An important constraint is that programming services should be provided as "public services". This expression is not defined, but clearly refers to the tradition of public service broadcasting. Another constraint is more restrictive: the BBC is required to obtain from the Government a licence to transmit and it must comply with the conditions that are imposed as a condition of

---

[1] See A. Briggs, *The History of Broadcasting in the United Kingdom,* Vol. 1 *The Birth of Broadcasting* (1961), pp. 352–353. See also BBC, *Annual Report and Handbook 1987* (1988).

[2] Department of National Heritage, *Copy of Royal Charter for the Continuance of the British Broadcasting Corporation* (1996) Cm. 3248 (hereinafter, "BBC Charter"), art. 8. See also (Beveridge) Broadcasting Committee, *Report* (1951) Cmd. 8116, paras 534–535, 624.

[3] See T. Madge, *Beyond the BBC: Broadcasters and the Public in the 1980s* (1989).

issuing the licence. In practice, it is the Agreement[4] containing these conditions which is the more important of the BBC's constitutional documents.

In many ways, the BBC's constitutional arrangements are rather quaint, but they are also complex and do not provide a comprehensive account of the Corporation's responsibilities and rights. The disadvantage of a Charter, which does not appear to have been considered in the 1920s, is that it is granted as an exercise of Crown prerogative, (the King's or Queen's residual common law powers of an executive nature). Much prerogative power is effectively controlled by the government of the day, however, so the use of a Charter allows the government considerable discretion about the way that the relevant institution is established. Furthermore, until recently, the courts have not been willing to review exercises of the Crown's prerogative.

There is a clear case for adopting a different approach and for placing the BBC on a statutory basis.[5] It would have the advantage of giving the BBC a permanent existence and of enshrining principles of public service. Such a statutory framework would also provide the BBC with a defence against improper pressures exerted by politicians, and enable some resistance to financial pressures to reduce its services. From the audience's perspective, a statutory framework could set out the standards and aspirations with which the BBC would be expected to conform, and it could provide a more explicit basis for rendering the Corporation accountable, including recourse to judicial review. There are disadvantages to the statutory approach, however. The framework would only be as valuable as the content of the statute, and some fear that Parliament might take the opportunity to engage in a radical overhaul of the BBC's remit. Yet the alternative may be no less favourable. The BBC reformed itself in anticipation of the recent Charter renewal in the context of wide political discussion of its future role. But its position is, constitutionally, as precarious as it ever was.

That public service broadcasters should be accountable for their activities has never been doubted, either by politicians or broadcasters

---

[4] Department of National Heritage, *Copy of the Agreement Dated the 25th Day of January 1996 Between Her Majesty's Secretary of State for National Heritage and the British Broadcasting Corporation* (1996) Cm. 3152, (hereinafter "BBC Agreement").

[5] This point was made in relation to the BBC's independence, above. For other discussion, see E. Barendt, "Legal aspects of BBC Charter renewal" (1994) 65 *Political Quarterly* 20–8.

themselves. Indeed, the BBC's service was started on the basis of public trusteeship. That principle, combined with a suspicious attitude to the potential of the new technology, led to the practice whereby the Corporation has never been formally established on a permanent basis; instead, its Charter has been granted and its Licence and Agreement issued for a succession of limited periods. As a result, the time for renewal has provided an opportunity for parliamentary and public discussion of the appropriate direction in which the service should be moving.

The general atmosphere of uncertainty which such accountability creates has fostered in the BBC what Burns has described as the "responsiveness and sensitivity — often amounting to anxiety — with which senior officials and programme staff relate to the world around them, especially to the noises and moves made by the larger and more powerful bodies in the immediate vicinity of the BBC."[6] As a counter to this, however, the programme-makers have had a special role in defining the generally accepted standard for accountability, a conception of public service revealed as some version of professionalism.

Against this background, the structure of accountability is not so important as the ethos of the Corporation. Most formally, it is responsible to the Secretary of State for the services and facilities that it provides and for any other activities that he or she requires from it. The ultimate sanction is dissolution. Under article 20, the grant of the Charter is expressly made on the condition that its provisions and those prescribed in the Agreement should be strictly and faithfully observed and performed. If it appears to the Secretary of State, as a result of representations made by interested parties or in any other way, that there is reasonable cause to suppose that the Corporation is not complying with any of its obligations, he or she may require it to show that it has done so and, if it fails to do this, a certificate may be issued to that effect and that in itself will be grounds for revoking the Charter. Connected with this provision is clause 15 of the Agreement, whereby the Secretary of State may revoke the licence should the Corporation fail to provide efficient broadcasting services or cease to observe the requirements of either the Charter, the Licence or the Agreement and not remedy the defect within a reasonable time. This is without prejudice to the Minister's general discretion to revoke the Licence under section 1 of the Wireless Telegraphy Act 1949 in any event.

---

[6] T. Burns, *The BBC: Public Institution and Private World* (1977), p. 32.

In practice, this provision represents a last resort which would be unlikely to be invoked, but it provides a salutary indication that the Corporation's activities are not wholly isolated from the political arena. While the point of establishing it by Royal Charter was precisely to distance it from day-to-day intervention by politicians, the minister's responsibility for its operations enable them to be discussed in Parliament. Nevertheless, ministers do accede to the convention that broadcasters' independence should be protected and, while they answer questions related to the issue of the licence and matters of general policy, they leave detailed issues of programming to the Governors. While their performance may be discussed when their Annual Report is submitted to the Secretary of State for consideration by Parliament, under article 18 of the Charter, it is their general approach rather than specific decisions which are assessed.[7]

The approach to accountability in the independent sector was modelled on that established for the BBC, but the differences between them reflect the fact that programmes are now made commercially under the supervision of the regulatory bodies, rather than by them. They, too, have to submit Annual Reports to the Secretary of State for laying before Parliament[8] but, again, the convention of political independence serves to limit the scope of debate. The existence of a statutory framework for the independent sector serves to provide better formal protection against interference by politicians for, if the regulators were thought to be failing in their duties, the normal source of redress would be judicial review rather than some vague appeal to the minister. Generally, because the relationship between programme-makers and Ministers has been institutionally buffered by the regulators, there has been less parliamentary discussion of independent broadcasting policy.

Internal Supervision

Since the various aspects of the media enterprise are combined into one body, the BBC's responsibility as a broadcasting authority, for disseminating programmes and for controlling and supervising their

---

[7] See (Annan), *Report of the Committee on the Future of Broadcasting* (1977) Cmnd. 6753, para. 6.8.
[8] Broadcasting Act 1990, Sched. 1, para. 15 and Sched. 6, para. 15.

content, has a domestic quality which is not found in the independent sector. In itself, that need not mean that supervision and accountability are any the less rigorous, and neither does the formal proximity of programme-maker to broadcaster necessarily have the effect of stultifying creative activity. But there is a latent ambiguity in the nature of the relationship, which the Corporation attempts to resolve through its internal organisation.

At its most basic, the relationship between broadcaster and programme-maker is one of employer and employee. The Director-General and his staff are appointed under article 14 of the Charter in order to manage the Corporation from day to day, but it is the Governors who bear the responsibility for the programmes that are released. Obviously, in practice, the degree of supervision exercised depends on the relationship between the Governors and their executive staff. In the early days of the Corporation, Reith took the view that the Governors should not involve themselves in the details of broadcasting, especially if that were to threaten the development of his conception of public service. In 1932, he secured an agreement from the Chairman, John Whitley, that the Governors' responsibilities "are general and not particular", allowing discussion of major matters of policy and finance, but leaving "the execution of that policy and the general administration of the Service in all its branches to the Director-General and his competent officers."[9] The Governors' role, then, was relegated to a rather vague protection of the public interest in broadcasting.

This rather doubtful interpretation of their constitutional role did not pass unchallenged. Some Chairmen attempted to exert their authority, most notably Lord Simon who failed, and Lord Hill who succeeded to a point.[10] In addition, both the Beveridge Committee and the Pilkington Committee saw the Governors in a different light, as akin to ministers responsible for the running of their departments and with an active role in mediating between the Corporation's executive and the public's opinions and criticisms. Beveridge, indeed, had gone further and suggested that the distinction between policy or principle and practice or execution was untenable.[11]

---

[9] Quoted in T. Burns, above, n. 6, p. 22, from the "Whitley Document." See also A. Smith, *The Shadow in the Cave* (1973) p. 144, referring to Lord Simon, *The BBC From Within* (1953).

[10] See Burns, above, n. 6; C. Munro, *Television, Censorship and the Law* (1979), pp. 18–19.

[11] See Beveridge, above, n. 2, paras 552–557; (Pilkington) Committee on Broadcasting, *Report* (1962) Cmnd. 1753, paras 404–409.

Nevertheless, the Governors have tended not to get involved in management, including programming, decisions. For one thing, they have limited expertise compared with the professional broadcasters. For another, the BBC's organisation was developed with a centralised and hierarchical administration, with decision-making being subject to constant internal scrutiny and referral upwards in cases of doubt. Of course, this gives greatest leeway to those with greatest certainty and, for the rest, there may be a tendency to anticipate the thinking at a higher level. But the result is that, by the time a decision reaches the Governors, "it is difficult to see how they can bring any new light or additional wisdom."[12]

What the Governors could, and still can, do is set the tone of the Corporation by employing the sort of management that they consider can best advance their view of the BBC's role. If they think that a Director-General is not managing the Corporation in a way which best serves the public interest, it is open to them to replace him or her. Normally, such a course of action would be unusual, but it has happened, most recently and dramatically in the case of Alistair Milne.[13] That decision followed the appointment of a new Chairman and, apart from its implications for the Corporation's independence, it was thought to indicate a new readiness on the part of the Governors to assert themselves. It is unlikely to mark a long-term shift in the internal relations of the Corporation, however, for the Governors cannot be expected to maintain a position of antagonism against the organisation which is a manifestation of themselves. Burns considered in 1977 that theirs was "an impossibly contradictory situation" and one which they had resolved in favour of accepting "the compliant, consultative role the Director-General, *and* the Corporation generally, needs of them and [. . .] has fitted them into." They speak, publicly at least, "for the Corporation to Parliament and its agents, to the Press and the public at large, and not as the chosen guardians of the public interest *vis-à-vis* the Corporation and its activities."[14]

Under the 1996 Charter, however, the functions of the Governors in representing the public interest have been made more explicit. At the same time, their task has been more clearly separated from the

---

[12] Burns, above, n. 6, p. 33.

[13] The circumstances surrounding his resignation were reported in *The Independent* and *The Guardian*, January 30, 1987 and in *The Observer*, February 1, 1987. See also his own account: A. Milne, *DG: The Memoirs of a British Broadcaster* (1988).

[14] Burns, above, n. 6, p. 53.

work of the professional broadcasters. Their responsibility is to oversee the BBC but not to manage it.[15] Thus,[16] the Governors are required to approve clear objectives and promises for the Corporation's services, programmes and other activities, and to monitor their attainment. They must ensure that the terms of the Agreement are carried out and determine the strategy of the BBC for its Home and Commercial Services. In respect of the latter, they must ensure that funding, operation and accounting are separate from the Home Services. Comments, proposals and complaints by viewers and listeners must be given due consideration and properly handled. The Governors also have duties to establish and maintain an Audit Committee to secure compliance with the highest standards of corporate governance. As before, it is they who appoint the Director-General and other key managers. The overall tone of these provisions is much less in the earlier tradition of public administration and more in the style of modern corporate management. Combined with the more transparent obligations contained in other parts of the Charter and of the Agreement, the Governors' functions provide a much improved basis for rendering the BBC accountable. The old problems will not disappear, of course, and it remains to be seen which of the interests of the audience or of the professionals will be defended best.

B. Regulatory Supervision

Regulation and Politics

Although direct political supervision of the media regulators is uncommon, the parameters of their decision-making is highly constrained by the political process. The ITC and R.A. are indeed formally independent, but they operate under a statutory mandate which reduces their scope for significant policy making. The 1990 and 1996 Broadcasting Acts established the broad framework for the commercial media in the United Kingdom, and the regulators'

---

[15] See Department of National Heritage, *The Future of the BBC: Serving the Nation, Competing World Wide* (1994) Cm. 2621 (White Paper). See also E. Barendt, above, n. 5.

[16] BBC Charter, cl. 7.

function is to implement it. It is true that they have considerable discretion in applying the detail, but there is little room for innovatory or strategic thinking. This is part of the British tradition of public administration.[17] Its advantage is that it places responsibility for policy in the democratic arena, but its disadvantage is that it reduces the potential to develop a principled approach to regulation appropriate to the industry. The broadcasting regulators are, to some extent, sheltered from the full impact of the political control which may be experienced elsewhere because of the historical significance of public service broadcasting and the political acknowledgement that freedom of speech is important. Nevertheless, there remain too many opportunities for political adjustments to be made to the regulatory scheme. One example is the power to make changes by secondary legislation to rules such as those on ownership or the financing of Channel 4. Another is the retention by government of control over frequency allocation and over telecommunications policy. One possible side-effect of this dimension to regulation is that the regulators themselves are able — or forced — to become adept at political lobbying. That may not always be a disadvantage for the regulatory scheme, if the regulators' views are respected by ministers; for example, the ITC had a significant influence on many features of the Broadcasting Act 1990. However, in general, it militates against the development of a reasoned and sustained media policy.[18]

Formal Arrangements

Formally, control of the services provided in the commercial sector is effected through the enforcement of conditions that are incorporated into licences by the regulatory bodies. Some conditions are specified in the 1990 Act,[19] but most will be determined by the regulators using their broad powers to include conditions as to the duties imposed by or under the Act, the payment of fees, the provision of information for them to carry out their functions, and such incidental and

---

[17] M. Loughlin and C. Scott, "The Regulatory State" in P. Dunleavy *et al.*, *Developments in British Politics — 5* (1997), pp. 205–219.

[18] On the inconsistencies in media policy development in the U.K., see L. P. Hitchens, " 'Get Ready, Fire, Take Aim' The Regulation of Cross-Media Ownership — An Exercise in Policy-Making" [1995] *Public Law* 620–621.

[19] For example, those relating to ownership restrictions or co-operation with the Broadcasting Standards Commission.

supplementary matters as they consider appropriate.[20] Typically, licences contain requirements to comply with the legislative scheme and, importantly, to honour the commitments included in the proposal to provide the service. Failure to comply with the terms of the licence may result in sanctions being applied, the ultimate one being revocation, and it is a criminal offence to provide a service without a licence.[21]

In relation to programme content, and unlike the position with the IBA, the current regulatory bodies do not have powers to preview programme services.[22] Whilst they have general duties to secure compliance with the Act and the terms of licences, they do not have responsibility for transmissions and relays, so programme providers do not have to seek their approval in advance. Instead, their role is that of an external enforcer, with the onus being on them to act upon any breaches that come to their notice. Inevitably, the control that they can exercise will be much less comprehensive. Although recordings of programmes may be monitored, and must be kept for 90 days for that purpose,[23] the resources needed for the task will be far greater than those used in pre-vetting schedules or scripts. In keeping with the lighter touch to regulation, their role is much more reactive than was that of the IBA. However, there is power available to them to issue directions in respect of matters specified in the licences.[24] This allows some flexibility in responding to unanticipated situations, for example, an impending takeover or a proposed change in the nature of a service or the scheduling of sensitive material.

The basis for enforcing licence conditions is to be found in sections 40 to 42 of the 1990 Act. Those sections apply to television programme services but, with some modifications, the same approach is adopted for other programme services and for radio.[25] A range of sanctions is provided, the more lenient being the requirement to publish an apology or correction and the most severe being revocation of the licence. The intention is to provide scope for a more flexible, graduated means of enforcement compared with the rather blunt power of revocation possessed by the IBA. One of the

---

[20] Broadcasting Act 1990, ss. 4 and 86.
[21] Broadcasting Act 1990, ss. 13, 82 and 97.
[22] *cf.* Broadcasting Act 1981, s. 6.
[23] Broadcasting Act 1990, ss. 11 and 95.
[24] ss. 4(2), 87(2).
[25] Broadcasting Act 1990, ss. 81 (local delivery services), 55 and 120 (additional services) and 109–111 (sound broadcasting services).

problems with such a heavy sanction is that it has to be reserved for the most serious cases, so that more trivial breaches can be committed with virtual impunity. Both regulators have demonstrated their willingness to use their powers, although they appear to prefer a more informal approach to securing compliance.

The power to direct corrections or apologies applies to broadcasts, whether terrestrial or satellite, where the ITC or R.A. are satisfied that a licensee has failed to comply with the conditions of the licence. In such a case, they may direct the inclusion of a correction or apology or both, if they are satisfied that such inclusions would be an appropriate remedy for the failure.[26] The sanction does not apply to complaints of unfairness or invasions of privacy, matters which are dealt with by the Broadcasting Standards Commission. Rather, it is intended to force a licensee to admit, publicly, that the service has fallen below standard. Whether an apology will have any effect on a recalcitrant company is open to doubt, however, for it will not indicate any shame where programming is commercially successful in attracting audiences and advertising, yet in doing so, falls below the thresholds of quality or diversity. Similarly, a correction is only likely to have an impact if it is interpreted in the broadest sense to mean that the deficiency in the service, rather than defects in particular programmes, must be put right.

Connected with this sanction is a power to direct a licensee not to repeat any programme that involved a breach of the licence conditions.[27] This applies only to television, although a similar provision could be incorporated into radio licences by the R.A. under its general power to incorporate directions. For radio, however, the regime can be stricter at this preliminary stage. Where it is satisfied that a licensee has failed to comply with the licence conditions or one of its directions, the Authority may serve a notice specifying a period, of not more than a year, during which a further failure to comply will trigger a power to preview programming material for up to six months.[28] Such potential for close supervision is at odds with the generally lighter touch to regulation in the statute and it is not clear why radio has been treated differently from television in this respect. The scale of operations may be smaller, and finance may be less secure, but those are not reasons to suppose that radio will be less responsive to regulatory demands.

---

[26] Broadcasting Act 1990, ss. 40 and 109.
[27] Broadcasting Act 1990, s. 40.
[28] Broadcasting Act 1990, s. 109.

The next level of sanctions, for which the model is contained in section 41 of the 1990 Act, is intended to have a financial impact on the service provider.[29] If the regulatory bodies are satisfied that a licensee has failed to comply with one of their directions or a condition of the licence, they may exact a financial penalty or shorten the licence period. In the case of terrestrial television, national radio, local delivery and additional services, there is a ceiling on the penalty for a first offence of 3 per cent of the qualifying revenue and 5 per cent for further offences. For other services, there is a fixed limit of £50,000. The latter was also the case with satellite television services but, in recognition of the disproportionate relationship between the fixed fine and satellite income, the 1996 Act has increased the penalty to whichever is the greater of £50,000 or the revenue-based penalties described above.[30]

The power to shorten the licence applies to all services other than Channel 4 and additional services. The licence period may be reduced by up to two years but the penalty is conditional in that, if the licensee's performance improves before the shortened period expires, it may be revoked. As with all penalties that have a financial impact, the effectiveness of these measures will depend on ability to pay and they are least likely to work where a service is failing because it is commercially weak. However they may also be ineffective if the operation is very profitable, as satellite television is likely to be, and penalties are treated as a tax on short-term gains.

The final level of sanction is revocation and the model is to be found in section 42 of the 1990 Act.[31] First, the regulatory bodies must be satisfied that the licensee is failing to comply with one of their directions or a licence condition and that the failure is such that, if it were not remedied, it would justify revocation. Secondly, the licensee has to be given time to take remedial steps. Thirdly, revocation can only occur if those steps have not been taken and revocation is in the public interest. Under section 89 of the 1996 Act, however, there is a special power of revocation which provides more immediate and effective control over satellite television services which breach the prohibition in section 6(1)(a) of the 1990 Act on programming material which is likely to encourage or incite to crime or to lead to disorder. It differs from the power in section 42 of the

[29] See also ss. 44, 55, 81, 110, and 120.
[30] Broadcasting Act 1996, s. 88.
[31] See also ss. 44, 55, 81, 111 and 119.

1990 Act by allowing an immediate suspension of the offending service, prior to representations, rather than threatening the licensee with revocation unless the failure is remedied. Otherwise, the power to revoke may also be used where the award of the licence resulted from information being falsely given or materially withheld with the intention to mislead,[32] or where a licence has been awarded for a service which will not, after all, be implemented.[33] In the latter case, for Channels 3 and 5, the ITC's discretion is a little more circumscribed should a licensee cease to provide the service before the licence expires; if it is satisfied that it is appropriate for it to do so, it must serve a notice of revocation.

With so many hurdles to surmount, it may be that it would take only the most formidable difficulties to emerge for revocation to be invoked at all, especially in relation to Channel 3. The central position of this channel in the independent sector is itself a disincentive to use the power although, where a regional licence is revoked, there is provision for the ITC to invite another regional licensee to take over the service on a temporary basis.[34] In addition, any Channel 3 revocation carries with it a financial penalty amounting to 7 per cent of the licensee's qualifying revenue, intended to make it expensive to renege on the commitment to provide the service.[35]

Regulatory Style

The fact that regulatory bodies have extensive powers at their disposal gives no indication, of course, about the way in which they will use them, if at all. Baldwin and McCrudden have summarised the issues as entailing three sets of basic choices. First, the regulator may decide between the informal path of education and negotiation or the more formal, interventionist enforcement of standards. Secondly, where enforcement is adopted, it must be decided whether to be "reactive", responding to complaints and problems as and when they arise in a piecemeal fashion, or to be "proactive", creating a

---

32 Broadcasting Act 1990, s. 42(5).

33 Broadcasting Act 1990, s. 18.

34 Broadcasting Act 1990, s. 42(8).

35 *ibid.*, s. 18. It replaced an earlier proposal to require that a performance bond should be secured by the licensee.

rational and comprehensive strategy in advance. Thirdly, there is a choice about methods of enforcement, either prospective, through rule-making and standard-setting, or on an individualistic case-by-case basis.[36]

Regulatory bodies do not, of course, have a free hand in the style that they present. Nor will they opt wholly for one alternative rather than another. To some extent, their options are limited by the framework of their enabling legislation, and the availability of resources will affect their potential to adopt a formal, proactive approach. But a major influence on their approach is likely to be determined by the identity of values between themselves and those that they regulate. This is not a matter of the agency being "captured" by the industry, for which there is little evidence despite much speculation.[37] Rather, it involves the extent to which the regulator has a sympathetic interest in the area of activity, an interest that can be developed and tested through discussion and negotiation with practitioners. In the media, for example, the IBA used its powers to nurture the ideal of public service broadcasting, just as the Cable Authority saw its role as that of promoting the cable revolution. Regulatory style is as much a question of the identity of the regulators and their objectives, then, as the methods available.

Nevertheless, the 1990 Act reconstituted the basis of television and radio regulation and, although there has been continuity of staff and outlook between the IBA, the ITC and the R.A., they have had to rethink their attitudes under the present regime. Formerly, the IBA had ultimate control over the programmes that were disseminated because they retained responsibility as the broadcasting authority. Programme-makers were precisely that, offering material for inclusion in the services provided by the Authority. It had the power to preview programme schedules and only broadcast the ones that it had approved. Most of the previewing was delegated to the IBA's

---

[36] See R. Baldwin and C. McCrudden, *Regulation and Public Law* (1987) pp. 8–9. See also R. Baldwin, *Rules and Governance* (1995); I. Harden and N. Lewis, *The Noble Lie* (1986), part 3; R. Cotterrell, *The Sociology of Law* (2nd ed. 1992), chap. 8; S.J. Breyer, *Regulation and Its Reform* (1982).

[37] See L. Hancher and M. Moran, "Organising Regulatory Space" in *Capitalism Culture and Economic Regulation* (1989), pp. 274–276; I. Ramsay, *Consumer Protection* (1989), pp. 77–79; Cotterrell, above, n. 36.

staff, with provision for monitoring their decisions,[38] and the procedure was made less formal through the working relationships that developed between its regional officers and the programme producers. Frequent consultation meant that the latter could anticipate the Authority's reaction to any programme but, in cases of doubt, it was possible to seek clarification in advance before time and money had been invested. If a programme contractor failed to comply with the IBA's directions, it could directly intervene to maintain the service.[39]

This informal style was carried over to the broader, financial aspects of regulation, but it sometimes left the IBA looking weak. The Annan Committee considered, for example, that the Authority was too reluctant to use its powers, even as a basis for negotiating improvements in performance, when attempting to enforce the rules governing the composition and ownership of programme contractor's companies. As a result, the financial and managerial difficulties experienced at London Weekend Television between 1968 and 1970 had been allowed to drag on too long.[40] Despite the implication that the IBA should have been more robust in the future, a similar, indecisive approach seems to have occurred when financial problems jeopardised the viability of the breakfast-time contract awarded to TV-am. By contrast, where the issue was seen not as one of enabling an unstable company to be rescued, but as one of preventing a stronger company from buying its way into a franchise, the IBA appeared to stand firmer, as it did when it refused to allow Rank to take over Granada.[41]

Under the current regime, the ITC and R.A. do not have such a stake in maintaining services and protecting companies. In addition, there are many more players to supervise and they are less likely to

---

[38] See the account in *R. v. IBA ex p. Whitehouse* (1985), *The Times* April 4, 1986. Lord Thompson, a former Chairman of the I.B.A., maintained that the commercial lobby did not take the lead in determining the regulatory style of the television industry. Rather, it shared the Authority's beliefs about the proper role of broadcasters. See "Thirty Years of Independent Broadcasting" (1985) 22 *Television* 212–218.

[39] Broadcasting Act 1981, s. 3(2). Use of the power was threatened in 1956 but never occurred: see Munro, above, n. 10, pp. 48–49.

[40] Annan, above, n. 7, paras 13.25–13.30.

[41] See IBA, *Annual Report and Accounts 1985–86* (1986), pp. 7–8. Similarly, the sale of Thames TV was blocked in late 1985. On the Rank bid, see *R. v. IBA ex p. Rank Organisation* (1986) *The Times*, March 14; it was held that the terms of Granada's programme contract justified the IBA's action. By contrast, in the radio sector in 1986, the I.B.A. was allowing foreign control of LBC and large foreign stakes in two other independent local radio stations. See *The Guardian* April 14, 1986.

share a consensus about the issues to be addressed. Consequently, the regulatory bodies are inclined only to respond to complaints.[42] The style that they have inherited is a conciliatory one, however, and it may be expected that formal process will be invoked relatively rarely. In any event, there are methods that fall short of that. One is the power to vary a licence. This may provide an opportunity for a licensee to retrench and provide a more realistic service; for example, a regional Channel 3 licensee may find that its resources are being stretched in fulfilling a requirement to supply programmes to the network.[43] If negotiation does not work, the regulators may be able to use the licence conditions which allow them to give directions to the licensee; for example, a company may be told to restructure to meet the ownership conditions in Schedule 2 or a particular form of advertising may be prohibited.[44]

In terms of formal process, much will depend on the way that the regulatory bodies are "satisfied" that there has been a "failure" to comply with the licence conditions and that, in turn, may depend on how tightly they are drafted. This gives the regulators considerable discretion in deciding whether or not to invoke sanctions and, as the later discussion shows, this has enabled them to create an intermediate level of informal sanction, the "formal warning". Under the various enforcement provisions discussed earlier, licensees have to be given "a reasonable opportunity of making representations" about the matters complained of; that is flexible, but it only reflects the vagueness of the common law.[45] Yet, apart from the initial notice of revocation, there is no provision for the giving of reasons. In addition, the new legislation erects a rather complex structure of sanctions without giving any clear indication why one approach is preferred for one service rather than another; for example, the terrestrial television services and radio are treated relatively severely but in different ways. Furthermore, the relationship between sanctions in terms of a tariff of seriousness may have to be resolved as familiar sentencing problems emerge in a different guise; it is by no means clear, for example, whether a conditional revocation is more or less severe than a financial penalty.

---

[42] That was certainly the role envisaged by the Home Office. See *Hansard* Broadcasting Bill, Standing Committee F, col. 835. For a review of the ITC's work in the context of utility regulation generally, see T. Prosser, *Law and the Regulators* (1997), chap. 9.

[43] See Broadcasting Act 1990, ss. 3(4) and 84(5). Not all variations are sanctions, of course.

[44] *ibid.*, ss. 5, 88, 89 and 93 respectively.

[45] See P. Craig, *Administrative Law* (3rd ed. 1994), pp. 292–302.

Generally, the regulators' style appears to be sympathetic to a "compliance" approach in which they seek the co-operation of licensees to provide a smooth-running service. However, they are not prepared to deal with issues informally, preferring to maintain some distance from their licensees; the tendency in the 1990 Act has been to formalise the relationship between regulator and licensee. As an intermediate solution, they operate a fairly rigorous approach to investigating and commenting on possible breaches of licenses, but they tend not to impose formal sanctions very frequently and sometimes take no action at all.

This approach is possible because the ITC and the R.A. have made considerable efforts to secure a consensual basis for the conditions and standards which they apply. Some of those are not open to argument, such as the statutory requirements. Some have been volunteered and incorporated into licence conditions. Other standards have been imposed in the form of the programme codes, but much of their content grew out of the public service ethos and represents many shared values — even in a commercial environment. Furthermore, those codes are more a repository of professional wisdom than a collection of mandatory rules (although some of them are mandatory). In this vein, a distinctive feature of the regulators' style is to consult extensively with the industry to learn about regulatory problems and to obtain comments on proposed changes in the rules or their practice. Generally, there is a high degree of transparency about policy objectives and the acceptable means of achieving them.

As for enforcement decisions, a study of the ITC's practice since 1993 shows that it has developed a graded set of responses to breaches of licence conditions.[46] Most enquiries about possible breaches arise because one or more members of the public complains, but a high proportion are began by the ITC on its own initiative. Most complaints are made in respect of matters of taste and decency, followed by violence, bad language, unfair treatment and inappropriate scheduling.[47] In responding to them, the ITC seeks representations from the licensee concerned before making an assessment of the issues and concluding whether a breach has occurred. In relation to some complaints or breaches, the ITC has

---

[46] The following comments are based on an analysis of the ITC's monthly *Programme Complaints and Interventions Reports* from 1992 to January 1998.

[47] See ITC, *Annual Report and Accounts* (annual).

used the opportunity to discuss broader issues of general significance. Examples are the use of knives in drama, undue prominence given to commercial products, invasions of privacy including the identification of child victims of sex attacks, and the issues surrounding the reporting of the shooting of Dunblane schoolchildren in 1996.

In respect of programmes which breached a licence condition,[48] the ITC took no further action in around 7 per cent of the total; this appears to imply that the breach was technical and not serious. In around 40 per cent of cases, the ITC offered "advice" to the licensee after finding a breach or expressing concern that a breach may have occurred. In those findings, the programme usually involved a situation which was not clearly covered by the codes and may have been open to reasonable differences of opinion or misunderstandings. Around a further 40 per cent of cases were resolved by the programme company giving undertakings to the ITC not to repeat the breach, or reporting that it had already taken pre-emptive action to prevent a recurrence. In those situations, the company's internal procedures for scrutinising editing and scheduling were usually at fault.

In about 6 per cent of cases, the first step towards formal sanctions was taken in the shape of a formal warning. An early example involved the showing of a kitchen knife used as a murder weapon in Channel 4's *Brookside*. Channel 4's *TFI Friday* and *The Word* were also the subject of formal warnings for particularly severe breaches of good taste and decency; as a result, *The Word* was not recommissioned and *TFI Friday* is pre-recorded. Other examples include Tyne Tees' revealing a child victim's identity, Live TV's giving undue prominence to a product, Yorkshire TV's showing excessive violence in *The Governor*, MTV's failing to schedule adult material appropriately and MedTV's failing to show due impartiality in news coverage. Recently, Channel 4 was issued with another formal warning in respect of four breaches of the Programme Code over a five week period and involving a promotional reference in a programme, inappropriate scheduling, indecent language and unfairness. The same action was taken against Live TV for invasion of privacy and Christian Channel Europe for showing scenes of exorcism and for breaking rules relating to on-screen fundraising. Instances of formal sanctions are relatively rare. Channel 4 was required to apologise for a grossly offensive remark made in a live

---

[48] Many programmes attract multiple complaints. Most complaints are not upheld.

interview with an American actor in *The Word* in 1994, for an invasion of privacy in its *Dyke TV* season in 1995, and for showing unacceptable incest scenes in *Brookside* in 1996 and for distorting the views of environmentalists in *Against Nature* in 1998. The severest sanction imposed so far is the fine. Granada was fined £500,000 in 1994 for giving undue prominence to commercial goods and services, and allowing excessive commercial interests in competitions on *This Morning*, and MTV Europe was fined £60,000 for three breaches of advertising and scheduling rules in 1995. At the beginning of 1998, Med TV was fined £90,000 for repeating the breaches mentioned earlier.

Although it regulates on a much smaller scale, the R.A. also operates a graduated set of responses to breaches. However, it appears more willing than the ITC to impose fines where informal methods have not apparently succeeded. Amounts have ranged from £500 imposed on local stations, for failure to provide an annual declaration, to £5,000 imposed on Talk Radio, for failure to provide log tapes and for broadcasting offensive and blasphemous material, and £10,000 imposed on Kiss FM and on Piccadilly 1152, for breaches of good taste and decency. Breach of promise performances such as, for example, broadcasting an insufficient amount of a musical genre which is supposed to characterise the station, but which is not mainstream pop, have attracted amounts of £1,000.[49]

So far, the regulators have demonstrated a willingness to enforce licence conditions in a commercial climate where companies are under severe pressure to maximise their returns. There is a power to vary the licences and it is occasionally exercised, but only to make minor adjustments to commitments.[50] A major confrontation was threatened in 1993 when some Channel 3 companies wanted to renegotiate their undertakings and reschedule *News at Ten* because it interfered with showing complete films during prime time viewing. Interestingly, the ITC's position in resisting the proposal was

---

[49] Details are to be found in the R.A.'s *Quarterly Bulletin* of complaints and their *Annual Report and Financial Statement*.

[50] For example, Channel 5's licence has already been varied to reduce the amount of original programming so that more money can be devoted to few productions to increase their quality. The ITC maintained, however, that viewers would benefit. The Channel was also allowed to show more repeats but was refused a request to increase its advertising and sponsorship minutage to that allowed for cable and satellite services. In 1993, GMTV's licence was modified to increase its commitment to factual programming following disquiet about the standard of its performance in current affairs.

supported by ministers and politicians, and the problem receded.[51] In the television sector, the ITC conducts annual performance reviews of the commercial terrestrial television licences and it has been quite critical of lapses in the quality of programming standards.[52] There seems to be a determination to maintain the standards which were undertaken when the franchises were awarded, notwithstanding financial constraints. Furthermore, in the 1996 Act, there is a new power given to the ITC to vary licence conditions on change of ownership where it considers that the change would have a prejudicial effect on the range and qualtity of regional programming.[53]

Transfrontier Broadcasts

These enforcement powers may be effective for services licensed in the United Kingdom, but they cannot control satellite programming which is uplinked from other countries and transmitted into the United Kingdom. By section 177 of the 1990 Act, a foreign satellite service may be proscribed by order if the ITC or R.A. consider that its quality is unacceptable because it "repeatedly" contains matter which offends against section 6(1) of the Act. When a proscription order is made under section 178, the effect is to make it a criminal offence for anybody to facilitate reception of the programme. Specifically, it is forbidden to supply equipment and decoders, programming material, advertising or publicity. An order may be made by the Secretary of State for Culture, Media and Sport provided it is in the public interest and is compatible with the United Kingdom's international obligations. So far, six such orders have been made, the first surviving a challenge by judicial review.[54]

However, the second condition has raised problems in relation to the Broadcasting Directive. As discussed earlier,[55] that instrument is

---

[51] See ITC, *Annual Report and Accounts 1993* (1994), p. 23.

[52] The *Performance Reviews* are published annually and are summarised in the ITC's annual reports.

[53] The Broadcasting Act 1996, s. 78 inserts a new s. 21A into the 1990 Act. The power may be used only to prevent a fall in standards, not to enhance existing provision.

[54] See *R. v. Secretary of State for National Heritage ex p. Continental Television Bvio and Others* [1993] 3 C.M.L.R. 387 (the "Red Hot Dutch" case). The other services were TV Erotica, Rendez-Vous, Satisfaction Club Television, Eurotica Rendez-Vous and Eros TV.

[55] Above, chap. 1.

based on the principle of mutual recognition by Member States of each other's laws provided they satisfy the minimum standards that it lays down. It means that, if the satellite is uplinked from an E.C. country, the United Kingdom is supposed to accept any programming which it transmits and, implicitly, to leave enforcement of standards to the uplinking country. However, Article 2 of the Broadcasting Directive allows one Member State to make a provisional derogation where a broadcast from another "manifestly, seriously and gravely" infringes provisions of Articles 22 or 22a dealing with the protection of minors or public order. There must have been at least two prior infringements in the past twelve months and efforts must have been made to reach an amicable settlement.[56]

The purpose of derogation is to allow the receiving state to take enforcement action where the uplinking state has failed to do so or has been ineffective. The problem arises where two countries take different views of what is required to satisfy the substantive provisions of the Directive. The ITC has so far recommended a proscription order in respect of six satellite channels and three of those involving E.C. uplinks have entailed derogations from the 1989 Directive, the only such derogations to have been made. The procedure allows the European Commission to determine whether a derogation is compatible with E.C. law and it has found in favour of the United Kingdom in two cases, with a third currently being investigated.[57] But the European Commission has hinted that the ITC may have been imposing higher standards than those in some other Member States, and has stressed that "The possibility of a difference in judgment between the authorities of the originating country and those of the receiving country is anticipated by the Directive."[58] However, the comparatively stricter provisions of the new Directive means that some other E.C. countries may have to tighten their laws to comply with it, although the possibility of greater control through technical devices means that the ITC may be required to relax its own stance.[59]

---

[56] Council Directive (89/552/EEC) of October 3, 1989 and Directive 97/36/EC of the European Parliament and of the Council (Consolidated Version, 1997), Art. 2(2). See above, chap. 3.

[57] European Commission opinions C(96) 3933 Final (the *Rendez-Vous* case) and C(95) 2678 Final (the *XXXTV,* formerly TV Erotica, case).

[58] European Commission, *Second Report from the Commission to the European Parliament, the Council and the Economic and Social Committee on the Application of Directive 89/552/EEC "Television Without Frontiers"* (1997) para. 4.2.

[59] See chap. 3.

C. Complaints: the Broadcasting Standards Commission

The Broadcasting Standards Commission (the BSC) was established by section 106 of the Broadcasting Act 1996. Consisting of up to fifteen members appointed by the Secretary of State, it constitutes a merger of the former Broadcasting Complaints Commission (the BCC) and the former Broadcasting Standards Council (the Council). Its powers and functions are set out generally in Part V of the Act.[60] The merger was prompted by criticism about the perceived weakness of the BCC, general public confusion about the roles of the two agencies, and the likelihood of making administrative savings.[61] The legislation maintains a distinction, however, between the former BCC's complaints functions, relating to fairness and privacy, and those of the former Council, relating to standards of decency. The government accepted, quite rightly, that the two tasks have important differences. The consideration of personalised complaints requires a dispassionate examination of the issues by a body without responsibility for programme-making. This contrasts with complaints about general standards of propriety that have no special impact on particular individuals. The new Broadcasting Standards Commission, therefore, will have two panels to deal with the separate channels of complaint that existed previously. The basis for mounting such complaints has not been altered by the new Act and, in essence, the work of the two former organisations will continue as before, but under one roof. However, the former Council's obligation to publish a code of guidance has now been extended to fairness and privacy issues and that may help to remedy one of the BCC's principal defects, that it did not articulate the principles on which their adjudications were based. Generally, however, the two panels may be expected to build on past experience and the following account will, therefore, deal with the two strands of complaints separately.

[60] Members work on a part-time basis. They are excluded from being associated with broadcasters, regulators or providers of licensed services. One half of the Commission's finance is provided by the BBC, the Welsh Authority, the ITC, and the R.A.; see s. 127.

[61] See: Department of National Heritage, *The Future of the BBC: Serving the Nation, Competing World-Wide* (1994) Cm. 2621 (White Paper), chap. 7; National Heritage Committee, *The Future of the BBC, Second Report*, (1993–94) H.C. 77-I, paras. 41–45.

Fairness and Privacy Complaints

The BBC set up the first body of this kind in 1971, following hostile reaction to a programme called *Yesterday's Men*.[62] This had adopted a partly satirical and therefore unorthodox approach to a documentary about the Labour Party in Opposition, following its loss of office after a General Election. It was claimed that the programme had not treated the issues as seriously as the participating politicians had expected and that material was used which it had been agreed would be cut.[63] These types of criticism were not new,[64] but the event proved to be a catalyst which prompted the Corporation to establish a Programmes Complaints Commission to head off the possibility of external supervision. Later in the year, the IBA followed suit with its Complaints Review Board.

Although these bodies represented some advance over the previous position, the Annan Committee was critical of their constitution and terms of reference. It considered that neither body commanded public confidence, despite being "scrupulous, judicious and impartial".[65] The fact that it was the broadcasting authorities who appointed their members, that complainants had to waive any relevant legal claims, that the BBC did not consider itself bound by the adjudications of its own commission, and that the IBA's board would not consider complaints about advertising, were all taken into account. Annan's recommendation for a single, independent commission was substantially accepted as the basis for the introduction of the BCC in 1981.[66]

The fairness and privacy remit of the Broadcasting Standards Commission follows the pattern which was established for the BCC. By section 110(1) of the 1996 Act, it has a duty to consider and adjudicate on complaints of unjust or unfair treatment in programmes or unwarranted infringements of privacy in, or in

---

62 The need for such accountability had been anticipated much earlier by the Beveridge Committee. It had gone much further, however, in recommending the establishment of a Public Representation Service that would be a special organ for self-criticism going beyond the receipt of complaints: see Beveridge, above, n. 2, paras 558–564.

63 Munro, above, n. 10, pp. 130–32

64 See M. Tracey, *The Production of Political Television* (1978).

65 Above, n. 7, paras 6.11–6.18.

66 By ss. 17–25, Broadcasting Act 1980. They were reconstituted by Part III of the Broadcasting Act 1981 and further reconstituted on the same basis by Part V of the Broadcasting Act 1990.

connection with the obtaining of material included in, programmes. The programmes affected are those broadcast by the BBC or the Welsh Authority, or included in a licensed service. If a complaint is upheld, however, the BSC cannot insist on an apology, the correction of a false impression, or financial redress. Its only sanction is publicity for its adjudications.[67]

The BSC's jurisdiction in fairness and privacy complaints is limited in important ways. A complaint about a programme transmitted more than five years after the death of the person affected cannot be entertained, unless it is considered appropriate in the circumstances.[68] This differs from the law of defamation, which provides no remedy at all to salvage a deceased person's reputation although, in fact, the point of most complaints of that kind has been the impact of the transmission on the feelings of family and relatives. There are also constraints relating to legal proceedings. Where it appears to the BSC that the complaint is already the subject of legal proceedings in the United Kingdom, it must not entertain it. Similarly, where such a remedy is available in respect of matter complained of, and it appears to the BSC that in the particular circumstances it is not appropriate for it to consider a complaint about the matter, it must also decline to entertain it.[69] These provisions appear to fall just short of requiring the complainant to waive his or her legal rights, a constraint which would be an unjustifiable interference with the individual's rights. The issue was discussed by the Annan Committee when it first recommended a complaints mechanism. It is possible that complaints could be used to rehearse a legal action and might well discourage co-operation from witnesses. However, the complainant should not have to choose between a public vindication or legal redress, and may be entitled to both. It is also possible that broadcasters would be exposed to double jeopardy, but the practical likelihood is that legal action would not be taken.[70] The Court of Appeal has, in effect, endorsed this view in holding that the BCC had wide discretion to weigh up the consequences for possible legal action of proceeding with an investigation. Generally, provided that it assessed properly the nature

---

[67] Broadcasting Act 1996, s. 119.
[68] Broadcasting Act 1996, s. 111(4).
[69] Broadcasting Act 1996, s. 114(2)(a) and (b).
[70] Annan, above, n. 7, para. 6.18.

and gravity of the complaint, there would be a strong expectation that it should proceed.[71]

While there is no formal limitation period set out in the Act, the BSC should refuse to entertain a complaint if it appears to it not to have been made within a reasonable time after the last occasion on which the relevant programme was transmitted.[72] The BCC indicated that it would normally expect a complaint to be made within three months of a television transmission and within six weeks of a radio transmission. Complaints after those times would not normally be entertained unless good cause were shown for the delay.[73] An example of good cause might be an absence abroad during a transmission whose content was only discovered on returning to this country. Finally, there is also provision for the exclusion of frivolous complaints and the BSC must not consider a complaint if " for any other reason" it is inappropriate for it to proceed with it.[74] The latter ground was considered, together with the nature of the subject-matter about which complaints may be entertained, by the Divisional Court in *ex p. Owen*,[75] discussed in chapter three.

The BSC's jurisdiction to hear complaints relating to unfairness or privacy is also constrained by limitations on those who have the standing to complain. A complaint "shall not be entertained by the BSC unless made by the person affected or by a person authorised by him to make the complaint for him."[76] A "person affected" is defined as "a person whose privacy is infringed" or "a participant in the programme in question who was the subject of [unjust or unfair] treatment or a person who, whether such a participant or not, had a direct interest in the subject-matter of that treatment."[77] The scope of the these provisions was considered by the High Court in the *Howard* case.[78] Mrs Howard was an expert historian who provided research material which was not used or referred to in a BBC programme about Churchill's decision, during the Second World War, to support

---

[71] The *Cohen* case: *R. v. Broadcasting Complaints Commission ex p. BBC* (1984) 128 S.J. 384.

[72] Broadcasting Act 1996, s. 111(5).

[73] *Report of the BCC 1994* (1993–94) H.C. 584, para. 11.

[74] Broadcasting Act 1996, s. 114(2)(c) and (d).

[75] *R. v. Broadcasting Complaints Commission ex p. Owen* [1985] 2 All E.R. 522.

[76] Broadcasting Act 1996, s. 111(1). The BSC retains the discretion, however, to refuse to entertain the complaint if it appears to it that the connection is not sufficiently close, by s. 111(7)(b).

[77] Broadcasting Act 1996, s. 130.

[78] *R. v. Broadcasting Complaints Commission ex p. BBC* [1994] E.M.L.R. 497.

Marshal Tito's partisans in Yugoslavia. She objected that she had been unfairly treated and the BCC upheld the complaint on the grounds that not mentioning her work might have indicated to other specialists in the field that her research was in some sense unsatisfactory. In proceedings for judicial review, Laws J. decided that there were two stages in determining the relationship between the complainant and the programme in question. First, the subject matter of the programme must be identified — that is, the contents of the broadcast which give rise to the claim of unfairness. This does not require a decision as to whether the programme was unfair or not. Secondly, it must be asked whether the complainant had a direct interest in that subject matter, again, irrespective of whether it can be shown to be unfair or not. It is only after such a direct interest has been established that the BCC may then proceed to consider the merits of the complaint. On the facts, it was found that Mrs Howard did not have a direct interest in the historical events portrayed by the programme, so her action failed. Laws J. said that it was not in the public interest to expand the scope of the BCC's jurisdiction to allow complaints about interests entirely collateral to any real interest which the complainant has in what has been broadcast. In essence, what Mrs. Howard wanted, and what the BCC seemed anxious to give her, was a right of access to the media. But freedom in communication does not entail that such a right should be provided for individuals, even if broadcasting freedom carries with it the responsibility to ensure that all notable views are portrayed.

Related to the issue of individual standing is the question of how far trade and representative organisations should be allowed to use the BSC to voice complaints about their members or products. The BCC's view was that such groups were not excluded from its jurisdiction and that the possibility that pressure groups will come to exert an undue influence on editorial autonomy is exaggerated. It stressed that the proportion of such groups who make complaints has remained constant since the Commission was established and that the basic need for a direct interest would be sufficient to exclude those who wish to use the complaints procedure to gain publicity for their cause.[79] However, its attitude to the standing of a representative organisation which does act in individuals' interests, but which may also have a wider political agenda to pursue, led to another challenge

---

[79] *Report of the BCC 1992* (1992–93) H.C. 83, para. 6; *Report of the B.C.C. 1991* (1990–91) H.C. 533, paras. 11–12.

in the High Court. In the *National Council for One-Parent Families (NCOPF)* case,[80] the BCC had taken the view[81] that the BBC *Panorama* programme, "Babies on Benefit", was unjust and unfair towards single mothers receiving social security benefits. The complaint had been brought by the NCOPF, and not by any individual mentioned in the programme, but the BCC regarded them as having a "direct interest" in the programme. The BBC was directed to broadcast a summary of the adjudication, but took the unusual step of also broadcasting a strongly worded rebuttal of the BCC's findings, believing that it had strayed into the general area of impartiality towards controversial matters. In proceedings for judicial review, Brooke J. held that the BCC should not have taken jurisdiction, but based his decision on the broad ground that Parliament had not intended the complaints scheme to be used to examine a programme's treatment of thousands of unidentified people. The result is consistent with the better argued test adopted by Laws J. On a broad view, the NCOPF might be regarded as part of the general social scenario which the programme portrayed. But unless the NCOPF played a part in the design of the benefits scheme, or suffered or benefited under it as an organisation, it is difficult to believe that its interest in complaining was anything other than collateral to the content of the programme. It stretches the idea of "direct interest" too far to allow anybody with an interest in a cause to be regarded as having a direct interest in a programme that is relevant to the cause. Furthermore, it would be a severe inroad on broadcasting freedom, enabling too many remote parties to have an effective veto on the general approach of programme-makers to selecting and editing material.

As for procedure,[82] the complaint must be in writing and, when it is received, the BSC must send a copy of it to the relevant broadcaster, regulatory body and licence-holder. They are obliged to comply with any requests from the BSC for tapes or transcripts, and for their representations. The BCC's practice was to hold a hearing, although there is a discretion whether or not to do so, but it must be in private. In recent years, the BCC streamlined its procedure by reducing the flow of complaints, replies and rejoinders between

---

[80] *R. v. Broadcasting Complaints Commission ex p. BBC* [1995] E.M.L.R. 241; [1995] C.O.D. 499.

[81] Reportedly, this was against the advice of its Secretary, but the Chairman has denied this. See *The Guardian* September 13, 1994 and September 15, 1994.

[82] Broadcasting Act 1996, s. 115.

complainants and the programmers, and by seeking to agree heads of grievance before the latter are approached. What it has consistently refused to do is to use a full hearing to allow cross-examination of the parties by each other. The process is regarded as informal and it has expressed concern at the time and expense that is being taken with the increased use of lawyers in furthering complaints.

As discussed in chapter three, prior to the 1996 Act there was no obligation to draw up a code setting out the principles for deciding claims of unjust or unfair treatment, or unwarranted infringements of privacy. But the BCC's practice demonstrated an increasingly interventionist approach to such issues, and it often left broadcasters frustrated and unsure of their approach.[83] Yet, if anything was noticeable about the BCC, it was its low profile. Despite there being a duty on the broadcasters and regulators to publicise its existence,[84] it was not used very often and its findings did not seem to have had a great impact. To a great extent, this may be because the broadcasters had already established strong internal controls on their practices in this area, and they had also developed alternative, informal mechanisms for dealing with complaints and heading off criticism. At the beginning, the BCC did not seek to antagonise the programme-makers and saw its role as not only safeguarding the public from unjust treatment or unwarranted infringements of privacy, but also safeguarding the media from unfair criticism.[85] Although it has tilted the balance since then, its work did not receive widespread public recognition and it failed to gain the respect of the programmers. It did not attempt to develop a caselaw and it did not link its remit with the programmers' codes of practice relating to fairness and privacy.

A major factor in rendering the fairness and privacy remedy inadequate was the ineffectual sanction at the BCC's disposal. This has been continued for the BSC.[86] All it can do, when a complaint is upheld, is require the offending broadcaster or licence holder to publish, at a time it directs, a summary of the complaint and its findings. The 1996 Act has bolstered this sanction, to a small extent, by providing that the offender should not publish a reply at the same time and by requiring a report to be made back to the BSC about the

---

[83] For a fuller analysis, see T. Gibbons, "The Role of the Broadcasting Complaints Commission: Current Practice and Future Prospects" (1995) 1 *Yearbook of Media and Entertainment Law* 129–159.
[84] Contained now, in respect of the BSC, in Broadcasting Act 1996, s. 124.
[85] BCC, *Report of the BCC 1982* (1981–82) H.C. 478, para. 13.
[86] Broadcasting Act 1996, s. 119.

action taken as a result of the adjudication.[87] This represents a missed opportunity because, if the new body is to have any credibility, it must be seen to have a more effective remedy, for example, the power to require apologies and corrections to be broadcast. In return, the BSC should not be able to uphold complaints in part, as the BCC used to do, by seizing on limited findings of unfairness or invasions of privacy regardless of their impact on the programme as a whole. At present, however, discussion of the BSC's work in this area has a marginal quality; the main constraints on programmers' practice are the broadcasters' and regulators' own codes.

Standards Complaints

The former Broadcasting Standards Council (the Council) was established on a non-statutory basis in 1988. The reasons why it should have emerged at that particular time are not easy to identify, however. As an idea, it had been pressed by the National Viewers' and Listeners' Association for many years.[88] It followed unsuccessful attempts to reform the Obscene Publications Act 1959,[89] it coincided with renewed arguments from the women's movement about the links between pornography and violence and, more generally, it marked the hardening of attitudes towards libertarian morality that was associated with the contemporary political trend to conservatism, notwithstanding its paradoxical association with economic deregulation.[90] Its creation was justified on the grounds that the public were becoming concerned that broadcasters had become slack in enforcing their own standards and that programming was placing the vulnerable (children and those susceptible to violence) at risk; in both cases, the evidence to support these claims was, at best, equivocal.[91] In addition, it was argued that external review would be

---

[87] Broadcasting Act 1996, ss. 119(4) and 120, respectively.

[88] See "Representing Britain's Semi-detached Values," interview with Mary Whitehouse by M. Brown, *The Independent* April 8, 1987. See also, M. Tracey, *Whitehouse* (1977).

[89] Bills were introduced by Churchill in 1985–86 and by Howarth in 1986–87.

[90] See generally, A. Gamble and C. Wells, *Thatcher's Law* (1989). The catalyst for the Council's creation seems to have been, however, the showing of scenes of rape and murder in the Jackie Collins saga, *Sins*, on a Sunday in September 1987 and before the family viewing watershed.

[91] See *Hansard* Standing Committee F, Broadcasting Bill, March 1, 1990, cols. 1097–1100.

good for the broadcasters, providing an extra safety net and even accountability.

Under the 1990 Act, the Council was placed on a statutory footing. Its remit has now been taken over by the BSC under section 108 of the 1996 Act. Its duty is to draw up a code of guidance about practices to be followed in connection with the portrayal of violence in programmes, practices to be followed in connection with the portrayal of sexual conduct in programmes, and standards of taste and decency for programmes generally. The duty applies to all television and sound programmes broadcast by the BBC and the Welsh Authority or included in a licensed service. In turn, the broadcasting and regulatory bodies have a duty to "reflect the general effect" of the BSC's code in their own codes of practice.

In fact, the relationship seems to have been reversed, in the sense that the Council's code reflected much of programmers' codes on the relevant subject-matter. The main difference between them is that the Council's code is more discursive and includes more examples and justifications, albeit together with more prescriptions, broad generalisations and controversial value judgments.

The BSC also has a duty to monitor broadcasting standards with a view to making general reports, including assessments of public attitudes and the way programming can affect them.[92] This duty extends to monitoring unlicensed services that are capable of being received in this country. In addition, it must consider any complaints made, by itself or the public, and adjudicate upon them, taking into account any relevant provision of its code.

As with fairness complaints, the statute sets out certain procedural requirements. Complaints must be made in writing and within two months in the case of a television programme, or three weeks in the case of sound. They must also not be the actual or potential subject of court proceedings in the United Kingdom, nor be frivolous or otherwise inappropriate for the BSC to consider. The programme provider must furnish the Council with a copy of the programme and a written reply. There is no requirement to hold a hearing to determine the complaint although, if one is held, it will be in private. This failure of due process was explained on the basis that the adjudication will not be a specific finding about a programme, but will address the general issue of the programmer's compliance with

---

[92] Broadcasting Act 1996, s. 109. It can no longer start the complaints procedure on its own motion, however.

the code.[93] While the statute gives no grounds for that interpretation, it is difficult to envisage findings that will not reflect judgments about particular programmes. Where a hearing is held, the complainant, the programme provider and programme-maker, any relevant regulatory body and any other person who might be able to assist are entitled to attend and be heard.

The BSC's decisions do not have a direct effect on the transmission of programmes. They are made known after the event and there is no power to prevent the offending programme from being repeated. It is also the policy behind the legislation, although it is not stipulated, that the BSC should be commenting on the broadcaster's or regulatory body's failure to comply with their own codes or that of BSC. The BSC's only sanction, or vindication if the complaint is unfounded, is to require the publication of a summary of the complaint together with its findings and general observations or a summary of them. Whether this will force programmers to change their practices depends on the moral authority that the BSC can command. At present, there is little evidence that the Council's moral criticism had much effect. Much more significant is the regulatory power of the ITC and R.A. to enforce sanctions and the development of good practice within the BBC through its Programmes Complaints Unit. Although there are sometimes differences of opinion, the regulators tend to adopt the same approach as the BSC (although neither refers to the other's findings).

For all attempts to justify its existence, then, the BSC's position is difficult to sustain in relation to standards complaints. Institutionally, its relationship with the broadcasters and regulatory bodies does not reveal clear channels of responsibility. Technically, the latter are independent but it is obvious that they will be expected to heed the BSC's advice. Indeed, the emphasis in the Council's work was very much directed towards making the programmers responsive to perceived public preferences, at the expense of editorial responsibility. The language of its first report contained much consumerist symbolism, with the relationship between broadcaster and audience being described as a contractual undertaking. The free speech principle was reinterpreted to mean that speech could be restricted for a cause "generally accepted" as a sufficient justification. At the same time, it asserted a number of strong values that reject an

---

[93] *Hansard*, Standing Committee F, March 6, 1990, cols. 1164–1166.

"ugly" society, acknowledge our "common humanity", decry the impoverishment of language and see the broadcasters in terms of visitors to the home. The BSC's dilemma is that it wishes to maximise individual autonomy whilst maintaining some standards. Although its own view of a good society is barely concealed, it cannot stipulate that, since it recognises the pluralism of our society. As a result, it tends to rely on the public's preferences, as revealed through market surveys and admittedly unrepresentative visits around the country, supplemented by empirical research on media effects. The reports of its complaints decisions are barely reasoned, being based on judgments about the relationship between programmes and the moral standards thought to be held by the general audience. It is not possible to make useful generalisations from them because they do not add to the provisions of the BSC's, or indeed the programmers', codes, and in respect of which there will always be reasonable differences of opinion.[94] The standards remit of the BSC could have great potential, if it had been established as a forum for open-minded discussion of media policy rather than a kind of enforcement agency. Instead, it will probably have the effect of making broadcasters more defensive and reluctant to allow the public to contribute to their own debates.

D. Self-regulation: the Press

Unlike the position with the programming media, the press is supervised through self-regulation. The organisation which used to be responsible for this was the Press Council.[95] It was established in 1953, as the General Council for the Press, in a rather belated response to the recommendations of the first Royal Commission on the Press and prompted by the introduction of a Private Member's Bill to achieve a similar result by statute. The Royal Commission had been established to examine the effect of increased concentration of ownership of the press on the quality of journalism and the furthering of free expression. Reporting in 1949, it found a number

---

[94] See generally, the BSC's monthly report, *The Bulletin*. For a survey of earlier decisions, see F. Coleman, "All in the Best Possible Taste: The Broadcasting Standards Council 1989–1992" [1993] *Public Law* 488–515.

[95] For an account of the Press Council's history, see H. P. Levy, *The Press Council* (1967); G. Robertson, *People Against the Press* (1983).

of deficiencies in newspapers' performances in terms of distortion of fact, political bias and a concern with sensationalism and triviality. In order to preserve what it considered the proper relationship between the press and society, if the press were to render a service to the public over and above the claims of commerce, it considered that the press itself should establish a body which would be responsible to the public for maintaining standards of integrity and professional conduct. The General Council of the Press was envisaged as building up a code of conduct in accordance with the highest professional standards, with particular attention being paid to complaints from the public, especially those relating to mistakes and invasions of privacy. In addition, it was hoped that some opportunity for the publication of views at odds with editorial policy could be encouraged. To enhance its moral authority, which was to be drawn from the press itself, the Council would have an independent chairman and would have a proportion of its members drawn from the public.[96] Furthermore, as Robertson emphasised, the Council was intended to be in the nature of a governing body which would represent press interests and constantly review the state of the industry, including its ownership and control.

In fact, the Council which did appear was a professional body consisting entirely of representatives of the newspaper industry and having as its Chairman a member of the press. It was financed wholly by the industry, as its successor is now. It did little to influence the development of professional standards and failed to draw attention to increasingly monopolistic tendencies in the industry, resulting in the setting up of a Second Royal Commission which reported in 1962.[97] That Commission was principally concerned with the Council's impotence in scrutinising the economic structure of the industry but, in addition to recommending that its objects and resources should be extended accordingly, it reiterated the First Commission's position on the Council's objectives and the need for an independent, lay element as a means of establishing its credibility. Furthermore, it suggested that, unless reform were quickly forthcoming, the case for legislative implementation of its proposals would be compelling. The outcome was a differently constituted Press Council which operated until 1991.

The Press Council's first object was to "preserve the established freedom of the Press". In the Younger Committee's view, this,

---

[96] Royal Commission on the Press, *Report* (1949) Cmd. 7700, paras 640 *et seq.*

[97] (Shawcross) Royal Commission on the Press, *Report* (1962) Cmnd. 1811.

together with its fourth objective to "keep under review developments likely to restrict the supply of information of public interest and importance", suggested that freedom for the press, rather than the interests of complainants, was considered the main priority.[98] This seemed likely because, at that time, the Council's membership consisted of 20 nominees of proprietors' and journalists' interests, and only five lay persons. Subsequently, following criticism from the Third Royal Commission which reported in 1977, lay membership was increased to 18, which constituted half the Council, but its concerns appeared to remain the same.[99]

The Press Council's second objective was to "maintain the character of the British Press in accordance with the highest professional and commercial standards." It did not manage to achieve any authoritative status in this regard, however. The First Royal Commission's hope was that it would develop a code of ethical conduct but this did not materialise. Indeed, the Council did not develop a set of rational principles to guide its adjudications on complaints, despite criticism on this point from the Third Royal Commission which drew attention to the way that "the standards they apply and the terms in which they are expressed fall short of what is desirable. In particular, we consider that adjudications do not contain sufficient argument, and that they sometimes make too many allowances for editorial discretion and errors of fact."[1] Nevertheless, the Press Council rejected the Commission's recommendation to produce a written code and to develop better reasoning for its decisions. Only when the National Union of Journalists withdrew its support for the Council in 1980 and it suffered criticism from some print unions in the following years did it offer to compile a code of past decisions, in return for the TUC's good offices in restoring harmony to its work.[2] Eventually, a digest of its decisions for the period 1953–84, *Principles for the Press*, was published in 1985, but it was a typology rather than a synthesis and it did not appear to be used as an authoritative source in its decisions.

Occasionally, the Council published declarations of principles. The one on privacy has already been mentioned, but there was also one on payments for articles, that is, cheque-book journalism. The main

---

[98] (Younger) *Report of the Committee on Privacy* (1972) Cmnd. 5012, para. 135.
[99] Judged by its chairmen's forewords to its Annual Reports.
[1] (McGregor) Royal Commission on the Press, *Final Report* (1977) Cmnd. 6810, para. 20.48.
[2] See Robertson, above, n. 95, p. 16.

declaration was made in 1966 and it was supplemented in 1975 to include indirect payments and in 1983 to include payments to the associates of criminals. The basic approach was that neither wrongdoers nor the press should benefit from the sale of stories to the press unless it is warranted in the public interest. In 1985, a declaration of principle was issued concerning financial journalism, essentially deploring any involvement by the press in insider dealing.

The third objective of the Press Council was to "consider complaints about the conduct of the Press or the conduct of persons and organisations towards the Press; to deal with these complaints in whatever manner might seem practical and appropriate and record resultant action." The basic procedure was that a complaint should first be addressed to the editor of the offending paper. If no satisfaction were obtained, the Council would then take action, initially offering conciliation but, if that failed, undertaking an investigation. As a condition of such action, if legal action was threatened or considered a possibility, the Council could ask the complainant to waive it in return for the editor's agreeing to co-operate in the inquiry and publish its findings. The only sanction for censured conduct was for adjudications to be sent to the paper for publication.

It will be noted that the objective relating to complaints was not wholly disciplinary, but also defensive. It was in the former aspect of the Council's work that most criticism was levelled, however, the main charge being that it failed to produce effective remedies for those who were aggrieved by press activity. The requirement of the waiver was especially controversial. It was justified on the basis that it prevented a newspaper or journalist from being exposed to double jeopardy. Both the Annan Committee and the Third Royal Commission criticised it because it unjustifiably restricted access to the courts and gave the impression that the Council was protecting the press from adverse comment.[3] In addition, as Robertson pointed out,[4] adverse adjudications by the Council did not jeopardise the press in any meaningful sense, since it had no legal powers. The disclosure of information in the course of a complaint would be unlikely to prejudice the press position in a legal action since the information would be disclosed through discovery and the court would, in any event, make up its own mind on the evidence. In

[3] See Annan, above, n. 7, para. 18; Royal Commission, above, n. 1, paras 43–49.
[4] Above, n. 95, pp. 29-31.

Robertson's opinion, only where the press might be threatened with criminal proceedings or where a journalistic source would be likely to be revealed would the waiver be justifiable.

Of course, all this assumes that access to the courts is a realistic option for most complainants. In most cases, however, the likely costs of legal action make double jeopardy remote and that suggests that more effort should be directed to providing a more effective alternative remedy. It may be that a self-regulatory body could have an important role simply by publicly condemning breaches of professional standards without exacting any punishment or compensation for the breach. Yet the Press Council did not even achieve that. As it was constituted, it lacked the support of the press for, as is still the case, there was no self-critical tradition, no moral compulsion, on which it could draw to enforce its pronouncements. Contrary to the Younger Committee's belief, it was not "respected, feared and obeyed".

Other criticisms of the Council referred to its procedures for adjudication. It adopted an adversarial approach which placed the onus on an aggrieved person, first, to make a complaint and then to pursue it against an opponent who would be usually wealthier and able to secure lawyers' advice and advocacy. In many cases, the complainant was asked to formulate the grievance in terms of an offence against recognised standards of press conduct, despite the Council's inability to clarify them. In addition, the press was entitled to an oral hearing, although the complainant was not, which added to an impression of unfairness. As a response to these kinds of difficulty, the Third Royal Commission considered that the Council should adopt a much more inquisitorial approach, especially in relation to persistent breaches of standards.

A further problem was the considerable potential, more often realised than not, for long delays to develop, because the Council allowed the parties to comment on and respond to each others' written submissions and it because it met infrequently. In 1984, the Council did introduce what it called a "fast track" procedure for the speedy correction of agreed significant factual errors or inaccuracies, or a speedy independent ruling where a complainant and the editor concerned disagreed. This was expected to produce a result within about 10 working days for people or organisations who were clearly identified. It was intended to demonstrate that the Council was effective in order to head off statutory control, but it was clearly of only limited scope, not least because it did not envisage the use of the telephone! Some of these shortcomings could be put down to a lack of finance from the industry, and the Third Royal Commission did recommend an increase in the Council's funds, but the main problem seemed to be a lack of commitment to make the organisation an effective force.

A principal reason why self-regulation in the press has persisted for so long, despite its patent inadequacies, is that both the press and its owners have been able to exploit the reluctance of government to be seen to interfere with free speech in a democracy. They have been able to identify the media's interests with the broader constitutional principle. Other reasons are ones that have been suggested to explain the preference for self-regulation in other spheres: the reluctance in British administrative culture to use legal controls, the political and economic weight of the industry in general, and the low party-political status of regulation, with MPs of all parties having interests in the industry. Substantively, the press has also been able to advance arguments to support self-regulation. In general, it is said that it is less costly to make rules, they can be tailored for the particular industry, enforcement is likely to be easier, and sanctions can be made more credible leading to greater compliance.[5]

For the most part however, the experience of the Press Council did not bear out these claims. As a result, its ineffectual nature and the contrast with responsible regulation in the programming media led to serious questioning of self-regulation and the official response was another inquiry into the standards adopted by the press, that of the Calcutt Committee.[6] This was set up following Parliamentary discussion of two Private Members' Bills, the Right of Reply Bill and the Protection of Privacy Bill, in 1989. Although the Bills were unsuccessful, the support which they received was considered to be evidence of widespread "public concern." Unfortunately, the Committee never substantiated the breadth of that concern, dwelling instead on relatively few incidents. One was the intrusion by the *Sunday Sport* into the hospital ward where the actor, Gordon Kaye, was recovering from surgery following an accident.[7] Another was an out of court settlement by *The Sun* in favour of the singer, Elton John. The Committee also emphasised evidence which they had

[5] See Ramsay, above, n. 37, pp. 91, 395–396.
[6] Home Office, *Report of the Committee on Privacy and Related Matters* (1990), Cm. 1102.
[7] This was the subject of litigation in *Kaye v. Robertson* [1990] F.S.R. 62. The judgment is reproduced as an appendix in the Calcutt Report.

received about the use by newspapers of stolen private correspondence and photographs.

For the purposes of this section, the main interest in the Committee's report lies in its discussion of the relative merits of the law, a regulatory scheme or self-regulation as the best means of maintaining standards in the press. It rejected a right of reply law on the grounds of practicality, as there would be difficulties in establishing the facts of a dispute in a suitably short time. It also rejected a general law of privacy for the familiar reasons offered by the Younger Committee, that it would be difficult to define, the need to incorporate some public interest defence would render its scope uncertain and the law would be unlikely to provide a simple and effective remedy. The choice, then, was between a voluntary commitment to ethical conduct or the imposition of a statutory complaints mechanism.

The Committee's preference was for a strengthened form of self-regulation in the shape of a Press Complaints Commission that would be financed by the industry but, in contrast to similar recommendations from Royal Commissions in the past, it suggested a legal framework for enforcing standards should the press not co-operate. The statutory route was envisaged, however, only if the new Commission failed to materialise by June 1991 or if there were a serious breakdown in the system whereby the Commission ceased to be effective. In the meantime, the possibility of giving the Commission statutory powers to enforce its rulings, should they be flouted, was seen as a preliminary move towards a compulsory scheme.

Unlike the Press Council, the Press Complaints Commission would not be an organisation campaigning on behalf of the press. Instead, its main duty would be to consider complaints in the light of a Code of Practice which it would be expected to publish. Such a code would have to be an improvement upon the Press Council's rather vague set of principles and the equally vague code that had been issued by the Newspaper Publishers' Association in 1989 in an attempt to soften the impact of reform proposals. Drawing on a revised code which had been adopted by the Press Council while the Committee was deliberating, Calcutt offered its own model which set out considerations relating to such matters as privacy, misrepresentation, harassment, intrusions into grief, the identification of victims and discrimination. The Press Complaints Commission was not recommended to have the role of a professional disciplinary body or a licensing agency, however, because it was considered that that would pose a danger for freedom of speech. Nor would it have any power to award compensation to aggrieved members of the public. Instead, it would provide a form of conciliation and adjudication with a more speedy procedure. Where a complaint was found to be justified, the Commission would be able to recommend that the offending newspaper should publish an apology.

These were severe recommendations[8] but, although the Press Council was reluctant to accept Calcutt's proposals, the Newspaper Publishers' Association and the Newspaper Society decided that it should be replaced by the Press Complaints Commission which started to receive complaints in January, 1991. However, two years later, Calcutt was asked to review the progress in securing protection for privacy. He strongly criticised the press for not implementing the recommendations of the earlier Committee.[9] In particular, they had not created an independent body for appointing members of the Press Complaints Commission; they had diluted the Committee's code of practice by introducing a version agreed by a panel of editors which had weakened the concept of "public interest"; they had not accepted that third party complaints should be investigated; and nor had they set up a "hot line" to provide a speedy resolution of grievances. Calcutt also made more detailed proposals for the statutory tribunal, which was envisaged as having powers to issue rulings, warnings and restraints on publication, powers to require apologies to be published and compensation to be paid and, ultimately, a power to impose fines to a maximum of one per cent of the net annual revenue of the paper concerned.

Following this review, Members of Parliament decided to examine the issue themselves and the National Heritage Select Committee produced a report which was much more sympathetic to media interests.[10] The Committee regarded the starting point for discussion as the public's "right to know". It thought that Calcutt's "cage of legal restraint" was inappropriate for regulating the media, preferring voluntary restraint combined with general laws not aimed solely and specifically at the media. Its proposals were intended to be implemented as a package; separate items were not to be introduced

---

[8] C. Munro, "Press Freedom — How the Beast was Tamed", (1991) 54 *Modern Law Review* 104–111.

[9] D. Calcutt, *Review of Press Regulation* (1993) Cm. 2135.

[10] National Heritage Select Committee, *Privacy and Media Intrusion* (1992–93) H.C. 94-I.

without the checks and balances of the others. This was because the cumulative effect of the law, especially that relating to official secrecy and defamation, was regarded as already adding to the media's difficulties in serving democratic interests. The first of the Committee's four principal recommendations was that there should be government action to extend access to information before any further measures should be introduced to constrain media activity. The second recommendation was for a Protection of Privacy Bill to cover all citizens, not just the media. Thirdly, it was recommended that voluntary regulation of the press should be strengthened by means of a contractual editorial responsibility for enforcing the industry's code of practice, the appointment of readers' representatives to adjudicate on complaints, and the establishment of a Press Commission with a brief to monitor complaints, but also to protect the freedom of the press (which is not within the PCC's brief). The Commission would be established by the industry, but would have powers to initiate complaints, adjudicate on them, enforce rulings through apologies or corrections, fines and compensation, and conduct research. It was expected that the industry would provide finance for the Commission's work and support its actions by accepting a revised code of practice which would recognise a zone of individual privacy and educate journalists accordingly. Fourthly, the Committee proposed a statutory Ombudsman to act as a bulwark against the inadequacies of voluntary regulation. Its role would be to investigate situations where the voluntary arrangements had broken down, supervise the Commission's work and, ultimately, enforce the code.

Soon after the National Heritage Committee's report, the Lord Chancellor's Department (LCD) published a consultation paper dealing with the case for introducing a general right to privacy in respect of conduct which constituted an infringement of a person's privacy, causing him substantial distress, provided such distress would also have been suffered by a person of ordinary sensibilities in the circumstances of the complainant.[11] However, the government decided against the introduction of privacy legislation.[12] Instead, it

---

[11] Lord Chancellor's Department (LCD) (and the Scottish Office), *Infringement of Privacy* (1993) Consultation Paper. A natural person's privacy was to be taken to include matters appertaining to his health, personal communications, and family and personal relationships, and a right to be free from harassment and molestation. There would be defences available to cover consent, lawful authority, absolute or qualified privilege, and disclosure in the public interest.

[12] Department of National Heritage, *Privacy and Media Intrusion: The Government's Response* 1995, Cm. 2918.

hoped that an improved process of self-regulation could be made to work. To this end, it suggested that the PCC should pay compensation, from a fund set up by the press industry, to victims of press intrusion (although this proposal has not been implemented), that a hot-line should be established between the PCC Chairman and editors, and that non-industry members should sit on the PCC committee responsible for drafting its code, which should be tightened.

Although the new Chairman of the PCC indicated a greater readiness to adopt a more rigorous approach,[13] the PCC was unable to make much progress in reducing press coverage of personal matters. Although it has appointed a Privacy Commissioner to investigate complaints, the public interest exception has given newspapers much scope. Stories about the Royal Family can be justified because it is a public institution.[14] Stories about hypocrisy by public figures can be justified because they reveal the way that the public is being deceived.[15] Furthermore, although it is possible to discover the outcome of PCC adjudications, there has been no attempt to mould them into a semblance of doctrine and they generally depend on the facts of the particular circumstances.[16] In any event, the PCC's sanctions continue to be limited. It may censure a journalist or newspaper, but it has no powers to impose a fine or award compensation. It may require a newspaper to publish an adverse adjudication, but it has no legal power to enforce that requirement. This lack of power has been reflected in the reactions of

---

[13] For example, in May 1995, the PCC upheld a complaint that the *News of the World* had breached its code in reporting Countess Spencer's bulimia problems. The chairman, Lord Wakeham, went further and wrote to the paper's proprietor, Rupert Murdoch, to express his concern. The paper's editor was publicly rebuked by Murdoch and apologised to the Spencers. More generally, see Press Complaints Commission, *Annual Report 1996* (1997).

[14] Examples are: the *Sunday Mirror* and *Daily Mirror* pictures of Princess Diana exercising in a gym; stories about nuisance telephone calls allegedly made by Princess Diana; accounts of love letters sent between Prince Charles and Camilla Parker-Bowles; and the *News of the World* story of the Princess's sister-in-law, Countess Spencer, and her battle with bulimia.

[15] Examples include various accounts of sexual immorality by persons of responsibility, those in high office, or those who advocate high personal standards; the *News of the World* has run a series of such stories in the late 1990s. Another topical set of examples is the publication, by many papers, of the details of National Lottery winners' personal lives.

[16] See L. Blom-Cooper & L.R. Pruitt, "Privacy Jurisprudence of the Press Complaints Commission" [1994] *Anglo-American Law Review* 133. The adjudications can be accessed at http://www.pccorg.uk/ .

the tabloids to PCC adjudications. Although they are normally published, they are given little prominence and the opportunity is sometimes taken to repeat the story which led to the complaint in the first place.[17] Following public discussion after the death of Diana, Princess of Wales, however, the PCC has streamlined its procedures, and tightened its code even further, as discussed in chapter three, but it is still too early to say how effective the new Commission will be. On the positive side, the new code provides a clearer foundation for the development of a more coherent body of guidance for acceptable practice by the press, provided that the Commission is willing to support it. The likelihood that newspapers will comply with the Commission's rulings is stronger, too, as there is a feeling that warnings that this is a last chance for self-regulation are more serious and will indeed be followed by legislation if it fails.[18] The need for change in a more hostile political climate has also been anticipated within the press and many newspapers have ombudsmen, some more apparently independent than others, to deal with complaints.

For all that, the main obstacle to reform will be the press itself. Self-regulation cannot succeed without its co-operation. Unlike broadcasting, there is less of a common culture within the press to enable discussion and acceptance of constraints on journalistic enthusiasm. News values tend to work in the opposite direction and it should not be surprising if there is resistance, both commercial and professional, to attempts to constrain the medium. Indeed, as an implicit acknowledgement that the code may be drafted too weakly, the PCC's Chairman has warned that newspapers should not place excessive reliance on the public interest defence.[19] Resistance to regulation may occur despite the fact that there is a much stronger editorial presence in the membership of the Commission than the Press Council, and a better cross-section of editorial styles, and that this latest effort at reform is backed by what have so far been the most realistic threats to legislate.

It would be worrying if further restrictions were placed on the press in the shape of sanctions which are external to its professional

---

[17] Examples are the *News of the World*'s re-publication of a story about the personal life of Clare Short M.P. following the PCC's ruling that it had invaded her privacy, and *The People*'s reproduction of secretly taken pictures of the Duke of York's daughter playing naked.

[18] See the Home Secretary's response to Calcutt's recommendations in *Hansard*, Vol. 174, col. 1124.

[19] PCC, *Press Release: Privacy and the Public Interest* November 21, 1996.

practice, because that practice is more likely to protect free speech and the dissemination of knowledge than a tribunal dedicated to preserving some interests at the expense of media scrutiny. However, the choice is not between complete liberty and total control. There are good reasons for demanding that the press should exercise a respect for such values as accuracy, privacy and non-discrimination, and there is a role for regulation to encourage the development of a professional recognition of their importance. The pressure for change must come from within the press, through its own public discussion of appropriate practice, but statutory support for the PCC's role — such as a requirement to publish the PCC's findings or a mechanism for it to impose financial penalties — should not be seen as interference with editorial freedom.

E. Other Forms of Accountability

The Political Process

For all that formal channels of accountability do exist, the political process can allow broadcasters to become remote from democratic supervision out of politicians' deference to either editorial independence or professional expertise. Yet the pressures to secure greater responsiveness continue, manifesting themselves in different ways. When politicians find themselves formally excluded from detailed debate about programming, it becomes attractive for them to voice their views as consumers. At the same time, when members of the audience find themselves unable to obtain satisfaction from broadcasters, it is natural for them to turn to their representatives in order to secure redress. Such moves are easy to make since each appears to be consistent with the concept of public service, with its ambiguous interest in both production and consumption. Yet it is being done at some cost to the media's independence by devaluing the importance of responsibility as a component of accountability and substituting, instead, a version of responsiveness that is more characteristic of the market than of the democratic process. Although criticism of programme content or timing is not new,[20] there has been a growing confidence in the use of informal public means, often by government and facilitated by the media itself, to air grievances.

---

[20] See C. Munro, *Television, Censorship and the Law* (1979).

One approach involves making views known in the course of general political discussion. An example is the controversy that developed during the Falklands campaign in 1982. Following two BBC programmes on the subject, the Prime Minister and the Foreign Secretary expressed concern that the approach to news and comment was too neutral in its treatment of the British and Argentinean positions. A number of MPs signed a motion condemning the Corporation's stance, although the Opposition defended it, and when the Chairman and Director-General designate went to the Commons to explain their own position, that the Corporation had to maintain its reputation for telling the truth, they received a lamentably hostile reception.[21] Another example, in 1985, concerned the BBC programme "Real Lives: At the Edge of the Union", which examined extreme nationalist and loyalist attitudes to the situation in Northern Ireland. The Prime Minister indicated her disapproval of the film and the Home Secretary said he believed that it would be contrary to the national interest to show it because it would give succour to terrorism, although neither had seen it. In the face of this criticism, the Governors of the BBC unfortunately decided to cancel the broadcast.[22] Another example was the disapproval that surrounded the showing of the Thames Television documentary "This Week: Death on the Rock". It dealt with the shooting in Gibraltar of three suspected IRA terrorists by the SAS and was condemned by the Prime Minister and the Foreign Secretary, on the grounds that it might prejudice an impending inquest on the deceased. Another programme on the same issue, transmitted by the BBC in Northern Ireland, was the subject of adverse comment by the Northern Ireland Secretary, the Foreign Secretary and, by implication, the Prime Minister.[23] In addition to these instances, MPs will often raise programming policy during parliamentary debate. Particular examples include the showings of

---

[21] See V. Adams, *The Media and the Falklands Campaign* (1986), pp. 8–14.

[22] See L. Curtis, "British Broadcasting and Ireland" in *Bending Reality* (J. Curran *et al.* eds., 1986). The film was subsequently shown, but with alterations intended to achieve greater balance. See also G. Philo, *War and Peace News* (1985); R. Negrine, *Politics and the Mass Media in Britain* (2nd ed. 1994), pp. 112-117.

[23] See *The Guardian*, April 29, May 3, 5, 7, 1988; *Hansard* (1987–88) Vol. 132, cols. 719–720, May 3 and cols. 1012–1013, May 5. Thames Television commissioned an independent inquiry which largely vindicated the programme but was rejected by the government. See *The Windlesham Report* (1989); *The Guardian*, January 27 and 28, 1989; *Hansard* (1988–89) Vol. 146, cols. 5w, 583w; the report was not discussed, but only lodged in the House of Commons Library.

"The Monocled Mutineer" and of "Tumbledown", together with an interview with the Sinn Fein leader, Gerry Adams.[24] More generally, the showing of sex and violence on television has occasioned much comment, especially during the debates on Mr Winston Churchill's Private Member's Bill to reform the Obscene Publications Act in 1986.[25]

As an alternative way of proceeding, politicians may make direct approaches to broadcasters. During the Falklands dispute, the Foreign Secretary asked viewers who were concerned to complain to the BBC, rather than get in touch with the Corporation himself. Yet, when Thames Television proposed to show an interview with the Argentinean General Galtieri about which the Cabinet was said to be deeply concerned, the Home Secretary telephoned the Director-General of the IBA who discussed the programme with the company before approving most of it for transmission.[26] In the case of "Real Lives" the Home Secretary made no direct contact with the broadcasters, but with "Death on the Rock" and the similar BBC documentary, the matter was different. The Foreign Secretary telephoned the chairmen of both the IBA and the BBC, asking them to postpone their programmes and, after the programmes had been screened, he wrote letters of protest to each.

Apart from ministerial interventions, the most notable complaints made by politicians to broadcasters have been allegations of bias towards particular parties. Again, such friction is not new, but a spate of objections during the 1980s were much more open and insistent. Examples include the SDP's concern that it was not being given sufficient credence as a third party in opposition, which culminated in litigation.[27] In addition, the Labour Party claimed that it has been treated unevenly by the BBC and objected to the IBA about the possible political content of advertising in support of the privatising of nationalised bodies.[28] The most concerted complaints during the period, however, were those made about and to the BBC by chairmen of the Conservative Party. In 1984, following a *Panorama*

---

[24] *The Guardian*, September 26, 1988.

[25] See the discussion of the Obscene Publications (Protection of Children, etc.) (Amendment) Bill. (1985–86) *Hansard* Vol. 88, col. 309, Vol. 90, cols. 566–619. Particular concern was expressed about the showing of the films "Sebastiane" and "Jubilee" on Channel 4.

[26] See V. Adams, *The Media and the Falklands Campaign* (1986).

[27] See above, n. 75.

[28] *The Guardian*, May 5 and 30, 1988.

programme about alleged extremism in the Party, the then chairman expressed the opinion that the programme was unsubstantiated and indicated that "very serious action" would have to be taken. He and the party's Chief Whip then arranged meetings with the BBC's Director-General, but were unable to reach any agreement about their differences. Two MPs who had been mentioned in the programme started actions for libel, which were settled in their favour two years later.[29] Soon afterwards, the BBC's treatment of news about the United States air raid on Tripoli in 1986 was the subject of complaint by another chairman of the Conservative Party. The Corporation was accused of bias and incompetence in a strongly worded attack, supported by a detailed analysis of its news coverage purporting to show poor editorial standards. The BBC was led to produce a firm rebuttal and, although that was initially rejected, the political will to continue the charges quickly evaporated.[30] More recently, a BBC *Panorama* documentary, about alleged gerrymandering in the borough of Westminster, was postponed following approaches from the Conservative Party. Interestingly, in explaining that the programme had been scheduled too close to local elections and denying that the BBC had bowed to political pressure, a senior BBC executive confirmed that such communications were not unusual and were received from both Government and Opposition sources.[31]

One interpretation of these incidents is that they were simply manifestations of democratic accountability. As institutions which are publicly financed, public service broadcasters and regulators are exposed to comment and appraisal, which they are well placed to rebut, by the public's representatives. Yet, if this were so, it was a form of scrutiny that is institutionally defective, as appropriate channels of accountability were not being followed. The Home Secretary was, typically, not involved as Home Secretary — the minister who was then responsible to Parliament for broadcasting and who could call on the advice and support of the Home Office in assessing the extent to which the broadcasting authorities were

[29] *The Guardian*, February 13, 14, 17 and 22, 1984; March 20 and 21, 1984; November 22,
1986.
[30] *The Observer*, October 26, 1986; *The Guardian* October 31, November 3, 6, 7, 12 and 17, 1986.
[31] Tim Gardam, speaking on Channel 4's *Right to Reply*, April 30, 1994; *The Observer*, May 1, 1994.

fulfilling their duties to Parliament. Significantly, where ministers do become involved formally, the type of pressure exerted alters, in order to avoid the inference that editorial independence is being compromised. Thus, the telephone call to the IBA about the Galtieri interview appears to have been more of a request to investigate the circumstances of the programme, with the IBA's eventual decision being accepted. In the "Real Lives" affair, the Home Secretary could only sustain his approach by arguing that he was merely expressing an opinion like any other citizen. In relation to the BBC's coverage of the Tripoli raid, the criticism petered out when the Chairman of the BBC suggested that, if the Governors could not be left to resolve the matter, it should be taken to the Home Secretary; it was not and, indeed, the minister reiterated his support for the Corporation's independence.

A more important reason for being cautious about this type of public scrutiny is that it does not clearly address the appropriate constitutional and regulatory criteria for judging the programmers' performances. Allegations of bias or publicising terrorism can be couched in terms of the duties to be duly impartial and not to encourage crime, but it is not so obvious how to locate calls for the media to be patriotic (in relation to the Falklands war) or to protect the integrity of coroner's courts (in relation to the Gibraltar shooting). Such issues cannot be soberly assessed when arguments are conducted through the media itself and transformed into debating points. Inevitably, in political discussion, interventions will be politically partisan.

One result of this tendency is that protection for broadcasters and regulators will come to depend on the calibre of the political opposition. Another result is that they are denied responsibility for their skills and knowledge, being expected to respond to popular preferences instead of explaining their actions in terms of political values about media practice. Many comments by politicians about broadcasting can actually be characterised in terms of market responsiveness. An example, already mentioned, is the Home Secretary's belief that he was only expressing a citizen's opinion in the "Real Lives" affair. In relation to the BBC's coverage of extremism in the Conservative Party and of the Tripoli raid, the complaints were advanced, albeit by chairmen of the party, on behalf of concerned consumers of the service. Communications by the Foreign Secretary or requests from Downing Street to view a tape seem to fall into the same category. Furthermore, the responses of the broadcasters, in agreeing to meetings with politicians and in making detailed replies to accusations, are as solicitous as those of a supplier in the market.

One positive effect of the new BBC Charter and Agreement will be the provision of a set of criteria for judging the Corporation's actions without needing to defer to populist political pressure. Already it is more noticeable that when MPs or ministers express concern about the Corporation, they do so in terms of its formal obligations.[32] The effect is to create a form of closure in respect of the BBC's existence and to move debate forward in terms of the application of its remit. A similar effect has been produced, for the regulators as well, in the growing practice of seeking judicial review in media matters.

JUDICIAL REVIEW

Earlier chapters mentioned the recourse to judicial review as a method of resolving grievances about media regulation. The process of "juridification" has been noticed in other areas of public law,[33] and it is by no means clear that it will have a positive effect since it has a tendency to polarise discussion about the purposes of media activity and the best way to achieve them.[34] Many decisions in media regulation require the balancing of a range of values and objectives. To shift them to the level of courtroom analysis allows the possibility that technical interpretation of statutes and procedural tactics may become unduly exaggerated. The advantages of judicial review are the external scrutiny and requirements of transparency and justification which it brings. Ideally, regulators should be developing and publicising principles for good practice in any event, but judicial review can encourage the process.

---

[32] For example, in March 1998, the public discussion of the BBC's decision to reschedule its coverage of Parliamentary broadcasting, and of its participation in a "scratchcard" competition in conjunction with the National Lottery operator, was conducted in terms of its obligations under its Agreement and the Governors' responsibility to enforce it.

[33] See M. Loughlin, "Law, Ideologies and Political Administrative Systems" (1989) 16 *J. Law & Society* 2; J. Habermas, *The Theory of Communicative Action,* Vol. 2 *Lifeworld and System: A Critique of Functionalist Reason* (1987) pp. 356 *et seq.*

[34] For a more optimistic view, see R. Craufurd Smith, *Broadcasting Law and Fundamental Rights* (1997).

When the Broadcasting Act 1990 was debated in Parliament, the possibility of judicial review was regarded as a correlative to the new articulation of competitive tendering rules. It was also regarded as a residual solution to ambiguities that could not then be resolved by ministers. As previous discussion has shown, however, the courts have continued the "hands off" approach which they adopted towards the media in the early cases against the IBA. The *Wednesbury* principle[35] of review, rather than appeal, has allowed a considerable margin of appreciation to the regulators. The courts have recognised that they do not have the expertise or mandate to intervene in issues of merit, as the strong warning in the *Virgin*[36] case shows. One disadvantage of this position is that it encourages regulators to concentrate on process rather than principle. As the good standards cases,[37] the licensing cases[38] and the election cases[39] indicate, it seems clear that, provided the regulators put in place adequate systems to consider all relevant issues, the judges will not intervene. The BCC cases[40] are different in depending on judicial interpretation of the authorising statute, but the same judicial attitude has allowed the complaints body to extend their jurisdiction quite far over broadcasters.

One issue which needs to be resolved is the amenability of the BBC and the PCC to judicial review. In the case of the BBC, the answer appears to be positive and a decision on the point appears a technicality.[41] In the PCC's case, the public status of the industry-created body is less clear but, given the importance of the press and the role of the self-regulatory scheme in deflecting legislative intervention, the arguments in favour of allowing review seem strong.[42] For both bodies, being subject to judicial review serves to focus attention on their constitutional documents, rendering them more significant and enforceable. The BBC may have cause to welcome the ability to use its Charter and Agreement as a defence against political criticism. Whether the press will want similar legitimacy to be credited to their code of practice is another matter.

---

[35] *Council of Civil Service Unions v. Minister for Civil Service* [1985] AC 374; *Associated Provincial Picturehouses Ltd v. Wednesbury Corporation* [1948] 1 K.B. 223.
[36] Above, chap. 4, pp. 167–168.
[37] Above, chap. 3, pp. 75–76.
[38] Above, chap. 4, pp. 164–165, 167–168, 171.
[39] Above, chap. 3, pp. 114–118.
[40] Above, chap. 3, pp. 91–93.
[41] *R. v. BBC ex p. Referendum Party*, *The Times*, April 29, 1997 and Lexis.
[42] See *R. v. Press Complaints Commission ex p. Brady* [1997] E.M.L.R. 185. The PCC's interpretation of its code was upheld without actually deciding the issue of jurisdiction.

Public Participation

Franchising

In the early days, it was thought that the parameters of broadcasting in the independent sector could be set by a body charged with promoting the public interest but without consulting the public. That this idea is unacceptable has been a consistent feature of critical comment about the IBA's (and ITA's) performance ever since. It arose in Parliament following the surprises which had occurred when the franchises were awarded for 1968, in an adjournment debate where a number of speakers argued that the extensive patronage of the Authority should be exercised in the open, with the bids being publicised, the criteria for selection being scrutinised by the public, and there being a right of appeal.[43] Although these points have sometimes been confused with the broader question of the extent to which contracts give rise to expectations of renewal, there was sufficient interest in the issue of procedures for the Select Committee on the Nationalised Industries to consider the matter in 1971 and make extensive recommendations. It emphasised the Authority's power over the industry and an important part of public life, and called for greater openness. This would be achieved by publishing more information about the criteria that it used and about major proposals for settling policy, in order to stimulate public debate. In addition, it suggested that applications for contracts should be published and that interviews with candidates should be held in public.[44]

The Annan Committee also discussed these issues. It recommended that public hearings should form part of the selection procedure and should be conducted in the areas in which the franchise would be held, in order to allow discussion of the past performance of the current programme contractor and the proposals of the new candidates.[45] In addition, it suggested that the IBA should publish the applications of the candidates who secured the television franchises after they had begun operation, similar to the practice that had been accepted with local radio contracts. In doing so, however, it did express some reservations about the protection of confidential

[43] *Hansard* (1966–67) Vol. 794, cols. 422–469.

[44] *Report of the Select Committee on Nationalised Industries* (1971–72) H.C. 465.

[45] Annan, above, n. 7, para. 13.24.

information, citing the example of the BBC person who had offered his services as programme controller to a franchise bidder.

Many of the points made by the committees were eventually incorporated into legislation but, in the meantime, the IBA began to plan its 1980 round of allocations with a much greater emphasis upon consultation and openness. It explained its proposed approach to the Select Committee on Nationalised Industries in its 1977 hearings,[46] and began to implement it in 1979. It involved arranging about 200 public meetings around the country in order to canvass the public's views before the contract particulars were settled. The meetings were intended to elicit information about public perceptions of the suitability of the contract area, the appeal of the service including the contribution of the local contractor, and the standard of quality and balance of programming. In addition, surveys of public opinion were conducted and written comments were invited from the public.

The exercise was well intentioned, but there remained doubt about its validity. It was not clear how representative the meetings turned out to be nor how vulnerable they were to lobbying by interest groups. The main concerns were apparently with programming policy, and there was little indication that the public knew or perhaps cared about the structure of independent broadcasting in a way which would make an informed contribution to questions about the network and the role of local companies. In the case of local radio, the procedure differed in that the meetings were held after applications had been received on the basis of "relevant factors" which the Authority had already announced.[47] That did not appear to have had the effect of making discussion more pointed, however, as no opportunity was allowed for detailed scrutiny of proposals. Altogether, the procedure does not seem to have been an effective way of securing public opinion at all, despite the IBA's Chairman's view that it was "as good public participation as you can get."[48] Better approaches might have been to rely on opinion surveys or to recognise that consultation with interested pressure groups would better reflect the way people tend to participate in political activity today.[49]

Under the 1990 Act, the extent to which the ITC and R.A. are obliged to incorporate consultation into their procedures for

---

[46] *Tenth Report of the Select Committee on Nationalised Industries* (1977–78) H.C. 637.
[47] See R. Baldwin, M. Cave and T. Jones, *The Regulation of Independent Local Radio and Its Reform* (1986) Brunel Discussion Papers in Economics No. 8603, p. 16.
[48] Quoted in A. Briggs and J. Spicer, *The Franchise Affair* (1986), p. 135.
[49] See I. Harden and N. Lewis, *The Noble Lie* (1986), chap. 6.

awarding licences is very much for them to decide. The only requirement placed on them is that they should publish information about the service they propose to license and the applications submitted to them.[50] The assumption is that representations will be made by those who feel the need to do so, but there is no onus put on the regulators to seek out views (although the R.A. will need to know local views to issue local radio licences). This is consistent with the adoption of public choice methods that has been identified in other areas of public law. Together with the use of tendering to award franchises, the supply of information is considered to provide sufficient transparency to render the process accountable.

As has been indicated already, this reflects a limited sense of accountability, one that is inadequate to deal with public issues of structure and quality that go beyond the satisfaction of preferences. To a small extent, the regulators have been sensitive to public interest in their decisions, and they have held informal meetings around the country during franchise rounds and distributed materials in public places such as libraries. More generally, they have adopted the practice of consulting widely on proposed changes to the regulatory scheme or codes of practice. Exactly what influence such consultation has on their deliberations is not, however, clear.

Programme Content

The broadcasting tradition has fostered a number of means, both formal and informal, that are intended to increase the accountability of its practitioners.[51] The BBC is required, under its Charter,[52] to establish a National Broadcasting Council and English Regional Councils. It has used its power to set up various advisory bodies and to provide a wide range of information and opinion which could be used in formulating policy. It remains uncertain, however, as to what extent these groups reflect public opinion or have any real influence. Although the former Advisory Councils were appointed by the BBC itself, they were required to be broadly representative of the public and the Corporation was making efforts to ensure that they were. It

---

[50] Broadcasting Act 1990, ss. 15, 50, 74. 98, 104 and 116.
[51] See T. Madge, *Beyond the BBC* (1989).
[52] Arts. 12 and 13. These replace the former General Advisory Council and Regional and Local Radio Advisory Councils.

is worth noting, however, that one of their functions was envisaged as providing a channel of communication for BBC views as well as a source of consumer information. The Annan Committee was sceptical of their impact on the professional broadcasters, but the BBC has been adamant that their comments are considered seriously, albeit without indicating whether they are likely to lead to action.

The BBC in fact regards the Councils and the advisory bodies as one end of a range of mechanisms for accountability, with increased use of feedback programmes and the answering of letters of complaint at the other. Under article 6 of the Charter, arrangements must be made so as to subject the BBC's work to "constant and effective review from without the Corporation", including the holding of public meetings around the regions in order to expose senior BBC personnel to relatively small audiences of interested persons. In addition, the Corporation conducts research which surveys both the size of the audience for each programme and the degree of satisfaction it produces; the former is important for scheduling decisions to achieve high ratings, while the latter helps to indicate the depth of appreciation of less popular or minority programmes. Although they provide much more representative information, they are necessarily cruder ways of securing accountability. Nevertheless, they contribute to a general impression the Corporation gives, supported by Madge's research, that public reactions to programming raise a presumption that its position must be justified. Such an attitude would appear to be a necessary precondition of accountability. It has to be remembered, however, that such justification occurs in the context of public service broadcasting, which is not only ambiguous but also rejects a simple populist approach to broadcasting choices. Under the 1996 Agreement, the transparency of such choices has been improved by the requirement that the BBC issues an set of promises about its aims by which it can be judged.[53] The Governors have responsibility for enforcing those promises, and they also oversee the new internal Programmes Complaints Unit which the Corporation has set up to improve its accountability by bringing transparency to its internal scrutiny and review procedures.[54]

Like the BBC, the IBA was assisted by a number of committees. It could appoint a General Advisory Committee and had to appoint

---

[53] BBC, *Our Commitment to You. BBC Statement of Promises to Viewers and Listeners* (1997).

[54] The Unit periodically publishes a *Programme Complaints Bulletin*.

local advisory committees for local sound broadcasts. In addition, it had to appoint national advisory committees for Scotland, Wales and Northern Ireland.[55] As regards the latter practice, which is similar to that of the BBC, the chairman of each of those committees was the Authority Member with special responsibilities for those areas. Unlike the BBC's National Broadcasting Councils, however, the Committees did not control the policy and content of programmes. Their function was to give advice on the conduct of television services in the area, so as to reflect as far as reasonably possible the range of tastes and interests of people residing there, albeit not necessarily their distinctive culture or language. They also gave advice about local radio services when requested to do so by the Authority. Supplementing these bodies were other advisory committees, but the IBA seemed to manage with considerably fewer than the BBC. Those relating to the allocation of charitable appeals were set up at the Authority's instigation, but the others were mandatory. There were committees to advise on religious and educational broadcasts, as well as on advertising, with a special medical advisory panel to comment on medical advertisements both in general and in relation to specific items. In all cases, the function of these committees was to tender advice to the Authority which they were free to accept or reject.

Under the 1990 Act much of this structure formally disappeared, although the regulators do have power to set up advisory committees as they think fit. The ITC has established Viewers' Consultative Councils and there are specialist panels to advise on advertising and sponsorship.[56] Indeed, it was the IBA's more specialist committees that appeared to be taken seriously in formulating policy on education and advertising although, in relation to religion, their informal panel of advisers seemed to be more important than the related advisory committee. It may be that particular advisers rather than committees will become the preferred method of consultation. As for more general advice, the loss of the IBA's General Advisory Council and its national committees may not be greatly felt because, although its discussions ranged over a wide variety of topics, such as television violence, young people's programmes, and racial issues, as well as particular programmes, the IBA did not profess such a high regard for them as the BBC. It may well be that "the best that can be said for them is that they are lightning conductors — opportunities

---

[55] Broadcasting Act 1981, ss. 16-18.

[56] Broadcasting Act 1990, Sched. 1, para. 16; Sched. 4, para. 14; Sched. 6, para 16.

for sectional interests and prejudices to be aired",[57] but that function is exactly what the relationship between professional broadcasters and the audience needs.

Unlike the situation with the BBC, there are no obligations on the ITC and R.A. to establish more informal methods of accountability, but they maintain that they are similarly responsive to public opinion. Criticism is taken seriously and, as discussed earlier, there is a well established complaints and interventions procedure. They also engage in audience research,[58] but their need to survey consumer preferences is less acute than the BBC's because the programming companies can be relied on to gauge the market. Indeed, while they will want to know about audience attitudes, their role is much more one of encouraging companies to maintain standards in the face of market demand to the contrary.

---

[57] S. Hood, quoted in B. Paulu, *Television and Radio in the U.K.* (1981) p. 140.
[58] This is required under the 1990 Act, ss. 12 and 96.

Chapter Seven

Prospects for Media Regulation

In considering regulation of the media in the United Kingdom, this study has extended over a broad range of issues and practice to reveal a complex set of relations between political objectives, media values and regulatory action. This chapter provides the opportunity to revisit some recurring themes and to offer conclusions about the future prospects for media regulation.

Convergence and Media Regulation

Convergence is the major developing issue in media practice. The European Commission published a Green Paper on the topic in 1997[1] and it follows earlier debates[2] and feeds into current inquiries.[3] Although convergences may be manifested in different ways, it is the convergence in platforms for delivery services that is of greatest interest. Digital technology enables infrastructures to converge

[1] European Commission, *Green Paper on the Convergence of the Telecommunications, Media and Information Technology Sectors, and the Implications for Regulation: Towards an Information Society Approach* (1997) COM (97) 623.

[2] See R. Collins (ed.), *Converging Media: Converging Regulation?* (1996); T. Prosser *et al.*, *The Impact of New Communications Technologies on Media Concentrations and Pluralism* (1997) (a study prepared for the Council of Europe); C. Murroni *et al.*, *Converging Communications: Policies for the 21st Century* (1996).

[3] The Culture, Media and Sport House of Commons Select Committee conducted a wide-ranging inquiry into audio-visual communications and the regulation of broadcasting during the 1997–1998 Parliamentary session. See Culture, Media and Sport Select Committee, *Fourth Report: The Multi-Media Revolution — Volume I* (1997–1999) H.C. 520–I.

because television, sound, information, computer file transfers and the human voice can all be carried along the same networks. At the consumer end, digital technology allows the possibility that the same equipment can be used for receiving programmes, sending messages by voice or by e-mail, browsing the Internet or conducting business transactions such as shopping and banking. The implications extend beyond the traditional media. Convergence opens new opportunities for business and commerce and offers new ways of working. Not least, it provides the scope for the development of an "information society" where citizens have the potential to gain access to, and thereby gain some control over, information resources which they need.

The possibilities for the information society naturally raise the implications of convergence for media regulation. In the course of this study, a number of situations have been noted where historically different regulatory regimes have acquired overlapping interests in media services. Because regulation has developed by accretion, as piecemeal responses to new technology, it has become complex and unwieldy. There is a variety of regulatory schemes and a proliferation of regulators, who often work in parallel but who have duties to consult each other where overlaps become manifest. This reflects — but also exacerbates — a lack of clarity about the appropriate regulatory approach. There are differing regimes for each of the television and radio services, depending on whether they are public service or commercial, analogue or digital, and terrestrial or cable or satellite services. Some logic can be detected: the BBC regulates itself in respect of all its programming, the ITC deals with commercial video programming and the R.A. deals with commercial radio, but they do not exclusively deal with complaints about programming and are overseen by the BSC. Nor is the BBC entirely self-regulating because its digital expansion, beyond its own multiplex, will require ITC licensing and its independent productions and fair trading in its commercial services are supervised by the Director General of Fair Trading. The latter's interest in competition policy also extends to the Channel 3 networking agreement and the bundling of cable and satellite programming and, where telecommunications are involved, OFTEL has a parallel concern. Indeed, where programming is distributed other than by broadcasting, OFTEL is one of the other bodies who have a major interest in media regulation. It has a direct role in licensing the infrastructure for local delivery services, just as the Radiocommunications Agency deals with allocation of electromagnetic frequencies.

In resolving the problems raised by such convergences, it is easy to assume that convergence itself should determine whether regulation is needed and, if so, how much. Although this study has focused on the media, it is not because the media in their present economic and technological forms are presumed to be permanent. On the contrary, the indications are that convergence will lead, in the long term, to considerable transformations of what we presently see the media to be. However, the underlying arguments for currently regulating the media will continue to be important. Convergence between platforms for delivering the services does not imply convergence of services, and it is the nature of service which should be the basis for regulatory intervention in the future.

The Need for Regulation

The development and adoption of new, especially digital, technology may raise the possibility that media regulation will no longer be necessary in the middle to long term, but that depends on characterising media products as purely commercial and without political and social significance. While it is true that the media are primarily concerned with entertainment, they also provide a major resource for communication and cannot be wholly shaped by market mechanisms. Indeed, it is the potentially *mediating* character of the media which makes them important and distinguishes them from simple information services. Newspapers, radio and television do more than convey ideas in a neutral way; they are part of our culture and provide a means of obtaining and presenting knowledge and engaging in political activity. As a result of their ability to select information and order priorities, they have a profound influence on the way we think about the world. Furthermore, it is doubtful whether information services can be completely neutral about the way they package material and make it available to consumers; they also select and shape what they convey. There is, therefore, a public interest in activities which are mediating, one which denies the mediators complete control over their goals and practices.

That is not to say that new forms of media will have no implications for media regulation, but the issue is one of re-regulation, rather than de-regulation,[4] the need to tailor regulation to

[4] See W. Hoffman-Reim, *Regulating Media* (1996); P. Humphreys, *Media and Media Policy in Western Europe* (1996); T. Prosser, *Law and the Regulators* (1997), chap. 10. See also Culture, Media and Sport Select Committee, above n.3, para. 116.

fit the values which are sought to be promoted. Here a functional approach is required, one which does not depend on technology or forms of delivery, but which recognises the nature of the service being provided and the character of the audience receiving it. The early justification for regulating broadcasting, that it was *broad*-casting, rests on the belief that material which is transmitted to a universal audience, both in terms of geographic reach and personal profile, requires special treatment. The reason is that the audience has no effective control over the scheduling and content of the material received. For universal programming, then, there will always be a need for sensitivity to audience membership, regardless of the public service or commercial quality of the content. To the extent that programming is made available in progressively segmented forms, either by "narrow-casting" or subscription, the case for content regulation becomes correspondingly weaker,[5] although there will continue to be a public interest in the overall provision of media output.

PUBLIC SERVICE BROADCASTING

Whether there should be free-to-air provision, and whether that should aspire to public service values, are separate questions from the need to regulate universal programming. It is difficult to tell whether public service values would have been created without Reith's BBC. But the contribution that such values have made to enhancing programme production, developing cultural and political awareness and generally raising levels of public knowledge about our society is too valuable to be squandered. There are few who would argue that we should not strive to achieve excellence and, if there has been paternalism and elitism in the past, it is because there has been insufficient accountability to the public in determining what criteria to apply. Public service has had a fundamental effect in creating expectations within the audience about what constitutes good programming, but that does not mean that it should continue to dominate media output and deny audiences the right to choose from the diversity of other material which the market is now providing.

[5] See J. Balkin, "Media Filters, the V-Chip and the Foundations of Broadcast Regulation" (1996) 45 *Duke Law Journal* 1131–1175.

There is no need for public service to be exclusive, only that sufficiently realistic conditions for its survival continue to exist. However, it is likely to continue to need protection from the full impact of market competition. This entails the provision of a secure source of public funding and there should be no expectation that public service should be required to compete with commercial companies across the whole range of its services. Public service broadcasting has a valuable role, then, in *complimenting* provision in the private sector.

Convergence and Regulatory Design

It follows from the earlier discussion that there is a strong case for rationalising media and related regulation by reference to the kinds of service which are being provided. The focus for regulation should be the product experienced by the end user, rather than the forms of delivery. It has been noted already that the overlaps between television, radio and telephony are increasingly extensive, for example between: mobile telephony and radio; digital audio broadcasting and visual information display; and telephony and video-on-demand. The aim should be to regulate according to the rationales for regulation. In this context, political and social regulation may be distinguished from economic regulation, so that modifications to market arrangements can be justified by reference to the media's special role in a democratic society

Such an approach would be a departure from the present arrangements whereby regulation is organised according to industry, combining both delivery platform and service offered. The R.A. and the ITC have argued that a specialist regulator is required to handle the particular problems of the radio and television industries respectively. That requires them to embrace a wide range of regulatory norms relating to programming, forms of delivery and competition generally. This raises a question about how much of a specialist a regulator can be expected to be. As the media industry becomes digitalised and ordinary market considerations become more relevant to its regulation, it does not make sense for media regulators to re-invent the wheel and develop afresh the experience gained over many years by the competition regulators. It is not obvious that programming and competition issues are so inextricably intertwined that dual regulation along different axes could not work. Certainly, there may be some increase in regulatory tension, if not conflict, as the different regulators seek to achieve their own agendas. However, for the most part, the regulatory bodies do already actively comply with their existing duties to consult with each other, and it is simply unrealistic to think that there will never be disagreements about policy.

Problems in deciding the appropriate scope of regulation may lead to the conclusion that the establishment of a single, "super" regulator would be the most effective solution.[6] The advantages would be that regulatory policy could be co-ordinated in one body and regulatory compliance would be made easier. However, there are strong arguments against such a move. It would be a delusion to believe that the existence of one regulator would remove any conflict between regulatory objectives. Instead, such conflict would be hidden from public gaze and become a matter of office politics rather than democratic debate. There would be a real risk that economic arguments would prevail, given the liberalising trends in the industry. There would also be a rather extreme concentration of power in one regulator for an industry which is so important to democratic aims. Both considerations suggest that it would be much healthier to have more than one regulator, with each defending its own corner through public and Parliamentary discussion. To create a single regulator would actually serve to pre-empt such debate, since it would not be policy-neutral.

Nevertheless, it would be advantageous to rationalise existing regulation by clarifying the scope of public interest and economic regulation, and assigning each sphere of regulation to separate bodies. In particular, there is a role for one agency to oversee the public interest sphere, to secure a minimum set of norms to protect freedom in communication and basic community standards, but without extending to matters of consumer preference. In practical terms, what is desirable is a media regulator which would take over the programme-related remits of the ITC and the R.A. together with the complaints functions of the Broadcasting Standards Commission, and which could also take jurisdiction over the BBC. Economic regulation, primarily directed at securing competitive practices, would be appropriate for one of the specialist agencies that already

[6] See R. Collins and C. Murroni, *New Media, New Policies* (1996) chap. 8. See also Culture, Media and Sport Select Committee, above, n.3, paras 158–159, recommending the creation of a Communications Regulation Commission.

exist. The aim of distinguishing between programme-related and economic regulation would be to reflect the functions of the different media services in providing mass or interactive services.[7]

The Regulatory Style

Assessing the development of media regulation this century, the pattern which emerges is one of political discourse qualified by professional expertise. The initial choice to treat the BBC as special, and therefore different from the press, was prompted by general political anxiety about its potential influence and governmental prudence in seeking to control its use. Over the years, political initiatives have tended to set the pace for the changes and reforms which have been devised in ministerial offices and implemented in legislative instruments. In many ways this has been a healthy and quasi-democratic process. One of the distinguishing features of broadcasting regulation has been the tradition of debate about its aims and practices. Within the medium itself, there is audience research, consultation with viewers and listeners, and opportunities for regional and local representations to be taken into account. Externally, there have been few years when an official committee or body has not been sitting and this has stimulated a prolific output of submissions and wide public discussion of media matters.[8] In its performance, broadcasting has attempted a practical resolution of what is a more general problem, that of maintaining legitimacy for technical expertise in a complex, highly specialised society.

The need for sensitivity to that issue arises from the many layers of discourse which are relevant to media practice, each of which can frame debate in different ways. Professional media knowledge has

---

[7] Although there are practical difficulties in regulating the international reach of the Internet and the case for self-regulation remains strong, the proposed regulator's remit, and the principles to apply in regulation, would be no different from other media services. For a discussion of the possibilities for self regulation, see Prosser *et al.*, above, n. 2. See also Culture, Media and Sport Select Committee, above, n.3, para. 114.

[8] " . . . in the past 30 years, there have been no less than 20 enquiries into the BBC and I calculated that 40 per cent of the time was spent either with enquiries or awaiting Government decisions on the enquiries." Lord Swann (former Chairman of the BBC) speaking the Royal Television Society "The Peacock Debate" (1986) 23 *Television* 223–233. Since then, there have continued to be discussions arising from, for example, investigations by Parliamentary select committees and initiatives from the E.C.

been especially significant in forming public service broadcasting values, albeit with continuing political endorsement. More recent discussion has switched to economic values and consumer sovereignty as the important criteria for determining regulatory objectives. At the same time, technological capacity determines what is possible (if not always chosen) and there has also been stronger awareness of legality in devising regulatory norms.

It would be pleasing to be able to say that there is an identifiable pattern in the different layers of debate and the point at which they impact on the whole regulatory framework, but the reality is much more untidy. Where political discussion dominates, for example, in devising primary or secondary legislation, there are few limits to the kinds of arguments which can be deployed. The debate is more free-ranging and allows creative and critical thinking, but it also enables decisions to be made on the basis of expedience or political popularity. In devising the latest ownership rules for the media, for example, it is clear that the shape of the scheme which emerged had as much to do with the pre-existing state of the industry as the principle of media pluralism. At the other end of the spectrum, judicial scrutiny of regulatory action is more constrained, unless the judges choose to stray beyond the limited arguments of judicial review. In between, the regulators are able to draw on a number of sources of guidance. For example, in devising rules about programme quality, they can speak to the professional producers about their values. In applying the rules of competitive tendering, the normative limits are economic at the final stage, but quality-based or technology-based at other stages.

How are these different normative frames reconciled in practice? The key actors are the media regulators and, to an extent, the BBC as a self-regulating broadcaster. It is they who can co-ordinate the various sources of guidance and assess their comparative importance. In doing so, they are able to introduce a reflexive dimension to the discussion. For example, the IBA's expertise in assessing what was possible, and on occasions desirable, was fed into the process of legislating the 1990 Broadcasting Bill with quite influential effect. When making decisions on policy or its application, the regulators have tended to incorporate law-derived requirements, to formulate clear procedures and to give reasons, into their everyday administrative practice. More specifically, when awarding some licences, the regulators' weighing of business plans includes an appraisal of the quality of service to be provided.

For all this, there is a rather passive aspect to the way media regulators carry out their tasks. Their function is to implement the legislation, manage the system and respond to demands from the market, consumers or politicians. If they have a formal agenda, it is to defend the mandate that Parliament has given them. Insofar as they co-ordinate different layers of debate about regulatory norms, it is to balance them as they apply them.[9] In all this, the media regulators are manifesting features of the traditional British approach to regulation, with its dependence on ministerial power and the expectation that regulatory discretion can be relied on to make the system work.[10]

Yet, in the media sector more than most, there is scope for developing a different and more mature model of regulation, one which would give a greater role to the regulator as an integrator — rather than co-ordinator — of normative frames. There exists a fairly stable set of political values relating to media activity: the importance of freedom of speech and pluralism is widely accepted, and the residual status of quality and public service in broadcasting is also widely recognised. Without compromising the equally important interest in democratic accountability, those values could form the basis of a regulatory mandate for the media. Within that mandate, but independently of direct political supervision, media regulators could themselves begin to develop policies and principles for shaping media activity. The structure of the industry and the extent of regulation in respect to different types of service could be assessed and organised in the light of those principles, free from the constraints of statutory detail and in flexible response to new developments in the industry. Independent media regulators of this kind would not be expected to ignore principles of good administration, of course, and would be anticipated to improve their procedures for rule-making, consultation and justifying their decisions. The function of regulator as integrator would facilitate the beginnings of a normative doctrine of media regulation, catering for the particular problems of media practice.

The idea of the regulator as integrator may appear radical in terms of public law tradition. It represents a move away from thinking that

---

[9] For an account of the more flexible Australian approach, see L. P. Hitchens, "Approaches to Broadcasting Regulation: Australia and United Kingdom Compared" (1997) 17 *Legal Studies* 40–64.

[10] On the "Westminster style of government", characterised by Parliamentarianism, "Club" government and the Diceyan tradition of law, see M. Loughlin and C. Scott, "The Regulatory State" in P. Dunleavy *et al.* *Developments in British Politics — 5* (1997) pp. 205–219.

regulation must be accommodated within a single, overarching legal environment. Yet it would be a natural evolution of the approach which has emerged for the media during this century. This book has traced a shifting discourse of regulation which has marked out the media as different and meriting special treatment. In the current practice of media regulation, the foundations of a coherent doctrine of regulation can already be detected.[11] That has served to give the media sector relatively greater independence and to protect it from excessive political interference. However, the values which justify that special treatment — media pluralism and democratic participation — need to be consolidated in a rapidly changing industry. The development of policy is increasingly vulnerable to the economic imperatives and political demands of the new media technologies and the new media markets. Yet much of the current tradition of media regulation remains relevant and the contribution of a specialist but accountable regulatory body needs to be recognised as central to the protection and promotion of medial values. A new basis is required, therefore, for a regulatory framework which can meet the challenges of media progress in the next century.

---

[11] On the importance for sociological studies of law to "explore the nature and conditions of regulation (and demands for regulation) that develop within the local milieux" of diverse social spheres, see R. Cotterrell, *Law's Community: Legal Theory in Sociological Perspective* (1995) p. 325–326.

Index